Table of Contents

Preface

This book is about violence, suicide, poverty, crime, sexism, racism, and other such problems: the shadow side of life in Canada, and elsewhere. So it is a bit depressing at times, and angering at other times. But it is also about reality: a reality which we cannot ignore, which we should try to understand, and which we can change.

It is also about ourselves, for most of us are (or will be) affected by most of these problems at some time in our lives, as victims or as victimizers, as avoiders or observers, as part of the problem or as part of the solution. We are therefore not discussing "them" in this volume, but "us" — to greater or lesser degree, depending upon the individual, and the problem.

The purpose of the book is threefold. First, it introduces the reader to the study of social issues and problems, with the operative word being "introduce." Shelves of volumes have been written on each of the topics discussed here, so this is not a comprehensive treatment. And many issues are not considered at all: pornography, prostitution, pollution, and others. This volume does not approach the "encyclopedia" method of tackling social problems: listing ten to twenty problems one after the other. But we do make a start in considering systematically some of the challenging dimensions of our lives. More useful, ultimately, than the analysis of lists is the investigation of how we construct our realities and *understand* our social problems. Which brings us to point two.

The second goal is to clarify the complexity of defining our social problems, for we all define them differently, as indeed we tend to see reality differently. I have identified three paradigms — the conservative, the conflict, and the feminist paradigms on society and social problems — and I try to show the strengths and uses of each model. The most important point in the analysis of social problems, in my view, is to try to understand the other person's point of view. No easy task, as we shall see later.

A paradigm, in the sociological sense of the word, is our world view: the pattern of our values, beliefs, assumptions, and expectations about our social world, including the nature of society and human nature, the value of the individual relative to the collective, the meanings of liberty and equality — the entire culture of our lives. As we shall see, and as you are no doubt already well aware, people do have different paradigms. And such paradigms conflict. Consequently, social problems are *doubly* problematical, for there is no consensus between the traditional patriarch and the feminist, the conservative and the socialist. I think that clarifying and delineating the conflicting paradigms will contribute more to understanding and ameliorating social problems than will repeated analysis of these problems.

Finally, we do have to consider the policy implications of these different issues, both at the individual and the societal levels. Poverty, crime, suicide, etc., are not going to disappear overnight, nor in the foreseeable future; so we have to recognize their reality, but also the possibilities of social change — according to whichever paradigm you find most useful.

The book is divided into two unequal parts. Chapters 2 to 4 outline the three paradigms and Chapters 5 to 9 are case studies of some of the principal issues that face us. The volume is framed by the first overview chapter, which discusses the paradigms and the dominant methodologies in more detail, and the final concluding chapter, which discusses the Weberian paradigm and the future. It is only the Weberian paradigm, it seems to me, which allows the possibility of entertaining more than one paradigm or model at a time, and prescinds from the politics of the others. Thus while each paradigm expresses one truth, so to speak, one prime value, one political orientation, it is above all Weber who permits the exploration of these competing paradigms — competing for legitimacy, that is — and allows us to see truths in all.

There are several caveats which I should enter here to explain some of the features of this volume. First I have tended to use, as necessary, newspapers and such popular magazines as *Maclean's* and *Time* to illustrate various points. This is partly because they have the most up to date information, and partly because they do articulate particular paradigms, but mostly because I try to integrate the media and academia. Our social problems are front-page news. They are not simply textbook issues of theory, methods, and statistics, far away and irrelevant; and while the mass media are no substitute for sociological research, they are often complementary. This technique will, I hope, help readers to develop further their "sociological eye."

Also, this book contains more classical and contemporary theory than is conventional in most North American texts, which in my opinion tend to present masses and masses of data with little chance for a reader to synthesize them with their own paradigms. In presenting some of the broad theories of society, as well as the narrower theories of particular issues, I try to locate our dominant paradigms in their historical and sociological contexts. It is necessary to see where we have come from, as well as useful to sharpen our minds on the ideas of the giants who have preceded us. The integration of theory and data therefore parallels, hopefully, the integration of media and academia mentioned above.

Finally, while the substantive chapters are organized along rather similar lines — which may be useful to scholars doing their own research on other problems or particular aspects of these ones — the paradigm chapters are not. The conservative paradigm (Chapter 2) is primarily theoretical, the conflict paradigm (Chapter 3) is partly theoretical and partly historical, and raises some of the substantive issues discussed later; and the feminist paradigm (Chapter 4) is primarily substantive, with some theory and some history. This integration (again!) of theory, history, and data is intended to create a holographic image of Canadian paradigms and problems: multi-coloured and multi-dimensional. Thus while each chapter is, inevitably, limited, the collection of three covers the spectrum.

There are tragedies in these topics, but also triumphs. The shadow side does imply the reality of the sunny side. One consolation is that most of us probably do not have all these problems all at the same time — we may just have them one after the other! But hopefully at the end we will have a better understanding of Canadian social problems and perhaps also have initiated some changes. It is trite but true that life is never problem-free for long, if at all; and it is not just Canadian social problems in the abstract which we are considering, but also our own and our friends' individual problems. Sociology is, and surely should be, useful as well as scientific.

ACKNOWLEDGEMENTS

Here I would like to acknowledge my thanks, to many people for many different things about this book. First I would like to thank my students at Concordia very much: I learn something from them every time we meet, and I hope they enjoyed our meetings as much as I have done.

Also I am extremely grateful to Clifford J. Jansen at York, Richard L. Ogmundson at Victoria and Dorothy Pawluch at McMaster who reviewed most of the manuscript with very great care and offered a number of constructive suggestions. While I could not accommodate all their points, and they are certainly not responsible for the weaknesses here, this volume is far stronger for their generosity, scholarship and wisdom.

At Concordia I would like to thank Rahel Eynan-Harvey, Caroline Knowles, Margaret Shaw and Joseph Smucker who read various chapters and made still more constructive suggestions; and Jeffrey Asher at Dawson College in Montreal was also extremely helpful.

Thanks also to all those at Prentice Hall who made this volume possible: Michael Bickerstaff, Marjorie Munroe, Kim Johnston, Norman Bernard and Lisa Berland.

Special thanks to so many friends and relatives and colleagues for their support and encouragement over the years, Barbara Adams, James and Zosia Aynsley, Frank and Hélène Edmonds, David Howes and Constance Classen, Carole Robertson, Jim and Daphne Hill, Anne Grahame, Jody Stavely, Gail Valaskakis, also to my sons John-Jasper and Nicholas, and especially to Hélène Tobin.

Anthony Synnott
1996

CHAPTER 1

SOCIAL PROBLEMS

Canada certainly has plenty of social problems. We can all rattle off a list after a moment's thought: poverty, crime, racism, sexism, suicide, prostitution, drug abuse, alcoholism, child abuse . . . . The list is long and depressing: wife-battering, the homeless, pornography, incest, illiteracy, violence, and so on.

The sociology of social problems seems fairly simple, at least in principle. The sociologist (you), or a government commission of inquiry, or a concerned group etc. researches a "problem," and makes appropriate recommendations; these recommendations are duly implemented, and the problem is, or should be, solved, or at least ameliorated. . . .

In fact, of course, things are rarely so simple. The political will may not exist. Financial resources may not be available. And the recommendations may be ignored, or rejected, and relegated to a dusty shelf with the other reports. Nonetheless, the sociologists can keep busy, and would seem to be doing important work.

Yet even this common-sense discussion of social problems is problematic. It does not take much research into social problems to realize that people do not always agree about what the problems are; nor about how important they are; nor about how to solve them, even if they agree about what they are. People define problems differently; and even if they agree on the definitions, they may not agree for the same reasons, and they may disagree also on the solutions. Thus what is a problem to some may be a solution to others; and what is a solution to some may be a problem to others.

Men and women, rich and poor, conservatives and radicals and feminists, and members of different ethnic groups, are all very likely to see "things," including social problems, very differently.

Poverty, for example, may have negative consequences for the rich, but it is obviously more of a problem for the poor. Suicide is a problem for some, but a solution to the problem of living for others. Prostitution may not be a problem for the call girl: it may be a solution to her problems. Abortion is a social problem for pro-life activists, but it is often a solution for others. And crime pays for some people: perhaps the poor who are having a hard time surviving, or wealthy bankers illegally laundering drug monies.

The definition, clarification, and solution of social problems therefore becomes immensely complicated in a pluralistic (heterogeneous) society; and recommendations from government committees, experts, think tanks or concerned citizens are often extremely controversial, and also sometimes in total disagreement with each other.

Indeed it is a salutary experience to ask any group of people (such as a classroom of students!) to rank the top five Canadian social problems. Few people will list the same five, and probably none will rank them in the same order. Nonetheless there is usually some consensus in that the top five often include poverty (unemployment, inequality, etc.), crime, and drug abuse (including alcoholism), with racism, sexism, violence, and child abuse further down the list.

It was this consensus and concern which largely, but not exclusively, determined the selection of topics for this volume.

Various points must be clarified at the start. The definition of social problems is *subjective*, i.e. individual and personal, as well as collective. A person who has been the victim of child abuse is probably more likely to rate it a social problem than one who has not. Definitions are also *relative*, relative to gender, socioeconomic status, value system, colour and so on. For example, women are more likely to define sexism as a social problem than men, the poor are more likely to list poverty as a major social problem than the wealthy, and visible minorities are surely more conscious of the reality of racism than, say, whites.

Also definitions and constructions change over time. Child abuse, for instance, was not recognized as a social problem until Dr. Kempe defined the battered child syndrome in 1966; until then, violence against children was considered an individual problem, rather than a social one, if indeed it was considered a problem at all, and not just a normal, routine method of discipline. Similarly, wife abuse was not recognized as a social problem in Canada until Linda MacLeod (1980) reported that one woman in ten was abused in domestic relationships. Definitions of social problems therefore change over time, and they are continually changing. Smoking is now widely defined as a social problem — it used to be a private pleasure! Drunk driving and environmental pollution have also been defined as social problems relatively recently. Homosexuality used to be considered a social problem; now it is not, but homophobia is. Suicide is widely believed to be morally wrong, and a social problem given the length of the casualty lists; yet some people now believe that suicide is a right.

Our values and standards keep changing, and as they do so we keep creating or constructing "new" social problems.

Given this process, what "new" social problems might we expect in the future? Several possibilities emerge. I would expect concern to increase over such issues as environmental abuse, elder abuse, animal abuse, and hate crimes — these issues have already been raised without yet being institutionalized. The new reproductive technologies are highly controversial and problematic. Some radical feminists have defined masculinity as problematic: we can expect some rancorous debate on that issue (see Chapter 4). Accidents may soon be defined as a social problem: they do not just "happen" but are highly correlated with age, gender, socioeconomic status, ethnicity, and also alcohol use; as such they are often life style risks and socially determined.

These definitional processes indicate that while certain problems may be ameliorated, nonetheless our changing values and rising standards will continually create new issues on the frontiers of our society: social problems are intrinsic to a plural and dynamic society. They will not just "go away" nor can they all be "solved" because we continually reevaluate our social lives by new criteria increasingly intolerant of human suffering.

Redefinitions of problems may be due to the actions of such "moral entrepreneurs" as Kempe and MacLeod, or due to changing realities (the homeless are also a new social problem, but this is not due to any "redefinition" of the data, but to the increased number of homeless in Canadian cities), or to changing expert opinion (e.g. on homosexuality, and smoking) or to changing public opinion (e.g. on divorce, animal experimentation etc.).

The final point I wish to emphasize is the applied consequence of the second, namely that what is, or is not, defined as a social problem is also *political*, i.e. definitions depend upon ideological orientations and also have various political and economic consequences. Conservatives, radicals, and feminists have very different paradigms of society and social problems, as we shall see. Indeed, this is the central focus of the book: that definitions and recommendations are political.

Different populations in society see reality differently, and "the truth," which may be so obvious to some, is not necessarily so obvious to others. Claude Lévi-Strauss was correct, I think, when he said: "True reality is never the most obvious of realities" (1964:61), which is probably not much more than a restatement of the old aphorism that "things are seldom what they seem."

One is reminded of the philosopher's trick question: "What shape is a dime?" The usual response is "Circular." Upon which the philosopher may show the full frontal dime to the audience, when it is indeed circular; but the dime may be turned around until it is varying *oval* shapes and finally a *rectangle*, and lying vertical or horizontal, or at any angle in between. The apparent shape therefore depends upon the perspective. The philosopher's point, however, is that many perspectives are possible and necessary, and that each alone is not only limited but even, in a sense, deceptive. Put more crudely, one might admit that the full frontal perspective is fine, but that there are other possibilities.

Let us make another analogy. The different perspectives on social problems and, more broadly, on society can be compared to different methods in photography: shooting from different angles and at different shutter speeds in various lights, with different lenses and filters. The variations lead to greater understanding, not to confusion, to strength rather than weakness.

These points about perspectives are worth making at some length and understanding in some depth, since beginners in sociology sometimes seem confused by the multiplicity of perspectives and the plethora of theories. We should surely recall our own maxims, that "there are two sides to every question"; or, more cynically, or perhaps more realistically, depending on your point of view, "there are three truths: my truth, your truth and the truth." The anthropologist Elsie Clews Parsons put the point very well: "Wisdom in ethnology, as in life, lies in having more than one method of approach" (1936:479).

The multiplicity of perspectives is particularly useful in the area of social problems. The business of sociologists in this area is not, in my view, to assert that A, B, and C are social problems, and that X, Y, and Z, respectively, are the solutions. This would be to adopt a simplistic and unrealistic model of society, as a sociologist. (As an activist, however, this may be quite appropriate.)

Social problems are not like maths problems in a textbook, which have the one correct answer at the back of the book. Society and people are more complicated than mathematical equations; and even if they were not, given the range of interests, values, and experiences, probably not even all the members of one family would agree completely on the definition, analysis, and "solution" of any social problem.

What sociologists *can* do is to consider *who* defines *what* as social problems, *why*, and *how* (i.e. by what criteria), and *so what* (i.e. what are the implications of these definitions? and for which groups?) Or: what is a social problem to whom, how is it a problem, why, and what do they suggest?

How we define reality or, in sociological terms, how we *construct* reality, will vary (Berger and Luckmann, 1967). Our constructions reflect our vested interests, our status, our political and religious beliefs, our values and goals in life, and so on. These may be unified and coherent, or multiple and complex, and even contradictory. But they determine our world view. They are the lenses through which we peer, possibly shortsightedly; they are the categories in and through which we understand. Given the range of values and goals and beliefs, it is not surprising that ten people might not agree exactly: disagreement should be *expected*; indeed disagreement is useful and may lead to the clarification of divergent interests and values.

The contribution of sociology in this discussion may be to compare our models of society and our world views, and to offer cost-benefit analyses of alternative proposals; but the choice of solutions rests with the politicians and the public: you.

METHODOLOGIES

Social problems can be studied in several ways. One way, perhaps the simplest and most obvious, is to make up a list of social problems, and just study. This method has been used very successfully in the text *Social Issues* (1983), edited by Dennis Forcese and Stephan Richer — although not all social issues are social problems. Their emphasis on social inequality as the theme linking the 13 issues discussed, however, does indicate that the issues are problematic. A more recent work, Subharas Ramcharan's *Social Problems and Issues* (1989) is equally wide-ranging. This method, known as the "objective" approach, is probably the most usual in Canadian and American texts: objective, in the sense that the assumption is that there are real, objective, problems "out there" which can indeed be studied, and solved.

A second method is chronological-historical. The Elizabethan Poor Laws of the late sixteenth century articulated the first state recognition that poverty was not simply an *individual* problem but also a social problem and that the state has a responsibility to alleviate that problem. From that date we can study the increasing role of the therapeutic state in the lives of citizens, with industrial reform and political reform particularly in the nineteenth century. The Great Depression of the thirties precipitated a rapid expansion of the role of government in Canada. Indeed the state is now increasingly involved, through legislation, federal, provincial, and municipal, in every sector of our public lives, and even our private lives. Health, welfare, education, occupations, transport, communications, sanitation, air and water, food and drink: all are governed by legislation, and often taxed too. Rules govern all: schoolrooms and games, universities and corporations, dress and undress and expletives, and certainly crime, suicide, prostitution, and violence.

This historical method has the advantage of clarifying the *changing* constructions of social problems, but this method is usually the domain of historians rather than sociologists as, for instance, Carrigan's (1991) history of crime in Canada.

A third approach to social problems is the "subjective" or the "social constructionist" method. This was developed originally by Malcolm Spector and Norman Kitsuse (1977) following earlier work by Herbert Blumer. The central insight of subjectivists is, as might be expected, that social problems are subjective, rather than objective, or given; i.e. they are socially constructed, and also reconstructed. "Social problems are what people view as social problems," as Joel Best puts it (1989: xvi). Problems are defined differently by different sectors of the population, redefined regularly, created and dissolved also. All knowledge is socially constructed, as Berger and Luckmann (1967) have shown; but it took a while before this insight was applied to such "obvious" phenomena as social problems. Constructionists therefore draw attention to the ways in which social problems are "created" and redefined, as is shown in their case studies of child abuse, AIDS, smoking, and other problems (Best, 1989). Sexism was not widely discussed as a social problem until the emergence of the second phase of the women's movement in the late sixties; now gender discrimination, pay equity, violence against women, and the lace ghetto, are widely discussed.

Similarly prostitution is legal in some places (West Germany, Holland, Nevada) and illegal in others (Canada, the United Kingdom). Homosexuality used to be considered morally deviant, and it used to be illegal to perform homosexual acts; today, however, despite residual homophobia, homosexuality is widely recognized as a legitimate sexual orientation; furthermore homosexuality, like prostitution, was or is institutionalized in many societies as a cultural norm. W.G. Sumner (1906) pointed out long ago that "the mores make everything right." Constructionists clarify how they do so, and how norms change.

The second major contribution of constructionists was to show that social problems often have little in common with each other, other than being defined as problematic. Unemployment, drug abuse, the destruction of the ozone layer, racism, suicide . . . and dozens of other social problems are too diverse in origin, too widespread internationally, and too long-standing to be easily theorized. Indeed Spector and Kitsuse state in the first sentence of their book: "There is no adequate definition of social problems within sociology, and there is not and never has been a sociology of social problems" (1977:1). Of course there has been; they simply mean that they do not care for it much! But certainly there is no one theory for all social problems within the objective tradition.

One might think of the objectivists and the constructionists as complementary; but their approaches are very different. To take the example of the homeless: objectivists tend to try to get estimates of the numbers first; this will give some idea of the seriousness of the problem. This means developing an acceptable working definition, which is itself no easy task. Then objectivists move on to analysis: who? what? when? where? why? Who are the homeless? What sorts of people (gender, age, background, types)? How and why did they become homeless? Where are they: in which cities, primarily, and which sectors of these cities? Is this population increasing or decreasing in numbers, or changing in composition? Why? What resources are available to them in terms of food and shelter? Are they sufficient? What are the municipal and provincial policies? What *should* they be? These are clear, straightforward and important questions.

Constructionists might enquire along very different lines. Who first defined homelessness as a social problem? When? Where? In the press, parliament, a documentary film, after a tragedy? How did these moral entrepreneurs or civic leaders define this problem? How was public opinion mobilized? What was the sequence of escalation? How was political action initiated and policy formulated? And why has attention been flagging recently (if it has — and how can this be measured)? These are very different questions.

One criticism of the constructionist approach is that it does seem to focus more on the process than the people, more on understanding than on action. Constructionists are more interested in understanding how a set of behaviours is defined as a problem, while objectivists are more concerned with solving or ameliorating a problem. There is therefore, I think, a conservative or passive bias in the constructionist tradition, useful though it is in other respects.

The approach I have adopted is a mixture of the constructionist and objective approaches, and is predicated on two assumptions. One, that there is a consensus on at least a broad prioritization of social problems; and two, that these problems tend to be perceived or constructed very differently, often along three principal political lines: conservative, radical, and feminist. So we are within the objective tradition in recognizing that there is widespread agreement that some social situations are problematic; but we are within the constructionist tradition in recognizing that these social problems are defined in various ways by different populations.

The volume begins by sketching the three political paradigms or perspectives on society and social problems, and then continues with the thematic analysis of selected problems within their historical contexts. I hope that this approach captures the insights of all three of the methods discussed earlier. We recognize that people do construct problems differently, and we try to consider how, and why, and what the consequences of these facts are. But we do recognize that there is a consensus and study a few concrete problems. The advantage of the historical method is that we can consider how definitions and constructions change over time. This approach is not particularly radical, but in so far as it uses three paradigms, it is likely to spark debate between students of different political opinions. From such debates, we learn.

HUMAN NATURE AND SOCIETY

Social problems of one sort or another are inevitable as no society is perfect, but the *degree* and *types* of problematics are highly variable. Crime rates vary enormously, for instance, and so do homicide and suicide rates. So the fundamental questions of this book are: "What causes these social problems and how can they be solved?" We ask these questions every day, after a particularly brutal homicide, or a rape, or an ugly incident of racism. How can such things happen? How can they happen in Canada? Who *are* these people? And what can be done to prevent such horrors recurring in the future?

These are emotional issues as well as academic, personal as well as sociological, and as such it is difficult to be "objective," "detached," and "scientific" — often regarded as the essential characteristics of the modern sociologist.[1]

On the other hand, neither conflict theorists nor feminist theorists are known for their detachment; indeed passionate involvement is now widely considered as essential as sound scholarship. These two characteristics are not mutually exclusive, of course, but my point is that sociology is not about books nor computers nor theories, however useful these may be; it is finally about people — who are all different, and there is not much agreement about them/us.

Two fundamental questions have to be raised here: do our problems originate in society or in human nature? sociology or psychology? the collectivity or the individual? This is not an easy question to answer, and perhaps these are false dichotomies, but we do need to consider the alternatives. If all societies have social problems, do they all stem from the innate selfishness, viciousness, and general nastiness of homo so-called sapiens? Certainly if humans are believed to be basically good and sapiens (wise), it is difficult to explain social problems. On the other hand it is easy to explain social problems if people are basically evil.

Do you believe that people are basically good or basically evil? Many people are likely to want to say "both" or "neither" or, to take refuge in the old evasion: "it all depends on what you mean by good and evil." But such judicious responses cannot be tolerated by any determined pollster.

Most of the students in my classes are optimistic and, like Rousseau, believe that people are basically good. So how do they explain the prevalence of so many social problems? Two ways: one — the problems are caused by a minority of villains, and/or caused (or at least not solved) by politicians. Such explanations suffice to start the debate. Only a small minority seem to believe that people are basically bad. For them social problems are not the problem, so to speak; they follow inevitably from the definition of human nature; their only difficulty is how to explain why our social problems are not worse. If people are evil, how come our levels of violent crime, for instance, are not *much* higher? Again, fear of punishment is not an entirely satisfactory response.

Both responses have long and honourable philosophical and sociological traditions, as we shall see in the next three chapters. On the one hand, Machiavelli, Hobbes and, with qualifications, Nietzsche and Freud have argued that *human nature* is flawed, or at least not nice, and we require society for our security and development. On the other hand the democratic and socialist traditions, pioneered by Rousseau, Marx and Engels, and more recently the feminist tradition, have argued that *society* is flawed and must be transformed.

Whether we blame "human nature" for our problems, however it is defined, or whether we blame society, however that is perceived is important; for presumably there is little we can do about "human nature" perceived as a biological given — but there is much we can do about society, which we ourselves continually create and recreate.[2]

The number and acuteness of our problems, or challenges as some would prefer to call them, raises a second, related question. Do we have a list of separate, discrete social problems, which can, in principle, receive social solutions — as we queried in the beginning of this chapter; or do we have *one* linked series of problems, a web of connected pathologies, symptomatic of a sick and problematic society? Opinions vary, as usual. Conservatives tend to the former view; radicals, including socialists and feminists, tend to the latter view for different reasons; so do many many peoples from disenfranchised ethnic groups and/or from disadvantaged regions. The implications of these opinions are serious. Conservatives are likely to be satisfied with Canada, perceiving only a few problems which can, in principle, be ameliorated.

Ironically, however, the Progressive Conservative Party of Brian Mulroney generated a new conservative reaction in the west with the Reform Party, and a nationalist reaction in Quebec with the Bloc Quebecois. The Reform Party has a long slate of proposals for social change: reduce government expenditure and central government itself to reduce the deficit and then the national debt, reduce welfare payments, introduce tougher crime policies, reduce immigration, perhaps charge user fees for medical care, perhaps restore the death penalty, and so on. The central problem with Canada in this view is Ottawa: out of control, out of touch, bureaucratic and even corrupt. Radicals, however, of the left, or feminists (the two are not mutually exclusive of course) are dissatisfied for other reasons and want other types of changes, seeing the whole system as (check one or more according to orientation) capitalist, sexist, racist, fascist, militaristic, centrist (the Ottawa/Toronto axis) and more.

The right wing desires change to maximize freedom, the left wing desires it to maximize equality. The former tends to want less government intervention, the latter tends to favour more to counterbalance the injustices of the free market and supply and demand economics. Is a balance possible?

Dissatisfaction with Canada, for whatever reasons of gender, class, ethnicity, language, religion, region etc. does not of course mean that people would necessarily want to live anywhere else, say in Ulster, Lebanon, or Russia; but it does suggest that people want change and may adopt a conflict paradigm on Canada.

Both our questions, therefore, about the causes of our problems, human nature or society, and their etiology, systemic or discrete, introduce us to the three paradigms on society and social problems.

THE THREE PARADIGMS

Every year *Maclean's* conducts a poll across Canada, surveying 1500 Canadians about different aspects of their behaviour, attitudes and values. Not all the questions are asked every year, but some of them suggest that Canadians entertain very different paradigms about Canada. Various questions from the 1994 poll indicate that levels of satisfaction and dissatisfaction vary widely (*Maclean's* 2.1.95).

Canadians were very satisfied with Canada. For instance 91% agreed that "Canada is the best country in the world in which to live" (83% in Quebec); 80% believe that "opportunities for women to move into senior positions in the workforce" have improved in the last ten years (as against 15% who think they have stayed the same, 4% who believe they have worsened, and 1% who do not know or gave no answer). Canadians were more divided about their own personal financial situations: 36% said it stayed the same over the last ten years, 33% said it improved and 31% said it worsened (and again, 1% did not know or did not answer).

On the other hand there were many areas of dissatisfaction: inequality, health care, immigration, youth, gender relations, politics, and crime. To simplify the statistics we will just compare the "extremes," omitting the relatively low scores for "Don't Know" and "No Answer", and the higher scores for "Stayed about the same". On *inequality*, 60% believe that the gap between wealthy and middle class Canadians has widened over the past ten years, as compared to 14% who think it has narrowed. 44% think that the *health care* system has deteriorated as against 21% who think it has improved. *Immigrants*: 47% believe that the quality of immigrants who have come to Canada has worsened, versus 14% who think it is better. And 43% believe that relations between immigrant and non-immigrant communities have worsened, while only 28% think they have improved. *Youth*: 76% think that the behaviour of young people has worsened in the last ten years, compared to only 6% who think it is better. *Gender*: 43% think that relations between men and women have worsened in the last ten years, a bit higher than the 36% who think that they have improved. *Crime*: the greatest consensus is that 85% believe that violent crime has increased in the last ten years, compared to only 4% who think it has decreased. *Politicians*: 77% think that "too many people who seek public office do so for financial gain"; only 22% disagree.

Although these questions do not isolate with surgical precision the adherents of the three paradigms, nor were they intended to do so, they do indicate some deep divisions in the population's perceptions of reality. Perhaps the deepest division is between optimists and pessimists. Nonetheless some believe that we are becoming more equal economically, the health care system is improving, youth are behaving better, gender relations and immigrant/non-immigrant relations are improving, violent crime has been decreasing, and politicians are not in it for the cash. . . . Happy souls! They are a minority, sometimes a minuscule minority (and we do not know whether they were consistently optimistic), but the poll does demonstrate the existence of different paradigms.

Evidently the satisfied and optimistic minority are more likely to adopt a *conservative* paradigm of society than the dissatisfied and pessimistic majority (on at least some issues), who see more conflicts, more problems, and must demand or hope for more change. Nonetheless, the overall satisfaction with Canada itself was the highest consensus of all (91%), so these "gripes" must be taken in that context of satisfaction.

The conservative paradigm is also known as the consensus model, from its central emphasis on consensus about norms and values as the integrating mechanism of modern society; we might also refer to it as the functionalist perspective, from the prevailing school within the paradigm. Indeed the "small c" conservative perspective is the dominant paradigm in Canada. Note that the conservative paradigm does not necessarily translate into votes for the Progressive Conservative political party; paradigms and parties are distinct phenomena. Indeed although the Liberal party may be more towards the left of the political spectrum, and Reform further to the right, all three parties subscribe to the consensus/conservative paradigm as sketched in Table 1-1, in that there is no demand for *violent* social change.

The conflict paradigm is also known as the activist, radical, or even Marxist model, from its prime ideologue. Not that all protesters and critics are Marxists, of course; but the most systematic and effective critic of capitalist societies in the nineteenth century, and there were many, was Karl Marx. The demise of communism has not negated the acuity of his insights, nor has capitalism (or communism) succeeded in eliminating poverty, abolishing exploitation and misery, or in solving our social problems. If we may extrapolate from the *Maclean's*/Decima data, it is reasonable to suppose that those who are most dissatisfied and pessimistic about their economic situation and their future, are also most likely to be dissatisfied with Canada in general. Certainly Canada has its dissatisfied groups and its critics from various perspectives: many native people, the poor and the unemployed, many feminists, Quebec nationalists, many Maritimers, especially those in the fishing industry, many Prairie farmers, members of some visible minorities, and others, have expressed their collective discontent with various aspects of Canadian life. This discontent may be partial, not total. Nonetheless these discontented Canadians, in so far as they work for change in their own interests, express conflict rather than consensus paradigms on society — and as such are likely to be perceived as *problematic* by other Canadians.

In Canada the conflict paradigm may not be the norm. In other countries, violent conflict itself, not "just" the paradigm, is the norm. Civil wars rage in many countries, and violent revolutionary movements flare up in others. People are fighting and dying to change their countries, to defend their rights, to acquire their basic human rights, to create a better world for themselves and their children. The status quo is believed to be unjust, unfair, illegitimate and even evil. In the last few years, dictators have been toppled, regimes over-thrown, and even the Soviet Empire has crumbled. Violence is an extreme form of the expression of political discontent; it is also normal, and it does not always succeed in changing society for the better for anyone, except perhaps arms deal-ers. More usually, the discontented *work* peacefully and energetically to reform society. Violence is a weapon of last resort, or a minority choice.

The point is that these paradigms are not simply academic matters of no interest outside the classroom. On the contrary, they are matters of our beliefs and influence our actions.

The third paradigm presented here, feminism, is also a conflict theory of society and social problems, but different in major respects from the radical para-digm — and also of course from ethnic and regional paradigms. The principal difference is that where radicals tend to regard capitalism as the major problem, the source and foundation of all (or most) of the others, feminists tend to regard patriarchy as the major problem.

All three paradigms are presented as ideal types in Table 1-1. Obviously they are vast over-simplifications of complex paradigms, so they are only the first words on the topic, not the last.

Probably most macro sociologists, and almost everyone if it comes to that, tend to fit ideologically into one or another of these orientations. The models describe constellations of ideas which *tend* to go together, more or less. No single individual may fit exactly into any one of these models, but most Canadians probably fit reasonably well into one or more of these categories.

Critical theorists, whether radical, feminist, ethnic or regional, examine what is wrong with society and its institutions, and query how it can be fixed. Consensus theorists are more inclined to exclaim "how sweet it is!", how much better it is now than it was in the past, and sing that it's getting better all the time. The two perspectives are not theoretically mutually exclusive, though in practice they tend to be; nor is one necessarily "right" and another "wrong" — although activists might not agree with that, nor with each other. The question really is, how useful is one or the other, and what are the practical/political implications of one paradigm or another.

The paradigms in Table 1-1 are not rigid, nor mutually exclusive. Marx, for instance, is usually described as an activist and a revolutionary, which he cer-tainly was, although in a literary rather than a physically violent mode. Yet his analyses of economic and political structure were in the highest traditions of sci-entific positivist scholarship, especially *Capital* (although largely outdated now); furthermore he wrote a superb, and probably satirical, functionalist analysis of crime (Marx, 1963:167-68), which is remarkably similar to later functionalist analyses of poverty (Gans, 1971) and crime (Merton, 1957). Also he himself stated that "communism is humanism," and his biographer describes him as a humanist (McClellan, 1971:112, 27). Marx, and especially Engels, also wrote

Table 1-1   Paradigms of Society

Variable	Conservative	Conflict	Feminist
Attitude to Society	Satisfied	Dissatisfied	Dissatisfied
Society	Body, order, organism, family	Battlefield, disorder	Battle of the sexes
Bond of Society	Consensus Division of labour	Coercion Violence	Coercion (by males/patriarchy)
Theorists	Burke, de Tocqueville, Comte, Spencer, Durkheim, Parsons and Merton, Functionalism	Machiavelli, Hobbes, Rousseau, Marx and Engels; Marxists; Freud Nietzsche; C.W. Mills; the union movement.	Wollstonecraft, Martineau, Anthony, the Pankhursts, Macphail, McClung, de Beauvoir, Millett, Greer, Steinem, NAC, CACSW
Goal of Sociology	Scientific understanding Prediction, Fine-tuning reforms as necessary	Action Revolution	Reform and/or radical reform Transformation
Nature of Society	A balance of multiple, specialized, inter-dependent institutions Basically fair and just	Competitive struggle for dominance. Class conflict Oppressive, exploitative, illegitimate	Patriarchy, Masculinist, Gender conflict Basically unfair and unjust
State	The State can solve social problems	The State *is* the problem: class rule	The State *is* the problem: male rule

early and important "feminist" critiques of nineteenth century capitalism. Positivist, functionalist, feminist and humanist (the labels are not mutually exclusive), but above all Marx was an activist . . . who lived the rather conservative life of a Victorian gentleman and scholar.

Emile Durkheim, the prime consensus theorist and founder of functionalism, was regarded as a wild radical in his time for seeming to justify crime, as we shall see. And certainly socialists and feminists fly many different ideological banners, as we shall see (cf. McLellan, 1983:9; Walby, 1990). Labels therefore have to be treated with care, and many different paradigms are possible.

Labels are not only academic: when used as short-hand, broad descriptions, they may also be pejorative. Indeed hostilities can be expected. The paradigms are mirror images of each other: diametrically opposed. The conservative paradigm sees reality from the top down: the goal is to conserve (or to recreate the society that once was), to maintain the status quo, and was initially developed by Comte, Spencer, and Durkheim. The two conflict paradigms, the Marxist and the feminist, see reality from the bottom up, from the point of view of the oppressed (defined by class or gender); the goals are to change, with the former stressing socioeconomic equality and the latter gender equality. Yet they too are often opposed: one blames capitalism, one blames patriarchy. It is no wonder that ideological conflicts generate heated rhetoric and vicious invectives: "dyed in the wool rednecks," "bleeding-heart liberals," "wild-eyed radicals," "shrill man-hating feminists," and "sexist pigs." Such labels should be understood for what they are: statements of paradigms.

The three paradigms of society will be understood better when perused again after reading Chapters 2, 3 and 4, but they are presented here to serve as a rough map for the following three chapters.

Paradigms are not new in sociology; as ideal-typical perspectives or world views, the dichotomous consensus and conflict paradigms were developed by Dahrendorf (1959), Lenski (1966), Cohen (1968) and others to compare Durkheimian and Marxist theories. Since then other paradigms have been articulated, particularly in Canada, where Marchak (1975) and Hiller (1976) have demonstrated the importance of regional, ethnic, religious, and cultural paradigms. More recently Burrell and Morgan (1985) have suggested four dominant paradigms in sociological theory; but they did not include feminism. I think that these three models suffice for the analysis of social problems, although they can of course be added to, or subdivided, as necessary to include, for instance, radical humanism and radical structuralism (Burrell and Morgan, 1985), or the various schools of feminism (Walby, 1990, Descarries-Belanger and Roy, 1991), or the regional, ethnic and other paradigms. Rich and poor, women and men, Maritimers and Ontarians, anglophones and francophones, etc., do not see Canada nor social problems in the same lights.

Not only do we probably see and construct social problems differently; we ourselves are also constructed as problematic: as friends or foes. Definitions go both ways. We define, and we are also defined. There is a long and valuable tradition that the sociologist is somehow "outside" our social problems: the objective, detached, scientific, and neutral observer, the expert, unbiased, impartial, and maybe all-knowing. Useful though this tradition is, I think we must realize at the outset that not only are we *not* outside the system, but we are all involved in our social problems; indeed all of us as citizens *create* our problems by our defining processes. Furthermore, to paraphrase Pogo (an old cartoon character): "I have seen the problem, and it is us!" We are all identified by others by virtue of our age, colour, language, gender, socioeconomic status and so on, as either friend or enemy, ally or fair game. To others, we may be readily identifiable as problematic. We not only do have vested interests which are problematic to others; but we have interests imputed to us, correctly or otherwise. And we do have our own biases, individual and collective. In studying social problems, therefore, we are studying ourselves . . . and we ourselves are being studied.

Note that the experts on, say, unemployment are probably neither the sociologist, nor the economist, nor the politician, but the unemployed; the experts on sexism and racism are primarily the victims, and also the victimizers. If we want to study social problems, text books are fine and helpful; but mostly we should talk to the people who live these problems, and listen to what they have to say, and read what they have written. With this in mind I have tried to include statements of individuals' experiences where possible.

Finally social problems are not academic matters, but often quite literally matters of life and death. As problems they can be quite depressing; but hopefully we can at least understand them better, and perhaps actively contribute meeting some of the challenges in our own lives. But the starting point is realizing that people do see things differently, and understanding (Weber's *verstehen*) how and why they do so. Then the action.[3]

ENDNOTES

1. Sociology neither is, nor can be, value free; nor should it be, conflict theorists might add, insisting that the point of sociology is to effect changes. Indeed, examining the three paradigms mentioned in this chapter is useful in clarifying the sets of values prevailing in sociology (and outside sociology too).

2. On paradigms of human nature and society see Stevenson (1987); Trigg (1988); and Burrell and Morgan (1985).

3. In practice, understanding and action are not so easily dichotomized of course.

THE CONSERVATIVE PARADIGM

Canada is a country that believes in freedom, dignity and respect, equality and fair treatment, and opportunity to participate. It is a country that cares for the disadvantaged at home and elsewhere, a country that prefers peaceful solutions to disputes. Canada is a country that, for all its diversity, has shared values.

This Committee of the Senate and the House of Commons paints a sunny portrait of Canada. Of course Canada is not perfect:

However, we must frankly and openly recognize that Canadian society has experienced gaps in its generosity and tolerance . . . Many political and legal battles have been waged by threatened communities, such as aboriginal peoples, women's groups, minority language communities and other disadvantaged groups.

Yet despite these "gaps" and these "battles", these shadows over the land, the sun still shines:

Canada is a peaceable society. It is a society based on civility, built not out of revolution but accommodation. It evolved through orderly progress . . . The frontiers would be harnessed largely by the rule of law, not the gun.

These quotations describe the Canadian mythology with passion: the "shared values" are clarified, the peace, civility, equality, fairness, order, tolerance, caring, freedom . . . (1991: 1, 23, 3. Cat. No. CP 22-29).

But is this portrait accurate? Or is it simply federal propaganda? Is this myth or reality?

We do have data which enable us to answer these questions. First we have the responses to the *Maclean's*/CTV 1994 poll, which we have just discussed, in which the vast majority of Canadians (91%) say that they believe Canada is the best country in the world in which to live (*Maclean's* 2.1.95). We also have the

1992 poll in which the majority say that they are satisfied with their personal economic situations (66%) and their future prospects (71%), compared with only 35% and 27% respectively who are dissatisfied (*Maclean's* 4.1.93). This gives us a rough "satisfaction level" of 66% to 91% as against a dissatisfaction level of 9% to 35%, depending on the precise question. This may coincide with a conservative-conflict paradigm split; and perhaps also with the "gaps in [Canada's] generosity and tolerance." At any rate, the majority is satisfied and seems to be proud of Canada.

On the other hand, dissatisfaction levels were very high with regard to some specific issues: crime especially (85%), politicians (77%) youth (76%), inequality (60%), immigrants (47%), and gender relations (43%). And the 1993 poll found that 39% of Canadians found that Canada was a worse place to live than it was ten years ago, compared to only 19% who said it was better. A majority (51%) were more pessimistic about the future than they were ten years ago, whereas only 32% were more optimistic. It is in these sectors of the population that we can expect to find the less conservative and more critical paradigms of Canada.

The second source of data, which complements this subjective data by its objectivity, is the United Nations Human Development (UNDP) annual reports. The UNDP has formulated a Human Development Index "which combines indicators of national income, life expectancy and educational attainment to give a composite measure of human progress." By this index Canada is number one in the world for 1994, (followed by Switzerland, Japan, Sweden and Norway), up from number two in 1993, but first also in 1992 (1993:19; *The Gazette* 28.5.94). Edmund Burke wrote over 200 years ago in 1790: "To make us love our country, our country ought to be lovely" (1986: 172) — sociologically lovely. By this criterion Canada is the loveliest country in the world, and Canadians have much to value, to be proud of, and to conserve.

Finally an international poll by the *Times Mirror* Group in 1994 found that Canadians were by and large very content with their dominant social institutions, Parliament, the Church and religious authorities, business, and the press, although not so content with unions, compared to people in other countries. Indeed Canada ranked highest of all eight countries polled in satisfaction with government and business, politics and economics — two critical sectors of social life, and Canadians were mainly satisfied with four of the five sectors polled. Indeed the only institution with which they were dissatisfied was the unions. Note, however, the high proportion of the "floating vote": the neither, both, or no opinion vote ranged from 17% to 25% (but in Germany this was elevated to a high of up to 62%!); also note that the dissatisfaction vote in Canada ranges from a low of 10% (the press) to highs of 35% and 48% (parliament and the unions respectively — an interesting juxtaposition since parliament is usually identified with the maintenance of the status quo and the unions with change!).

The data presented in Table 2-1 indicates not only the comparative international contentment, so to speak, but also the sectoral comparison, the range of dissatisfaction and the floaters.

All in all, these three surveys, *Maclean's/CTV*, the UNDP report and the *Times Mirror*, indicate high levels of achievement (UNDP) and satisfaction (*Times Mirror*) with Canada, despite some concerns over specific issues and for the future (*Maclean's/Decima*). This picture tends to support the analysis of the Committee of the Senate and the House of Commons (1990). The conservative paradigm would seem to have widespread support, with good reason, but with some dissenters on specific issues. The myth is the reality.

Conservatism, as its name implies, legitimizes the conservation and preservation of a given status quo, with such reforms as may be necessary to alleviate specific problems or achieve new goals. Usually identified with the right of the political spectrum (and the blue of the light spectrum), conservatives are most inclined to be relatively satisfied with society as it is. Other things being equal, they are more likely to be "haves" than "have nots," although there are working class conservatives and middle class radicals (like Marx and Engels). The distinguishing features of conservative ideology include, as we saw in Table 1-1, the belief that society is, or is like, an organism, a living body, in its unity, growth, and in the interdependence of its parts; a concern with order, in tension with an interest also in change and progress; and a confidence in hierarchy as the most appropriate and efficient method of government in politics, economics, and bureaucracy.

The origins of the essentially sociological enterprise of describing and analyzing society, lie in the conservative reaction to the turmoil of the French Revolution, and in the problems generated by rapid industrialization and change. In this chapter we will trace the conservative tradition through Burke, Comte, de Tocqueville, Spencer and Durkheim to North American functionalism, and conclude with the Canadian conservative, George Grant. At the same time we will draw out some of the implications of the conservative paradigm on society and its problems by contrasting it with the conflict perspective of Marx, Engels and the activist tradition, which will be developed more fully in the next chapter.

EDMUND BURKE (1729-97)

The founder of conservative ideology is generally considered to be the Irishman, Edmund Burke. A marginal man, Irish but living in England, Anglican but of Catholic background with Catholic family, at odds with one political faction after another, he was also politically complex. He approved of the abdication, as he called the expulsion, of James II in 1688, and the secession of the 13 colonies in

Table 2-1 Institutional Satisfaction in Eight Countries 1994

"I'd like your opinion of some groups and developments in [your country]. For each that I name, tell me if you think they are having mainly a *good influence* on the way things are going in this country or mainly a *bad influence* on the way things are going in this country."

The Parliament/Congress/National Assembly

	Canada	France	Germany	Italy	Mexico	Spain	U.K.	U.S.
Good influence	44	40	23	13	38	42	27	39
Bad influence	35	30	16	55	15	23	43	44
Neither, both or no opinion	21	30	61	32	47	35	30	17

The Church/Religion/Religious Attitudes

	Canada	France	Germany	Italy	Mexico	Spain	U.K.	U.S.
Good influence	61	39	24	45	73	48	41	73
Bad influence	18	34	14	19	5	21	22	15
Neither, both or no opinion	21	27	62	36	22	31	37	12

Unions

	Canada	France	Germany	Italy	Mexico	Spain	U.K.	U.S.
Good influence	31	36	25	20	45	35	32	42
Bad influence	48	39	17	41	13	32	32	37
Neither, both or no opinion	21	25	59	39	42	33	36	21

Business Executives/Management

	Canada	France	Germany	Italy	Mexico	Spain	U.K.	U.S.
Good influence	51	43	27	29	50	27	31	44
Bad influence	24	23	14	32	10	27	26	37
Neither, both or no opinion	25	34	39	39	40	46	43	19

Newspaper

	Canada	France	Germany	Italy	Mexico	Spain	U.K.	U.S.
Good influence	73	59	47	37	70	71	38	74
Bad influence	10	12	6	19	4	3	29	13
Neither, both or no opinion	17	29	47	44	26	26	33	13

Source: *Globe and Mail* 16.3.94

1776, but he was appalled by the outbreak of the French Revolution in 1789, and quickly published his *Reflections on the Revolution in France* (1790).

Many of Burke's contemporaries were absolutely delighted by the Revolution. They believed it was the triumph of liberty, democracy, reason and the enlightenment over monarchical tyranny and the papacy. Wordsworth was happy: "Bliss was it in that dawn to be alive, but to be young was very heaven." He changed his mind later when war broke out.

Burke was more cautious, and more prescient; and after the arrest of Louis XVI and Marie Antoinette he put his political reputation on the line:

> I tremble for the cause of liberty, from such an example to kings. I tremble for the cause of humanity, in the unpunished outrages of the most wicked of mankind. (1986: 177)

In Burke's view:

> Society is indeed a contract . . . a partnership not only between those who are living, but between those who are living, those who are dead, and those who are to be born. (1986: 194-95)

This contract is historically rooted in the Magna Carta (the charter signed by King John in 1215 which guaranteed certain political and civil liberties and restricted royal power); and he said that it is willed by God as "the necessary means" of the perfection of human nature (1986: 196); and it is also psychologically founded in, and developed from, the family:

> We begin our public affections in our families. No cold relation is a zealous citizen. We pass on to our neighbourhoods, and our habitual provincial connections. These are inns and resting-places. (1986: 315)

The state begins in family affections, therefore, and love:

> To be attached to the subdivision, to love the little platoon we belong to in society, is the first principle (the germ as it were) of public affections. It is the first link in the series by which we proceed towards a love to our country and to mankind. (1986:135)

In France what Burke saw was not the steady expansion of love, reason, and human perfection from the family to mankind, but "rage and phrenzy," and not democracy but mob rule:

> Rage and phrenzy will pull down more in half an hour, than prudence, deliberation and foresight can build up in a hundred years. (1986: 279-80)

The result in France:

> Laws overturned; tribunals subverted; industry without vigour; commerce expiring; the revenue unpaid, yet the people impoverished; a church pillaged, and a state not relieved; civil and military anarchy made the constitution of the kingdom. (1986: 126)

Burke's conservatism was not well received at first; but two points are important. When he wrote, the revolution was still in its first year, with the King and Queen arrested. The English had already executed one King, Charles I in 1640, and banished another, James II in 1688; so this perhaps was "no big deal." (It was for Burke, however, who was a great admirer of the Queen of France.) But Burke predicted that things would get worse; and when they did, with the September 1790 massacres, the executions of the King and Queen, the Terror, and then the Napoleonic wars which devastated Europe until the final defeat at Waterloo in 1815, then admiration for his wisdom and foresight, and his conservatism, increased rapidly. The final irony was the restoration of the Bourbons in the period of Louis XVIII.

Burke's second point was not about France, but about Britain: he advised his readers that "this could happen here." Aye! There's the rub! And as the violence escalated in France, so initial sympathies gradually transmuted into distaste, fear, and eventually war against the French — and more sympathy for Burke's notions of gradualism, order, tradition, hierarchy, and affection. The European blood bath that was the French Revolution for more than a quarter of a century, from 1789-1815, determined Conservative thought from Burke through de Tocqueville and Comte, for a generation (until the radical reaction of Marx and Engels in 1848).

ALEXIS DE TOCQUEVILLE (1805-59)

One of the foremost conservative theorists of the nineteenth century, and a precursor of sociology, was Alexis de Tocqueville. A French aristocrat, he had lost many of his family to the Terror; perhaps it was this experience which made him wary of democracy. In 1831 he visited the United States, studied politics, religion, the justice and penal systems, race relations, and the attitudes and values of the locals, and finally published a massive two-volume work, *Democracy in America*. In his first sentence he sets the theme of the book, and also its limitations:

> Amongst the novel objects that attracted my attention during my stay in the United States, nothing struck me more forcibly than the general equality of conditions. (1966, Vol. 1: xxxv)

This "general equality of conditions" among the [white] people [males?] caused de Tocqueville some unease, despite some admiration. Reviewing history, he noted that:

> The noble has gone down on the social ladder, and the [commoner] has gone up. The one descends and the other rises. Every half-century brings them nearer to each other, and they will very shortly meet. . . Whithersoever we turn our eyes we shall witness the same continual revolution throughout the whole of Christendom. (1966, Vol. 1: xxxiii)

But what did this equality mean? Where was Christendom going? For de Tocqueville, equality was not an end in itself, nor was it necessarily progress, as it was for his contemporaries Marx and Engels. He confessed that he felt "a kind of religious dread" at the prospect of "so irresistible a revolution" (1966, Vol. 1: xxxix). Why this dread?

For one reason: he was not at heart a democrat, but an aristocrat. He wrote

> I have an intellectual preference for democratic institutions, but I am an aristocrat by instinct; this means that I detest and fear the masses. I love with passion freedom, legality, the respect for rights — but not democracy . . . Liberty is my foremost passion. That's the truth! (1966, Vol. 1: v)[1]

Liberty and equality are contradictory goals in this view. As R.H. Tawney put it later, "Freedom for the pike is death for the minnows" (1964:164). There's not much equality in being food for something else. After the Terror and the Napoleonic wars he was perhaps skeptical of the value of the slogans of the revolution: "Liberté! Egalité! Fraternité!," and of Rousseau's beliefs, enshrined in the American Declaration of Independence, that "All men are created equal." In his most famous phrase, he feared "the tyranny of the majority" (1966, Vol. 1:248).

Although de Tocqueville was perhaps nostalgic for a lost aristocratic order, and in dread of an egalitarian future, his main concern was to point out the *dangers* of equality and of democracy (1966, Vol. 2: 350; cf. 106).

He was a noble, and descending the social ladder. No doubt that was part of his concern with the dangers. But only part. The dangers were real and obvious. And de Tocqueville was also a sociologist of race relations who reported bitterly on the degradation and destruction of the native Indians and Blacks by the majority Whites. On American Indian policy he states:

> The Spaniards were unable to exterminate the Indian race by those unparalleled atrocities which brand them with indelible shame, nor did they even succeed in wholly depriving it of its rights; but the Americans of the United States have accomplished this twofold purpose with singular felicity; tranquilly, legally, philanthropically, without shedding blood, and without violating a single great principle of morality in the eyes of the world. It is impossible to destroy men with more respect for the laws of humanity (1966, Vol. 1: 347-48).

Except perhaps in Canada, some might add. Small wonder that de Tocqueville feared the tyranny of the majority. So did the Indians, and with reason.

And in his continuing critique of democracy in America, de Tocqueville summed up his analysis of the state of black-white relations succinctly: "I reserve my execrations for those who, after a thousand years of freedom, brought back slavery into the world once more" (1966, Vol. 1: 375).

Having identified the problem, the white majority, de Tocqueville then clarified the further problems to be expected in the future:

> By the choice of the master, or by the will of the slave, it [slavery] will cease; and in either case great calamities may be expected to ensue. If liberty be refused to the negroes of the South, they will in the end seize it for themselves by force; if it be given, they will abuse it ere long. (1966, Vol. 1: 375)

That is, granted freedom, the Blacks will struggle for equality and declare war against the tyrants: the majority.

De Tocqueville predicted:

> The negroes may long remain slaves without complaining; but if they are once raised to the level of free men, they will soon revolt at being deprived of all their civil rights; and as they cannot become the equals of whites, they will speedily declare themselves as enemies. (1966, Vol. 1: 372)

As indeed so many have done, both in the United States, with Malcolm X among others, and to a lesser degree perhaps in Canada. The problem of racism persists. And de Tocqueville's relatively unenthusiastic analysis of democracy and equality must be complemented by his relatively radical analysis of race relations, and a liberal-conservative view of gender relations. He devoted four chapters to the equality of the sexes.

> There are people in Europe who, confounding together the different characteristics of the sexes, would make man and woman into beings not only equal, but alike. They would give to both the same functions, impose on both the same duties, and grant to both the same rights; they would mix them in all things, — their occupations, their pleasures, their business. It may readily be conceived, that, by thus attempting to make one sex equal to the other, both are degraded; and from so preposterous a medley of the works of nature, nothing could ever result but weak men and disorderly women. (1966, Vol. 2: 223)

Not so in America, said De Tocqueville. He subscribed to the separate *but equal* theory of gender, and to the notion that each gender had its own sphere of power: men in the public world, at work, and women in the private world, at home. He contrasted what he described as the greater equality and freedom of American women favourably with the French norms of "contempt of women" (1966, Vol. 2: 226). He was therefore not as conservative as the majority norm in France. Admitting that women in the United States are confined and dependent, he concluded:

> I have nowhere seen woman occupying a loftier position; and if I were asked, now that I am drawing to the close of this work, in which I have spoken of so many important things done by the Americans, to what the singular prosperity and growing strength of that people ought mainly to be attributed, I should reply, — to the superiority of their women. (1966, Vol. 2: 226)

De Tocqueville's conservatism is therefore not simple; furthermore his concerns for "the tyranny of the majority" were surely well-founded, not only in the Terror in France, and the then prevailing patterns of race relations in the US, fully supported by the (white) majority, but also later. Only 100 years later, Hitler was duly elected by the fully enfranchised German people on a clearly stated platform of racism, violence, and world conquest.

Democracy and equality are, if not a problem, then problematic, for gender, race, and class. And de Tocqueville concluded his work enigmatically, with a sigh for the old hierarchical order:

> The nations of our time cannot prevent the conditions of men from becoming equal; but it depends upon themselves whether the principle of equality is to lead them to servitude or freedom, to knowledge or barbarism, to prosperity or wretchedness. (1966: Vol. 2: 331)

We have seen, and still see, both. In de Tocqueville's view, equality was not a panacea. Nor was it for Comte.

AUGUSTE COMTE (1798-1857)

August Comte is usually considered the founder of sociology partly because he coined the term, but also because he established, or tried to establish, the new discipline on a firm scientific foundation of empirical methods which he called Positivism. The term was intended to emphasize the distinctiveness of sociology, which he first named social *physics*, from metaphysics and historicism. In his first major work, *Cours de Philosophie Positive* (6 vols., 1830-42), Comte reported his discovery of the law of human progress, namely that the human mind has passed successively through three stages: the theological, the metaphysical, and is now finally in the scientific or positive stage. This law of the three stages postulates that in past millennia people believed that phenomena are directly produced by God or gods; in the second stage they believe they are produced by "abstract forces," like nature; now people study the laws governing phenomena. "Reason and observation are the means of this knowledge" (1975: 71-72).

Evidence of this, he suggests, is that societal evolution is mirrored in the three stages of individual development: "Now, each of us is aware, if he looks back upon his own history, that he was a theologian in his childhood, a metaphysician in his youth, and natural philosopher in his manhood" (1975: 73).

Comte dates the origins of positivism to the scientific renaissance pioneered by Bacon, Descartes, and Galileo, and the establishment of astronomy, physics, chemistry, and biology. But "Nothing was said of social phenomena . . . They are the most individual, the most complicated, the most dependent on others . . . This is what men have now most need of, and this it is the principal aim of the present work to establish" (1975: 76-77). The purpose of sociology, in his view, is to discover the laws of human society, and of human progress; he did believe that there were such laws, and that they were progressive. Sociology he described as "the queen of the sciences"; the most important of them all, its goal is clear: "Savoir pour prévoir et prévoir pour pouvoir." To know in order to foresee, and to foresee in order to act (cf. 1975:88). The sociologist is therefore, in this view, the equivalent of the philosopher-king in Plato's Republic: a gratifying thought to many sociologists, surely.

Comte was also the first sociologist to apply the organic analogy to society: the notion of the nation as the *body* politic.[2] It is an ancient idea in philosophy and theology, articulated by Plato in the *Republic* and developed by Paul with the doctrine of the Mystical Body; but Comte attempted to give it scientific legitimacy, influenced both Spencer and Durkheim, and thus pioneered the basic conservative paradigm. Having defined the individual organism as the subject of biology, and the social organism as the subject of sociology, Comte argued:

> If we take the best ascertained points in Biology, we may decompose structure anatomically into *elements, tissues* and *organs*. We have the same things in the Social Organism; and may even use the same names. (Comte, 1966, Vol. 2: 240)

So Comte described this Social Organism as composed of families, "the true elements or cells"; classes or castes, "its proper tissues"; and finally Cities and Communes "which are its real organs" (1966, Vol. 2: 242). From this organicism, with its intrinsically conservative bias, it is but a short step to functionalism: what are the functions of cells? families? tissues? inequality?

Comte's second major work, *Système de Politique Positive* (4 volumes) was published from 1851 to 1854 and reflected an entirely new set of values. By this time he had married and been widowed and these experiences seem to have changed his life. Under the rubric "We tire of thinking and even of acting; we never tire of loving," Comte still continued trying to develop "the science of society," but he also aimed for the "spiritual reorganization" first of Europe and then of the world, to be supported principally by women and the working classes. To this end he developed a "Religion of Humanity." The goals of positivism have changed: "L'amour pour principe, l'ordre pour base, et le progrès pour but." "Love . . . is our principle; Order our basis; and Progress our end" (1966, Vol. 1: 257). Furthermore the methodology has changed. No longer is the emphasis on observation, experimentation, and comparison, as in the sciences. Comte emphasized the subordination of the intellect to the heart, and of reason to feeling (1966, Vol. 1: 257; 13-16). This he described as the subjective principle of positivism, in contrast to the objective principle which is science.

Comte suggests that: "Our highest happiness consists in Love [of humanity]; and we know that more than any other feeling Love may be strengthened by exercise . . . To love Humanity may be truly said to constitute the whole duty of Man" (1966, Vol. 1: 283, 285). Positivism therefore substitutes "the Love of Humanity for the Love of God" — a point that Feuerbach or Marx might have appreciated had not Comte raised a new religion to replace Christianity, with himself as Pontiff. He concluded his discussion with a call to "pure" self-sacrifice, and the assertion that: "Placing our highest happiness in universal Love, we live, as far as it is possible, for others" (1966, Vol. 1: 321). Paradoxically this sociological ideal is virtually identical with the Christian ideal to love thy neighbour as thyself (Matthew 19: 19) which Comte so deprecated. It seems that the positivist stage of human progress had come full circle back to the first stage, the theological.

So what does Comte contribute to the understanding of social problems? First, his conviction that social science can understand, predict and control social interaction. Second, his insistence on the scientific method, rather than theology or metaphysics. Later he switches to the personal rather than the scientific: love, yet allied with reason. Indeed his insistence on both reason/science and love/the affective faculty is perhaps his greatest legacy: a sociology that does not care about people may be scientific, but it may also be morally bankrupt; methodologically sophisticated perhaps, but useless in practical terms. Such warrior sociologists as Marx and Spencer would no doubt have scoffed at Comte's affectionate sociology; but Durkheim might have noted that love is surely the principle bond of society (although he did not), stronger than the division of labour or religion. "All you need is love," sang the Beatles much later, and Burke had thought the same much earlier; but Burke and Comte began with the family, which Durkheim did not.

More fundamentally, efforts at social change are informed by goals and values — they are not, and indeed cannot be, value-free. Comte reminds us that human values exist, and should be articulated.

Comte's emphasis on order, organicism, hierarchy, and religion are no doubt traditional conservative themes in the analysis of society, and in the resolution or amelioration of problems; but others disagreed with his paradigms — notably Marx.

Comte and Marx were contemporaries, both of them caught up in the political and economic turmoil of the Industrial Revolution in Europe, and both of them intent on solving the problems they saw. But they defined the problems differently and, therefore, conceptualized different solutions. Both had rejected the religions of their youth, but Comte remained committed to secular religion, while Marx was committed to atheism. Comte, who had seen the consequences of the French revolutionary slogan of "Egalité," believed that hierarchy was essential to order, whereas Marx believed in equality. Both believed in progress, but for Comte this could only be achieved by the triumph of social science in a rapidly changing society, while Marx believed progress could only be achieved through class conflict and revolution. Comte believed in science, and above all, love; Marx in political action and violence. And the differences could be multiplied. Problems for the one were solutions to the other, and vice versa.

HERBERT SPENCER (1820-1903)

Spencer is most well-known now for his Social Darwinism and his dictum: "The survival of the fittest." Yet he developed his theory of the evolution of society through war, "the struggle for survival," long before Darwin's *Origin of Species*. Indeed Darwin's theory of natural selection could well be known as "Natural Spencerism" — the application of Spencer's model of social conflict to the natural world. Darwin himself graciously described Spencer as "about a dozen times 'my superior'" (Coser, 1971: 110).

Spencer's conservatism is rooted in his individualism, his organicism, and his evolutionism; and it begins with his first book, *Social Statics* (1851), subtitled "The Conditions Essential to Human Happiness," which nailed his values to the mast! Here he formulated the law of equal freedom: "Every man has freedom to do all that he wills, provided he infringes not the equal freedom of any other man" (1969: 103). This liberty of action is "the first essential of happiness," says Spencer, and this law is "the *primary* law of right relationship between man and man" (1969: 88-89). It is also essentially individual — and one of the sources of Spencer's conservatism.

The role of government is simply to enforce this law. Thus government is "a necessary evil"; it is "an institution originating in man's imperfection; an institution confessedly begotten by necessity out of evil" (1969: 311, 14-15). The least government is the best government. This, of course, has implications for social policy, as we shall see: conservative ones. Government should not be involved in the solution of social problems; social problems are an individual matter and call for individual solution.

This ties in with his theory of societal evolution through war. He argues that humanity has progressed over the millennia, from despotism, "feudalism, serfdom, slavery — all tyrannical institutions . . . springing out of, and necessary to, a bad state of man," to democracy, constitutional government, and political freedom. "Thus, as civilization advances, does government decay. To the bad it is essential, to the good, not" (1969: 13-14). He distinguished between savage or primitive man, "whose happiness is obtained at the expense of the happiness of other beings," and the ultimate, ideal or civilized man, who respects the law of equal freedom, "who can obtain perfect happiness without deducting from the happiness of others" (1969: 413). He believed that, all in all, we were evolving out of the state of war, but that war itself was the mechanism of this progress: "from the very beginning, the conquest of one people over another has been, in the main, the conquest of the social man over the anti-social man; or strictly speaking, of the more adapted over the less adapted" (1969: 416-17). War is useful, therefore, in this view, and contributes to progress and social evolution.

This is "the struggle for existence" (1969: 228. Spencer's phrase before Darwin's); and the way humans advance towards greater "individuation" — a progressive journey "from the one extreme in which the state is everything and the individual nothing, to the other extreme [and goal], in which the individual is everything and the state nothing" (1969: 435-36). Obviously, however, the cost of progress is high.

Spencer was particularly impressed by the "analogy between the body politic and a living human body," as Plato and Hobbes had been before him. In his essay "The Social Organism" (1860) he discussed their similarities: both increase in size as they grow and evolve, increase in complexity, increase in the mutual interdependence of their parts, and survive beyond the lives of their component parts. He went on to compare the circulation of blood to the circulation of money; blood vessels are like roads, the double channels of arteries and veins are like the two tracks of railways, the brain performs parallel functions to Parliament, while nerves are comparable to telegraph wires (1969: 195-233).

The implications of this rather fanciful comparison are serious, for it is the brain that orders the body, as it is Parliament that rules the body politic; conversely disorder is action against Parliament. The conservative bias of the organicist metaphor is obvious. Indeed Spencer's conservatism was most harsh: he was deeply contemptuous of the amiable, the beneficent, the do-gooders and what we would now call the welfare state philosophy:

> Pervading all nature we may see at work a stern discipline, which is a little cruel that it may be very kind. That state of universal warfare maintained throughout the lower creation, to the great perplexity of many worthy people, is at bottom the most merciful provision which the circumstances admit of. (1969: 322)

This "universal warfare" applies not only in nature but also in society. Spencer does not shrink from the hard consequences of his logic, that human suffering and death are, in the long run, beneficial to humanity:

> The well-being of existing humanity, and the unfolding of it into this ultimate perfection, are both secured by that same beneficent, though severe discipline, to which the animate creation at large is subject: a discipline which is pitiless in the working out of good: a felicity-pursuing law which never swerves for the avoidance of partial and temporary suffering. The poverty of the incapable, the distresses that come upon the imprudent, the starvation of the idle, and those shoulderings aside of the weak by the strong, which leave so many "in shallows and in miseries," are the decrees of a large, far-seeing benevolence. It seems hard that an unskilfulness which with all his efforts he cannot overcome, should entail hunger upon the artizan. It seems hard that a labourer incapacitated by sickness from competing with his stronger fellows, should have to bear the resulting privations. It seems hard that widows and orphans should be left to struggle for life or death. Nevertheless, when regarded not separately, but in connection with the interests of universal humanity, these harsh fatalities are seen to be full of the highest beneficence. (1969: 322-23)

This is early functionalism in the extreme. In this view, poverty, suffering, and even death are functional for the well-being and ultimate perfection of existing humanity — which must have been a great consolation to the dying! And the oppression of the weak by the strong is actually benevolent: a law of nature fostering the struggle for existence and the evolution of society from savagery towards civilization, as he saw it. In *The Study of Sociology* Spencer was even more dogmatic:

> For if the unworthy are helped to increase, by shielding them from that mortality which their unworthiness would naturally entail, the effect is to produce, generation after generation, a greater unworthiness. . . .

> Fostering the good-for-nothing at the expense of the good, is an extreme cruelty. It is a deliberate storing-up of miseries for future generations. There is no greater curse to posterity than that of bequeathing them an increasing population of imbeciles and idlers and criminals. To aid the bad in multiplying, is, in effect, the same as maliciously providing for our descendants a multitude of enemies. (1961: 313,314)[3]

While allowing for private altruism, Spencer insists that public agencies should not support "good-for-nothings" nor prevent their deaths: "that . . . natural process of eliminations by which society continually purifies itself" (1961: 315). This is where Spencer's philosophy begins to anticipate Nazism, and the "ethnic cleansing" by the Serbs in Bosnia. But not preventing is not the same as actively causing death.

Yet Spencer was no fascist attempting to justify his privileged position, the class and race stratification system, and Victorian imperial policy. He did oppose the Poor Laws, intended to mitigate the lot of the poor, but he supported the extension of the vote to the working class, he advocated equity for women long before J.S. Mill, and he bitterly opposed British imperialism.[4] These seemingly inconsistent policies are yet entirely consistent with his individualism, evolutionism, and organicism, and his theory of struggle.

Spencer is complex, and would no doubt have been appalled at the way in which he has been used ideologically. He himself was optimistic: "Progress . . . is not an accident, but a necessity . . . so surely must the things we call evil and immorality disappear; so surely must man become perfect" (1969: 65). He did not see himself as a conservative: "The two feelings answer to the two sides of our present mixed nature [savage and civilized] . . . Conservatism defends those coercive arrangements which a still lingering savageness makes requisite. Radicalism endeavours to realize a state more in harmony with the character of the ideal man" (1969: 469 cf. 427). By his own criteria, therefore, he is a self-defined radical, but perhaps he is more a naturalist.

Charles Darwin appreciated and developed many of Spencer's ideas in *The Origin of Species* (1859), notably the struggle for survival and, through natural selection, the survival of the fittest. All this he formulated as "one general law, leading to the advancement of all organic beings, namely, multiply, vary, let the strongest live and the weakest die" (1968: 263). The similarity to Spencer is apparent. Darwin concluded his volume on an optimistic, even poetic note:

> Thus, from the war of nature, from famine and death, the most exalted object which we are capable of conceiving, namely, the production of the higher animals, directly follows. There is grandeur in this view of life, with its several powers, having been originally breathed into a few forms or into one; and that, whilst this planet has gone cycling on according to the fixed law of gravity, from so simple a beginning endless forms most beautiful and most wonderful have been, and are being, evolved. (1968: 459-60)

Nature and society mirror each other, in this view; and "nature red in tooth and claw," in Tennyson's immortal phrase, is mirrored by Hobbes' war of all against all and Spencer's state of universal warfare.

Conservatism therefore has many different ideological and personal roots, and various meanings also. That of Burke and De Tocqueville was rooted in their fear of the majority, Comte's in his intellectual elitism and Spencer's in his libertarianism and organicism despite his occasional radicalism. All of them cared profoundly for the love and happiness of the human species, each in their own style, but they evidently disagreed in their recommendations to achieve this happiness. Where Adam Smith had been the apostle of laissez-faire economics and the free market and hence of capitalism, Herbert Spencer was the apostle of laissez-faire politics, the survival of the fittest and hence of conservatism.

Spencer's work is no longer widely read: his rampant individualism, militarism, elitism, implicit racism, and total lack of compassion are out of step with the development of the welfare state after the great depression of the thirties. Nonetheless strands of his ideas are continually resurfacing and he remains a fundamental sociologist of conservative ideology.

EMILE DURKHEIM (1858-1917)

If Comte's principal purpose in sociology was to discover the laws of society by scientific methods, Durkheim's interest lay in the relation between the individual and society. Three of his four books were devoted to that topic: *The Division of Labor in Society* (1893), *Suicide* (1897) and *The Elementary Forms of Religious Life* (1912). This concern, he emphasized in the Preface to *The Division of Labor*, was not speculative but practical (1964: 33):

> We should judge our researches to have no worth at all if they were to have only a speculative interest. If we separate carefully the theoretical from the practical problems, it is not to the neglect of the latter; but, on the contrary, to be in a better position to solve them.

And in *Suicide* he insisted that "The progress of a science is proven by the progress toward solutions of the problems it treats" (1952: 35).

The first topic Durkheim tackled was that of the division of labor because it involved "the question of the relations of the individual to social solidarity" (1964: 37). It also enabled Durkheim to deal directly with contemporary society, avoiding the speculative questions of evolutionism, historicism, and diffusionism that interested some of his contemporaries. (His debt to Comte was acknowledged in 17 references.) But above all, it becomes clear, he believed that the division of labor "is the principal bond" of modern societies (1964: 173).

Durkheim posited two types of solidarity which he called "mechanical" and "organic." In the first the "collective conscience" is strong, he defined this as "the totality of beliefs and sentiments common to average citizens of the same society" (1964: 79); there is little division of labor; and the society is homogeneous. This solidarity is characteristic of traditional societies. Societies characterized by organic solidarity have extensive division of labor and are, therefore, highly heterogeneous with multiple roles. The collective conscience is weaker, and individualism is consequently stronger. This modern society poses the problem of anomie, or normlessness. This term, together with Marx's concept of alienation, has become part of the public vocabulary.

The solution? Durkheim half-ducked it, at first (1964: 23):

> The work of the sociologist is not that of the statesman. We do not have to present in detail what this reform should be. It will be sufficient to indicate the general principles as they appear from the preceding facts.

But later he becomes impassioned. After describing how many of the old bonds which united people to one another (religion, geography, family, collective conscience, etc.) have weakened, he explodes (1964: 28):

> A society composed of an infinite number of unorganized individuals, that a hypertrophied state is forced to oppress and contain, constitutes a veritable sociological monstrosity. . . . A nation can be maintained only if, between the State and the individual, there is intercalated a whole series of secondary groups near enough to the individuals to attract them strongly in their sphere of action and drag them, in this way, into the general torrent of social life. We have just shown how occupational groups are suited to fit this role, and that is their destiny.

Note the vast difference between the views of Durkheim and Marx on the division of labor: for Durkheim it is integrative, for Marx it is alienating.

He returned to the themes of individualism, anomie and bonding in *Suicide*, which is discussed in more detail in Chapter 7, but it should be mentioned that his study of suicide is still a classic.

"Social life," says Durkheim, "comes from a double source, the likeness of consciences and the division of social labor" (1964: 226), i.e., common values and mutual interdependence. Egoistic suicides are consequences of inadequate bonding between the individual and society, and anomic ones of confused or changed bonds. Religion is one powerful bonding force, and in the *Division of Labor* he had already commented on the role of religion in mechanical solidarity (1964: 169):

> Originally, [religion] pervades everything; everything social is religious; the two words are synonymous. Then, little by little, political, economic, scientific functions free themselves from the religious function, constitute themselves apart and take on a more and more acknowledged temporal character. God, who was at first present in all human relations, progressively withdraws from them; he abandons the world to men and their disputes.

In *Elementary Forms*, Durkheim develops his ideas further. Religion, he says, is symbolically the worship of society; as such it is both necessary and useful for the well-being of the individual and of society. For example, Durkheim observed that "nearly all the great institutions have been born in religion" (1974: 418-19): law, schools, hospitals, art, and more. Furthermore, the psychological benefits of religion are many (1947: 416-17).

> The believer who has communicated with his god is not merely a man who sees new truths of which the unbeliever is ignorant; he is a man who is *stronger* . . . Whoever has really practiced a religion knows very well that it is the cult which gives rise to expressions of joy, of interior peace, of serenity, of enthusiasm, which are to the believer an experimental proof of his beliefs.

In Durkheim's view, religion strengthened the moral, psychological, social, and institutional bonds which unite individuals with each other and with society; and, as he had shown earlier in *Suicide*, the weakening of these bonds can result in anomie and higher suicide rates. To paraphrase Voltaire, if religion did not exist it would be necessary to invent it (which, of course, is what Comte had tried to do in his own terms).

Finally, in a ringing challenge to the ghosts of Marx and Engels, and to Freud, Durkheim affirmed: "There are no religions which are false. All are true in their own fashion; all answer, though in different ways, to the given conditions of human existence" (1947: 3). And again: "Our entire study rests upon this postulate that the unanimous sentiment of the believers of all times cannot be purely illusory" (1947: 417).

Contrast these views with those of Marx and Engels, who argued that religion is "the opium of the people" (Marx, 1963: 41). Freud, like the functionalists, conceded that: "Religion has clearly performed great services for human civilization. It has contributed much towards the taming of the asocial instincts. But not enough." Despite making some people happy some of the time, "comforting them, reconciling them to life and . . . making them into vehicles of civilization," religions are ultimately infantile, wish-fulfillment, "the displacement of man's will on to God" and indeed "mass delusions" (1985: 219, 225, 269). Religion, which was a solution to Comte (in a secular form) and to Durkheim, was a *problem* for Marx, Engels, and Freud.

Finally, the last social fact that Durkheim examined was crime. If suicide is a break with social solidarity, so is crime (1964: 70). Crime, he said, is "normal" and indeed "inevitable . . . due to the incorrigible wickedness of men." But it is also "an integral part of all *healthy* societies" (emphasis added). Furthermore, "Crime is . . . necessary," and it "plays a useful role" in the evolution of society, particularly in facilitating social change. Thus, "Crime, for its part, must no longer be conceived as an evil that cannot be too much suppressed." Durkheim insisted that this analysis was not an apology for crime, and "it does not follow that we must not abhor it" (1962: 67-74). The principal function of crime, however, is that it "brings together upright consciences and concentrates them." People unite in their indignation, horror, and fury at the crime; and then demand punishment, whose "true function is to maintain social cohesion intact" (1964: 102, 108).

Ironically, the first functionalist analysis of crime had been written, albeit as satire, not by Durkheim, but by Marx. Crime is functional for society — although, as you will see, it is a little embarrassing to quote the text:

> A philosopher produces ideas, a poet verses, a parson sermons, a professor textbooks, etc. A criminal produces crime . . . The criminal produces not only crime but also the criminal law; he produces the professor who delivers lectures on this criminal law, and even the inevitable textbook in which the professor presents his lectures as a commodity for sale in the market [N.B.: him, as well as me, and perhaps you too]. There results an increase in material wealth. . .
>
> Further the criminal produces the whole apparatus of the police and criminal justice, detectives, judges, executioners, juries, etc., . . . Torture itself has provided occasions for the most ingenious mechanical inventions, employing a host of honest workers in the production of these instruments.

Marx continues in this proto-functionalist, and also satirical, vein. The criminal produces not only crime, but also professions, wealth, new technology; he (the criminal is male) also "renders a 'service' by arousing the moral and aesthetic sentiments of the public" — a point that Durkheim made later, as we have mentioned; he inspires "art, literature, novels, and the tragic drama, as *Oedipus* and *Richard III*." Furthermore: "The criminal interrupts the monotony and security of bourgeois life"; and he keeps employment rates high! In this panegyric Marx's theory of crime seems remarkably similar to Durkheim's theory of religion. Certainly in this (satirical) paradigm we should be grateful to the criminal for crime! Indeed, if criminals are so useful, one might logically conclude that they should apply to the Canada Council for grants to continue their work . . .

Yet the sting is in the tail, and Marx removes the mask to unveil the brutal reality: "Crime, by its ceaseless development of new means of attacking property, calls into existence new measures of defence . . ." of that unequal division of wealth so characteristic of high capitalism. (Note the redefinition of crime by contemporary feminists as attacks on *women*, not property, — or as attacks on women as property. See Chapters 4 and 6.) Then Marx internationalized the problem of crime:

> Leaving the sphere of private crime, would there be a world market, would nations themselves exist, if there had not been national crimes? (1963: 167-68)

Would Canada exist, if there had not been national crimes? A conflict paradigm question. It may have particular poignancy not only in Canada, but also in Eastern Europe where new nations are being formed, founded on what the United Nations has described as crimes against humanity.

Where Durkheim described the "incorrigible wickedness" of criminals, and Marx emphasized, satirically, their usefulness in producing crime, Engels insisted that capitalism produces those criminals: the problem is not criminals but the "incorrigible wickedness" of capitalists:

> In this country, social war is under full headway, every one stands for himself, and fights for himself against all comers, and whether or not he shall injure all the others who are his declared foes, depends upon a cynical calculation as to what is most advantageous for himself. It no longer occurs to any one to come to a peaceful understanding with his fellow-man; all differences are settled by threats, violence or in a law-court. In short, every one sees in his neighbour, an enemy to be got out of the way, or, at best, a tool to be used for his own advantage. And this war grows from year to year, as the criminal tables show, more violent, passionate, irreconcilable. The enemies are dividing gradually into two great camps — the bourgeoisie on the one hand, the workers on the other. This war of each against all, of the bourgeoisie against the proletariat, need cause us no surprise, for it is only the logical sequel of the principle involved in free competition. (1969: 161-62)

What is particularly interesting here is not only Engels' application of Hobbes' old aphorism (see Chapter 3), and his anticipation of many of the ideas usually attributed to Marx, but especially his view of crime as the "logical sequel" and, in his view, entirely justifiable sequel, of inequality. Whether this view still applies in Canada, or not, is a matter of some debate (see Chapter 6).

Durkheim was the founder of functionalism. The title of Book One of his first book is "The Function of the Division of Labor." In his second book, *The Rules of Sociological Method* (1895), Durkheim goes into more detail, distinguishing clearly between cause and function (1962: 97):

> to explain a social fact it is not enough to show the cause on which it depends; we must also, at least in most cases, show its function in the establishment of social order.

It is this interest in *"social order"* which is so characteristic of the conservative paradigm. Durkheim's research on the division of labour, religion, crime and suicide, clarified how society maintains and perpetuates itself both by ideological consensus: the collective conscience, and by economic, legal, and religious structures. (The activist tradition, however, concentrates on how society *changes* and even breaks down, and how structures oppress, rather than integrate, the individual.)

Durkheim seems to have lost heart after his son was killed in the trenches in 1915. His theories of social order and mutual interdependence must have seemed completely irrelevant as World War I devastated France. Unlike Marx, Spencer and Darwin, Durkheim had no theory of war. He died in 1917, only 59 years old.

NORTH AMERICAN FUNCTIONALISM

The functionalism Durkheim had developed did not die with him but was developed further by the British anthropologists Bronislaw Malinowski and A. R. Radcliffe-Brown. They visited the United States in the 1930s by which time all Durkheim's books had been translated, and functionalism was increasingly adopted into North American and European sociology.

Functionalism or structural-functionalism, as a theoretical perspective, has been characterized, to a greater or lesser degree, by a number of interlocking ideas: that society is a unity of interdependent institutions; that, like a body, each institution functions to maintain the social structure; and that the prime concern of sociology is with the problem of order and system-maintenance. The principal exponent of functionalism in North America through the fifties and into the sixties, when the paradigm was challenged, was Talcott Parsons. He basically introduced Durkheim and Weber to North America in his first book, *The Structure of Social Action* (1937), and developed functionalism as a theory in *The Social System* (1951). Parsons' prime concern with stability is apparent in his inimitable, and almost unintelligible, prose:

> This integration of a set of common value patterns with the internalized need-disposition structure of the constituent personalities is the core phenomenon of the dynamics of social systems. That the stability of any social system . . . is dependent on a degree of such integration may be said to be the fundamental dynamic theorem of sociology. (1964: 42)

Every sociologist seems to have a favourite "dynamic theorem," and Parsons' is that stability depends on a close fit between social values and individuals' perceived needs. Thus he devotes only one chapter to social change, in which he suggests that *"a general theory of the processes of change of social systems is not possible in the present state of knowledge"* (1964:486). And anyway, he adds defensively that, "If theory is *good theory* [it should] be *equally* applicable to the problems of change and to those of process within a stabilized system" (1964: 535). Perhaps. But why "stabilized"? At any rate Parsons, following Durkheim, identifies four principal integrative mechanisms: common values, the division of labour, religion, and force, to which only two pages are devoted (1964: 151-67, 41-42). To which conflict theorists might add that such mechanisms integrate when they integrate, and disintegrate when they disintegrate.

In a classic organicist metaphor worthy of Spencer, Parsons suggests that money too integrates society:

> Money could thus be regarded as a mechanism through the circulation of which economic activities are controlled, in a manner analogous to that in which the circulation of hormones in the blood controls certain physiological processes. (Hamilton, 1983: 122)

Robert Merton, a former student of Parsons, developed functionalism further in *Social Theory and Social Structure* (1949) which included innovative work on deviance (see Chapter 6), anomie, and distinguished between manifest and latent functions, and dysfunctions (processes tending towards systemic disintegration) (bad!) and eufunctions (processes tending towards systemic order and integration) (good!). The volume was popular in its time, going through three editions, and was followed by *Social Problems* (1961), which he edited with Robert Nisbet, a survey of 15 social problems which is still valuable today. While in general the "objective aspect" of these problems is central, Merton does note the importance of the "subjective aspect" (Merton and Nisbet, 1971: 1); but by the third edition, functionalism had evolved far beyond the stereotype or the straw man of some of the critics.

One major and controversial functionalist work was the paper "Some Principles of Stratification" (1945) by Kingsley Davis and Wilbert Moore, in which they pointed out the ubiquity, necessity, and utility of social inequality, although they did not attempt to justify it. Davis later summed up the functionalist argument as follows: "Such inequality is thus an unconsciously evolved device by which societies ensure that the most important positions are conscientiously filled by the most qualified persons" (in Lenski, 1966: 15). The paper did not go unchallenged (Tumin, 1953), but it established a precedent for what would eventually be seen as a conservative, even fatalistic, orientation in functionalism. If all problems are functional, i.e., useful, necessary, and responding to some social need, then what can be done about inequality? crime? racism? suicide? What can anyone do? And how is change possible?

An early functionalist-type work was John Dollard's *Caste and Class in a Southern Town* (1937). Without using the concept of function he described the economic, sexual, and prestige "gains" of the White middle class achieved at the expense of the lower class Whites and the Blacks; he also noted the costs, in a climate of Whites' fears, and Blacks' aggression. This method of cost-benefit analysis, borrowed from economics, has proved extremely useful, particularly for policy recommendations, but also for integrating consensus and conflict paradigms.

Discussing the economic gains of the White middle-class, Dollard (1957: 100) suggests:

> If the reader would get a vivid sense of this gain, let him remember the last time that he had a ten- or twelve-hour stretch of monotonous and low-paid physical work to do, such as engine wiping, strawberry picking, or pushing a wheelbarrow. It will help to bring the realization that the wish for status advancement is not only a prestige suction from above; there is also the squeeze of disagreeable work from below to urge him toward managerial, intellectual activities.[5]

Suction and squeeze: Dollard had a highly tactile theory of social mobility. A more recent functionalist theory of poverty, rather than wealth, was offered by Herbert Gans (1971). He argued that the poor are not only exploited, but that they are *useful* (or functional) for the affluent — which is why poverty persists, and will continue to persist until either the poor "become dysfunctional for the affluent or powerful, or when the powerless can obtain enough power to change society." He listed thirteen functions of poverty, economic, social, and political: the poor do the dirty work; they subsidize the affluent (by freeing up their time, by paying a higher proportion of their income in property and sales taxes, by being guinea pigs in medical research, etc.); they create jobs (in the penal and police systems, for instance, but also as dope dealers, in numbers rackets, as "pentecostal ministers, faith healers, prostitutes, pawn shops, and [in] the peacetime army"); they buy the goods no one else wants, and also "provide incomes for doctors, lawyers, teachers, and others who are too old, poorly trained, or incompetent to attract more affluent clients"; and more. He does not say that poverty *should* exist, nor such extreme poverty, but he provides enough evidence "to support the functionalist thesis that poverty, like any other social phenomenon, survives in part because it is useful to society or some of its parts" (1976: 191-97).

His article was extremely controversial, not only for the apparent conservative bias, but also for the tone of it. I suspect it was written in haste. But a conflict theorist would have paid far more attention to the *costs* of poverty, to the poor, to the rich, and to the country as a whole.

In recent years functionalism has declined in significance for three reasons. Firstly, society has changed. The late sixties and seventies (and arguably through to the present), were times of disorder, conflict, and change: in France the Paris revolution of 1968; in the United States the Civil Rights movement, Black Power and Red Power, the Hippie movement, the Women's movement, the protests against the Vietnam War, and of course Woodstock. In Canada we witnessed the Quiet Revolution, the F.L.Q., the October Crisis (1970) and the declaration of

The War Measures Act, the victory of the Parti Québecois (1976) — all in Quebec. The First Nations rejected a proposed White Paper of the Federal Government in 1969; Harold Cardinal published *The Unjust Society* (1970), a damning indictment of white majority Canadian society; and The Royal Commission on Bilingualism and Biculturalism, compelled to recognize a new and changing Canada, recommended a policy of multiculturalism, which was implemented in 1971. By the seventies, theories of change and conflict were required.

Secondly, new methods and new schools have emerged: ethnomethodology, symbolic interaction, phenomenology, dramaturgy, and especially more quantitative (positivist) research and now postmodernism. And thirdly, functionalism has been sharply criticized for its apparent conservatism, lack of comparative perspectives and, on occasion, its lack of historical and comparative perspectives, its inattention to change, force, and power, and its complacency (Cohen, 1968: 47-68; Turner and Maryanski, 1979). Nonetheless, the new schools have not modified the prevailing conservative and consensus orientations of most North American and European sociology.

Indeed these conservative orientations have been compatible with the dominant political orientations of important nation states: the Thatcher-Major years in the U.K., the Reagan-Bush years in the U.S.A. and the Mulroney reign in Canada. There is indeed much of value to conserve, as Edmund Burke would be the first to insist.

GEORGE GRANT (1918-88)

Perhaps the most distinguished Canadian conservative thinker in recent years was George Grant, whose *Lament for a Nation* was first published in 1965. "This lament mourns the end of Canada as a sovereign state," he wrote. The effort to *conserve* Canada as separate from the United States, as envisioned by Sir John A. Macdonald, has failed, in his view. The dream has died. "To be a Canadian was to build, along with the French, a more ordered and stable society than the liberal experiment in the United States" (1971: 2, 4). But the lure of technology and capitalism has attracted the Canadian economic and political elites so strongly that continentalism has triumphed over nationalism, and "greed" over the order and stability which Grant loved.

Conservatism, for Grant, was Canadian nationalism, defended against American imperialism. He seems to have believed that the war was already lost, and that Canada was a satellite state and a branch plant of the U.S. economy. That this was regrettable was obvious; in a second edition Grant noted the militarism of the U.S. evident in the Vietnam War, the carelessness for the future (the spontaneous combustion of the river in Cleveland and the pollution of Lake

Erie), the high levels of racial conflict, the decay of the inner cities . . . in such circumstances nationalism seems necessary. Yet, he adds, "Like most other human beings, Canadians want it both ways. We want through formal nationalism to escape the disadvantages of the American dream; yet we also want the benefits of junior membership in the empire" (1971: ix). But we cannot have both, and the elites have chosen.

"Capitalism is, after all, a way of life based on the principle that the most important activity is profit-making" (Grant, 1971: 47). Thus capitalism leads to continentalism and is sustained by liberalism, and the Liberal parties. The old East-West axis from Canada to the UK, "from the prairies, down the Great Lakes and the St. Lawrence, to Western Europe" was destroyed by the successive hammer-blows of World War I, the Depression and World War II; and the death of the lion was evident in the fiasco of the Suez invasion of 1956. This axis was cross-cut by the North-South axis which has increasingly pulled Canada into its orbit: the orbit of "progressives," looking to the technological future, with no intention of conserving the past, and apparently reckless of the present. In this view Canadians have an American future: prosperity mingled with disorder and chaos.

As with Canada, so with Quebec, Grant believed. "French-Canadian nationalism is a last-ditch stand . . . Those who want to maintain separateness also want the advantages of the age of progress. These two ends are not compatible, for the pursuit of one negates the pursuit of the other" (1971: 76). This "progress" is American. Industrial civilization homogenizes and bureaucratizes, but control and power remain at head office: New York, Chicago, Tokyo. This may ultimately be "good" or "bad" — Grant did not know; but he laments the passage of an indigenous culture and a unique tradition.

Nationalism is usually located on the right wing of the political spectrum, from its historical identification with Nazism, fascism, anti-Semitism and racism and its contemporary identification with the Neo-nazis, ethnic cleansing and the white right.

Grant's nationalism however was not so much ethnic as polyethnic and geographical, and although he was deeply critical of US domestic and foreign policies he was, he insisted, not so much anti-American as pro-Canadian. His slim volume was enthusiastically received and served to fuel the economic nationalism of the sixties. Ironically Grant's influence as a conservative was most strongly felt in the socialist NDP. Thus his nationalism crossed over from right to left.

The end of the story, so far, was the demise of economic nationalism with the Free Trade Agreement with the USA in 1992 in the Mulroney era (Mulroney has been described in the spirit of Grant as the greatest American Prime Minister Canada has ever had!), and in 1994 the collapse of the National Party of Canada founded in 1992 by Mel Hurtig, which failed to win a seat in the 1993 federal election.

CONCLUSION

The conservative paradigm assumes the legitimacy and value of the status quo. Indeed most Canadians believe that Canada is the best country in the world, as the *Maclean's/*CTV poll indicated; they are very satisfied with their principal institutions, as the *Times Mirror* survey showed; and they have every reason to be satisfied with a Canada which tops the world, as the UNDP report indicated. The system seems to be working for most of the people most of the time.

The characteristic tenets of conservative ideology are the emphasis on individualism, gradualism, hierarchy, organicism, piecemeal reform by a minimalist state, reliance on the market, competition, and the profit motive as the driving forces of the economy, liberal democracy as the political system, and overall an insistence on order, and a belief in the civility, equality, fairness, tolerance and freedom of life in Canada. Yet many of these tenets are, or may be, challenged by more radical conflict theorists or feminist theorists, as we shall see.

Social problems of course exist; but to mainstream sociologists they can each be isolated and resolved, one by one, or at least contained before they become unduly destructive. *Reform* is the key to societal survival and to the conservation of a social order which is believed to be, on the whole and by and large, about as fair, just, and equitable as is humanly possible. Canadian social problems are believed to be minuscule compared to those of many other nations around the world, and we are continually exhorted to *conserve* and value what we have in the finest country in the world! — as validated by the UN Development Program (1994).

The response of the conflict theorist is succinct: "If you think the system is working, ask someone who isn't!" Does the system work? or does the system stink? For the latter view, read on.

ENDNOTES

1. Indeed it is this emphasis on liberty, so characteristic of both Burke and Spencer, which is one mark of the Conservative. Conflict theorists tend to emphasize equality as the prime value.

2. Plato was the first to compare society to a human body, and his political philosophy, outlined in the *Republic,* states that three parts of the body (head, heart, and belly) rule three different types of people who are therefore suited for different occupations and roles in the state. The three types are the philosopher-kings (ruled by the head), the warriors (ruled by the heart), and the peasantry and crafts people (ruled by the belly). Plato also refers to them as the gold, the silver, and the bronze respectively. Obviously, it is the philospher-kings who are considered to be the natural and rightful rulers. Plato therefore articulated a conservative, elitist, and undemocratic theory of rule which has legitimized hierarchy down through the ages (*Republic* Bks 3, 4, 9; also *Phaedrus* and *Timaeus* 69-70, 89-90; cf. O'Neill, 1985; Synnott, 1993).

3. Spencer summarized this view more epigrammatically: "The ultimate result of shielding men from the effects of folly, is to fill the world with fools" (*Essays,* 1891, Vol. 3: 354). This ethic is far removed from the Christian ethic of loving thy neighbour as thyself, and the parable of the good Samaritan; but it clarified his individualism.

4. On Spencer's liberalism, see *Social Statics* (1969: 155-71, 232) and his dictum that "no man can be free till all are free; no one can be perfectly moral till all are moral; no one can be perfectly happy till all are happy" (1969: 456). In *The Man Versus the State* (1891/1969) he vigorously attacks "the socialists," and insists that "The root of all well-ordered social action is a sentiment of justice, which at once insists on personal freedom and is solicitous for the like freedom of others" (1969: 334) — which is uncannily similar to the vision of Marx and Engels in the *Manifesto*: "We shall have an association, in which the free development of each is the condition for the free development of all" (1967: 105).

5. It is a measure of the effectiveness of the feminist paradigm that you probably noticed Dollard's sexist language, and that it probably grated.

THE CONFLICT PARADIGM

Canada is a battlefield, according to the conflict paradigm, and conflict and violence are the norm. The struggle for power is not only an individual matter, as conservative theorists suggest, it is also a group issue, affecting every sector of society (economics, polity, law, the quality of life, and the age of death) and creating many of the social problems discussed in this text.

Every day the television and newspapers dramatize different conflicts: class struggles, the battle between the sexes, ethnic clashes, conflict between federal and provincial governments, political parties, francophones and anglophones, police and criminals, east and west and center, gays and straights, and so on. We have a war on crime, a war on drugs, a war on (children's) poverty, a half-hearted attack on pollution, and so on. The military metaphors abound. And there are fights in schools and families, factories and offices, playgrounds and neighbourhood streets, and virtually everywhere that people meet. Such conflicts usually involve words rather than blood, but often enough both.

Society, in the conflict paradigm, is not a relatively harmonious social order, as the functionalists would have us believe; it is a battlefield where contending armies struggle for power. In this view, society — or Canada, since this is our frame of reference — is not held together by a consensus on moral values and by structural interdependence, as Durkheim and Parsons had argued, but by violence and the threat of violence, force and the threat of force.

The conflict paradigm is not widespread in Canada where, as we have seen, most people are relatively satisfied with their lives. It is much more prevalent in high tension societies, countries where there is a state of civil war or a guerrilla insurgency, and here we have an alphabet of carnage: Afghanistan, Angola, Bosnia, Cambodia, Colombia, India, Iraq through to Rwanda, Somalia, South Africa, Sri Lanka, Sudan, Tajikistan and Yemen. Indeed if a war is defined as a situation in which 10,000+ people have been killed in factional conflicts in the last 25 years, then a state of war exists in 24 countries, including all of the above plus Guatemala and Peru in the Americas; Croatia (and almost Ulster) in Europe; Indonesia and the Philippines in Asia; and Burundi, Chad, Ethiopia, Liberia, Mozambique (and almost Zaire) in Africa. Every country has some conflicts, but some are much bloodier than others; some have continued for centuries, others began in the 1990s.

Nonetheless the conflict perspective does have resonance in some sectors of Canada. Which groups are, do you suppose, most dissatisfied with Canada? Without research data, one might expect the following to be most dissatisfied with Canada: the First Nations, Quebec nationalists, women, the old, the poor and the unemployed, and all those in the Maritime provinces formerly engaged in the fishing industry.

Certainly the relation between objective social position and subjective perceptions of reality is complex, and "common-sense" expectations can be erroneous; nonetheless, as we read in Chapter 2, a substantial proportion of Canadians are dissatisfied with the present and fearful of the future.

Canada is a divided country, in this view, — divided economically, politically, regionally, linguistically, ethnically, and by gender. The major fault lines sometimes converge and coincide and sometimes cross-cut, as the case may be: divisions within divisions, solitudes within solitudes.

Fundamentally these conflicts are about *power*, and the unequal distribution of power in Canada. The notion that Canada is free, equal, civil, peaceful, tolerant, compassionate, loving, and so on, is laughable to many conflict theorists, as we shall see; and to dismiss the high levels of conflict and violence as due to "gaps in [Canada's] generosity and tolerance" is not only plain silly in this view but betrays a profound misunderstanding of the nature and dynamics of Canada. This is the mythology from the *top*. Canada may stack up well against Gabon (bottom of the UNDP list) and the USA next door (number eight), but there is a long way to go. The greater misfortunes of other societies do not justify complacency.

Conflict theorists are of two types: some focus primarily on areas of conflict that have been identified, that is, social problems of various sorts: (e.g., crime, racism, etc.), while others are primarily interested in problems within systems not usually identified as social problems in themselves: the *education* system (high drop-out rates, high illiteracy rates, low achievement levels particularly in maths and the sciences, violence in schools); the *health* system (high and rising costs, unnecessary procedures — many caesarians, hysterectomies, circumcisions; doctors' strikes, the abuse of patients, over-reliance on high-tech medicine, misdiagnoses); the *legal* system (failure to reduce crime rates, miscarriages of justice, e.g., the Marshall case, long delays and high costs and interminable appeals); the *family* (wife battering, child abuse, incest, women's double burden, unwanted pregnancies, nonpayment of child support) . . . and so on.

The other type of conflict theorists, more notorious but also more rare, are the revolutionaries and activists who wish to promote radical social change and perhaps revolution, and to exacerbate social conflict. Among recent activists in Canada we might include the FLQ in Quebec in 1970, and the Mohawk warriors in 1990. Others, who may be equally radical in their demands for major change, but have not usually resorted to violence, include leaders of the women's movement, the First Nations, the union movement, and such single-issue activists as Greenpeace, animal rights activists, and indeed all who define themselves as activists in some cause.

The contrasts between the conservative and conflict paradigms are rooted in different attitudes towards Canada, different theories of human nature and society, different perspectives on history, and different ideas about methods of social change.

HISTORICAL BACKGROUND

The history of Canada is a history of violence and bloodshed, from the point of view of the conflict paradigm. In the 16th century the first European explorers kidnapped numbers of Indians and Innu and brought them back as "souvenirs" or slaves, including Gaspar Corte Réal who took fifty from Newfoundland or Labrador back to Portugal; Martin Frobisher who captured one Innu in reprisal for the loss of two of his own men; and Jacques Cartier who abducted some native men while founding Montreal. In the 17th century while cementing his alliance with the Huron, Champlain related how they attacked the Iroquois League and he himself shot and killed or wounded various chiefs. The Iroquois in their "turn" destroyed Huronia in 1648-49. The First Nations, the English, and the French were in virtually continuous conflict with each other, military and economic, for decades. These conflicts included French attacks on Iroquois lands, the Jesuit martyrs (1642-49), the Iroquois attack on Dollard des Ormeaux and 60 others killed in 1660, and King William's war (1689-97) between the French and the English.

The eighteenth century was bloody also, with Queen Anne's War (1702-13), King George's War (1744-48) and the Seven Years War (1756-63), which included Pontiac's Rising (1760), possibly the first known episode of germ warfare with the allegation that General Amherst sent smallpox-infested blankets to Pontiac's people, and the deportation of the Acadians (1760).

Slavery was established in Canada in the earliest years, both of Blacks and of Indians; and although slavery was virtually ended by 1800, it was not legally abolished until 1834 by the British Parliament (Trudel, 1966).

English, French, Indians, Blacks . . . but the Americans were also involved. The forces of the new United States invaded Canada in 1775-76 and again in the War of 1812, and were defeated on both occasions. And there were many brush fires: the Aroostook War in 1839, the Pig War in 1859, and the Fenian Raids in 1866.

In 1827 the last of the Beothuks of Newfoundland died: Nancy Shanawdithit. The entire nation had been exterminated by the English especially, the Micmac, and the French. This is one example of tribal genocide in the history of Canada: a quite startling achievement which was, by an amazing coincidence, simply not mentioned in 25 out of 27 Ontario high school text books in 1971 (McDiarmid and Prat, 1971). Teaching history, it appears, is *Teaching Prejudice*, which was the title of their book.

Rebellions flared in Upper and Lower Canada in 1837, led by W.L. MacKenzie and Louis-Joseph Papineau respectively. Lord Durham, sent by the British government to report on the situation after "pacification," reported of the Lower Canada revolt in 1844: "I found two nations warring in the bosom of a single state." The war persists, although it is usually a war of words in different languages, and so relatively painless; but it flares up occasionally in violence, and always in politics.

Conflict continued after Confederation: the Red River Rising (1870) in Manitoba, and the Northwest Rebellion (1885) in Saskatchewan, ending in the execution of Louis Riel (1885) — a hero to the French and the Métis, and a villain to the English. Meanwhile the expropriation of Indian lands continued, by force, but more usually it seems by the threat of force; and the First Nations were increasingly relocated to a scattering of "reserves" across Canada.

The twentieth century opened with the transference of military conflict beyond our borders. Internal wars were followed by international wars: the South African War (1899-1902), the First World War (1914-18: over 650,000 Canadians served; 62,374 were killed); the Second World War (1939-45: over one million served, 41,992 were killed); the Korean War (1950-53: over 25,000 served, 412 fell); the Vietnam War (over 12,000 Canadians volunteered, and over 1,000 were killed); and the Gulf War (1991: no Canadians killed). So far ten Canadians have died in peace-keeping activities in Bosnia (*Maclean's* 12.12.94).

Ethnic conflicts have been endemic in this century, and racism has thrived. Chinese immigrants, for instance, who were first recruited to help build the Canadian Pacific Railway, were later, from 1884, forced to pay "entry" or "head" taxes, rising from $50 finally to $500 in 1903, in an effort to restrict immigration. Mackenzie King, then Deputy Minister of Labour and later Prime Minister, commented in a 1908 report:

> That Canada should desire to restrict immigration from the Orient is natural, that Canada should remain a white man's country is believed to be not only desirable for economic and social reasons but highly necessary on political and national grounds. (Ferguson, 1975: vii)

Then on 1 July, 1923, the Chinese Immigration Act was passed, which virtually blocked further immigration until its repeal in 1947. This is known in the

Chinese community as Humiliation Day. The 1947 Chinese Immigration Act did not open the door to the Chinese; it permitted only the reunion of families. Then in 1962 new legislation normalized immigration. The Chinese, who helped build the railroad, were then abandoned by the CPR, were the only people subject to a head tax, and the only people explicitly banned from Canada (Tan and Roy, 1985).

The Japanese also suffered from widespread Canadian racism. Not only was the franchise restricted but also, as Peter Ward (1982: 10) has noted, they endured "A major race riot in Vancouver in September 1907, [against the Chinese also], limitations upon employment opportunities, immigration restrictions, discriminatory housing covenants, and segregation in public accommodation." After the Japanese attack on Pearl Harbour in December 1941, attitudes hardened rapidly, and the King government ordered the evacuation of all Japanese from the coasts of British Columbia: 21,000 Japanese, most of them Canadian born, and others naturalized citizens, who constituted 90% of the Japanese population, were relocated. Most went to detention camps, some were sent to the Prairies to work on the sugar beet farms, others constructed roads, and some were interned as enemy aliens. All fishing boats, cars, trucks, cameras, and radios were confiscated and later sold. Finally all houses and property were also liquidated, at giveaway prices, with the proceeds being held for the owners, less administration fees. "They lost their jobs, incomes, property and accumulated savings" (Ward, 1982: 14). Within a few years of the end of the war, however, the Japanese were awarded some compensations for their losses, and they were enfranchised. Times and attitudes have changed.

The white Canada immigration policy applied not only to the Japanese and the Chinese but also to the (East) Indians. An agreement with Japan reduced Japanese immigration; the head tax, and an order-in-council requiring all Asians to have $200 on hand when landing had dried up Chinese immigration. Another 1910 order-in-council aimed to stop Indian immigration by requiring a "continuous journey" from India to Canada; since no shipping lines operated this route, Indian immigration was, the government believed, impossible. Stephen Leacock commented: "as smart a piece of legislation as any that ever disenfranchised negroes in the South." Even smarter, however, was a Sikh entrepreneur who chartered the Komagata Maru in 1914 to bring nearly 400 Sikhs to Canada. Canadian authorities refused them permission to land, and public opinion was extremely hostile. The Premier of B.C. told the press on the night the ship dropped anchor:

> To admit Orientals in large numbers would mean in the end the extinction of the white people, and we always have in mind the necessity of keeping this a white man's country. (Ferguson, 1975: 10)

And a journalist for the Vancouver *Sun* managed the feat of double racism, insulting both the Sikhs and the Irish at once:

We do not think as Orientals do. That is why the East Indians and other Asiatic races and the white race will always miscomprehend each other . . .

[The Sikhs] are like the Irish raised to the nth or the fourth dimension. They are remorseless politicians and disturbers. (Ferguson, 1975: 46)

The arithmetic of such racism was typical of the Social Darwinism of the times. In the end, after two months at anchor, after much hardship on board, violence, threats of lawsuits, and the arrival of a cruiser, the freighter steamed away from Canadian shores.

The Black community — communities is the more appropriate term — have immigrated to Canada principally from Africa, the Caribbean, and the United States: the first communities were established by Black Loyalists in Nova Scotia and New Brunswick during the American Revolution; the Maroons from Jamaica were settled in Nova Scotia in the 1790s, but most migrated on to Sierra Leone; more Blacks fled from the United States during the War of 1812, and still more, fugitive slaves, took the Underground Railroad north from 1840 to 1860 to freedom "under the lion's paw" in Ontario. Following the immigration reforms of the 1960s many Blacks, and indeed all shades and ethnicities, have come to Canada from the Caribbean, Africa and elsewhere. Blacks have there-fore been accepted into Canada, to a degree — but they have also been rejected to a degree. An informal apartheid has prevailed in this century:

It usually shocks modern Canadians to know that legally-segregated schools existed in Nova Scotia and Ontario, that white Christian churches discouraged black membership, that certain beaches, parks, restaurants, hotels, theatres and even cemeteries refused admission to blacks. (Walker, 1984: 22)

Discrimination against Blacks is widespread as numerous surveys and stud-ies have demonstrated (Walker, 1984: 18-19); and relations with the police, par-ticularly in Toronto and Montreal, are very poor. Consensus theorists believe that "the ignorance [of racism] is being overcome" (Walker, 1984: 24). Conflict theorists may not be so sure.

The Jews have also experienced prejudice and discrimination in this centu-ry. Fascist movements sprang up across the country in the thirties, as they did almost everywhere in the Western world: some examples are Nazi Germany, Mussolini's Italy, Franco's Spain, and Mosleyism in the UK. Swastika clubs were formed in Ontario and the Canadian Union of Fascists was established in Manitoba; in Quebec Adrien Arcand established the National Social Christian Party in 1934. Anti-Semitism was institutionalized and endemic in Quebec, but also across Canada where "Gentiles Only" signs and "No Jews or Dogs Allowed" dotted the landscape of beaches and resorts. Jewish refugees from Nazi Germany were effectively excluded from Canada, and thereby sentenced to death. "None is too Many" was the verdict of an Ottawa civil servant (Betcherman, 1973;

Delisle, 1993; Abella and Troper, 1982). Anti-Semitism is much reduced now (but see Chapter 8).

Canadian racism was institutionalized against the Chinese, Japanese, Blacks, Jews and Native People, and also the English and French, in immigration policy, land policy, law, education, jobs, voting rights, and attitudes, and it is still a significant conflict in varying dimensions. The principal differences between the first and last decades of the century, however, have been the efforts of federal and provincial governments to combat rather than to legitimize racism (see Royal Commission, 1984; Committee, 1984).

Ethnic conflicts can be tangled with language and political conflicts. The Conscription Crisis of 1917 and 1942 polarized English and French, Canada and Quebec. Then the violence of the FLQ from 1963 to 1970, minimal compared to that of the IRA, climaxed in the kidnapping of James Cross and the murder of Pierre Laporte, and the Declaration of the War Measures Act in 1970. The nationalist Parti Québecois, led by René Lévesque, was elected in 1976, two years after the same voters had overwhelmingly re-elected the federalist Pierre Trudeau. Lévesque, updating Lord Durham, informed the Americans that: "Canada and Quebec cannot continue to live like two scorpions in the same bottle" (1979: 75). Many voters in Quebec agreed, and in the 1993 federal election the sovereigntist Bloc Québécois, winning 14% of the popular vote, won 54 seats in the House and so became Her Majesty's Loyal Opposition.

The 1993 election is itself a case study in conflict, pitting five principle political parties against each other, each with its own distinct ideology and program; also highlighting divisions within Canada, not only of party but also of region, language, gender, and ethnicity, as well as the apparent inequity of the electoral system itself. Given our first-past-the-post system, the election results can be very unrepresentative of the Canadian political will. For instance, the Bloc with 14% of the vote won 18% of the seats, but the Conservatives actually won a higher percentage of the vote with 16%, yet won only 1% of the seats. And the Reform party won 19% of the vote but only 52 seats. One conflict issue is therefore the disparity between votes cast and seats won. A second is how the results reflect schisms in Canada, with Liberal success in Ontario and the Atlantic provinces, Bloc victory in Quebec, and Reform conquest of the West (50 out of 85 seats): a triple solitude of regions. A fourth solitude, from the point of view of gender, is that women, 51% of the population, won only 18% of the seats: 54 women were elected, 16 more than in the 1988 election. Radical feminists may tend to see this as the persistent politics of exclusion. Conservatives may point to the 42% increase as an emerging politics of inclusion. Finally visible minorities and the aboriginal peoples are also statistically under-represented: six members of visible minorities were elected, more than ever before apparently; but they constitute about 8% of the population (1991) and only 2% of the House. Three native people were elected: 1% of the House for about 4% of Canadians. Injustice or progress?

The battle of the sexes has been political and economic as well as physical: the struggle for the federal and provincial franchises, the struggle for the right of appointment to the Senate, finally recognized in the Persons Act of 1929, and the continuing struggles for pay equity, occupational mobility, adequate protection . . . and a new political agenda. These issues, including male violence against women, are discussed further in Chapter 4.

Class conflict is manifest so often and in so many ways it is impossible to summarize; but one obvious measure is the frequency, duration, and intensity of strikes and lockouts. In 1990 Canadians lost 5,154,000 person-days in work stoppages, strikes or lockouts, legal or illegal — this is proportionately the highest rate in the industrialized world, except for Italy. This number is up from 1985 (over 3 million) but down from 1980 (about 9 million) and fluctuates widely depending upon economic conditions (Statistics Canada, 1991. Cat. 11-210, p. 38). While these figures do seem to indicate high levels of industrial conflict, this is far less than the amount of time lost due to absenteeism, sick leave, and holidays. In the first half of this century most strikes were directed primarily at the achievement of union recognition; more recently the goals have been working conditions and wage rates. One of the most significant strikes in Canada was the Winnipeg General Strike (1919), which mobilized 22,000 workers and resulted in the election of J.S. Woodsworth as the first socialist M.P. in 1921. He later became the first leader of the CCF in 1926.

Violence is not simply a matter of history. The army was called into Quebec, again, during the Oka and Kahnawake crises of the summer of 1990. Indeed the protests of First Nations leaders have escalated in recent years, over forest-cutting, dam-building, land-expropriation, exclusion of their interests in the Meech Lake Accord, and many voted against the Charlottetown Accord. Blacks protest the real or alleged racism of police in Toronto and Montreal who have shot and killed six Blacks (out of 12 victims) from 1990-92. And Native People on the Prairies have made similar complaints — complaints which have been validated by the Manitoba Justice Inquiry and Alberta's Casey Report.

According to the conflict paradigm, there is something violent at the very core of Canada, which was built on violence, and is sustained by violence, whether legitimate or illegitimate, depending upon one's political values. Conflict is not simply a matter of history, but is everyday, normal, routine: the stuff of our daily press and the TV news. Each day exposes more violence: personal, institutional, class-based, gender, ethnic, economic, political, military or criminal. It is a violent world we live in, and which "we" have created. Nobody else.

Americans, Canadians, French, English, the Indian nations and Inuit, Blacks, Chinese, Japanese, Jews, Catholics and Protestants . . . political parties, corporations, sexes, families, regions, interest groups, and just plain criminals . . . the list could go on, but we have to stop sometime . . . everyone has been fighting someone for centuries, using physical violence or military wars, tariff wars or trade wars, legal battles, immigration legislation, political fights, as well as the battle of the sexes. Conflict is the norm, in the conflict perspective. To describe Canada as "a peaceable society . . . based on civility" is very strange indeed.

THE HOBBESIAN WORLD

Some theorists see the roots of the problem of conflict in an evil human nature. Machiavelli (1467-1527) had a jaundiced view of humanity: "all men are bad," he explains in *The Discourses* (Chapter 3):

> All those who have written upon civil institutions demonstrate (and history is full of examples to support them) that whoever desires to found a state and give it laws, must start with assuming that all men are bad and ever ready to display their vicious nature, whenever they may find occasion for it. (1950: 117)

In *The Prince* (Chapter 17), Machiavelli makes the same point in more detail, but stresses the practical implications:

> . . . it may be said of men in general that they are ungrateful, voluble, dissemblers, anxious to avoid danger, and covetous of gain; as long as you benefit them, they are entirely yours . . . but when [danger] approaches, they revolt . . . And men have less scruple in offending one who makes himself loved than one who makes himself feared. (1950: 61)

Cynical or realistic? He is more concise later: "men will always be false to you unless they are compelled by necessity to be true" (1950: 89).

But Machiavelli was above all an authority on power: how to get it, how to keep it, how to use it. He was essentially a realist rather than an idealist; hence the word machiavellian. It is to him that is credited (or otherwise) the doctrine of "Might is Right." Ethics is secondary to power. The father of power politics advocated deceit, and even evil, to stay in power: "A prudent ruler ought not to keep faith when by so doing it would be against his interest" (think of election promises!); but he goes on: "If men were all good, this precept would not be a good one; but as they are bad, and would not keep faith with you, so you are not bound to keep faith with them." Also "it is necessary . . . to be a great feigner and dissembler [for] one who deceives will always find those who allow themselves to be deceived" (1950: 64-65). His eighteenth chapter in *The Prince* is the classic example of the politics of expediency: "it is well to seem merciful, faithful, humane, sincere, religious, and also to be so; but you must have the mind so disposed that when it is needful to be otherwise you must be able to change to the opposite qualities." Indeed he insists that the prince must "not deviate from what is good, if possible, but be able to do evil if constrained." Finally, the excuse offered by so many for their evil actions as revolutionaries or despots of all sorts: "the end justifies the means" (1950: 65-66).

Thomas Hobbes (1588-1679), writing at the time of the English Civil War, shortly after the execution of Charles I, wrote in similar terms. Since his country was literally a battlefield, he was, not surprisingly, particularly preoccupied with the problem of order and the causes of war. He found the causes of war in human nature:

> in the nature of man, we find three principal causes of quarrel. First, competition; secondly, diffidence [defence]; thirdly, glory.

> The first, maketh men invade for gain; the second for safety; and the third for reputation. The first use violence, to make themselves masters of other men's persons, wives, children, and cattle; the second, to defend them; the third, for trifles, as a word, a smile, a different opinion, and any other sign of undervalue . . .

> Hereby it is manifest, that during the time men live without a common power to keep them in awe, they are in that condition which is called war; and such a war, as is of every man, against every man . . . and the life of man, solitary, poor, nasty, brutish and short. (Pt 1, 13: 1960: 81-82)

The solution to these problems lay, for Machiavelli, in a strong prince; and for Hobbes in Leviathan, a "mortal god": absolute rule (1960: 112, ch. 17); i.e., the use of force.[1] Violence, in these views, is intrinsic to human nature, and *also* to the state.

This war of all against all must seem foreign to nice, peaceable people (like ourselves), and it seems particularly alien to the Christian tradition in which both Machiavelli and Hobbes, and also probably most Canadians, have been raised.

Christ advised his disciples to "love thy neighbour as thyself" (Matthew 19: 19), even to "love thy enemies" (Matthew 5: 44), and to "do unto others as ye would have them do unto you" (Matthew 7: 12). But even if Christians or non-Christians follow this ethic, they are also likely to follow another ethic which flows from this Machiavellian and Hobbesian world view.

Consider the advice we routinely give our children:

- Don't talk to strangers.
- Don't take candy from strangers.
- Don't get into a car with anyone you don't know.
- Be back before dark.

No doubt we also give advice compatible with the Christian ethic: Be good, don't steal, don't hit, tell the truth, and so on. But in practice we recognize a Hobbesian world where people are often not good, do steal, hit, lie, and indeed kill. We teach our children to fear their fellows, and to be careful. We teach them that the world is dangerous.

Furthermore our adult folk-wisdom expresses the same fears of humanity, and the same warnings:

- "Caveat emptor!"
- It's a jungle out there.
- Mind your back.
- Don't get involved.
- It's a dog eat dog world.
- Count your change.
- Lock up.
- Don't hitch-hike.
- Don't pick up hitch-hikers.
- You never know who you can trust.
- Fight fire with fire.
- The first law: "Do unto thy neighbour as he would do unto you."
- All's fair in love and war.
- Every man for himself.
- Business is business.
- Read the small print.
- It's the survival of the fittest.
- Believe nothing of what you hear, and only half of what you see.
- You have to look out for number one.
- There's a sucker born every minute.
- Never give a sucker an even break.
- Nice guys finish last.
- The weakest go to the wall.

We may like to *believe* that most people are basically nice and good; but we *behave* as though they are not. There are a thousand warnings about the dangers from other people, and the evil nature of Homo (for want of a better word) Sapiens. We take precautions, we reserve judgement, we do not necessarily believe what we are told, we are careful. And we know we have to fight hard for survival. There is a struggle for existence, as Spencer and Darwin said.

But not everyone believes that people are basically evil. Some believe that people are basically good, but that *society* is evil (or at least the particular structure of society in place then, and now). This is the tradition established first by Rousseau and then elaborated by Marx and Engels. Either way, conflict is the norm, individual or societal.

JEAN-JACQUES ROUSSEAU (1712-78)

Jean-Jacques Rousseau, the apostle of democracy, as he saw himself, was convinced that humanity is good: it is society that is vile. He opens *Emile* (1762) with the definitive statement: "God makes all things good; man meddles with them and they become evil" (1974: 5, cf. 1963: 222). This was an attack not only on Hobbes and Machiavelli but also on the Christian doctrine of original sin. The reasons for social conflict, in his view, lie not in an evil human nature but in society itself. He articulated this view clearly in the famous opening sentence of *The Social Contract* (1762): "Man is born free; and everywhere he is in chains" (1963: 3). The chains, and social inequality, originate in property.

> The first man who, having enclosed a piece of ground, bethought himself of saying "This is mine," and found people simple enough to believe him, was the real founder of civil society. (1963: 192)

People are naturally "good" and "born free," but with the establishment of civil society emerge its "inseparable attendants" of "growing inequality" and all manner of "evils" (1963: 203, 181). He adds, in Hobbesian mode: "We may admire human society as much as we please; it will be none the less true that it leads men to hate each other in proportion as their interests clash . . . we always gain more by hurting our neighbours than by doing them good. Nothing is required but to know how to act with impunity" (1963: 222-23). Crime, violence, injustice, and slavery are all institutionalized therefore, in and by this inequality, beginning with the first enclosures of land and private property. In the end the corruption of government dissolves the social contract by which civil society was initially established, and the despot is overthrown by the very violence through which he ruled. "As he was maintained by force alone, it is force alone that overthrows him" (1963: 219).

Rousseau's ideas were enormously influential. His philosophy was instrumental in legitimizing the American Revolution and the French Revolution; the US Declaration of Independence, "We hold these truths to be self-evident, that all men are created equal . . .," and the French Declaration of the Rights of Man stem particularly from his insights. The conquest of colonial powers and of royal powers are both due in part to Rousseau.

The contrast between the conservative and the conflict paradigms can be summarized briefly. If humanity is basically evil, as Machiavelli and Hobbes argued, then civil society is necessary and useful for the benefit of everyone and the protection of all. The status quo is legitimate, whether ruled by the strong prince or Leviathan. On the other hand if people are fundamentally good, as Rousseau argued, then civil society is hardly necessary, and should be minimal; but if evils are generated by inequality, as Rousseau also argued, then conflict is institutionalized, change and violence become the norm, and revolution is not only a possibility but perhaps also a necessity. And here Rousseau influenced Marx and Engels.

In sum, Rousseau was the first to see social problems of various sorts as rooted in the *society*, not in the *evil* nature of human beings, as in the traditional Christian viewpoint and in Hobbes' view. Anne Frank, the 13-year-old Jewish girl who wrote *The Diary of a Young Girl* while in hiding from the Nazis in Holland, wrote in the spirit of Rousseau: "in spite of everything I still believe that people are really good at heart" (1972: 237). She was discovered, and killed.

KARL MARX AND FREDERICK ENGELS

The first proponents of a systematic conflict theory were Marx and Engels. In 1845 Engels published *The Condition of the Working Class in England*, a devastating criticism of laissez-faire capitalism; and in 1848 Marx and Engels wrote *The Communist Manifesto*, perhaps the single most important document of the nineteenth century, influencing millions on every continent for almost 150 years.

They begin the *Manifesto* with their interpretation of world history as a struggle between oppressor and oppressed, culminating in the present epoch (1848) in the class struggle between the bourgeoisie, who are the owners of the means of production, the capitalists, and the proletariat, or workers:

> The history of all hitherto existing society is the history of class struggles.
>
> Freeman and slave, patrician and plebeian, lord and serf, guild-master and journeyman, in a word, oppressor and oppressed, stood in constant opposition to one another, carried on an uninterrupted, now hidden, now open fight, a fight that each time ended, either in a revolutionary reconstitution of society at large, or in the common ruin of the contending classes. . . .
>
> Our epoch of the bourgeoisie, possesses, however, this distinctive feature: it has simplified the class antagonisms. Society as a whole is more and more splitting up into two great hostile camps, into two great classes directly facing each other: Bourgeoisie and Proletariat. (1967: 79-80)

But what is the relevance of these long-dead writers for modern Canadian society? You may well ask. Certainly contemporary Canada is very different from the Germany and England of the 1840s; and the collapse of the Soviet Empire perhaps implies the intellectual bankruptcy of Marxism-Leninism, as well as the economic bankruptcy of the state it underpinned. On the other hand their ideals still inspire the labour movement and social democrats, as well as socialists, and their insights may still be valuable. Society has changed, but much remains the same. Class struggles persist. Oppression persists. And the fight continues: in Haïti, for democracy; among the Zapatistas in Mexico, for land and justice; and in Canada.

Marx and Engels attacked the "naked, shameless, direct, brutal exploitation" of the working class, which "has left no other nexus between man and man than naked self-interest, than callous cash payments." Despite its vast achievements, capitalism has created a class of labourers "who live only so long as they find work, and who find work only so long as their labour increases capital." Alienated, the worker becomes "an appendage of the machine" (1967: 82, 87). Furthermore capitalism is not simply an economic system; its lust for gold determines every sector of society.

Politics

Capitalist society cannot be reformed, in their view, for there are no mechanisms for reform. None in politics: "Political power . . . is merely the organized power of one class for oppressing another" (1967: 105). Again: "The executive of the modern state is but a committee for managing the common affairs of the whole bourgeoisie" (1967: 82).

Abraham Lincoln could pray in his address at Gettysburg in 1863 that "government of the people, by the people, for the people shall not perish from this earth." But for Marx and Engels and other conflict theorists, capitalist politics was, and still is, government of the middle class by the middle class for the middle class. And in 1863 neither Blacks nor women had the vote in the USA.

Law

The legal system in their view, is just as unjust as the political system. They informed the bourgeoisie that: "Your jurisprudence is but the will of your class made into a law for all" (1967: 100). Justice is not blind, but clear-sighted, exercised in the interests of the bourgeoisie, and administered and enforced by that same class. In 1845 Engels offered an incisive analysis of law, as differentially perceived by the bourgeoisie and the workers:

> . . . the law is sacred to the bourgeois, for it is his own composition, enacted with his consent, and for his benefit and protection. He knows that, even if an individual law should injure him, the whole fabric protects his interests; and more than all, the sanctity of the law, the sacredness of order as established by the active will of one part of society, and the passive acceptance of the other, is the strongest support of his social position. Because the English bourgeoisie finds himself reproduced in his law, as he does in his God, the policeman's truncheon which, in a certain measure, is his own club, has for him a wonderfully soothing power. But for the working-man quite otherwise! (1969: 253)

Given the "soothing power" of the club, "working-men do not respect the law" (1969: 254). Why should they? The law, in this view, does not respect them, neither in 1845 nor in the 1990s; nor, in the conflict paradigm, does the law respect women, the First Nations, visible minorities, the poor. . . .

The French author Anatole France (1894) explained caustically: "The law, in its majestic equality, forbids the rich as well as the poor to sleep under bridges, to beg in the streets, and to steal bread."

Crime

Engels offered a radical analysis of crime in England, entirely different from the Durkheimian perspective on crime. The criminal is not a villain, but the defiant victim of capitalism. He described the worker as follows:

> He is poor, life offers him no charm, almost every enjoyment is denied him, the penalties of the law have no further terrors for him; why should he restrain his desires, why leave to the rich the enjoyment of his birthright, why not seize a part of it for himself? What inducement has the proletarian not to steal? It is all very agreeable to the ear of the bourgeoisie to hear the 'sacredness of property' asserted; but for him who has none, the sacredness of property dies out of itself. Money is the god of this world; the bourgeois takes the proletarian's money from him and so makes a practical atheist of him. . . . Want leaves the working-man the choice between starving slowly, killing himself speedily, or taking what he needs where he finds it — in plain English, stealing. And there is no cause for surprise that most of them prefer stealing to starvation and suicide. (Engels, 1969: 145)

Violence

As the poor starved to death (and they did, as Engels and numerous government reports showed), so the bourgeoisie prospered; and so the crime rate increased and the class war escalated. Indeed, England was in a state of war, in his view:

> The social war, the war of each against all, is here openly declared . . . people regard each other only as useful objects; each exploits the other, and the end of it all is, that the stronger treads the weaker under foot, and that the powerful few, the capitalists, seize everything for themselves, while to the weak many, the poor, scarcely a bare existence remains.

> What is true of London, is true of Manchester, Birmingham, Leeds, is true of all great towns. Everywhere barbarous indifference, hard egotism on one hand, and nameless misery on the other, everywhere social warfare, every man's house in a state of siege, everywhere reciprocal plundering under the protection of the law, and all so shameless, so openly avowed that one . . . can only wonder that the whole crazy fabric still hangs together. (Engels, 1969: 58)

Marx summed up his view: "One capitalist always kills many" (1963: 150). What is to be done?

In Engels' view, "all hope of a peaceful solution of the social question for England must be abandoned. The only possible solution is a violent revolution, which cannot fail to take place" (1969: 285).[2] Marx and Engels concluded the *Manifesto* with the famous slogan: "Let the ruling classes tremble at a Communistic revolution. The proletarians have nothing to lose but their chains. They have a world to win. Working men of all countries, unite!" (1967: 120).

Marx (1963: 80) explained why revolution is necessary:

> Revolution is necessary not only because the *ruling* class cannot be overthrown in any other way, but also because only in a revolution can *the class which overthrows* it rid itself of the accumulated rubbish of the past and become capable of reconstructing society.[3]

The Future

The revolution would create (they believed) the classless, equal and free and peaceful society, the well-known but unfortunately named dictatorship of the proletariat: "We shall have an association in which the free development of each is the condition for the free development of all" (1967: 105). After the revolution the slogan will be "From each according to his ability, to each according to his needs" (Marx, 1963: 263). A noble vision. Furthermore, as the revolution is achieved in country after country around the world, so will national and international peace be achieved:

> In proportion as the exploitation of one individual by another is put an end to, the exploitation of one nation by another will be put an end to. In proportion as the antagonism between classes within the nation vanishes, the hostility of one nation to another will come to an end. (1967: 102)

For materialists, these two friends were remarkably idealistic; but Marx was 30 and Engels only 27 when they wrote their *Manifesto*.

Inequality

The Communist Manifesto was not only a call to arms to achieve the revolution, it was also a clear statement of aims: "The theory of the Communists may be summed up in the single sentence: Abolition of private property" (1967: 96). Marx and Engels added a stinging critique on the inequality of distribution of wealth in capitalist society (1967: 98):

> You are horrified at our intending to do away with private property. But in your existing society, private property is already done away with for nine-tenths of the population; its existence for the few is solely due to its non-existence in the hands of those nine-tenths.

This, of course, is sheer rhetoric, and totally inapplicable to Canada today. But is it? The wealthiest 10% of all Canadians own 51% of all privately owned wealth — more than the other nine-tenths put together. The poorest 40% of the population own 2% of the wealth (see Chapter 5).

Perhaps the insights of conflict theorists on inequality, politics, justice, and crime have more immediate significance than might be apparent, particularly for the poor, for women, for native peoples, for the old, for visible minorities. . . .

Fundamentally, however, the distinctive feature of the conflict paradigm is the need for change; as Marx phrased it: "The philosophers have only *interpreted* the world in different ways; the point is to change it" (1963: 84).

Marx died in 1883 soon after his wife and his favourite daughter; but his ideas have lived on, still inspire some, still have resonance and are still controversial. Marxist doctrines have legitimized, to greater or lesser degrees, the Mexican, Russian, Chinese and Vietnamese revolutions; and they still inspire countless political parties of various stripes from Communist in France and Italy to Labour in the UK and the NDP; and Liberation Theology, a blend of Christian faith and Marxist sociology, is becoming increasingly prevalent and powerful in Central and South America.

DARWIN AND NIETZSCHE

Marx and Engels were not the only conflict theorists, nor was class the only conflict issue. Other theorists saw life very differently. Both Darwin and Nietzsche, neither of whom were sociologists, have certainly influenced sociological theory.

Charles Darwin, the son of a Shropshire clergyman, was educated at the universities of Edinburgh and Cambridge. He was always a naturalist, to the despair of his father: "You care for nothing but shooting, dogs and rat-catching, and you will be a disgrace to yourself and all your family" (Darwin, 1887: Vol. 1: 32). His enthusiasm and skills stood him in good stead, however, as after his graduation he was recommended for a job as a naturalist on board HMS Beagle, which was commissioned by the Admiralty to survey the coasts and waters of South America. This voyage lasted five years (1831-36) and enabled him to collect raw data for what became his theory of evolution. On his return he wrote *The Voyage of the Beagle* (1845); he also married his cousin, and the couple had 10 children. *The Origin of Species* was published in 1859, and was followed by *The Descent of Man* (1871). His theory of evolution by natural selection through the struggle for existence transformed the understanding not only of nature but also of society. In a chapter entitled "The Struggle for Existence" in *The Origin*, Darwin suggests:

> A struggle for existence inevitably follows from the high rate at which all organic beings tend to increase. . . . [A]s more individuals are produced than can pos-

sibly survive, there must in every case be a struggle for existence, either one individual with another of the same species, or with the individuals of distinct species, or with the physical conditions of life. It is the doctrine of Malthus applied with manifold force to the whole animal and vegetable kingdoms. (1968: 116-17)

Darwin's argument was that, in nature, different species lived on, and off, each other, and the survival of one was dependent not only on the other, but also on what the other was dependent on, and so on. For instance, red clover was only fertilized by the humble-bee (or bumble bee), but the survival of humble-bees was dependent upon the predations of mice; the prevalence of mice was in turn dependent upon the prevalence of cats. "Hence it is quite credible that the presence of a feline animal in large numbers in a district might determine, through the intervention first of mice and then of bees, the frequency of certain flowers in that district" (1968: 125). Not to mention the dogs, which chased the cats, which ate the mice, which. . . .

Species compete with each other for survival, but also depend upon each other. As Darwin put it: "Battles within battles must ever be recurring" (1968: 124). The reference to Hobbes seems obvious, but was never explicit. Others, however, drew the seemingly obvious conclusions. Marx, for instance, wrote to LaSalle, a well-known French socialist, in 1861:

> Darwin's book is very important and it suits me well that it supports the class struggle in history from the point of view of natural science. One has, of course, to put up with the crude English method of discourse. (Oldridge, 1983: 233)

So the "struggle for existence" of red clover, the humble-bees, the mice, and the cats, and no doubt the dogs, becomes the epitome of the class struggle between the bourgeoisie and the proletariat! Darwin never said this, nor anything like it; but Herbert Spencer's phrase "The survival of the fittest" seemed to suggest that in the societal "struggle for existence" the cream rises to the top by an ineluctable law of nature, while the dregs fall to the bottom. (The good democrat will surely note that the scum also rises, and that gold too falls to the bottom!) Spencer's theory of conflict and struggle is complex, as we have seen; but he distinguished between personal violence, which infringes on the rights of others, and is savage and requires state control; and institutional violence, which is a law of nature, beneficent, providential, part of the struggle for existence and contributes towards human progress: war is the classic example. In this respect, he was both a conservative and a conflict theorist.

Engels (1892) also insisted that the regional, national, and international class struggle "is the Darwinian struggle of the individual for existence transferred from Nature to society with intensified violence. The conditions of existence natural to the animal appear as the final term of human development" (Marx and Engels, 1969, Vol. 3: 140). Both Marx and Engels believed in the congruence of social and biological evolution: history and biology following the same laws (cf. Marx and Engels, 1969, Vol. 1: 101; Vol. 3: 162).

Communists used Darwin to justify the struggle for power and the use of violence in this struggle, and fascists also used him for the same ends. Adolph Hitler was a case in point. His autobiography, titled *Mein Kampf* (My Struggle) (1924), shows that he was particularly influenced by the German philosopher, Friedrich Nietzsche (1844-1900). Like Darwin, however, Nietzsche was not responsible for those who abused his thinking.

Nietzsche had tried to develop a philosophy based, not so much on how people said life *should* be lived, but on how it actually *is* lived. Machiavelli had tried to do the same, as we have seen. This required him to capsize the Christian philosophy. Life is a battle in his view; and he declared that: "The free man is a warrior" (1977: 271). Furthermore,

> life is essentially appropriation, injury, overpowering of the strange and weaker, suppression, severity, imposition of one's own forms, incorporation and, at the least and mildest, exploitation. . . . 'Exploitation' does not pertain to a corrupt or imperfect or primitive society: it pertains to the *essence* of the living thing as a fundamental organic function. (1977: 229-30)

For Nietzsche, human nature is not evil, it just is — and it is violent. Life is not modeled on Christian precepts; life is "appropriation," "injury," and "over-powering." So there are no social problems; there is only a Hobbesian war, a life of mutual exploitation (as Engels had indeed described in England). The only solution to life is death, and he recommended suicide (1977: 267) (see Chapter 7). He did not follow his own advice, however, and went mad before he died of, probably, tertiary syphilis.

SIGMUND FREUD

Freud was not a sociologist, of course, but a psychoanalyst and therefore he should not, strictly speaking, be included in a discussion of conflict theorists. But his insights on civilization and society have been important, and must be considered in any discussion on the roots and origins of violence and social conflict. Freud strikingly rejected Rousseau's view of the goodness of humanity. Indeed he argued that *Homo homini lupus*: Man is a wolf to Man (1985: 302):

> . . . men are not gentle creatures who want to be loved, and who at the most can defend themselves if they are attacked; they are, on the contrary, creatures among whose instinctual endowments is to be reckoned a powerful share of aggressiveness. As a result, their neighbour is for them not only a potential helper or sexual object, but also someone who tempts them to satisfy their aggressiveness on him, to exploit his capacity for work without compensation, to use him sexually without his consent, to seize his possessions, to humiliate him,

to cause him pain, to torture and to kill him. *Homo homini lupus*. Who, in the face of all his experience of life and of history, will have the courage to dispute this assertion?

Indeed he echoes Hobbes as he refers to "man's natural aggressive instinct, the hostility of each against all and of all against each" (1985: 313). He calls this aggression the Death instinct, which may be directed externally, in murder and war, or internally, in suicide and suicidal behaviour. Opposed to this instinct is Eros, the Life instinct, "whose purpose is to combine single human individuals, and after that families, then races, peoples and nations into one great unity, the unity of mankind" (1985: 313).

Freud died in 1939, before the outbreak of World War II which caused the deaths of about 44 million human beings: a triumph of the Death instinct. Nor was it a war to end all wars, for it was swiftly followed by wars in Korea, Vietnam, the Falklands, Afghanistan, Cambodia, Ethiopia, the Gulf, Bosnia, and Chechnya, not to mention countless raids, revolutions, civil wars and insurrections around the world from Northern Ireland to Somalia, Peru, and India.

Despite Freud's "instinct" theory, sociologists have tended to argue that violence rates are cultural matters (Montagu, 1968). The homicide rate in Detroit, for instance, is ten times higher than in Windsor, Ontario, just across the river. And the homicide rate in the United States is about three times higher than that of Canada, whose homicide rate is in turn is about three times higher than that of the United Kingdom. Most homicides in these countries are committed by males, as feminists particularly have noted (Miles, 1991). Nonetheless the range in homicide rates is so great from one country to another that it is obviously impossible to blame them all on human, or male, "instincts." Male biology is much the same everywhere; the violence rates are very different. Furthermore most men do not commit homicide, and some women do.

In the physical sciences conventional wisdom avers that nature rather than nurture, biology rather than culture, is the determining factor in the etiology of violence (Wilson, 1979; Moir and Jessel, 1991: 75-87). But whether the balance is 60:40 or 30:70 one way or the other, or just 50:50, does not matter unduly because (a) no one knows, and (b) everyone agrees that both the sociological and the biological etiologies are probably relevant. All activities are physical and social.

MICHEL FOUCAULT

An alternative theory of violence has been proposed by Michel Foucault. In his view, violence is a necessary, and ubiquitous social control system. He began *Discipline and Punish* (1979) with a detailed account of the execution of the regicide, Damiens, in Paris in 1757. The poor man was burned at the stake, tortured, torn apart by horses and finally quartered: the immense pain inflicted on the body was intended to be commensurate with the pain inflicted on the body politic. The state punishes offenders physically and violently. Similarly in every sector of society authority figures train subjects, with rewards certainly, but also with violence. Starting in the family, then the school, the factory or office, the military, the state, in ever widening circles of power, parents, teachers, bosses and foremen, officers and, at the national level, police and the penal system have the power to inflict different types of punishment, often physical, on offenders. Penalties may range from a light slap to capital punishment; and the end result is the production of what Foucault calls "docile bodies."

The means to this end is constant surveillance. "Inspection functions ceaselessly. The gaze is alert everywhere" (1979: 195). Everyone watches everyone. Cameras, electronic eyes, spy satellites, binoculars and spectacles are everywhere. Life is not so much a struggle, as Marx, Spencer and Nietzsche argued; nor is it solidarity and interdependence as Durkheim thought; nor is it acting, despite Goffman. Life is prison, "the panoptic machine" (1979: 217; cf. Synnott, 1993).

Foucault's insistence on *discipline* as the key mechanism of social control focuses particularly on power over the physical body: the tiniest movements of the human body are political, they are watched as symbolic of the self, and they may evoke a powerful and violent response. Power over the body is power over the self.

Violence, therefore, in Foucault's view, is not instinctive as Freud thought, nor an element in the struggle for societal existence, or biological survival, and he avoids entirely the old nature-nurture debate — it is just a mundane instrument of power in every sector of society and at every level. The "carceral system" is a continuum extending "from the smallest coercions to the longest penal detention," from which it is difficult to escape (1979: 303). Even Woodstock had its Hell's Angels as security.

Foucault therefore shifted the focus on violence from the perspectives of deviance or sin or biology or "masculinism" to violence as routine, normal, necessary and useful. This is not to say of course that he justifies homicide, war, or indeed any violence at all; he was a professor of history not a soldier; but he does offer some insights into the "whole technology of power over the body" which he says, quite correctly I think, that "the educationalists, psychologists and psychiatrists" have failed to consider given their priority in "the technology of the 'soul'" (1979: 30).

Foucault is not a conflict theorist in the usually accepted senses of the term discussed earlier; but he was one of the foremost theorists of violence and social control, writing fine studies on power and control of the mad (1967), the bad (1979) and sex (1980) and as such he merits consideration here.

VIOLENCE

Physical violence is the most extreme and most feared form of conflict. Theorists of violence have recently tended to blur the issue of physical violence by including in their definitions of violence such issues as "verbal violence," "psychological violence" and even "spiritual violence." Useful though these ideas are, speaking a four-letter word is not the same as shooting someone, nor is a put-down as serious a crime as rape. We should not confuse the metaphorical and the literal; and in this final section we will explore the roles and types of violence in contemporary Canada which, in the conflict paradigm (and in reality) must be acknowledged.

First, there are many types of physical violence, which can be differentiated by sectors, albeit very briefly. This is routinely reported in the media, and we no doubt take it for granted as the shadow side of life. Examined *cumulatively*, however, in all our spheres of existence, it becomes apparent that violence is not so much the exception as the *norm*: violence and the threat of violence.

Economic violence

Violence on the picket line is not that unusual in Canada; and sexual harassment, which is often very physical, is almost routine in many offices, factories, and workplaces across the country. The moral violence of firing workers without due notice, or requiring overtime work without pay, or failing to provide adequate facilities for people — these are not at issue here although they may have physical consequences. Two recent examples of economic violence are the murder of six miners at the Golden Oak mine in Yellowknife: the miners were strike-breakers. From the other side of the power divide: two executives of Westray mines have been accused of gross negligence leading to the deaths of 26 miners in Cape Breton in 1992.

Violence in the workplace ranges all the way from molesting in boys homes (the Mount Cashel case) to murder in mines underground (the Golden Oak case), or universities, or National Assemblies.

Accidents happen; and they are, by definition, physically violent. Accidents are the leading cause of death among young people, and while they often occur on the road and in the home, they also occur at work. Work-related accidents may not be intentional, but there is often responsibility or culpability involved in the sinking of a fishing vessel, the crashing of a plane or the derailment of a train, as the enquiries and coroners suggest.

The point is not only that working can be hazardous to your health, nor even that some occupations are far more hazardous than others, and that physical violence is implicit in both observations; but there is also deliberate, intentional violence institutionalized in competitive labour markets and in labour-management relations. Marx and Engels noted this long ago but, even though conditions have improved substantially since then and occupational mortality rates are far lower, the point is still worth reiterating.

Political violence

The classic examples of political violence in recent years are the FLQ activities from 1963 to 1970, the October Crisis and the declaration of the War Measures Act in 1970 with the murder of Pierre Laporte and the kidnapping of James Cross. More recently in 1990 we experienced the Oka crisis between the Mohawks and the Quebec government, and the Mohawk blockade of the Mercier bridge into Montreal. Each crisis highlighted areas of national tension; and on each occasion police forces were deemed inadequate to resolve the situation and the army was called in.

Political tensions are usually resolved or lessened by holding municipal, provincial, or federal elections, or by meetings in or out of court between conflicting parties. Still, tensions may require, or seem to require, more direct action.

Many native bands, for instance, have blockaded logging roads, the TransCanada, the CN rail tracks, or construction projects in recent years to protest their grievances. Greenpeace have sunk one whaling vessel recently, have visited Germany to protest B.C. logging policies and have protested, violently or otherwise, their political views. Some environmental activists have been convicted of hammering spikes into trees about to be logged, which could result in injury and death to sawmill operatives. Others risk their own lives climbing buildings or chimney stacks to protest pollution. The Clayoquot Sound confrontations and arrests in 1993 symbolize the clash of political values.

From Davis Inlet — where the Labrador Innu have protested with occasional and predictable violence the appalling situation of their community — to Clayoquot Sound, Canadians continually protest their political grievances with violence and with more or less success.

Gender violence

Marc Lépine is the classic example here, the rejected student who shot and killed 14 women at l'Université de Montréal and injured another 11 students. Gender violence is expressed also in sexual assaults, sexual harassment, and domestic violence. The categories overlap of course: gender violence is also criminal, may be domestic, may be political, etc.

The battle of the sexes, as the popular phrase goes, is only one aspect of the relations between males and females. But with the rise of the second phase of the women's movement in the seventies to challenge the patriarchal status quo, and spurred on by the legal recognition of the "battered wife syndrome," gender equity legislation, and the recent acquittal of Lorena Bobbitt in the US, the "battle" has been heating up.

Domestic violence

Linda MacLeod (1980, 1987) has demonstrated the vast range and the devastating impact of domestic violence in Canada, most particularly in wife-battering by males. This will be discussed in more detail in Chapter 4. The Badgley Report (1984) has also reviewed the data on child sexual abuse, usually by family members. The battered child syndrome is now a phrase that has been absorbed into the sociology lexicon like the battered wife syndrome: a sad commentary on the prevalence of domestic violence.

Between one-third and one-quarter of all homicides occur within the family, loosely defined. The home is a dangerous environment and, considering child abuse, sex abuse, and violence, family members are the most violent people in our environment. But such violence is still the exception rather than the rule.

Sports violence

Sports violence is loved by Canadian spectators, particularly in hockey, boxing and occasionally in soccer, baseball, and football. Hockey would not be the same without it, nor obviously would boxing. This is violence for profit — and will continue to be so until victims of violence sue successfully for damages in civil court.

The stabbing of tennis star Monica Seles and the attack on ice-skating star Nancy Kerrigan have introduced new dimensions of violence to hitherto very physical but non-violent sports. So many millions of dollars are now at stake that sports competitions may be taking new forms. Where winning is everything, then the Hobbesian war is declared. "All's fair in love and war!"

Violence in the media

The media perpetually glorify violence, romanticize and idealize violence, and eternally portray violence. A film without violence is rare. An evening's television without violence is not rare: it does not exist. A front page without conflict does not exist.

Media violence begins for children with the cartoons and escalates to the graphic violence of the Rambo and Terminator movies, the horror movies, and all this for fun and profit. Even "The Piano," a supposedly sensitive movie, has an entirely gratuitous finger-chopping scene. Much of the violence is against women to begin with, and ends with the revenge of the avenging justice-seeking males. The sequence of good women being violated by bad guys who are in turn violated (justifiably, presumably) by good guys is pretty routine. And it likely encourages the violation of women as well. Although the hypothesis that violent movies cause violent behaviour is virtually impossible to prove with any scientific certainty, it seems so obvious as to be scarcely worth discussing.

But to blame the media is not sufficient. The media are responsive to popular demand. *We* pay to watch the movies and the videos and the violent TV programs. Do we protest? If there is a problem with the media perhaps it is we who are the problem.

Virginia Larivière, a fourteen year old girl whose sister was abducted on her way to the corner store, then raped and killed, collected over a million signatures to her petition to protest violence in the media. One result was the effort by the federal government to require limitations on the amount and type of violence shown on television, on threat of stations losing their licenses. Larivière achieved more than a thousand editorials. One activist may accomplish more than journalists and academics combined.

Roles of Violence

These different types of violence occur *everywhere*, in school yards and on university campuses, in mines and in offices, on sports fields and TV screens, in video games and on the streets, in bars and banks and bedrooms and battlefields. Cumulatively, the utility of the conflict paradigm can hardly be under-estimated.

What does such violence achieve? The roles of violence in contemporary Canada remain much as they have throughout our history, and can be summarized as follows:

1. To maintain the status quo and to keep power: the penal system, and discipline.

2. To change the status quo and to acquire power and all that goes with it, wealth, status, and respect. Change may be effected by ballots or bullets or, in Malcolm X's famous phrase, "by any means necessary."

3. For profit, as in robberies and criminal gangs. Crime pays. So does violence in sports. Violent films make money. The armaments industry is big business.

4. For sexual gratification, as in child sexual abuse, rape, and sexual harassment.

5. To achieve political change: the FLQ, Oka, Greenpeace, Clayoquot . . .

6. To express a grievance, real or imagined, justified or not: Lépine, Fabrikant.

7. To express hatred: this overlaps with previous categories no doubt, but would include such *hate* crimes as killing prostitutes and gays, probably the

rare serial killers and mass murderers whose rage is turned outwards, and such ethnic crimes as racial and anti-Semitic attacks.

8. For love, perhaps, and rarely, as in mercy-killings, at the request of the victim or not, and in assisted suicides (cf. Chapter 7). That people have a right to life is well known; that we may also have a right to die is more controversial and may require a renegotiation of the relation between individual and state rights as well as the concept of violence.

9. For fun, as in the Stanley Cup riots of 1986 and 1993 in Montreal, and similar disturbances in other cities. Such riots can be used for profit, or even provoked, by "criminal elements" or "outsiders," as is often alleged, but they may be enjoyed by others.

10. Finally, violence often provokes counter-violence in an escalating spiral, self-defensive measures of various sorts, and an increasing infringement of personal liberties for the entire society. Violence and the threat of violence keep people home after dark, put bars on windows, require more security alarms, "justify" students carrying knives or guns and using them, anaesthetize our moral sensibilities, blur our concepts of reality making us believe that violence is more "normal," and therefore more "right," than in fact it is, trigger mimic violence, acclimatize us to new norms, and ultimately create an even more violent society.

CONCLUSION

Long ago the Greek philosopher Heraclitus stated that "war is Father of all, King of all" (Barnes, 1987: 102). That is the conflict perspective. In his view this is realism. No doubt this philosophy was buttressed by his jaundiced Machiavellian view of human nature: "most men are bad and few good" (Barnes, 1987:110). (Discuss!)

Conflict theorists tend to have not only a very different view of history from consensus theorists, who emphasize the happy order rather than the blood, but also different views of society and also of human nature. Conflict theorists are particularly sensitive to conflict: class, ethnic, gender, sectarian, regional, language and other — all of which are deep rooted in contemporary Canada.

A conflict theorist is not one who *wants* conflict necessarily: such a theorist is one who *studies* it as an instrument of social change or as a marker of social tension and attempts to understand it, explain it, perhaps actively mediate and alleviate it. It is the radical or the revolutionary who *advocates* conflict, violent or non-violent, to effect desired social changes in the structure of society.

To sum up some of these theories of conflict and violence: Some theorists have explained violence and social conflict by the evil (Machiavelli and Hobbes) or totally amoral (Nietzsche and Freud) nature of humanity. Others have explained it as the logical or defensive response to an inequitable, "evil" society (Rousseau and Marx) — which is also violently oppressive. Spencer regarded violence, not so much as a necessary evil — necessary given either the state of human nature or the state of the state — but as providential: a *good* for the evolution of society and of humanity (though tough on fools and losers). Where Rousseau, and particularly Marx and Engels, had stressed the utility and morality of violence from the bottom up: revolutionary violence (as so many anarchists and revolutionaries have done since, from Bakunin to Fanon, Malcolm X, the IRA and the FLQ); Foucault emphasized the necessary role of violence as an instrument of discipline, control and punishment, from the top down, but strangely for a Frenchman he neglected the reverse role of violence in revolution. Feminists have concerned themselves primarily with the role of male violence as an instrument of the control of women.

In recent years feminists and sociologists (and the categories overlap of course), have tended to avoid the speculative debates about the good or the bad in human nature and society and have focused more on either the micro-level: socialization and gender roles, or the macro-level: cultural values and social structures. Feminists in particular have offered numerous recommendations on the control of violence (see Chapter 4).

Theorizing conflict is not an academic or philosophical game: it does make a difference to how we live our lives, to policy formulations, and to our expectations of others. It matters whether we understand societal conflict as a consequence primarily of a flawed human nature or a flawed society; whether we believe that people are basically good, requiring minimal government, or basically bad, requiring maximum coercion; whether we perceive social conflict as legitimate or illegitimate; and whether social conflict is to be used to maintain or to change a given status quo. Violence itself may be seen as rare and as morally deviant or as normal and natural and fairly common, depending on one's experiences perhaps, but also on one's sense of history.

We recognize, at least sometimes, that life *is* a struggle, it is a problem, and one damned thing after another. But we think it *ought* to be wonderful, loving, and peaceful and a bowl of cherries. Caught between the "is" and the "ought," reality and our expectations of that reality — people can get frustrated and unhappy. While no doubt we should count our blessings in this war of all against all (in the conflict paradigm), we could also develop more realistic but not necessarily lower expectations. Fairy tales after all are for children; and happy endings are for Walt Disney movies — but so powerful is our socialization that we still expect them; yet there are no final happy endings — there are only new beginnings.

Whether sociologists attend to conflict or not, and whether people advocate violence or not, conflict and violence do exist, do persist and cannot be ignored.

Conflict is not everything, and not everything is conflict. But conflict theorists argue that such a paradigm is more realistic and more useful sociologically (and philosophically) than the conservative paradigm which sees conflict as deviant, or exceptional, or individual, or as a passing shadow on the sunny "peaceable" face of Canada.

ENDNOTES

1. How this Leviathan, composed of naturally quarrelsome and warlike people, would create a peaceful, pleasant society was a problem that Hobbes could not resolve. The greater power of Leviathan can control the lesser power of the individual; but who controls Leviathan?

2. Ambrose Bierce, the American satirist, defined Revolution as follows: "In politics an abrupt change in the form of misgovernment." And Conservative: "A statesman who is enamoured of existing evils, as distinguished from a liberal, who wishes to replace them with others."

3. Towards the end of his life Engels revised this view and came to believe in the possibility of a peaceful transition to socialism through the suffrage, parliamentary activity, and expanding membership of the party (cf. McLellan, 1978: 70-2).

THE FEMINIST PARADIGM

The women's liberation movement identified women as an oppressed group, demanded equality in all social, economic, cultural, judicial, and sexual matters, and looked critically at scientific and other theories to examine to what degree they bolstered and maintained patriarchy while at the same time often claiming to be value free and neutral.

. . . At the most fundamental level, feminist scholarship is committed to understanding and improving the situation of women.

Margrit Eichler's (1985: 619, 624) concise formulation of the feminist paradigm clarifies the major differences between the feminist paradigm and the conservative paradigm in particular, while the notions of oppression and radical social change point to its identity with the conflict paradigm, the Marxist origins of which we discussed in the previous chapter.[1]

A waitress told Gloria Steinem a briefer and more personal formulation: "Now I see that feminism is about strengthening women from the inside too" (Steinem, 1993: 338).

The achievement of these goals is a struggle. For feminists (as for other conflict theorists), society is neither fair, nor just, nor equal, nor, as Durkheim argued, a relatively harmonious system characterized by organic solidarity, linked by the interdependence of mutually supportive parts and "shared values." On the contrary, it is a battlefield where the war between the sexes is fought out, in sector after sector, with different types of weaponry (law, words, humour, organizations, votes, protests) and often enough in blood: a war between women and men or, some might say, between feminists (women and some men) and patriarchs, traditionalists, chauvinists, sexists, and conservatives (men, and some traditionalist women).

Feminist perspectives range from left to right along the political spectrum, and heterosexual to lesbian along the inclusivist-exclusivist spectrum; and since "the personal is political," sexual orientation does have political implications. Sylvia Walby (1990) has distinguished four basic feminist orientations: Marxist, radical, liberal, and dual-systems (Marxist-radical). Scholars with these different orientations all theorize about patriarchy, but differ about its relation to the economy, family, culture, sexuality, violence and the state, to name Walby's six areas of investigation.

Feminists therefore may be united in their agreement about the oppression of women, but there can be lively disagreement about the modalities of this oppression, the most appropriate tactics of resistance, the nature of the ideal society, and of course the political party or other mechanisms best suited to achieve these goals. Feminists work in each of the three main federal parties, but also outside them; thus while there is no one voice for women (nor for men, if it comes to that) there is nonetheless a powerful consensus on the need for change.

THE WOMEN'S MOVEMENT

The beginnings of the modern women's movement lie in the international out-pouring of protest against the oppression of women during the sixties. The remoter origins lie further back, in the French Revolution. Revolted by the 1789 Declaration of the Rights of *Man*, Olympe des Gouges published her Declaration of the Rights of Women in 1791 insisting that "Woman is born free and her rights are the same as those of man." She was guillotined two years later (O'Faolain and Martines, 1973: 307). Meanwhile in England Mary Wollstonecraft published her classic work *A Vindication of the Rights of Women* (1792/1985), an attack on the French Revolutionary Declaration on the Rights of *Man*, as well as a critique of the oppression of women and an argument for emancipation. Harriet Martineau, described by her biographer as the first woman sociologist, visited and studied the United States just after De Tocqueville, from 1834 to 1836. She deplored the "Political Nonexistence of Women," and was appalled at their condition:

> The Americans have, in the treatment of women, fallen below, not only their own democratic principles, but the practice of some parts of the Old World . . . While woman's intellect is confined, her morals crushed, her health ruined, her weaknesses encouraged, and her strength punished, she is told that her lot is cast in the paradise of women: and there is no country in the world where there is so much boasting of the 'chivalrous' treatment she enjoys. (Hoecker-Drysdale, 1992: 63)

This verdict flatly contradicted the almost sycophantic praise offered by De Tocqueville (as we have seen) which perhaps helps to account for his greater contemporary renown.

In the United States the beginnings of the movement are usually ascribed to the first Women's Rights Convention held at Seneca Falls in 1848. Their Declaration of Sentiments parodied the US. Declaration of Independence:

> We hold these truths to be self-evident; that all men and women are created equal . . . The history of mankind is a history of repeated injuries and usurpations on the part of man towards woman, having in direct object the establishment of absolute tyranny over her.

The Declaration listed a series of grievances, and demanded the franchise. A few men agreed with the feminists about the existence of what Wollstonecraft described as "the state of warfare which exists between the sexes" (1985: 285), notably Frederick Engels and J.S. Mill; but most did not. The struggle continued with the suffragettes and culminated in the federal enfranchisement of women in Canada in 1918, and the election of Agnes Macphail to the House of Commons in 1921, where she sat until 1940.

Election to the house did not mean the possibility of appointment to the Senate however; and in the celebrated "Persons Case," brought by Nellie McClung and others, the Supreme Court of Canada unanimously decided in 1928, that women were not "persons" in law, and could not hold public office as senators. The suit was appealed to the British Privy Council, which reversed the Supreme Court decision in 1929, describing the exclusion of women from public office as "a relic of days more barbarous than ours."

World War II effected a massive gender displacement of the labor force. As men, and women, were mobilized for war, women moved in to the labor force to fill their places in an expanding economy, and were as rapidly displaced again at the end of the war. Into this turmoil came Simone de Beauvoir's *The Second Sex* (1949; English 1953). Betty Friedan followed with *The Feminine Mystique* (1963), and in 1966 she co-founded the National Organization for Women (NOW), and modern feminism had its first organizational base in the United States. The first mass protests soon followed at the Miss World Beauty Pageant in New York in 1968.

Other influential works appearing at this time were Kate Millett's *Sexual Politics* (1969), Germaine Greer's *The Female Eunuch* (1970), Robin Morgan's *Sisterhood is Powerful* (1970), and Shulamith Firestone's *The Dialectic of Sex* (1970). It was Germaine Greer (1970) who first identified the enemy explicitly:

> Women have very little idea of how much men hate them . . . Men do not themselves know the depth of their hatred. (1971: 249, 271)

Meanwhile in Canada the National Action Committee was formed in 1971; then an umbrella organization of 30 women's groups, it now includes about 300 member groups from across the country and is the largest and most powerful women's organization in Canada.

It was in the seventies that the first feminist journals and newsletters were founded, the first courses on women were offered at universities, the first chairs of women's studies were established, and the first books were published (Eichler, 1985). A significant development was the Report of the Royal Commission on the Status of Women, tabled in 1970, listing 167 recommendations concerning the economy, education, family, taxation, poverty, public life, criminal law, immigration, and citizenship. One of the recommendations was the establishment of a federal Status of Women Council which was implemented in 1973 with the creation of the Canadian Advisory Council on the Status of Women (CACSW).

With the understanding that the women's movement was solidly established by the seventies, we will now proceed to examine such changes as have occurred in Canada, and how they are interpreted according to the feminist paradigm. We will consider successively the economy (including participation rates and distribution, and income), politics (including power and gendered agendas), the law, the university, and violence against women; we will conclude with a note on the apparent definition of *men* as a social problem, and the masculinist paradigm.

THE ECONOMY

Participation

Women's participation in the labor force has increased substantially in the last two decades; 38% of women were employed in 1969. This figure rose to 49% in 1979 and to 58% by 1989. Men's participation has been relatively stable at 77%. As a result of these changed rates, women now constitute 44% of the total labor force, up from 33% in 1969 (Parliament, 1990: 18).

Distribution

Distribution within the labor force is very uneven, however, and very unequal. Indeed the occupational distribution is usually described as sex segregation or, more emotionally, as occupational apartheid. Women are disproportionately represented in the so-called pink colour jobs or the lace ghetto. These jobs are usually characterized by relatively low pay, low skill requirements, few prospects for advancement and low rates of unionization.

This is clearly demonstrated in Table 4-1 which shows that 53% of the female labor force is concentrated in clerical, sales and service occupations, whereas only 26% of the male labor force works in these occupations. Conversely 46% of the male labor force works in the primary occupations (farming, fishing, mining, etc.), processing, construction, transportation and handling whereas only 11% of the female labor force works there. Men and women seem to be fairly evenly divided in the managerial sector (36% of women and 28% of men), but the category is very broad and camouflages a hierarchical stratification within the occupational category.

The professions are defined as those occupations which require a minimum of a bachelor's degree for entry. Some professions are male-dominated: over 90% of all engineers and physicists, 88% of judges, 79% of physicians and surgeons, 86% of dentists, and 78% of lawyers are male. Some professions, by contrast, are female-dominated: 96% of dietitians and nutritionists, 85% of physiotherapists, 81% of elementary and kindergarten teachers and 81% of librarians are female (1986 data). However there is mobility. Women constitute (1986) 45.1% of all professionals, up from 42.5% in 1981 (Marshall, 1989: 15). At this rate of change, we have probably achieved professional parity now; but certainly not economic nor occupational parity.

Indeed the occupational picture may change rapidly. At present women represent between 45% and 50% of students enrolled in law, medicine, and commerce, although only 14% of the enrollment in engineering. This profession has been scrutinized closely in recent years, in an attempt to remedy this low enrollment pattern and the misogynous behaviour of engineering students at many campuses across the country, especially since the massacres at l'Université de Montréal in 1989 and Concordia in 1992. Some blame the virtual exclusion of women from the profession (only 3% of engineers are female) on socialization: we are taught to be masculine or feminine, and engineering is not seen as com-

Table 4.1   Labor Force by Occupation and Sex, Canada, November 1994

	Female Thousands	Male Thousands	Total Thousands
Managerial and Professional	2,262	2,168	4,430
Clerical	1,615	390	2,005
Sales	620	734	1,354
Service	1,129	845	1,973
Primary Occupations	138	508	646
Processing, Machining, etc.	348	1,352	1,700
Construction	20	807	827
Transportation	43	485	528
Material Handling	125	379	505
Unclassified	66	46	113
Total	6,366	7,715	14,081

Source: Statistics Canada, 1994. *The Labor Force*. December. Cat. No. 71-001.

patible with a feminine image. Some blame the public school system; in Alberta, for instance, only 14% of high school graduates have taken the prerequisite courses of maths and physics, and only one-third of those are women. Some blame the engineers. A student at Toronto stated: "I don't know how many times I've been told that things have changed and that the profession wants women. But it doesn't. The welcome is lip service." An engineering faculty member explains:

> The tribe has little time for human or social values . . . You have to ask why any thoughtful person — especially one who happens to be female — would want to have anything to do with them. (McKay, 1992: 39-41)

Gloria Steinem once remarked: "There are not really many jobs that actually require a penis or a vagina, and all other occupations should be open to everyone."

Income

The good news is that the female-to-male earnings ratio for full-time full-year workers rose to 72% in 1993. This represents a slow but steady closing of the gender income gap for full-time adult workers, from 58% in 1967 to 62% in 1977 and 66% in 1987 (Statistics Canada, 1994; 1989; Cat. No. 13-217). Despite this gap, the female-to-male earnings ratio for single never-married earners is 99%, i.e., virtually identical incomes.

The bad news is that only 51% of female workers are full-time, full-year workers compared to 65% of working men; for the other half of the female labor force, wages went *down* in absolute terms. Also, the closing gap was not so much due to structural change in the gendered economy (i.e. to increasing equity) as to massive lay-offs in the predominantly male manufacturing and construction sectors. The same Statscan report showed the feminization of poverty: 37% of women earned less than $10,000 in 1991, compared to 23.9% of men; and 15.7% of men earned more than $50,000 compared to only 3.7% of women (Statistics Canada, 1993. Cat. No. 13-217). Furthermore, there is still a 28% wage gap.

Two related questions spring to mind. What accounts for these income differentials? How much of this gap is due to discrimination?

Statistics Canada have emphasized that a number of factors are operative in explaining these earnings differentials. They reflect mostly the type of jobs performed, the number of hours worked per week, and the number of weeks worked per year; they also reflect the differences in age, the numbers of years in the labor market, years of education, the proportion of unionized jobs, and so on. All of these variables would have to be factored in to isolate the effect of gender alone.

Despite the complexity of the issue, some of the data are startling in their simplicity. Statistics Canada (1994. Cat. No. 13-217) notes, with no comment:

> A male with eight years or less of schooling earned $28,019 compared to $55,567 for a university graduate. Corresponding data for females were $20,580 (grade eight or less) and $41,228 (university degree).

This shows the economic benefits of a university degree, but also that men enjoy a $8,000 advantage over women after eight years of school; this rises to $14,000 upon graduation from university. Put another way, after eight years of schooling women earn 73% of men's earnings, after university 74%. Many of the variables listed by Statistics Canada do not apply at the first stage in the life cycle. The critical variable in explaining income differentials appears to be gender, which explains the *initial* inequality, and then streams the population into different sectors of the labor market, with different wages attached; this *reinforces* the initial disparity.

The Human Rights Commission of Canada states that 50% of this income differential is due to discrimination (*The Gazette* 2.2.88); the other 50% is therefore presumably a matter of personal choice.

Room at the Top?

Although women constitute 44% of the paid labor force, they hold fewer than 10% of the directorships and top management jobs in major Canadian corporations. Léo-Paul Lauzon, a professor of accounting at l'Université du Québec, surveyed 676 public and Crown corporations. His principal conclusions are as follows:

- Women held only 4.7% of the 7,076 directorships listed in company annual reports in 1990 (but this is up 74% from the 2.7% reported in 1985).

- Women held only 6.7% of the 5,091 top executive positions (but this is more than three times the proportion, 2%, reported in 1985).

- 42% of these firms (299 in total) had no women executive officers or members of the board (Globe and Mail 30.6.92).

There is movement in the corporate hierarchy, but whether glacial or rapid is a matter of opinion. Either way, women are over-represented among the poor in Canada, and under-represented at the top.

"When will women get to the top?" This was the title of a cover article recently in *Fortune*, the leading business magazine in the United States. The answer was "not for a long time yet," according to the 201 (all male) chief executives of the largest corporations surveyed. Since many of these corporations are multinationals, the responses have relevance for Canada. When asked "How likely is it that your company will have a female CEO in 10 years," 82% said it was not likely; when asked if this would happen in 20 years, 81% said it *was* likely. For the young today, such timing would be quite convenient.

The biggest barrier may be discrimination. One CEO explained: "It shouldn't be this way, but too many senior managers, and particularly CEOs, tend to want to pass their jobs along to someone who's the image and likeness of themselves." Another agreed: "The problem with women advancing has more to do with men than with women. Men have dragged their feet." Despite discrimination, an increasing number of women are making it in corporate America: as of 1991 women constituted 4.8% of senior management in the 201 previously mentioned corporations — not a lot, but better than the 2.9% in 1986 (Fisher, 1992: 44, 46).

Another *Fortune* writer, Nancy Perry, while conceding that there is still discrimination, advises against "female victimitis" which she says is characteristic of "ardent feminists." "Far better," she writes, "to adopt the attitude: if you can't join 'em, beat 'em" (Perry, 1992: 58-59).

In *The Equality Game*, Nicole Morgan studied the history of women in the Federal Public Service, Canada's largest employer. She shows that the equality issue has been a "game" for most of the history of the civil service; only in the last 15 years or so has the service "begun to respond." Yet women are nowhere near equality. Using data for the Ottawa region only, she found that the number of women at the executive level more than quadrupled from 1976 to 1985 (from 81 to 345), but that they still constituted only 8.7% of the total number of executives, although this was up substantially from 2.8% in 1976. They also constituted 16% at the second rank of senior managers (up from 7%), 24% of middle management (up from 13%), and 61% of the lowest rank, and by far the largest category, of non-managers (up from 52%). Upward mobility everywhere, it seems, but the vast majority of women (83%) are in the lowest category whereas most men (56%) are in the top three ranks. Despite some progress, therefore, there is still polarity and inequality — and now much bitterness among both genders. One male remarked: "All it takes to be a deputy minister is to be female, Black, handicapped and part Indian." The male backlash against affirmative action which many men perceive as reverse discrimination is in evidence. And some women believe that a witchhunt is in progress, particularly against feminists. Francophone women face a double jeopardy: "Not only do we not manage like men, but we also do it the French way. This means that we are often too frank. We're immediately perceived as aggressive. Just think! Not only women but Latin women!" (Morgan, 1988: 39-64).

Rosabeth Kanter's study of gender relations in the Industrial Supply Company (a fictitious name), complements Morgan's work. She distinguished between five types of male responses to the "woman problem": the angry competitors (usually the young), the relaxed (usually older), the avoiders, the chivalrous, and the accepters ("few"); but also she perceived four types of role-traps for the token women executives at Indsco: the mother, the seductress, the pet, and the iron maiden. She notes that women executives "said they worked twice as hard to prove their competence" (Kanter, 1977: 42-43, 233-37, 216).

One problem is that the face of business is quintessentially male. Since big business especially has always been male, this is not so surprising; but as the world turns, this may have negative effects on women's aspirations. In Calgary, for instance, the number of businesses which employ "Mr." in their business names outnumber those with Mrs., Miss, or Ms. by 6 to 1, and in Toronto the ratio is 13 to 1. These include such classics as Mr. Shower Door, Mr. Drain, Mr. Crankshaft, Monsieur Muffler, Mr. Tasty Burgers, and Mr. I Buy Almost Anything in Halifax (*Maclean's* 12.10.92:11). The equation of masculinity and power is sometimes decidedly odd. (In Montreal there are almost as many businesses with Miss as with Mister — but they are almost all restaurants or boutiques in a classic polarization of genders.)

POLITICS

In the Communist Manifesto (1848), Marx and Engels insisted that "every class struggle is a political struggle" (1967: 90). Similarly feminists insist that the battle of the sexes is a political struggle, as well as an economic struggle.

Women constitute about 51% of the population, but they held only 18% of the seats in the House of Commons in the last election of 1993 — although this was up considerably from 13% in 1988 and 0.4% in 1968. Similarly they held only 15% of the seats in the Senate — but this is up from 0% until 1931, when Cairine Wilson was appointed to the Senate. Representation tends to be high in provincial politics, ranging from 3.8% in Newfoundland in 1989 to 25.6% in the 1990 Ontario election won by the NDP. And representation is even higher in municipal politics: up to 43% and 54% in Calgary and Edmonton (1989) (Maillé, 1990: 6, 12-14, 23). So there is much inequity, some parity, and much change.

The list of political pioneers is long. In 1974 Pauline McGibbon was appointed Lieutenant Governor of Ontario, the first woman to hold that office. In 1980 Jeanne Sauvé became the first woman to be Speaker of the House of Commons, and in 1984 she was the first woman to be appointed Governor General of Canada. Bertha Wilson was the first woman appointed to the Supreme Court of Canada, in 1982. In 1989 Audrey McLaughlin was elected the first female leader of a national political party. In 1991 Rita Johnston became the first female premier of a province, British Columbia, on the resignation of Bill Vander Zalm, and the Northwest Territories legislature elected Nellie Cournoyea as its leader, the first woman to lead the Assembly. In 1992 Louise Frechette was appointed Canada's ambassador to the UN, the first woman to hold that position. In 1993

Catherine Callbeck became the first woman elected Premier of a province in Canada, in Prince Edward Island. Also in 1993 Kim Campbell succeeded Brian Mulroney as Prime Minister of Canada: the last major political post not hitherto held by a woman. While this is not parity, it is change since Agnes Macphail was first elected to Parliament in 1921.

In 1994 Victoria Matthews became the first female Anglican bishop in Canada; Maureen Kempston Darkes was appointed CEO of General Motors, the largest corporation in Canada. And Wendy Clay, a doctor and a pilot, became the first woman to attain the rank of major-general in the Canadian Armed Forces; she was also the first woman to earn her wings in the Forces, back in 1974. So the barriers are crumbling, one by one, in politics, church, business, and the forces.

Are women winning? Radicals may tend to dismiss all these changes as "tokenism," and point to the still remaining considerable inequities. Liberals tend to believe that this goes "beyond tokenism" and constitutes a real, if partial, structural change. Whichever the paradigm adopted, it is apparent that the rate of change is far more rapid in politics than in economics. That Roberta Bondar was the first Canadian woman to fly a space mission in 1991 does not necessarily change the gendered world.

While men were enfranchised in the nineteenth century in North America and Western Europe, women did not get the right to vote until the second and third decades of this century in Canada, Britain, and the United States (see Table 4-2); and then only after militant protests by the Suffragettes. Quebec was the last province to grant women the right to vote in provincial elections in 1940 (Brodie and Vickers, 1982; Maillé, 1990).

Change was facilitated by The Human Rights Act (1977) which made sexual discrimination illegal, and by Section 15 of The Canadian Charter of Rights and Freedoms, passed in 1985, in which government recognized the principle of sexual equality (Maillé, 1990: 25). Enfranchisement does not guarantee economic equity however, nor does it guarantee equal political representation; and it does not mean that government is representative of women's interests.

Lincoln defined democracy as "government of the people by the people for the people." Socialists have described western democracies as "government of the wealthy, by the wealthy for the wealthy." Feminists define the system as "government of men by men and for men."

Certainly the political agendas of the governing parties in Canada do not reflect women's priorities. Issues of particular concern to women, as defined by CACSW, are the following:

- economic equity
- abortion
- child care

Table 4-2   Years Women Gained the Right to Vote

Selected Countries

New Zealand	1893	South Africa	1930
Australia	1902	Spain	1931
Finland	1906	Brazil	1932
Norway	1913	Thailand	1932
Denmark	1915	Turkey	1933
U.S.S.R.	1917	Philippines	1937
Austria	1918	France	1944
Canada	1918	Italy	1945
Germany	1918	Japan	1945
Poland	1918	Yugoslavia	1945
Belgium	1919	Bulgaria	1947
Great Britain	1919	China	1947
Holland	1919	Indonesia	1955
Ireland	1919	Algeria	1958
Sweden	1919	Iran	1963
U.S.A.	1920	Kenya	1963
India	1926	Switzerland	1971
Pakistan	1926		

- maternity leave
- the new reproductive technologies
- women's shelters
- violence against women

The priorities of the federal government (or the bourgeoisie, or the men, depending on one's perspective) have been, and still are, very different:

- Free Trade
- Meech Lake (1991)
- G.S.T.
- The Gulf War (1991)
- The Constitution (1992)
- The economy (1993)
- Quebec (1994, 1995)
- The Deficit

Furthermore women's political agendas are not necessarily restricted to Canada. Some women have argued that Canadian aid and development programs should be tied to civil rights and political reforms and to the abolition of abuses against women around the world. Such abuses include female circumcision, the right to kill (alleged) adulteresses, forced marriages, unequal rights of inheritance, denial of property rights or alimony for divorced women, lack of custody rights of mothers over their children, female infanticide, the compulsory sterilization of women, wife-burning . . . Such issues are rarely mentioned on men's political agendas.

We conclude where we began, with Agnes Macphail: "I do not want to be the angel of any home; I want for myself what I want for other women, absolute equality" (CACSW, 1988: 21). And Charlotte Whitton, Mayor of Ottawa in the fifties and sixties: "Whatever she does, woman must do twice as well as any man to be thought of just half as good . . . Luckily, it's not difficult."

LAW

"The Law is a ass — a idiot," pontificates Mr. Bumble in Dickens' novel, *Oliver Twist*. The Lord High Chancellor in the opera *Iolanthe* disagrees: "The law is the true embodiment of everything that's excellent." Somewhat more radical, Oliver Goldsmith wrote in "The Traveller" that "Laws grind the poor, and rich men rule the laws." Marx and Engels were more analytical, and in *The Communist Manifesto* they harangued the bourgeoisie: "Your jurisprudence is but the will of your class made into a law" (1848/1967: 99-100).

More recently, Justice Bertha Wilson, the first woman appointed to the Supreme Court of Canada, described some aspects of Canadian law as "little short of ridiculous":

> [In some areas of law] a distinctly male perspective is clearly discernible and has resulted in legal principles that are not fundamentally sound and should be revisited as and when the opportunity presents itself. Some aspects of the criminal law in particular cry out for change since they are based on presuppositions about the nature of women and women's sexuality that in this day and age are little short of ludicrous.

Basically, she says that the law is an ass, and that men rule the laws. Only 9% of the 850 federal judges are women, but, Wilson suggested, "Perhaps they will succeed in infusing the law with an understanding of what it means to be fully human" (*The Gazette*, 9.2.90).

Certainly more and more complaints are being lodged against judges. In its annual report for 1991-92, The Canadian Judicial Council noted that 115 complaints were lodged against judges: up 35% from the previous year and a record number to date. Although most complaints were dismissed as unfounded or inappropriate, two judges have resigned and others were reprimanded. Some of the cases involved sexism. One judge stated that "At times no may mean maybe or wait awhile"; another was accused of saying Indians lie all the time; one judge stole two antique brass door-knobs from the courthouse for his own office; and another was seen drunk in a hotel: he was wearing a black bra, panties, and nylons at the time (*Globe and Mail* 31.7.93). Another has been accused of sexual assault (*Globe and Mail* 27.7.93). One judge remarked that "Rules are like women, they're made to be violated." Another, trying to explain that rapes in the north are different from the rest of the country because they usually occur when a woman is drunk and passed out, stated: "The man comes along, sees a pair of hips and helps himself." Another informed the court that "Sometimes a slap in the face" is all a woman needs, and that this "might not be such unreasonable force" (*The Gazette* 10.2.90).

In Toronto a Justice of the Peace, 65, married with five children is reprimanded for "gross, disgusting" and sexually suggestive remarks to two young women; and a judge's misconduct is deemed "tantamount to sexual assault" in another case (*Globe and Mail* 4.2.94; 25.11.93). In Quebec a judge tells a worried woman: "If the gentleman assassinates the lady I won't lose any sleep over it and I won't die. Don't worry I won't suffer from a depression either, because it's not my responsibility." A female judge sentenced a man to a lenient 23 month sentence for sodomizing his nine-year-old stepdaughter over a period of two and a half years, on the grounds that the man had spared the child's virginity (*Globe and Mail* 9.12.93; 29.1.94). And so on. With judges like these, where are women to find justice? But anecdotal evidence must be used cautiously; it is not clear how representative of the total these examples are: these judges may be the rare exception rather than the rule.

These examples may be dismissed by some as the occasional aberrations of an all-too-human legal system, or they may be perceived as symptomatic of the institutional oppression of women by a patriarchal system of jurisprudence that is totally congruent with the economic and political systems. Indeed Harriet Martineau was perhaps the first to criticize the entire structure of the legal system from a feminist perspective:

> The question has been asked, from time, in more countries than one, how obedience to the laws can be required of women, when no woman has, either actually or virtually, given any assent to any law. No plausible answer has . . . been offered; for the good reason that no plausible answer can be devised. (Hoecker-Drysdale 1992: 63)

But the problem is not only the singular stupidity of some judges; it goes beyond that to the systemic structure of legislation and jurisprudence. The relatively small proportion of female legislators in the federal and provincial governments, and the relatively small proportion of female judges, suggests that patriarchy will persist for a while, but the proportions are changing.

On the other hand the allegedly patriarchal federal legislature, and the various provincial governments, have adopted a wide range of equity legislation, including the Employment Equity Act (1986), the Federal Contractors Programs, the Public Service Employment Equity Program, and the Public Service Reform Act (1993). The results have been twofold: a reevaluation of salaries in the public and the affected private sectors, which have usually resulted in higher salaries for women, and a slow but steady upward mobility for women and, to a lesser degree, the other target groups: natives, visible minorities, and the disabled.[2]

These changes are reflected in public opinion. The 1994 *Maclean's*/Decima poll asked Canadians, "Have opportunities for women to move into senior positions in the workforce improved or worsened over the past ten years?" The responses were: improved, 80%; stayed about the same, 15%; worsened, 4% — with men slightly more positive at 85% than women at 75% (*Maclean's* 2.1.95).

THE UNIVERSITY

Students

Universities were not open to women in Canada until the 1870s. At that time women could not vote in federal or provincial elections and were virtually excluded from much of the paid labor force.

Debates about admitting women to the university were extremely acrimonious. They hinged ultimately on definitions of the nature of women and men, and their appropriate roles in society. Many patriarchs believed that university education was neither necessary nor useful to women, that women could not handle such hard work, that they would become less feminine, and that anyway the mixing of the sexes would create moral disorder, etc.

Yet by 1992, 57% of all bachelor's degrees were awarded to women, up from 44% in 1975; plus 48% of all master's degrees — which is almost parity — and 32% of doctoral degrees, up from 28% and 16% respectively in 1975 (Stout, 1992/Statistics Canada, 1993 Cat. No. 81-220). These dramatic increases in women's share in the educational system, rising to numerical dominance at the BA level, are not evenly distributed through the various fields, but the distribution is more even than it was. Of the 18 professions classified as male-dominated, in 1975, six are now reclassified as in the neutral zone in 1990. Two of the most interesting changes are in commerce: in 1975 women were only 13.3% of commerce graduates but by 1990 they were 45.8%; and in veterinary medicine, the proportion of women graduates increased from 20.8% to 61.9%. Lesser increases are apparent also in zoology, law, medicine, and political science. Women's enrollment is particularly low in engineering, physics, and forestry, and suffered a decline in computer science (Stout, 1992). The most obvious consequences of these quantitative and qualitative changes in the university is the possibility of women gaining increased access to traditional male occupations, with the possibility of increased mobility and income

Faculty

Women hold 19.2% of tenure and tenure-track positions in Canadian universities (1991-92 data), up from 17.2% in 1989-90 when the distribution ranged from 6.8% at the full professor rank to 52.4% of the lecturers, according to the recent report of The Canadian Association of University Teachers (Quebec data was not available. CAUT, 1991, 1993). When we extrapolate from these data we see that as senior male faculty retire, and junior female faculty move up through the ranks, the university will include a majority of women in the near future. We are therefore seeing the beginning of the feminization of the university.

Predictions are complicated by the uneven distribution of gender among those who have been granted doctoral degrees. Women earned 31.9% of the 1,000 doctorates granted in 1992, ranging from 11.2% in Engineering and the Applied Sciences and 16.8% in Mathematics and the Physical Sciences to 48.2% in Fine Arts and 54.5% in Education (see Table 4-3).

The most recent data for 1991-92 indicate that women constitute 35.8% of those enrolled in doctoral programs, with lows of 10.8% in engineering and the applied sciences to highs of 49% in sociology, 57% in anthropology, and 64% in psychology (CAUT, 1993).

Table 4-3   Number and Proportion of Women Granted Doctorate Degrees by Major Discipline, Canada, 1992

Discipline	N	%
Education	171	54.5
Fine Arts	13	48.2
Humanities	133	38.4
Social Sciences	271	44.5
Agriculture and Biology	107	28.4
Engineering, Applied Science	56	11.2
Health Professions	138	41.2
Mathematics, Physical Sciences	99	16.8
Total[1]	1,000	100

[1]Includes 12 for which the discipline is not known.

Source: Canadian Association of University Teachers 1994. *Bulletin* April. From Statistics Canada, Education Culture and Tourism Division. Postsecondary Education Section.

Women are evidently underrepresented at senior levels, and unequally distributed through faculties and departments. Some of this (real and/or apparent) inequity derives from gender stereotyping and systemic discrimination in social and educational gender streaming, and some no doubt from women's autonomous choices. Feminists suggest more of the former, conservatives more of the latter.

Indeed, the university is a gender-stratified and polarized institution in the feminist perspective: men dominate the higher levels, and women are disproportionately clustered in the lower ranks; most of the administrators and full-time faculty members are male, most of the secretarial staff are female.

The university has changed, however, not only in the increased proportion of female students and faculty, but also in the building of new structures, especially in recent years: these include women's studies programs, status of women officers or committees, employment equity policies, sexual harassment policies, and gender-equity hiring policies. Ideologies have also been changing as activists monitor course contents, gender stereotyping in texts, sexist language, and bias-free communication, and sensitize the generally male professoriate and administration to the feminist paradigms.

VIOLENCE

On December 6, 1989, Marc Lépine shot and killed 14 women and wounded 11 other women and two men at the Université de Montréal. He then killed himself. This was the largest mass shooting in Canada, and the first mass murder in North America, or anywhere, to deliberately target only women. This one act therefore displayed new dimensions of both sexism and violence.

Violence against women is nothing new, and Lépine is only the last in a long list of men who have killed women. Some of the more notorious mass murderers of women, and serial killers of women are the following:

- Jack the Ripper, never identified, killed six women in London in 1888.
- Ted Bundy was convicted of murdering two women, but was suspected of killing at least 21 women, perhaps as many as 67, between 1974 and 1978.
- The Yorkshire Ripper, Peter Sutcliffe, killed 12 women between 1975 and 1980 in the UK.
- Christopher Wilder murdered between 10 and 13 women from Florida to Nevada to New Hampshire before being killed by his own gun in a scuffle with police in 1984.
- In the Green River killings, about 48 prostitutes have been murdered since 1981 in the Seattle and Vancouver areas. The killer has not been apprehended.

- Paul Teale has been charged with the first degree murder of two Ontario teenagers in 1991; 48 sexual assault charges were also laid against him, dating back to 1987.
- Joel Rifkin killed 17 women in New York state between 1990 and 1993.
- Frederick West was charged with murdering 12 women, including his first wife and his two daughters, in England. He has since committed suicide. His second wife is charged with nine murders.

These serial killers and mass murderers are just the tip of the bloody iceberg in violence against women. Physical violence is predominantly a male phenomenon, with men accounting for the majority of both perpetrators and victims; in this chapter, however, we will be considering only violence against women. The issue was first brought to national attention by Linda MacLeod's study for CACSW, *Wife Battering in Canada: The Vicious Circle* (1980), and her follow-up report, *Battered but not Beaten: Preventing Wife Battering in Canada* (1987). Since then, and particularly since Lépine, violence against women has received increasing attention.

In 1991 the Committee on the Status of Women submitted a report to the federal government entitled *The War Against Women*[3]. Note the escalation of the definition: wife battering (1980) to war (1991). The Committee cited the Lépine Massacre at l'Université de Montréal in 1989, and the 119 women murdered by current or former husbands or partners in 1989. The Committee offered a broad definition of violence:

> Violence against women is a multifaceted problem which encompasses physical, psychological, and economic violations of women which is integrally linked to the social/economic/political structures, values and policies that silence women in our society, support gender-based discrimination, and maintain women's inequality. (1991: 3)

Homicide is relative rare in Canada compared to the US, for instance, and spousal homicide is even more rare; yet spousal homicides constitute about 15% of the total, 38% of the total of female victims, and 6% of the total of male victims, according to a review from 1974 to 1992 by Wilson and Daly (1994). Defining the word spouse loosely to include married, common-law, and legally separated and divorced, they found that 1,435 women and 451 men were killed by their spouses, giving a male to female homicide ratio of 3.2 to 1. Although rates vary widely across the country, they have remained relatively stable over these 18 years at 17 victims per million couples per annum. In 1991, for instance, 85 men killed their wives and 25 women killed their husbands (*Globe and Mail* 31.10.92).

Spousal homicides are not only *quantitatively* different by gender, however, they are also *qualitatively* different it is often suggested. Wives sometimes killed their husbands in self-defense or in defense of their children, and sympathetic courts are now not only handing out reduced sentences to battered wives who kill their abusive husbands, but also acquitting them completely even in cases of "pre-emptive strikes," i.e., not simply when under attack, but when in fear of a future attack.

Jane Stafford shot and killed her husband, a notoriously abusive man, after he passed out drunk in his truck, having threatened to kill her and her son. She was acquitted by a jury, but the Nova Scotia Court of Appeal ruled in 1983 that no one has the right "in anticipation of an assault that may or may not happen, to apply force to prevent the imaginary assault;" and she was sentenced to six months in jail and two years probation. In 1990, however, in another landmark case, Angelique Lyn Lavallée of Winnipeg was acquitted of murder after she blew the back of her boyfriend's head off with his shotgun when he threatened to kill her. In a unanimous decision written by Bertha Wilson, the Supreme Court recognized the battered woman's syndrome, accepted expert testimony, and refused to accept the premise of the Nova Scotia court which effectively sentenced women to "murder by installment." In several other cases, courts have recognized past abuse as grounds for self-defensive action, although not all claims for such are necessarily recognized. In June 1990, in Manitoba, a woman was given six months for stabbing an abusive boyfriend to death. In August 1991, in Manitoba Emily Brown received a three-year suspended sentence for shooting her abusive partner; the judge argued that she had "served that period of incarceration" during the 10 years she lived with the man. And in June 1991 Skeeter Paul, also in Manitoba, was charged with murder after her husband attacked her (for asking him to move his feet so she could clean up some spilled pickle juice); but after hearing testimony about the man's violence and brutality, the Crown simply dropped the case. Needless to say, all this does not give women a license to kill real or alleged abusive partners; but it does signal men and women, that times have changed (*Globe and Mail*, 31.10.92).

The clemency movement is having some success in redefining the homicides perpetrated by the victims of abuse as self-defense and a legitimate act: a tragedy more than a crime. In the United States the American Medical Association, supported by the US Surgeon General, declared that violent men constitute a major threat to women's lives, and children's too. Between 33% and 50% of all female homicide victims in the US are killed by their spouses or lovers, compared to 4% of all male victims; between 22% and 55% of females' visits to hospital emergency rooms are due to domestic violence; and more birth defects are caused by male violence than by diseases. Furthermore the average sentence for a man who kills his spouse is 2 to 6 years while for a woman it is 15 to 20. These issues were raised by cover stories of *Time* (18.1.93) and *Maclean's* (11.11.91), and although they are certainly not solved, they are receiving far more attention.

In general, women are much more likely to be killed by someone domestically related to them than are men (67% to 27% respectively); and they are also much more likely to be killed in their own homes (62% to 40%) (*Juristat*, June 1987: 5). In sum, most female victims of homicide are killed by their loved ones in their own homes; most men are not. Family and home are much more dangerous to women than to men.

Men are not only (sometimes) dangerous to their wives and children, they are also dangerous to themselves. After the killings, men are much more likely to kill themselves than are women (Daly and Wilson, 1988: 523). Lépine is a case in point.

Homicide is relatively rare of course. Lesser forms of violence are far more common, especially in the home (Lupri, 1989). The Committee reported the details of this war:

- In 1989, 12,970 sexual assaults were known to the police. Between 1983 and 1989, the number of complaints of sexual assault made to the police increased by 93%. Every 17 minutes there is a sexual assault committed in Canada, and 90% of the victims are female . . .

- Of aboriginal women surveyed in a recent study by the Ontario Native Women's Association, 80% had been assaulted or abused. In Toronto secondary schools, 20% of girls reported having been sexually assaulted and 11% reported physical violence while dating . . .

- At least one in ten women is physically and/or sexually assaulted each year by a husband, ex-husband or live-in partner. A woman is hit by a husband or partner an average of 30 times before she even calls the police . . .

- In 1989, 48% of Canadians reported that they personally knew of situations in which women were physically abused by husbands or live-in partners . . . Research found that the rate of wife-beating was 1,000 [times] higher for men who had observed violence in childhood than for men who had not had similar experiences. (Committee, 1991: 6-7)

Violence and the threat of violence, and a permanent climate of fear, are part of the everyday life for women, as they are not for men. Yet physical violence is itself only a small part of the more general *abuse* suffered by women. Not that men do not suffer violence and abuse from women, physical and/or emotional. Feminists insist, however, that the dimensions of such violence that can be measured and identified are vastly different. Furthermore, the *degree* and *range* of abuse against women amounts to *institutional* oppression, and reflects and reinforces their unequal status in Canada.

The physical consequences of violence against women are evidently enormous, varying from broken bones, black eyes, knife and gunshot wounds, to death. The psychic costs are also high: loss of self-esteem, fear, worry, and emotional pain. These too have consequences. The Committee reports that: "Women who have been sexually assaulted are approximately five times more likely to have a nervous breakdown, six times more likely to attempt suicide, and eight times more likely to commit suicide or die prematurely." They are also more likely to abuse drugs or alcohol. Furthermore the violence does not cease with the victim: the ripples spread to others. The second generation, the children of the original victims, are likely to repeat the process either as perpetrators or as victims. Violence breeds violence, it has often been remarked. And over 80% of women interviewed in federal penitentiaries had been either physically or sexually abused, and mostly both (1991: 11-12).

The costs of such pervasive physical violence are therefore not only physical, not only psychic, and not only multi-generational, but they are also economic:

> Medical costs to doctors' offices, hospital emergency wards, and mental health clinics; in criminal justice costs for police services, courts and corrections; and, in social service costs for welfare, housing, and day care. As well, given that women are a major part of the labor force, employers pay for violence against women in high absenteeism costs and low productivity rates. (1991: 11)

The Federal Government responded rapidly to the Committee Report, accepted virtually all the recommendations made, listed the initiatives that were then and are now being implemented, and established a goal of "zero tolerance" for violence against women. The Status of Women report, entitled *Living Without Fear . . . Everyone's Goal, Every Woman's Right* (1991) made 25 recommendations focusing particularly on prevention and education, law enforcement, and the provision of services to abused women, violent men, and their families.

Both the Committee on the Status of Women (1991) and the Federal Status of Women report (also 1991) recommended the establishment of a Federal Task Force to fully analyze violence against women. The Canadian Panel on Violence against Women was established in 1991, held hearings across the country in 1992, and presented its report *Changing the Landscape: Ending the Violence–Achieving Equality* in 1993. It is probably the most thorough analysis of such violence anywhere, sickening in its content, and articulating the voices of thousands of women in 139 communities. The report also goes far beyond simple statistical questions about the frequency with which physical violence is inflicted on women to include the entire range of issues related to the inequality of women, issues which facilitate violence against women and permeate the entire society, including racism, homosexuality, poverty, health, education, media. Here are two examples illustrating both the violence *and* the institutional complicity:

> My husband struck me on our honeymoon. He killed our first child by kicking the four month child out of my uterus. My doctor asked me what did I do to make him so mad, our Anglican minister reminded me that I had married for better or for worse, the lawyer wanted to know where I would get money to pay the fees, and my mother told my husband where I was hiding.

> Twenty-two assault charges were laid against my husband, a few were dropped, but in most cases he was convicted. He never went to jail — he was merely sentenced to varying terms of probation. (1993: 5)

The Panel distinguished between physical including sexual violence, psychological or emotional violence, financial violence, and spiritual abuse (e.g., the residential school system and religious exclusionism). These dimensions of violence can overlap and intersect, and these women's stories testify that they do.

But the Panel not only reported horror stories of the most appalling brutality, it also specifically adopted what it called

> a feminist lens through which violence against women is seen as the consequence of social, economic and political inequality built into the structure of the society and reinforced through assumptions expressed in the language and ideologies of sexism, racism and class. (1993: 3)

It is this lens which enabled the Panel to elaborate their analysis of institutional violence of different types in the workplace, the health care system, the social service system, the legal system, the military, the education system, the media, the Christian church, and in government.

Committed to the two goals: "the achievement of women's equality, and the elimination of violence against women," the Panel proposed a zero tolerance policy (1993: Part 5: 3). The Panel also made 494 policy recommendations to government, police, the courts, hospitals, unions, churches — every sector of society, especially to men; and it suggested that violence against women could be ended by the year 2000. (See Fekete, 1994, for a critical review.)

The Canadian Panel Report was followed swiftly by the Statistics Canada report, "The Violence Against Women Survey. Statistics Canada conducted telephone interviews with 12,300 women across the country, randomly selected to ensure a representative sample with results that are generalizable to the female population as a whole. Violence was defined as "experiences of physical or sexual assault that are consistent with legal definitions of these offences and could be acted upon by a police officer."

The results were horrific and the seven principal findings are reported here, verbatim, from the survey:

- One-half of all Canadian women have experienced at least one incident of violence since the age of 16.

- Almost one-half of women reported violence by men known to them and one-quarter reported violence by a stranger.

- One-quarter of all women have experienced violence at the hands of a current or past marital partner (includes common-law unions).

- One-in-six currently married women reported violence by their spouses; one-half of women with previous marriages reported violence by a previous spouse.

- More than one-in-ten women who reported violence in a current marriage have at some point felt their lives were in danger.

- Six-in-ten women who walk alone in their own area after dark feel "very" or "somewhat" worried doing so.

- Women with violent fathers-in-law are at three times the risk of assault by their partners than are women with non-violent fathers in law.

The total number of "violent incidents" reported by the 12,3000 women was 20,543. However the vast majority of these, 82%, resulted in *no* injuries. And of those incidents that did result in injuries (3,685), that vast majority did not receive medical attention; i.e., of the 20,543 incidents, only 1,026 (5%).

While the survey has been roundly criticized by John Fekete (1994), it nonetheless remains a matter of selected emphasis, and paradox, whether one insists that 51% of women have been victims of "violence," or that 82% have never been injured, by men.

MEN AS A SOCIAL PROBLEM?

There is a substantial agreement among feminists that women are oppressed, marginalized, and abused. In this chapter, we have tried to consider some of the effects this oppression has on economics, occupations, the university, politics, law, and the family; some of the consequences in physical violence and even death; and the origins and development of the Women's Movement to counter this oppression, to create new ways of life, and to empower women.

For many feminists, and many women, *men* are a social problem. For others the problem is, more indirectly, patriarchy. *Newsweek* (28.5.90) stated authoritatively, and perhaps articulated North American popular culture:

> Women, after all, are not a big problem. Our society does not suffer from burdensome amounts of empathy and altruism, or a plague of nurturance. The problem is men — or, more accurately, maleness.

But what is "maleness?" Are there men who do not have it? and women who do? This is not entirely clear. The same theme is reiterated by Rosalind Miles in *The Rites of Man* (1991) in which she refers (rather dramatically) to men as "the death sex" compared to women who, presumably are the life/love/altruistic/nurturing sex — i.e., really much better and far superior sex. She says that "To explain violence is to explain the male. The reverse is also true" (1991: 8, 12). The last chapter of her book is entitled "Killer Male," and she asks, rhetorically I think, "What remedy for men, maleness, masculinity, manhood?" (1991: 234). This is the construction of men as a disease!

Andrea Dworkin makes a similar point: "*Men love death*. In everything they make, they hollow out a central place for death, let its rancid smell contaminate every dimension of whatever still survives. *Men especially love murder.* In art they celebrate it, and in life they commit it" (1988: 214. Emphasis added). She notes that "Not one of us could have imagined . . . the rapacity of male greed for dominance; the malignancy of male supremacy; the virulent contempt for women that is the very foundation of the culture in which we live" (1988: 20). Indeed she argues that "sex and murder are fused in the male consciousness, so that the one without the imminent possibility of the other is unthinkable and impossible" (1988: 21). Dworkin admits to being "very hostile" to men, and this may be explicable partly in terms of the appalling brutality of her ex-husband (1988: 58, 100-06); but she is not alone.

Marilyn French is also very hostile to men: "I believe patriarchy began and spread as a war against women." And referring to" the widespread war against women" she insists that "it cannot be an accident that everywhere on the globe one sex harms the other so massively that one questions the sanity of those waging the campaign: can a species survive when half of it systematically preys on the other?" (1992: 14, 18). The war is not only universal, in her view, but it begins early: "Men start repressing females at birth: only the means vary by society. They direct female babies to be selectively aborted, little girls to be neglected, underfed, genitally mutilated, raped or molested; they sell adolescent girls to men in marriage or slavery" (1993: 197). And throughout their lives women work hard but earn little; she cites a UN report which affirms that women do between two-thirds and three-quarters of the work world wide, and produce 45% of the world's food, but receive only 10% of the world's income and own only 1% of the world's wealth (1993: 30).

"To be female is to walk the world in fear," says French (1993: 197). She says that a woman is beaten every 12 seconds in the USA; four women are beaten to death every day; and that the "United States has one of the highest, if not the highest rate of rape in the world" (French, 1993: 187, 191). If so, there is good reason for this hostility. About men: "All men are rapists and that's all they are" (in Farrell, 1993: 309).

Not only are men themselves a problem, so are the societies they create. Mary O'Brien, one of the foremost and evidently outspoken Canadian feminists, states:

> Patriarchy is not healthy. It legitimates violent solutions to historical problems in ways which casually destroy whole species, the natural environment and the well-being of individuals; it is pre-occupied with death and infatuated with power; it claims to transcend contingent nature while it invents sexism, racism, and genocide. (1989: 299, cf. 25)

The questions raised by radical feminism are searching, and provoke hot debates. The contribution to scholarship has been immense: the research on new topics with fresh methodologies, values, and goals has had wave effects that are transforming attitudes and social structures, as we have seen. The status quo is not what it was.

At the same time attitudes have hardened. Bumper stickers may be humourous: "A woman needs a man like a fish needs a bicycle"; "When God made man she was only kidding"; "Men are the speedbumps on the highway of life." "I suffer from PMS: Putting up with Men's Shit"; "Men are like diapers, always on my ass and full of shit." T-shirts explain: "10 Reasons Why a Beer is Better Than a Man." Joke books are published: *Men and Other Reptiles* (1993). Sometimes the humour is affectionate, but sometimes it is aggressive, like the bumper stickers "Dead Men Don't Rape!" and "The Only Good Man is . . ." Anyway, the downfall of men from god-like beings to shit has been as pervasive as it has been rapid. Anti-male jokes are "in"; anti-female jokes, of which there have been so many over the centuries, are "out." This is part of the current rethinking of gender which still remains a puzzling process for many people. A Flin Flon, Manitoba, woman complained to Meg Luxton: "Sometimes I think men are really stupid, or they hate women or at least there's no point in trying with them" (1984: 33).

Murderers and misogynists, stupid, rapists and racists, the death sex, full of shit, destroyers, violent, a problem — the bitterness, anger, fear, and even hatred of men is clearly articulated by some radical feminists.

Not all feminists agree, however; not all of them deplore patriarchy, or men, deplore capitalism, or anything else necessarily. Camille Paglia has this to say:

> One of feminism's irritating reflexes is its fashionable disdain for "patriarchal society," to which nothing good is ever attributed. But it is patriarchal society that has freed me as a woman. It is capitalism that has given me the leisure to sit at this desk writing this book. Let us stop being small-minded about men and freely acknowledge what treasures their obsessiveness has poured into culture.

> We could make an epic catalog of male achievements, from paved roads, indoor plumbing, and washing machines to eyeglasses, antibiotics, and disposable diapers. We enjoy fresh, safe milk and meat, and vegetables and tropical fruits heaped in snowbound cities. When I cross the George Washington Bridge or any of America's great bridges, I think: *men* have done this. Construction is a sublime male poetry . . . If civilization had been left in female hands, we would still be living in grass huts. (1991: 37-8)

Paglia is, admittedly, controversial. But not only does she praise capitalism and patriarchy and even men, she also viciously attacks what she calls the "Infirmary Feminism with its bedlam of bellyachers, anorexics, bulimics, depressives, rape victims, and incest survivors. Feminism has become a catch-all vegetable drawer where bunches of clingy sob sisters can store their moldy neuroses" (1994: 111).

This range of invectives is not usually found in Canada, although Barbara Amiel, a columnist for *Maclean's*, has forcefully denounced what she describes as "the feminist reign of terror in Canada." This has resulted in the creation of "kangaroo courts," the presumption of male guilt, convictions too "in circumstances that would have been laughed out of court when common sense still prevailed in Canada," and the silence of female elites, as Canada proceeds towards "the authoritarian matriarchal state" (1994: 13).

The Masculinist Paradigm

One of the consequences of the women's movement has been the massive structural changes which have occurred in Canada during the twentieth century; a second has been the ideological change by which men have been reconceptualized as a social problem by some feminists; a third consequence has been the development of the men's movement: a paradigmatic critique of and challenge to the feminist paradigm.

The beginnings of the men's movement is usually ascribed to the appearance of the poet Robert Bly on Bill Moyers' PBS show, and the publication of his book *Iron John* in 1990. This was quickly followed by Sam Keen's *Fire in the Belly: On Being a Man* in 1991. Special interest men's groups had been organized before, of course; but in the nineties men began to realize their common interests. There are some similarities in their approaches to gender relations. Both wrote primarily for and about men, but both specifically included women in their discussions, and positively rather than negatively. Thus Keen insists: "We are more profoundly united by our common humanity than separated by gender" (1991: 10); further the notion of fire is not exclusively masculine, as one might imagine from this title: "Good men and good women have fire in the belly. We are fierce" (1991: 194).

Both authors also praise men and masculinity. Bly says: "Men have been loved for their astonishing initiative: embarking on wide oceans, starting a farm in rocky country from scratch, imagining a new business, doing it skillfully, working with beginnings, doing what has never been done" (1990: 60). And Keen adds: "I know of no single honorific that defines a man so much as the verb 'to husband' . . . To husband is to practice the art of stewardship, to oversee, to make judicious use of things, and to conserve for the future" (1991: 180). "It is important to be able to say the word *masculine*" says Bly "without imagining that we are saying a sexist word" (1990: 234).

But both men also note that something is wrong, not only the shadow side, the violence and so on which has been publicized widely by feminists, with reason, but something else. Bly refers to the prevalence of "the soft male," the passive male: "They're lovely valuable people — I like them — . . . But many of these men are not happy. You quickly notice the lack of energy in them. They are life-preserving but not exactly life-giving" (1990: 2-4). And Keen diagnoses "the spiritual disease of modern men" as "lack of joy" (1991: 171). Although they do not agree on the causes of this "disease" (Bly blames the absent fathers, Keen rather vaguely blames "THE SYSTEM" (Keen, 1992: 207), their approaches are complementary, I think, rather than contradictory.

Keen criticizes some feminists as "animated by a spirit of resentment, the tactics of blame, and the desire for vindictive triumph over men that comes out of the dogmatic assumption that women are the innocent victims of a male conspiracy" (1991: 196). This is what some masculinists have described as "the new sexism."

Keen does not describe *all* feminists as vindictive, nor even most — this point should be stressed — merely those who polarize and demonize males; and he cites approvingly two Canadian psychologists: "although we have been quick to reject stereotypes that view women as man's inferior, we seem now reluctant to challenge stereotypes . . . that view woman as man's superior" (1991: 203).

Warren Farrell's *The Myth of Male Power* (1993) is less poetic than *Iron John* and less personal and autobiographical than *Fire in the Belly*, and it is far more statistical and sociological. Farrell's credentials for discussing gender relations are impeccable: he served for three years on the Board of Directors of NOW and more recently serves on the board of three national men's organizations. He insists at the outset on the immense contributions of the women's movement to social change and the humanization of society: Farrell is not a patriarchal dinosaur, he spent ten years fighting to help achieve these goals. On the other hand he is not uncritical either:

> Feminism suggested that God might be a "She" but not that the devil might also be a "she." Feminism articulated the shadow side of men and the light side of women. It neglected the shadow side of women and the light side of men. And neglected to acknowledge that each sex has both sides *within* each individual. (1993: 15)

He adds that: "Our anger toward men as victimizers blinds us to men as victims" (1993: 221). And men are victims, just as women are, but in different ways. His subtitle is: "Why men are the disposable sex." Farrell supports his thesis with data, only a small portion of which can be presented here, all of which suggest that many men do *not* have power (which he defines as "control over one's own life" 1993: 48) — and many women do. We live in neither a patriarchy nor a matriarchy, he argues, but in both — and women too are often disposable, but in different ways (1993: 18).

Farrell swamps us with statistics on disposability: one million *men* were killed or wounded in just one battle, The Somme, in 1916. Only men are eligible for the draft and it is principally men who are killed in war. In Panama 23 American men were killed, no women: a 100% male casualty rate. In the Gulf War, 86% male casualty rate. Is this equality?

As at war, so at work: 94% of deaths at work occur to men. Men are in the most hazardous occupations, risking their lives for their families or their communities. Young men are 24 times more likely to be killed in farm accidents than young women. Garbagemen are two and a half times more likely to be killed on the job than police officers — there are very few garbage collectors who are female. 80% of all municipal firefighters are *volunteers*, and 99% of them are men. This is a high-risk job: risk of injury, cancer, early retirement, communicable diseases including AIDS and of course death by fire. Why volunteer? The more hazardous the job, the higher the proportion of (powerless and disposable) males.

Males account for about 85% of the homeless, about 90% of those in federal prisons, 90% of those with AIDS; men are only half as likely as women to receive treatment for mental illness, they are 20 times more likely to receive the death sentence for homicide or manslaughter than women, they have higher death rates in all 15 of the major causes of death, many of which are stress-related, they work longer hours than women, including in- and out-of-home labor (nine hours more per week on average) according to the University of Michigan Survey Research Center, they commit suicide more than four times more often than women, they are more likely to be victims of violent crimes even when rape is factored in to the statistics, and they live on average seven years less than women. Furthermore this longevity-gap has increased 600% since 1921 when women lived on average "only" one year longer than men. Is this oppression?

And the much vaunted "war against women?" from 1985 to 1988, 4,986 men were killed by women and 10,190 women were killed by men (1993: 414). If there is a war, it is not equal in casualties certainly, but it is not one-way either; and Farrell's statistics are very different from French's. But these statistics just open, they certainly do not end, the debate.

Farrell's point is that we often forget the male victim of war, "accidents," jobs, suicide, alcohol, prison, crime, . . . gender roles generally . . . and the new sexism. Some men do dominate the pinnacles of power, but the vast majority do not. And men do *not* hate women; on the contrary, they have been trained to protect women, and to support their wives and families, their communities (e.g. volunteer firefighters) and their countries. That they do not always do so is well-known; but some forget that they often, indeed usually, do so, to the best of their ability. Male altruism, creativity, and heroism are everywhere, and the violence is far outweighed by the life-saving.

He suggests that we are both "slaves" to each other, "but in different ways" but "we should be celebrating rather than blaming" (1993: 41). And he concludes with the challenge of his book: "To go beyond woman [women] as sex objects and men as success objects to both sexes as objects of love" (1993: 371).

Farrell defines himself as "a men's liberationist (or 'masculist') when men's liberation is defined as equal opportunity and equal responsibility for both sexes.

I am a feminist when feminism favors equal opportunities and responsibilities for both sexes. . . . Ultimately I am in favor of neither a women's movement nor a men's movement but a gender transition movement" (1993: 19).

Ironically and paradoxically, however, precisely the same list of problems that some members of the men's movement cite to "prove" the point of their victimization by society — higher rates of suicide, alcoholism, crime-victimi-zation, imprisonment, murder-victimization, capital punishment, combat deaths, industrial accidents, homelessness, and lower life expectancies, all indicative of *powerlessness* — are often used selectively by feminists, as we have seen, (plus crime rates, rape and homicide rates, misogyny and sexism, and arguably pollution, racism, war and ecocide) to "prove" that men themselves are a social problem. In this feminist view, men are not the victims of society, society and especially women and children are the victims of men.

CONCLUSION

One does not expect conservatives and radicals to agree with each other's paradigms, nor would one expect feminists to agree totally with the masculinist paradigm; but whether this masculinist paradigm is simply dismissed as male backlash or studied as a cooperative and complementary mutual gender empowerment, the debate should be rewarding. There may be long and acrimonious arguments about statistics and therefore "reality," and about "competitive" victimization and altruism; but if feminists and masculinists listen to each other and try to understand how each conceptualizes their reality, and if feminists can stomach Farrell and Bly, and masculinists can digest Miles and French, then Max Weber's "verstehen" or empathetic understanding (see Chapter 10) becomes possible.

Alternatively, or in addition, both "sides" can read Gloria Steinem's latest contribution on self-esteem, *Revolution from Within*, written for both men and women as she insists, reversing the old adage that "the political is personal" (1994: 17). And in Canada we have the quarterly journal *Balance*, published by The Movement for the Establishment of Real Gender Equality (MERGE), committed to "the vision of full equality and understanding between the sexes."

ENDNOTES

1. Sources for further research on the women's movement in Canada include the following: The Canadian Advisory Council on the Status of Women, 110 O'Connor Street, 9th floor, Box 1541, Ottawa, Ontario, K1P 5R5; there are regional offices in Montreal and Calgary. They publish a quarterly newsletter, *Fine Balances*, and a num-

ber of research monographs and background reports. Status of Women, Canada, is located in Suite 700, 360 Albert St., Ottawa, Ontario, K1A 1C3; they also publish a newsletter, *Perspectives*. The Canadian Council on Social Development publishes *Vis-à-Vis*, a national newsletter on family violence. Their address is Box/CP 3505, Station/Succ. C, 55 Parkdale, Ottawa, Ontario K1Y 4G1. The provinces and territories also have their directorates. The Ontario Women's Directorate, for instance, contributes to the costs of *Health Sharing*, a Canadian women's quarterly; and in Quebec, le Conseil du Statut de la Femme publishes *La Gazette des Femmes*. Other Canadian journals include *Resources for Feminist Research, Canadian Woman Studies/les cahiers de la femme, Atlantis*, and the *International Journal of Women's Studies*. Two Statistics Canada publications might also be mentioned: *Perspectives* (Cat. No. 75-001) and *Canadian Social Trends* (Cat. No. 11-008). Other organizations include the Canadian Research Institute for the Advancement of Women (CRIAW) at 151 Slater St., Ottawa, and the National Action Committee (NAC); but there are many more. Also useful is Statistics Canada, 1990, *Women in Canada*. Ottawa. Cat. No. 89-503.

2.   A recent evaluation of the impact of the Employment Equity Act by CACSW (1992: 4) argues that it has had *no* significant effect on the progress of women's economic situation from 1986 to 1990.

3.   Some thought that the word "war" was too strong. But three years later the cover story of *US News and World Report*, a magazine not noted for its radicalism nor its feminism, was precisely this: "The war against women: women are falling further behind in country after country — and their men like it that way" (28.3.94). *Make* it that way too.

POVERTY

Is poverty a social problem? Who says so? and why? and what sort of a problem: economic? political? moral? Who are the poor? and why are they poor? More generally, what are the causes of poverty? and what the remedies, if any? Obviously, to answer all these questions would require a book, or two, not a chapter; and equally obviously the range of possible answers is potentially highly controversial. Indeed the first and most basic question is surely: what is poverty? We must define our terms. And this itself is controversial.[1]

Over four million Canadians live in poverty today, including 1.2 million children: one in six children. This includes a poverty rate of 20% for seniors and 62% for lone-parent mothers. About one and a half million Canadians are unemployed and about three million are on welfare. Poverty is deep and widespread in Canada and the rate of poverty is about the same as it was 20 years ago, although the composition of the poor and the dynamics of poverty have altered, as we shall see.

DEFINING POVERTY

This is poverty, according to 67-year-old Mary S.:

> If you're really interested, I'll tell you what it's like being an old woman alone who's only got the government pension to live on . . . It's wearing out your second-hand shoes going from one store to another trying to find the cheapest cuts of meat. It's hating having to buy toilet tissue or soap or toothpaste, because you can't eat it. It's picking the marked-down fruits and vegetables from the half-rotting stuff in the back of the stores that used to be given away to farmers to feed their animals. It's hunting the thrift shops and Salvation Army stores for half-decent clothes.

Emergencies come up; grand-children have birthdays; clothes wear out; cleaning products run out; bus rates go up. How do we manage? We pay our rent and utilities and we eat less.

We live in fear. Fear of the future, of more illness, less money, less pride. Fear that the cheque won't arrive and we won't be able to work our way through the red tape in time to pay our rent. Fear that we will run out of food before the next cheque comes in.

So, fear holds you in line. It is our punishment for getting old and sick. (National Council of Welfare, 1979: 12-13)

Poverty is doing without, it is fear, it is worry, it is malnutrition and ill health, depression perhaps and isolation, scrambling to live and maybe wanting to die . . .

Eugene, a street kid, the poorest of the poor, tells Marlene Webber: "It's a free society, man. We're free to die down here and nobody gives a shit" (1991: 248).

Poverty is lack of money, most obviously, and all that this implies in human as well as economic terms. The Economic Council of Canada does not debate these powerful subjective definitions: "While the poor can be defined as those who lack the resources required to enjoy the basic necessities of life, there is no broad consensus on how to measure resources and the necessities of life (1992: 1). In Canada the poor might have an old television, an old car, and indoor plumbing — but these would be considered luxuries in many Third World countries.

We must first distinguish between *absolute* and *relative* poverty. Absolute poverty is the state of being absolutely without essentials to the degree that life is directly threatened: without food, water, clothing, shelter, and the necessities for survival, as in Somalia and so many other countries around the world. There is little absolute poverty in Canada — this is not what we are talking about. Poverty in Canada is defined as poverty *relative* to the normal standard of living, as determined by standards set by the Federal Government which we will discuss below.

We must also distinguish between *objective* and *subjective* poverty. The objectively poor are those whose incomes fall below the low-income cut-off levels determined annually by the Federal government. The objectively poor are enumerated in government statistics on old age pensioners, the unemployed, minimum wage workers, most single mothers, the homeless, those on welfare, and many of the First Nations — just to mention some of the principal sectors of this population. But, many of these people, defined objectively as poor, do not define *themselves* as poor. Subjectively they are not poor. This may well make an enormous difference to their self images and therefore to their life chances. The working poor and the welfare poor may receive the same amount of money per month; but their feelings about this may be very different.

These are important distinctions. Three researchers might go into the same community and return with very different conclusions — because they define poverty differently. Thus one sociologist might go into the community, check the hospital records and the medical records as to the causes of death, and conclude that there is little or no (absolute) poverty because no one has died from starvation, or malnutrition, or was homeless and froze to death. This scenario is not so farfetched, for the economist Christopher Sarlo in his book *Poverty in Canada* (1992) has applied essentially similar criteria in reaching his estimate that only about 4% of Canadians (about one million) are poor, in contrast to federal estimates of about 16%. His criterion is absolute poverty; the federal one is relative poverty. Another sociologist might enter the same community, interview the locals and conclude, quite correctly, that there is no poverty because no one admitted to being poor. This often happens: "I'm not poor, but poor old Fred down the road . . . ." In our terms, however, there may be high levels of objective and even absolute poverty, but low levels of subjective poverty. People don't *feel* poor if they are working, and everyone is in the same boat. A third sociologist may go to the same patient community, check the census tracts, the income breakdowns for the area, wage rates, welfare and UI rates and conclude, again quite correctly, that poverty is widespread: by objective criteria a high proportion of the population is below the poverty line. Three observers reach three different conclusions, all correct, but all define their terms differently and use different methodologies.

To give another example: some students are living below the poverty line, but they might not feel poor, nor identify themselves as poor; i.e., they would be objectively but not subjectively poor. If they were in absolute poverty, they would likely *feel* poor as well.

The most widely used measures of poverty are the low-income cut-off lines developed by Statistics Canada. Canadians who spend more than 56% of their income on clothing, food, and shelter are defined as low income (i.e., 20% above the Canadian norm of 36%); the limits vary by size of population and with the size of the family, and are changed every year. Statistics Canada insists that these LICOs are not measures of poverty itself, but they are widely accepted as such by the media and by such organizations as the National Council of Welfare.

The low-income cut-offs are in many ways an unsatisfactory measure: they have to be adjusted regularly as the prices of different commodities (rent, oil and gas, etc.) rise and fall at different rates in different parts of the country, and they also have to be adjusted for inflation. Statistics Canada has recently introduced a new Low Income Measure (LIM) (AA: acronyms abound), based on one-half the median income. This measure is widely used in comparative international analysis, is far simpler to use, and emphasizes poverty relative to the Canadian norm. Also the results by this criterion are very similar to those produced by the low-income cut-off lines. By this standard 39% of the poor are men, who constitute 47% of the population; 61% of the poor are women (Statistics Canada 1991, Cat. 13-207, p, 155; cf. Spector, 1992). Being female therefore increases the chances of being poor by about 15%. This is part and parcel of the feminization of poverty.

WEALTH AND INCOME

The world is not an equal place. Indeed there are about 358 billionaires in this world, not including royalty and dictators, according to the annual listing by *Forbes*. The top six are presented in Table 5-1 for your envy.

The US has about one-third of these billionaires, 120: Germany has 42, Japan 36, and Canada 6 (see Table 5-2).

Table 5-1 The Wealthiest Billionaires, 1994

Name	Net Worth $ Billion	Source	Country
du Pont family	9.0	DuPont Co.	US
Hans and Gad Rausing	9.0	Packaging	Sweden/UK
Yoshiaki Tsutsumi	8.5	Real estate	Japan
Bill Gates	8.2	Computers	US
Warren Edward Buffet	7.9	Stock Market	US
Sacher-Hoffman family	7.8	Pharmaceuticals	Switzerland

Source: *Forbes* 18.7.94

Table 5-2 The Wealthiest Canadian Billionaires, 1994

Name	Net Worth $ Billion	Source
Kenneth Thompson	5.2	Publishing, Hudson's Bay
Irving family	4.0	Lumber, oil
McCain family	3.0	Food
Charles Bronfman	2.0	Liquor
Edward Rogers	1.3	Telecommunications
Galen Weston	1.0	Food, groceries

Source: *Forbes* 18.7.94:198; *Maclean's* 6.9.93

Other authorities reach slightly different conclusions, depending on their selection criteria. *Forbes* does not include royalty, for instance; but both the *Sunday Times* (London) and *Fortune* (US) do include royalty. Thus the richest person in the world is the Sultan of Brunei with a fortune of £28 billion (roughly double that for dollars), including a fleet of 165 Rolls Royces — I suppose just in case 164 of them break down simultaneously. The Queen is also in the top ten with about £5 billion. Families are difficult to assess, since they can fall apart into individual rather than collective packages of wealth; but the Walton family is estimated to be worth about $23.6 billion, and the Mars family (candy) about $9 billion. For comparative purposes Paul McCartney is worth only $400 million, Elton John $130 million, and Mick Jagger $90 million (*Sunday Times* 10.4.94; *Fortune* 28.6.93).

The distribution of wealth in Canada is presented in Table 5-3. Several points are of interest. First the immense inequality: at the top of the heap, the wealthiest 10% own 51% of the wealth, *more* than the other 90% put together! At the other end of the spectrum the poorest 40% of Canadians, over six million people, own only 2% of the Canadian wealth; and of these the bottom 10% are in debt. They own less than nothing, in economic terms.

Wealth is defined as the value of total assets less total debt. Assets include savings, stocks, bonds, shares and investment holdings, real estate including vacation homes, and also consumer durables such as cars, yachts, antiques, jewelry, stamp collections, televisions, coin collections, silver, and so on. Income *creates* wealth; and wealth *generates* income. In general, the higher the income, the

Table 5-3   Distribution of Wealth in Canada, 1984 (Families and Unattached Individuals)

Wealth Deciles	%
1 (highest)	51.3
2	17.5
3	11.6
4	8.2
5	5.7
6	3.6
7	1.8
8	0.6
9	0.1
10 (lowest)	-0.4

Source: Statistics Canada, 1987. Changes in the Distribution of Wealth in Canada, 1970-1984. G. Oja. Cat. 13-588, p. 25.

greater the wealth; but equally, the greater the wealth, the higher the proportion of unearned income (Statistics Canada, 1978). For the rich, life can be a vir-
tuous circle; for the poor a vicious circle, hard to break out of.

The Federal study cited above, however, has two limitations; first, the
author notes, it "excludes important personal assets such as equity in pension
funds, insurance policies, and the value of collectibles (for example, art, stamps,
jewelry), as well as the value of many consumer durables (other than cars,
trucks and recreational vehicles)." Also wealthy people are more likely to refuse
to respond to the survey (Statistics Canada, 1987. Cat. 13-588, pp. 5, 18). In
other words, the degree of inequality is much greater than Table 5-3 suggests:
the rich are much richer than they seem.

The average wealth in Canada, according to this survey, was $85,344; and
the median was $39,876. The most valuable asset, for most people, is their home
(Statistics Canada, 1987. Cat. 13-588, p. 28) . . . if they own one.

The distribution of wealth in absolute terms is presented in Table 5-4. Note
that 9% of the population have net assets worth under $1,000 and another 8%
are in debt, while 10% have net assets conservatively estimated at over
$200,000.

James Davies, who has extensively researched the distribution of wealth,
calculates that there are about 100,000 families in the top one per cent, whose

**Table 5-4   Distribution of Wealth, Canada, 1984 (Percentage
Distribution of Families and Unattached Individuals)**

300,000+	5.1
200,000-299,999	4.4
150,000-199,999	5.0
100,000-149,999	9.7
75,000-99,999	8.5
50,000-74,999	11.4
30,000-49,999	11.3
15,000-29,999	9.5
5,000-14,999	9.8
1,000-4,999	8.7
$0-999	8.9
Negative	7.5
Average Wealth:	$85,344
Median Wealth:	$39,876
Average Income:	$29,113
Median Income:	$24,894

Source: Statistics Canada, 1986. The Distribution of Wealth in Canada, 1984:32,29. Cat. 13-580. See
also Statistics Canada, 1979. The Distribution of Income and Wealth in Canada, 1977. Cat. 13-570.

average wealth is about $1.5 million; but only 0.5% are millionaires; and one or two hands can enumerate the billionaires (Davies, 1993: 109).

By comparison in the United States the richest 1% of households owned 37% of private net worth in 1992, up from 31% in 1983, according to the Federal Reserve Board. These 834,000 households had more wealth ($5.7 trillion) than the bottom 90% ($4.8 trillion) (*Globe and Mail* 22.4.92. cf. Chawla, 1990). The rich get richer.

One has to wonder: is there a limit? Can the rich continue not only to get richer, for some of the increase is due to inflation, but to capture a larger and larger slice of the pie? When should it stop? What does it cost in human terms? Is it fair? If not, what do you do?

INCOME

Income is more evenly distributed than wealth in Canada, but it is by no means equally distributed. (See Table 5-5). The highest income quintile earned 41% of all incomes earned after tax, i.e., more than the poorest three quintiles put together; while the poorest 20% earned only 5.5% of all the incomes earned, i.e., only about one-quarter of their "fair share" in an equal society. So the wealthiest quintile earned about seven times more than the poorest. The inequality is even greater of course if we compare deciles, the top and bottom 10%. Using 1991 data, CCSD shows that the top decile earns 27% of total income (including transfer payments) while the lowest decile earns 1.6%: an inequality ratio of 17 to 1 (Ross, Shillington, Lochhead, 1994: 91).

Note that although Canadians do have a progressive tax system, i.e., the wealthy are taxed at higher rates than the poor, nonetheless the tax system is not very progressive. The wealthiest quintile lose only 3% of their share of the

Table 5-5   Distribution of Income by Quintiles All Units, Before and After Tax, Canada, 1992

Quintiles (20%)	Before Tax	After Tax
Highest	43.6	40.8
2	24.8	24.7
3	16.7	17.5
4	10.3	11.5
Lowest	4.6	5.5
Total	100	100

Source: Statistics Canada, 1994. *Income After Tax, Distributions by Size in Canada*. Cat. 13-210, p. 28. See also Ross, Shillington and Lochhead, 1994.

pie, and the poorest only receive 1% more. It does not do much, the radical might say; the conservative might add that this 1% nonetheless constitutes a substantial 20% more than what the poor had before.

Incomes earned in any one year may be considerable. In 1993 Bryan Adams made $35 million, Joe Carter $7 million, Lawrence Bloomberg (neither an athlete nor a singer but a company director) $6.9 million; by comparison Jean Chrétien's salary is just $157,600. In the States top incomes are higher: Michael Eisner, the manager of Walt Disney, earned $260 million in 1993; entertainment figures can do well: Oprah Winfrey ($66 million), Steven Spielberg ($53 million), Kevin Costner ($34 million) and Bill Cosby ($33 million) (*Maclean's* 7.31.94).

Athletes can also do well. *Forbes* has published the top 40 incomes in sports for 1994 (19.12.94). From the top these are Michael Jordan, basketball, $30 million; Shaquille O'Neal, basketball, $17 million; Jack Nicklaus and Arnold Palmer, golf, $15 and $14 million; and Gerhard Berger, auto racing and Wayne Gretzky, whom you know, $14 million each. Most of this money is from endorsements or franchises. Only two women made the top 40, both tennis players: Steffi Graf with $8 million at number 19, and Gabriela Sabatini at number 39. There is considerable mobility among the very rich, however; eight baseball players who were in the top 40 in 1993 did not make it into the 1994 list due to salary caps and to the strike.

At the international level, the United Nations has reported that the richest one-fifth of the world population, including Canada, receive 82.7% of total world income; and the poorest one-fifth only 1.5% of total world income; and these chasms have widened in the last 30 years (1993: 34-47). Again, the rich get richer.

The same process is reflected in Canada where the CCSD analysis indicates that from 1981 to 1991 the highest income quintile increased its share of the disposable income pie to 36.6% (up 1.3%) while the lowest income quintile decreased its share to 7.3% (down 0.5%) (Ross, Shillington and Lochhead, 1994: 93). This polarization is worrisome, and both social and economic consequences are likely to be negative unless the trend can be reversed.

Yet there is nothing necessary or inevitable about these rates of poverty and these inequalities. Comparative international research using standardized data from the OECD presented in Table 5-6 shows that Canada ranks very poorly in its poverty policies compared to other countries.

Indeed the poverty rate in Canada among all working families is about *twice* that of France and Germany and *three* times that of Belgium and the Netherlands. The poverty rate for lone-parent families ranks eight out of ten, only better than Australia and the USA. Youth poverty rates are high also: eight out of ten (Ross, Shillington and Lochhead, 1994: 111). In discussing the conservative paradigm in Chapter 2 we noted Canadian authorities who cited our "compassion." Is not Table 5-6 an objective measure of this *lack* of compassion?

Table 5-6   Relative Rates of Poverty for Ten Countries, Nonelderly Families, Various Years

Country	Year	All Families %	Couples/ Children %	Female Lone-Parent/ Children %	Families under 25 years %
Australia	1985-86	15.7	12.2	66.4	26.2
Belgium	1985	5.4	13.6	17.1	12.6
Canada	1987	15.4	10.5	52.1	30.1
France	1984	8.9	7.5	21.9	11.9
Germany	1984-85	8.5	5.5	38.8	25.9
Italy	1986	10.1	11.7	21.1	23.6
Netherlands	1987	4.7	4.8	10.6	10.3
Sweden	1987	12.1	3.2	6.0	31.0
UK	1986	12.4	14.5	30.4	18.8
USA	1986	18.7	14.2	59.8	37.3

Source: Michael Forster, cited in Ross, Shillington, Lochhead, 1994: 111.

One of the explanations for the differential poverty rates from country to country is the differential expenditures on social programs by various countries. This in turn reflects national values and also tax policies. In general, the higher the tax rate, the higher the proportion of GNP spent on social support and the lower the poverty rate. It seems simple, but due to the extraordinary financial mismanagement of the Canadian economy by both the Liberals and the Conservatives over the last 20 years, which has left us with an annual deficit of about $40 billion and a national debt of about $700 billion, the servicing of which takes about one-third of our annual GNP, the possibility of increasing social expenditure to reduce poverty rates seems at present very remote. Canadian compassion has its limits.

Some examples of rates of social spending (excluding health and education) as percentages of GDP for seven of the ten OECD nations listed in Table 5-6: France, 21.3; Netherlands, 18.6; Italy, 15.4; UK, 10.7; Canada, 10.3; USA, 8.5; Australia, 7.8 (ECC 1992: 9). (Data for Belgium, Sweden, and Germany are not available.) Note that Canada is at the low end of the spectrum and the poverty rates correlate closely with expenditure rates. Note also that France, Netherlands, Sweden, Italy, and the UK, and most other countries in the OECD, have higher tax rates than Canada (taxes constitute 35.3% of GDP, 1989) whereas of the ten countries cited, only the USA and Australia are lower (ECC 1992: 10).

In this sense we may see Canadian poverty rates as a matter of calculated political choice reflecting specific Canadian/voter priorities.

These inequalities of wealth and income reflect a number of other inequalities, of which we will discuss four: provincial economic inequality, ethnic inequality, the feminization of poverty, and child poverty.

The critical question here is: is inequality inequitable? The answer determines the political paradigm.

REGIONAL INEQUALITIES

There is considerable economic variation from region to region. Some provinces are much wealthier than others. This is presented in Table 5-7.

The points to note are which are the "have" and which the "have not" provinces. The average family income in Ontario is 39% higher than in Newfoundland, and the 31 point spread from the Canadian average equals $16,000 dollars. Indeed the incomes gap between Newfoundland and the Canadian average is about the same as the gender incomes gap.

Regional inequalities breed regional friction, however; and the "have" provinces are increasingly expressing their concern about the dollar transfer payments to the "have not" provinces — particularly since poverty rates are still high even in the wealthier provinces. Indeed the household poverty rate in Ontario is 18%, compared to 20% in Saskatchewan and Alberta, 21% in B.C., 18% to 21% in the Atlantic provinces and highest in Manitoba at 24% and

Table 5-7   Distribution of Income by Region

	(Family income) 1992	
	$	%
Ontario	57,071	109
British Columbia	55,089	105
Alberta	53,538	102
Manitoba	49,545	94
Quebec	48,060	92
Saskatchewan	47,720	91
Nova Scotia	45,541	87
New Brunswick	45,049	86
Prince Edward Island	44,519	85
Newfoundland	40,993	78
Canada: Average Income	52,504	100
Median Income	46,479	

Source: Statistics Canada, 1994. *Family Incomes.* Cat. No. 13-208 pp. 24-5. See also Statistics Canada, 1994. Cat. No. 96-318.

The harsh consequences of poverty for children was spelled out by the Canadian Institute of Child Health using 1986 data:

- Infant mortality rates are twice as high in the poorest quintile as in the richest.

- Mortality rates for all children (under 20) are 56% higher among the poorest than the wealthiest quintiles.

- Deaths from fires, drownings, homicide and suicide, and pedestrian-motor-vehicle accidents are from two to ten times higher among the poor than the rich (depending on the sex of the child and the type of incident. 1981 data for children aged 1-14). (Avard and Harvey, 1989: 98-9)

In sum, poverty kills. And when it does not kill, it maims, both physically, as in illness and accidents, and also mentally and socially. Psychiatric disorders and school-related problems (failed grades, learning disorders, conduct problems, need for remedial classes, hyperactivity) are twice as high for children on welfare as for those not on welfare — some of which may be due to much higher nutritional deficiency levels among the poor (Avard and Harvey, 1989: 102-03). Which in turn "feeds" into poorer health, and the vicious circle. The vicious circle also works the other way: sickness, mental illness, and accidents also cause poverty. The causal processes are reciprocal.

Native children have a particularly hard time surviving in Canada. So do their parents. Aboriginal peoples, including Métis, Inuit, and status Indians, in general have far lower incomes than other Canadians. In 1990 52% of Canadians who had incomes had less than $20,000, compared to 73% of aboriginals; but only 28% of Canadians had less than $10,000, compared to 47% of aboriginals. The Canadian Council on Social Development calculates that poverty rates are 20% higher for aboriginals than the Canadian average (Ross, Shillington and Lochhead, 1994: 40-41).

The implications for children are devastating, as CIOCH and the 1991 Senate Report indicated. Data are the latest available, from the mid-1980s, and include the registered Indian population only, i.e., Inuit, Métis, and non-status Indians are not included.

- 51% of all aboriginal children live in poverty.
- The stillbirth rate is three times higher among native people than the Canadian average.
- Infant mortality rates are double the Canadian average.
- Injuries and accidents are the main cause of death for all young people (aged 1-19), but the rates are six times higher for native children (1-4) and four times higher for native adolescents (15-19).

- The accidental death rate overall is more than three times higher in the 1-14 age group; this includes drowning: 4 times; fire: 6 times; falls: 2 times; traffic: 1.6 times.

- Suicide rates are three times the national average; but five times higher for those aged 10-14, and seven times higher for those aged 15-19 and 20-24.

- Several infectious conditions are much higher among native children: tuberculosis, meningitis, hepatitis A and B, pneumonia, and gastroenteritis.

- All this translates into lower life expectancy. Native children born in the 1980s can expect to live 68 years on average, eight years less than non-native children. (Avard and Harvey, 1989: 98-105; Senate Committee, 1991: 9-11)

To be born native in Canada means to be at higher risk of being stillborn, and then to be at far higher risk of infectious diseases, suicide, accidental deaths by falls, drowning, fires or traffic, and to live on average eight years less than other Canadians. Is that fair?

THEORIZING POVERTY AND INEQUALITY

Theories of poverty and inequality abound. The most ancient theories are those of Greek philosophy and Christian theology, which still have resonance today. For Plato it was obvious that the origins of inequality lie in the fact that people are biologically different. In *The Republic* he said that there are men of gold, men of silver, and men of bronze — he said men, but the theory applies to women also. They are ruled by different parts of the body: head, heart, and belly respectively. They seek different values: wisdom, glory, and the gratification of their physical desires; they are therefore fitted for different occupations in the *polis*: rulers, soldiers, and workers or farmers. The socioeconomic stratification system therefore synthesizes biology, ethics, and occupations in a legitimate meritocracy: the best rule and the worst are ruled.[2] This is no doubt a conservative philosophy of inequality which Karl Popper (1966) has defined as a root of fascism and racism in modern times; and it does permeate Social Darwinism, Hitler's *Mein Kampf* (1942) as well as South African apartheid ideology.

The traditional teaching of the Christian church has been that poverty is ordained by God, and must be endured and sanctified. This is epitomized in the lives of Job, and of Christ himself, who was born poor, lived in poverty all his life, and is the role model for Christians. Monks, nuns, and the religious still renounce their wealth and take vows of poverty. In this view poverty is a grace from God, and its practice is a virtue. This teaching is well expressed by one verse in the Anglican hymn, "All Things Bright and Beautiful":

The rich man in his castle

The poor man at his gate

God made them high and lowly

And ordered their estate.

As fine a legitimation of social inequality and poverty as the wealthy might have wished for! Such an ideology has been challenged by Liberation Theology, which has emphasized the secular implications of Christ's mission, as enshrined in the one commandment (to love thy neighbour), the Lord's Prayer, and the criteria for salvation applied at the last judgement. But poverty and inequality remain highly controversial in ecclesiastical circles, with clergy and laity divided between conservative and radical theories of poverty. Nonetheless the conspicuous achievement of the early Church was the assertion of the *spiritual* equality of all: this was a radical challenge to the ideology and practice of Greece and Rome, but the secular implications of this spiritual equality are still debated.[3]

Biologically determined or divinely ordained: these were the two prevailing theories of inequality up until the Enlightenment. Philosophical beliefs and religious convictions do not constitute sociological theories, however; and the first modern thinking about inequality began to emerge in the eighteenth century in relation especially to colonialism and monarchism in the American and French revolutions, and then in the nineteenth century with the abolitionist, reform, and suffragette movements.

During the Enlightenment the ideology of human equality was increasingly institutionalized as a core value in western civilization; conversely institutional inequality, whether imperial, royal, racial, class-based or gender-based, was increasingly, but by no means universally, regarded as illegitimate.

Jean-Jacques Rousseau was one of the first to declare this equality (see Chapter 3); and the doctrine of universal equality is now enshrined in the first paragraph of the UN Declaration of Human Rights: "All human beings are born free and equal in dignity and rights."

This statement of sublime moral principle coexists with the hard reality of an economic stratification system of supreme inequity and inequality. The conjunction of egalitarian ideology and inegalitarian structure is surely a contradiction.

Certainly the poor have been of concern to government, for humanitarian, economic, and other reasons. The Elizabethan poor laws of the sixteenth century were the first recognition by the state that it was responsible for the citizenry, and beyond that, that individuals could not always be held responsible for their impoverished situations. The Depression of the 1930s validated this perspective and finally resulted in the creation of the welfare state.

Engels and Marx

Among the first to study the new urban-industrial stratification of the nineteenth century was Friedrich Engels. The son of a wealthy German cotton-manufacturer, Engels published *The Condition of the Working Class in England* in 1845, when he was 24. This was a devastating critique of high capitalism drawn both from his own extensive travels and from official sources. He described the long hours, the exhausting labour in mine, foundry, and mill by men, women and children, the dangerous working conditions, the housing conditions, the occupational diseases, the deaths from overwork and preventable accidents, the violence of the capitalists dealing with protests, the conspiracy of interests between capitalists, politicians, police, and judges against the workers, and he concluded that: "The only possible solution is a violent revolution, which cannot fail to take place" (1969: 285). He described capitalism as institutionalized murder:

> When society [the ruling class] places hundreds of proletarians in such a situation that they inevitably meet a too early and an unnatural death, one which is quite as much a death by violence as that by the sword or bullet; when it deprives thousands of the necessaries of life, places them under conditions in which they *cannot* live — forces them, through the strong arm of the law, to remain in such conditions until that death ensues which is the inevitable consequence — knows that these thousands of victims must perish, and yet permits these conditions to remain, its deed is murder just as surely as the deed of the single individual; disguised, malicious murder, murder against which none can defend himself, which does not seem what it is, because no man sees the murderer, because the death of the victim seems a natural one [accidental], since the offence is more one of omission than commission. But murder it remains. (1969: 126-7)

Such passion cannot have endeared him to his father. He also described England in Hobbesian terms as in a state of war: "The war of each against all, is here openly declared" (1969: 58).

Engels and Marx wrote *The Communist Manifesto* (1848) for the First Communist International in Paris. In terms of power per page this short monograph has to rank as one of the most important documents of the nineteenth and twentieth centuries, inspiring as it did the Mexican (1910), Russian (1917), Chinese (1949), Cuban (1958) and Vietnamese (1960s) revolutions, as well as communist, socialist, and labour parties and unions around the world, affecting the lives of billions, for better *and* for worse; and not least for initiating a fresh paradigm on poverty and inequality which has been labeled the conflict paradigm.

In the *Manifesto*, Marx and Engels stated emphatically: "The theory of the Communists may be summed up in the single sentence: Abolition of private property" (1967: 96). Marx later defined this in *Capital* as "the expropriation of the expropriators." They added: "You are horrified at our intending to do away with private property. But in your existing society, private property is already done away with for nine-tenths of the population; its existence for the few is solely due to its non-existence in the hands of those nine-tenths" (1967: 98). Hence the logic of the famous and ringing conclusion to the *Manifesto*: "Let the ruling classes tremble at a Communistic revolution. The proletarians have nothing to lose but their chains. They have a world to win. Working men of all countries, unite!" (1967: 120-21).

Marx went into far more detail in *Capital*, mixing complex mathematical equations with passionate appeals, and sarcastic asides; but his hatred of contemporary capitalists was explicable perhaps in terms of his humanitarianism. He objected if women, especially, were mere substitutes for steam, horse, water, or mule power: cheaper too (Vol. 1, Ch. 15; 1969: 372); indeed he summarized the process of capital accumulation and economic growth: "One capitalist always kills many" (Vol. 1, Ch. 32; 1969: 714). This referred not only to the conquest of the Americas, Africa, and India, the Chinese opium wars, the slave trade and slavery, and to the Irish question, but also, at home, to the Enclosure Movement and the Industrial Revolution.

Britain at that time was "the workshop of the world"; and Marx's and Engels' identification with the workers exploited by capitalism was mirrored by many others, including the Romantic poets like Blake and Wordsworth, and such socially conscious authors as Dickens; his Scrooge in *A Christmas Carol* is the archetypal capitalist, *Oliver Twist* is a critique of the poorhouse system, and *Bleak House* satirizes the legal system.

But then as now, not everyone sees the same things the same way. Comte, for instance, writing in France at the same time, was impressed by the peacefulness of economic growth, in contrast to the constant state of war in France from the Bastille to Waterloo, 1789 to 1815:

> . . . in industrial states, where wealth is acquired by other ways than violence, the law is evident. And with the advance of civilization it will operate not less but more strongly. Capital is ever on the increase, and consequently is ever creating means of subsistence for those who possess nothing . . . The few provide subsistence for the many. (1957: 238)

Contrast this, "The few provide subsistence for the many" with Marx's view: "One capitalist always kills many" (1969: 714). Engels described capitalists as murderers; yet Comte described capitalists as "the nutritive organs of Humanity" in whom we should take "pride" (1957: 411).

Marx and Comte did not debate: they just had different paradigms about, and probably experiences of, poverty and capitalism. Durkheim also disregarded Marx and Engels; indeed Marxism did not become salient as an ideology until the Russian Revolution in the year of Durkheim's death.

Emile Durkheim

Durkheim was no Marxist. For him the division of labour is constitutive of society, and an integrating not an alienating force. "Social life comes from a double source, the likeness of consciences [shared values] and the division of social labor" (1964: 226). Modern industrial society is characterized by what Durkheim called organic solidarity: organic as in a living, physical body characterized by many interdependent organs, each with specific and distinct functions for the growth and development of the body. Traditional or, in Durkheim's evolutionary term, "lower" societies are held together more by common values, whereas modern industrial societies are held together more by the division of labour. "What gives unity to organized societies . . . is the spontaneous consensus of parts." Indeed the division tends to fragment the common values by centrifugal force (1964: 360-61).

Durkheim's principal concern was with the relation of the individual to society (1964: 37). He did not concern himself directly with inequality or poverty. But he thought that the broad sweep of progress and increasing organic solidarity would result inevitably in greater equality and greater justice: "The more we advance on the social scale . . . the more these inequalities tend to become completely level" (1964: 378).

Durkheim distinguished between internal and external inequality, that is, individual and social inequality. The point is, the "fit" between the two. He concedes that "the unequal merit of men will always bring them into unequal situations in society"; and the division of this (unequal) labour will function to increase solidarity "if society is constituted in such a way that social inequalities exactly express natural inequalities" (1964: 377, 384). This is the "cream and dregs" theory of inequality. And Durkheim believed that (some) poverty is functional for solidarity.

But is such a society possible? Is it even desirable? Durkheim believed that we have almost achieved the perfect meritocracy, where everybody on the ladder is where they *deserve* to be . . . and they know it.[4]

Conservatives probably tend to believe that this is fair. Spencer certainly did. People at the bottom of the ladder probably do not. Certainly Mary S., whose definition of poverty opened this discussion, disagreed.

But Durkheim did argue that equality is important, not only "to attach each individual to his function, but also to link functions to one another." He insisted that "there cannot be rich and poor at birth without there being unjust contracts," and consequential injustice and civil conflict (1964: 381, 384). Indeed he described social inequalities as "the very negation of liberty" (1964: 387). Too much inequality, therefore, may be *dysfunctional* for solidarity.

Where Durkheim, and later Davis and Gans (Chapter 2), have argued that poverty is functional, more recent theorists have argued that poverty is dysfunctional and *costly*. Not only does inequality have high social costs, but it also carries high economic costs. An uneducated labour force acts as a brake on economic growth rates. This is a labour force which is not only lost to production, but has *also* to be maintained by UI or welfare: a double cost. Add on the social and economic satellite costs of ill health and higher mortality rates for the poor, and also it *seems* (the data is not always crystal clear) higher crime rates, suicide rates, and alcoholism rates (triple costs), then it becomes more apparent that inequality is "hurting" the Canadian economy, the society and the future.

"The task of the most advanced societies is, then, a work of justice." Durkheim argued with some passion: "Our ideal is to make social relations always more equitable, so as to assure the free development of all our socially useful forces" (1964: 387). He envisages a future society "where each individual will have the place he merits, will be rewarded as he deserves, where everybody, accordingly, will spontaneously work for the good of all and each" (1964: 408).[5]

Meanwhile, until this utopia has been achieved, there will be inequality and conflict. Arguing that "it is neither necessary nor even possible for social life to be without conflicts," given human nature and/or inequitable social structures, Durkheim still insists that the class wars, "the conflict between capital and labor," the industrial and commercial crises and business failures of his time — all were "exceptional and abnormal" and due to either "anomic" or "forced" divisions of labour (1964: 354, 365, 372). In these anomalous situations, "Machines replace men," and workers are mechanized: "He is no longer anything but an inert piece of machinery." And there is conflict, but: "it is always the law of the strongest which settles conflicts, and the state of war is continuous." Here he sounds like Marx and Engels, and before them, Hobbes. He adds that "one cannot remain indifferent to such debasement of human nature" (1964: 370-71). And he wasn't. Hence his demand for equality.

Max Weber

Weber and Durkheim were almost exact contemporaries, but they did not engage with each other's work; Weber was more interested in debating with Marx — disagreeing with much of what he wrote. In his most famous work, *The Protestant Ethic and The Spirit of Capitalism* (1905), Weber argued that the Protestant virtues of hard work, frugality, sobriety, saving, and honesty facilitated the accumulation of wealth, which was the spirit of capitalism. Poverty, once a virtue, now became a "vice" (as it so often is today, to some conservatives, a sign of laziness); conversely wealth, an impediment to salvation in the teaching of Christ and Paul, now became, if not a virtue, then a sign of God's blessing. John Wesley, the founder of Methodism, explained this synthesis of Protestantism and capitalism succinctly:

> We ought not to prevent people from being diligent and frugal; we must exhort
> all Christians to gain all they can, and to save all they can; that is, in effect, to
> grow rich. (Weber, 1968: 175; his emphasis)

The new Christianity and the new capitalism therefore introduced the new
ethic of poverty in which the victim is blameworthy, and blamed.

Marx had attacked Hegel for his idealism, and argued that dialectical materialism is the motor of history. Weber in turn attacked Marx for his materialism,
insisting that ideas, like the Protestant ethnic, are also "effective forces in history" (1968: 90); but he advised that he did not intend to "substitute for a one-
sided materialism an equally one-sided spiritualistic causal interpretation of
culture and of history" (1968: 183).

Weber also took issue with Marx on the class structure. Where Marx identified two main classes, the bourgeoisie and the proletariat, Weber attended more
to the middle class. Where Marx stressed that economic power dominated other
forms of power, Weber added political power and "status" power (broadly, interest groups, for example, religions) as alternative power bases which might cross-
cut class lines. Marx was convinced that the capitalist system was built on
violence and maintained by violence; Weber thought it was built by hard work
and a different ethic. Marx expected increased alienation, leading ultimately to
revolution and the dictatorship of the proletariat; but Weber described a process
of increased rationalization, leading ultimately to bureaucratization and the dictatorship of the official. In the last resort Marx was an optimist with a happy picture of an egalitarian future; Weber was a pessimist, fearing an "iron cage" of
bureaucracy (Weber, 1968: 181; see Grabb, 1990: 52-70).

Durkheim believed that equality is, or would be, functional for the new
industrial state. Weber saw a future, not of equality and justice, but of a rational
bureaucracy: hierarchical, impersonal, and anti-egalitarian.

Inequality and poverty may be in the eye of the theorist; and theorists disagree: Marxists and radicals, Durkheimians, including Davis and Gans,
Weberians, and feminists all conceptualize the nature of poverty, its origins, and
the policies needed to deal with it, in different ways (see Table 5-8). Which do
you agree with most? But, equally important, can you understand the logic of
the alternative paradigms? Can you refute them with data? or not?

POLICY

The NCW Brief on Child Poverty (1990) states:

> There is no magic solution to child poverty. Children are poor because their par-
> ents are poor, so to eradicate child poverty we have to get at the roots of family
> poverty. That will require a *war on several fronts*: the income security system,
> employment policy, education and social services. (1990: 5. Emphasis added)

TABLE 5-8 COMPARATIVE PERSPECTIVES ON POVERTY

	Religious	Functionalist	Conflict	Feminist
Who are the poor?	Divine Providence ordains	The lazy, the handicapped, the unlucky and those in depressed areas or declining occupations	The working class	Disproportionately women
Poverty	Poverty a virtue and a grace	Inevitable, necessary, useful (functional) (Durkheim, K. Davis, H. Gans)	Evil, unnecessary, not inevitable	Ditto
Cause	God	Society; human nature	Capitalism, greed	Patriarchy, sexism
Solution	Heaven? Not applicable for (Liberation Theology which is often Marxist)	Reform Tinkering with programs and fine-tuning	Revolution or radical reform	Reform, but radical, economic, political, educational, occupational and social

This involves federal fiscal and monetary policy, industrial policy, and community development policy: all difficult issues. This "war" (that word again) against child poverty and therefore family poverty will cost. In times of recession and/or slow growth will Canadians support tax hikes to pay for this war? It seems unlikely. It was not a platform on any of the major political parties "fighting" the 1993 election (except the NDP, who were crushed).

The Canadian Council on Social Development has noted that poverty in Canada "is the result of an unequal distribution of riches rather than a lack of riches" (1994: 1) — but few voices demand the redistribution of these riches, apart from the CCSD.

Many committees, councils, and advocacy groups have made lists of recommendations for the alleviation of poverty since the Croll Report (Senate Committee) and the more radical *The Real Poverty Report* both came out in 1971 — but the poverty rate has remained about the same for the last 25 years or so. While some might become fatalistic and conservative, others redouble their efforts to reduce poverty and to help those who need help.

Among the recommendations of the NCW (1990) are the following:

- restoring full indexation of child-care benefits.
- implementing a national child-care system.
- developing a fairer, more progressive tax system.
- changes to the welfare system, including raised rates and indexation.
- reform of the divorce legislation both for equity-entitlement and child support.
- and especially reducing unemployment, in combination with pay equity and affirmative action legislation.

These recommendations are in substantial agreement with those of Avard and Harvey of the CICH (1989) and the two Senate Committee Reports (1991, 1980), although the emphases on child care, divorce reform, and equity reflect the stronger feminist influence.

The CCSD (1994) has emphasized that government should pay more attention to job creation and to the adequacy of the wages in these jobs than to transfer payments. The Council notes the immense importance of such transfers for low income families, but insists that Canadians must have the right and the opportunity to earn their own living. This is why poverty has been so intractable. Indeed, many full-time jobs pay such low wages that welfare is a more economic choice. Most non-poor families now have two income earners: one is no longer sufficient (1994: 120).

Areas of particular concern identified by the Council are the very high poverty rates of single parents, the *declining* incomes of young families, the increasing child poverty rate, and the emergence of the "educated poor." Almost one-third (29%) of poor families had some post-secondary education — double the rate in 1981. Neither a job nor an education therefore guarantee an escape from poverty (1994: 121-3).

On the other hand there has been some progress. The poverty rate for seniors has been almost halved over the last ten years, due principally to higher transfer payments (1994: 117). Nonetheless the *increasing* polarization between rich and poor, the increasing impoverishment of the poor, and the poor state of the Canadian economy do give cause for grave concern.

What of the future in the new millennium? That depends on Canadians. Various scenarios are possible. First, the utopian option. The hearts of Canadians will be touched by the plight of the million children in poverty, the exclusion of the First Nations, the plight of the unemployed and of those on welfare, the homeless, the need for food banks, the impoverishment of the female-headed single-parent families and the feminization of poverty. Perhaps . . . or perhaps not. If Canadian hearts have been touched, this has not translated into touching the pockets, or at least not sufficiently to alleviate poverty in the last 20 years nor to galvanize politicians in the 1993 election campaigns.

Scenario two: pressure tactics. Special interest groups, notably the Assembly of First Nations and the women's movement, will organize and pressure provincial and federal governments to initiate effective social policies. Indeed they are already doing so, with some positive results. Such pressure tactics may or may not include occasional violence. Violence as a strategy of social change in Canada seems usually to be perceived as unnecessary, illegitimate and, especially, as counterproductive; but such perceptions are not universal, and may change.

Scenario three: the choice. The Senate Committee (1991) advised that the quality of Canada's economic future is in jeopardy if the quality of life of Canada's *human* future, our children, is not substantially improved. In this view, whether change comes from above (scenario one — an enlightened citizenry and political leadership) or from below (scenario two) may not really matter; but change must be initiated and poverty alleviated or Canada itself will be impoverished. Canada will survive (perhaps not at the top of the UNDP list), and the quality of life will not be quite as good as it might have been.

ENDNOTES

1. A bibliography on poverty might include the various reports by the National Council of Welfare (Cat. Nos. H67 and H68), and occasional articles in *Perspectives* (Cat. No. 75-002) and *Social Trends* (Cat. No. 11-008). Particularly useful is James Curtis *et al* (1993), also some articles in Forcese and Richer (1983). On theory see Grabb (1990); and on unemployment see Clarke (1986) and Burman (1988). Also The Economic Council of Canada (1992), Sarlo (1992), Canadian Institute of Child Health (1989),

The Senate Reports (1980, 1991), and the Canadian Council on Social Development (Ross *et al*, 1994).

2. See books 3: 414-15; 4: 440-42; 9: 580-82; 1963: 659, 683-84, 806-9. Also *Phaedrus* and *Timaeus* 69-70, 89-90. The idea that people are "naturally" unequal is as immensely persuasive as the opposite idea; and Plato develops it to its logical conclusions.

3. The secular, egalitarian, and radical implications of Christianity as "tidings of great joy" are emphasized in Liberation Theology.

4. See Michael Young's brilliant satire, *The Rise of the Meritocracy* (1961).

5. Note how similar Durkheim's ideal utopia is to that of Marx and Engels: "We shall have an association in which the free development of each is the condition for the free development of all" in the *Communist Manifesto* (1967: 105), and also to that of Spencer (see Chapter 2).

CRIME

Crime is endemic in Canada. The crime rate has increased over the last ten years; the violent crime rate has increased even more rapidly. Canadians are becoming increasingly violent, and the future looks more violent still.

Furthermore crime costs an estimated $14 billion per year, according to the Solicitor General. This breaks down fairly evenly into $8 billion in the visible costs of the justice system, including the police, prisons, the courts and legal aid, and $6 billion in the invisible costs of insurance claims, theft, and shoplifting — not to mention the high costs of human pain, suffering, and loss (*The Globe and Mail*, 11.3.93). Crime is expensive, deadly and increasing.

In the United States, however, with ten times the population and three times the violent crime rate, crime costs about $425 billion a year. This includes $90 billion on criminal justice (police, the courts, prisons), plus $65 billion on private protection (security systems, alarms, guards), plus $50 billion in urban decay (the cost of lost jobs and fleeing residents), plus $45 billion in property loss (the value of stolen goods), plus $5 billion in medical care for victims of crime, plus $170 billion in shattered lives (the economic value of lost and broken lives): total $425 billion (*Business Week* 13.12.93).

The human costs of crime cannot adequately be measured in purely economic terms of course: consider the fear, the pain, the loss, the death. But the dollar figures do allow us, indeed force us, to confront the direct and indirect costs of crime to society, and the tangible and intangible damages.

Why is this? What *are* the causes of crime? and what can be done? Theories of criminality abound: biological, psychological, and sociological. The debates are endless; everyone has their own opinion; and the experts often seem to disagree. Where does one start?

In the case of crime, I think the place to start is the self. Confidential self-report surveys indicate that 99% of us have committed criminal acts, crimes, of one sort or another. A *Psychology Today* survey (Table 6-1) found that 93% had

Table 6-1   Survey on Cheating, Lying, Stealing and Immorality[1]

Driven faster than the speed limit	93%
Told little white lies in the past year	88%
Taken home office supplies or other materials in the past year	68%
Cheated on examinations or school assignments (when possible)	67%
Parked illegally	60%
Taken sick days from work although well enough to go in during the past year	47%
Had extramarital sexual intercourse	45%
Driven while drunk or under the influence of drugs	41%
Tried to save money on tax returns by lying or withholding information (in the past five years)	38%
Gone through Customs purposely not declaring an item	38%
Made personal long-distance telephone calls at work in the past year	38%
Deceived best friend about something important in the past year	33%
Cheated on an expense account in the past year	28%
Cut into line or failed to wait for turn in a public place	19%

[1]Data exclude those to whom the items did not apply.

Source: Hassett, 1981:41

driven faster than the speed limit, 68% had stolen from the office, 41% had driven drunk or on drugs, and over one-third of the sample had made false declarations on their tax returns, smuggled items through customs, and so on. A confidential class survey might produce interesting results. Why did *you* do it? (or me, if you insist!). This may be the most appropriate place to begin, plus it has the added advantage that we begin to realize that in discussing criminals, we are also discussing ourselves. "They" are "us"!

First we will consider the crime data, and the problems with the statistics. Then we will examine types of crime, and some of the principal perspectives and theories of crime. We will conclude with examining some of the recommendations for reducing the crime rate, particularly theories of punishment.

CRIME IN CANADA[1]

Thousands of activities are defined as illegal by Federal, Provincial, or Municipal legislation. They range from murder to betting, contravening building codes, to letting your dog foul the sidewalk. Table 6-2 indicates the number of crimes committed, and the crime rates, as reported by Statistics Canada.

In 1993 over three million criminal offences were reported by the police. Most of these were crimes against property (53%), 10% were crimes of violence, and 27% were Other, including prostitution and arson. In addition to these

Table 6-2   Crime Rates Canada 1993

	Number	Rate per 100,000
Violent Crimes		
Homicide	630	2
Attempted Murder	988	3
Assaults	238,470	829
Sexual Assaults	34,764	121
Other Sexual Offences	4,170	15
Abduction	1,204	4
Robbery	29,961	104
Total	310,187	1,079
Property Crimes		
Breaking and Entering	406,582	1,414
Motor Vehicle Theft	156,811	545
Theft over $1,000	117,758	410
Theft under $1,000	768,859	2,674
Have Stolen Goods	36,186	126
Fraud	113,054	393
Total	1,599,250	5,562
Other Criminal Code		
Mischief	415,645	1,446
Bail Violation	66,197	230
Disturbing the Peace	54,499	190
Offensive Weapons	18,672	65
Prostitution	8,520	30
Arson	12,526	44
Other	250,600	872
Total	826,659	2,875
Total Criminal Code	2,736,096	9,516

Source: Statistics Canada, 1994: *Canadian Crime Statistics 1993.* Cat. 85-205.

Criminal Code violations presented in Table 6-2, there were about 198,000 traffic crimes (7%), 57,000 drug offences (2%) and 48,000 offences against other Federal statutes (e.g., the Immigration Act, Excise Act, Canadian Shipping Act, etc.).

Despite the widespread and apparently escalating fear of crime, the Criminal Code crime rate actually fell in 1993, for the second consecutive year, although it is still 13% higher than it was 10 years ago. The violent crime rate also decreased slightly, a reversal of direction for the first time in 15 years. If these trends continue the future begins to look brighter.

Now we will consider some of these crimes in greater detail.

Homicide

In 1993 630 homicides were reported, a decline for the second consecutive year from 732 in 1992 and 753 in 1991. Of these homicides 80% were cleared by charges, and another 50 were also cleared, usually by the death of the suspect. Of those charged, 473 were men, 75 were women; these figures include 36 youths (Statistics Canada 1994:31). In general about one-third of all homicides are within the family, over half are committed by friends or acquaintances and only about 15% by the much feared stranger.

Despite the fear of homicide and despite the frequency of homicide in the media, homicide is not only rare, but the present homicide rate is 27% lower than it was in 1975 (Statistics Canada, 1994:31).

Homicide rates vary widely across the country, as Table 6-3 indicates, rising steadily from east to west and much higher in the Northwest Territories than anywhere else in Canada. Note that there were no homicides in the Yukon in 1993.

Many homicides are committed within a criminal subculture. Previous research studies indicate that 67% of the accused and 45% of the victims had criminal records. Homicide is also principally within the male domain: about 90% of the accused are male, and 64% of the victims (Wright, 1992; Statistics Canada 1989 Cat. No. 85-209).

Sexual Assault

Over 34,000 sexual assaults were recorded in 1993. The Criminal Code distinguishes between three levels of sexual assault. Level one "involves no serious bodily harm or physical injury to the victim," although there may be psychological trauma. The vast majority of sexual assaults, 96% to be precise, are Level one. Level two involves a greater degree of force or threatened force (e.g., with a weapon and/or injury). Level three involves wounding, maiming or disfiguring the victim, or endangering the life of the victim. Rape is Level three sexual assault.

All this data is an underestimate of the actual numbers, as is well known, since victims often do not report such assaults to the police. Why not? For many reasons, depending on the level of the assault. Some respondents informed Statistics Canada that the assault (in the legal sense) was too minor, also they wanted to keep it private, or were ashamed, or feared a "second rape" by the

Table 6-3   Homicide by Number, Rate per 100,000 and Province, 1993

Province	Number	Rate
Newfoundland	7	1
PEI	-	2
Nova Scotia	19	2
New Brunswick	11	1
Quebec	159	2
Ontario	193	2
Manitoba	31	3
Saskatchewan	30	3
Alberta	49	2
B.C.	122	3
Yukon	-	-
Northwest Territories	7	11

Source: Statistics Canada 1994, Cat. 85-205.

police or the courts, or feared the perpetrator — a host of possibilities (*Juristat*, 1994, Vol. 14, No. 7, Cat. No. 85-002). Increasingly, however, women are testifying in public. The rape trials of William Kennedy Smith and Mike Tyson in 1992 in the United States did much to publicize the issue.

Both the number and the rate of Level three sexual assaults have declined since 1983 (357 incidents in 1993, down from 550); and the clearance rates have increased from 63% to 75% (Statistics Canada, 1994; Allen, 1992).

Prostitution

This is an interesting crime in the sense that it is not a crime to be a prostitute, but it is a crime to communicate for purposes of prostitution in a public place. It is also controversial: many authorities argue that prostitution should be decriminalized, just as suicide has been (Shaver, 1985). A *Maclean's* poll showed that 49% of Canadians believe that prostitution should be legalized, 44% disagree, and 8% had no opinion or did not answer (*Maclean's* 2.1.94). The Fraser Committee Report on Pornography and Prostitution (1984), which undertook the most extensive research on prostitution in Canada to date, recommended that prostitution be institutionalized, regulated, and taxed, as it is in other parts of the world; but its recommendations were rejected.

We know a fair amount about prostitution now, particularly female street walkers; rather less about male prostitution, and sex-trade workers in massage parlours, strip clubs, hotels and escort services and call girls, as well as the customers or "johns."

In an original article, Frances Shaver has argued that prostitution is primarily a male crime rather than a female crime as is so widely believed, since 96% of the people involved, mostly clients but also pimps, are male. She protests the sexism which permeates the occupation: "it is the act of selling sex that is denounced, not the act of buying it"; and it is the original economic disadvantage of women which makes prostitution an option (1993:165; also Lowman, 1991:113-34).

The 1993 crime data indicate that the majority of those charged with prostitution offences were male (51%) (Statistics Canada, 1994:50). This is a major change in enforcement policy from a few years ago and perhaps indicates a wider acceptance of the feminist paradigm on prostitution (also Wolff and Geissel, 1994).

We cannot discuss all the details of every type of crime, however, so we will move on to consider the accuracy of our data.

Crime Statistics

These statistics seem neat and clean and clear. In fact, however, they are highly inaccurate. In 1976 the Law Reform Commission of Canada stated bluntly that: "The state of statistics and information on the nature of crime and the administration of justice in Canada is simply deplorable." And five years later another commission of inquiry reiterated the same point (Statistics Canada, 1981: 5, 10).

Our crime statistics are based on police reports from across the country submitted to Statistics Canada. But by no means all crimes are reported to the police, for any number of reasons:

- the crime may never have been discovered. This is probably particularly true of "white collar" crime.

- even if a crime is discovered, a victim may fear reprisals (physical violence, being fired, etc.) from the boss or the Mafia.

- crimes which do not involve victims, in the usual sense of the term, are particularly likely to go unreported. Where two or more parties voluntarily engage in crime to their mutual benefit, as in prostitution, drug-trafficking, illegal gambling or off-track betting, then both parties are satisfied. No one complains. No one reports the crime.

- the activity may not be regarded as criminal, e.g., a bar-room brawl, or a fight in a game of hockey.

- the offence may be regarded as private: "keep it within the family," as in wife-battering or child abuse.

- the offence may be too embarrassing or painful to report, e.g., a theft in a brothel, or a policeman being robbed. Nine out of ten rapes, it is estimated, are not reported.

- people may think it is not worth the time and trouble to report the crime, particularly if they suspect that the offender will not be caught. Often an offence is only reported for insurance purposes; and if insurance money is not involved, it will not be reported.
- police are not likely to report their own crimes, if any, from illegal wiretapping to accepting bribes or beating up a suspect.
- and there are the widespread attitudes: "Mind your own business" and "Don't get involved."

Probably most people can think of crimes they have witnessed, or even experienced (not to mention committed), which they have not reported to the police. Further evidence of underreporting was provided by the Statistics Canada General Social Survey (GSS) in 1993, in which a sample of 10,000 adults were interviewed about their experience of crime in 1992. Essentially this was a Victim Survey, which discovered data differing from the statistics in the police reports on which the crime data presented in Table 6-2 are based. The salient feature of the GSS for our purposes is that the victims only reported 48% of the crimes they had experienced. Given this rate of underreporting crime, it may be that the official statistics on violence should be multiplied by a factor of two for greater accuracy (Gartner and Doob, 1994; cf. Wright, 1995).

Furthermore, even if crimes are reported to the police, they may not be recorded, and again for a wide variety of reasons. If the offence is not too serious, the police may simply warn or just ignore an offender, depending on how busy they are, the age of the offender (juveniles' offences are sometimes not recorded), the offender's status (a working-class drunk may be arrested, and a middle-class one dropped home — or vice versa), the police's estimation of whether or not the problem is over (e.g., a marital dispute with allegations of assault), or the sheer futility of the exercise (e.g., minor theft — unless insurance money is involved). More relevant is that the police file their reports for the most serious offence only. So if someone breaks into a house, steals some money, assaults two people and murders a third, only one crime is reported in the statistics.

A text on crime portrays the relation between crime and the statistics on crime as a funnel, or an inverted triangle. At the top is the totality of crimes committed, but, the authors advise, "not all actual crime is detected, not all detected crime is reported, not all reported crime is recorded, not all recorded crime results in arrests, not everyone arrested is brought to trial, not everyone tried is convicted, and not everyone convicted is sentenced" (Silverman, Teevan, Sacco, 1991: 55; cf. Hagan, 1991:41). Certainly self-report studies and victimization studies present very different realities of crime than the Uniform Crime Reports submitted by the police; and our official crime rates are underestimates, with some offences more underestimated than others. Variations from province to province or changes over time may therefore be due to:

- more or less crime
- more or less efficient police detection
- more or less complete public reporting
- more or less complete police recording
- some combination of all these.

What our crime statistics do give us is a picture of crime as *recorded*; and this is the data we have to work with, inaccurate though it is. Working with all three sets of data (including self-reports and victim surveys) however, reduces some of the inaccuracies.

TYPES OF CRIME

The police and Statistics Canada categorize offences against the Criminal Code as "crimes of violence," "property crimes" and "other" (as in Table 6-2); but there are other categories which may be more useful sociologically. Some of these dimensions will be considered here.

Victimless Crime

Crimes of violence and property crimes have obvious victims: people lose their lives, their money. The offence is clear. However, a number of crimes seem to have no victims: prostitution, illegal gambling and betting, possession of drugs, and the use and sale of drugs — all these crimes involve willing participants. No one suffers, so it seems, in these supposedly purely private matters. So why are they crimes? Should the Criminal Code be amended?

The issues are extremely controversial. Many people do not believe that gambling is wrong; some believe that prostitution should be legalized and that smoking pot should be allowed. Furthermore, legislation against such victimless crimes is extremely difficult to enforce, since neither party is likely to complain, or *can* complain without self-incrimination. Finally legislation against so-called victimless crimes can, and often does, generate a ripple of secondary crimes *with* victims, as innovators try and satisfy public demands for now illegal actions.

Prostitution, for instance, is sometimes regarded as a "victimless" crime: it is a consensual act as two individuals agree to trade assets. Yet prostitution does have many victims. Many street workers were sexually abused as children, many come from dysfunctional families of one sort or another, many are runaways, many are drug addicts. Victimized by families, they may be further victimized, physically and psychologically, by pimps, and also by clients. In Vancouver one study found that over one-third of female prostitutes had been physically assaulted, and 21% had been raped. Similar rates of violence were reported from Montreal (Gomme, 1993: 304). Furthermore in 1991 and 1992, 22 female prostitutes were murdered, and 10 others were implicated in the murders of eight people (Wolff and Geissel, 1994: 22; also *Juristat* 1993, 13(4)).

But if some women are forced into prostitution, others especially at the upper end of the profession, may make clear and rational decisions to choose this job: it can pay well (Stein, 1974; Shaver, 1993).

Other controversial areas in which the public is deeply divided or in which the law does not reflect public opinion are abortion and euthanasia. Not everyone, however, would agree that abortion or euthanasia are crimes; but nor would everyone necessarily agree that there are no victims.

Male and Female Crime

Males constituted 89% of those accused and charged with crimes of violence and 81% of all offences against the Criminal Code (Statistics Canada, 1994, Cat. No. 85-205). Crime is therefore principally a male matter, particularly violent crime.

However 19% of all those charged with Criminal Code infractions were female, an increase from 15% in 1978. Women did not constitute a majority in any category except infanticide (three cases in 1993), but they were a large proportion of those charged with prostitution (49%), shoplifting (44%) and fraud (30%) (Statistics Canada, 1994).

The female crime rate is not only quantitatively different from the male crime rate, it is also perhaps qualitatively different. Some researchers suggest that "a considerable proportion [of violent acts committed by women] consists of acts of rebellion or retaliation against men in abusive or exploitative situations." Further: "The criminality of women may also be understood as symptomatic of a sense of futility with a desperate life situation, such as poverty, homelessness or abuse" (Johnson and Rodgers, 1993:102). The majority, they say, are "non-violent offenders who commit petty crimes for economic gain . . . Many women are at the same time victims" (Johnson and Rodgers, 1993:112).

Shelley Gavigan has suggested that: "Until recently it was possible to condemn criminologists both for their near silence on criminal law, and for their sexism when they did speak" (1993:215). Such a blanket condemnation is no longer possible due, in her view, to the rise of feminist criminologies. Nonetheless as Dorothy Chunn and she have argued elsewhere, intense debate surrounds a number of issues with respect to female offenders, notably numbers and types of crime, motivation and the relation to gender inequality, the ideological bases of criminal law and the implications for treatment and/or punishment of offenders (Chunn and Gavigan, 1991).

Men are far more likely to be aggressive and destructive and to make a career out of crime within an organization; and they are far more likely than women to be violent within the home. Spousal homicide is clearly different by gender, again not only in numbers (three to one), but also in rationale; we considered the battered wife syndrome in Chapter 4. Nonetheless the differences should not be overestimated. Women have contributed to the ranks of international terrorism: Leila Khaled, a Palestinian, hijacked a Tel Aviv-bound aircraft in 1969; Kim Hyon Hui blew up 115 people on a Korean flight in 1987 — but she had been trained for years, and her family in North Korea would have been killed had she refused. Susanna Ronconi of the Italian Red Brigade was as ruthless as the women in the Baader-Meinhof gang in Germany (MacDonald, 1992). But they are still a small minority in the ranks.

Just as patterns of criminality are different, so also are patterns of victimization. 24% of Canadians were victims of at least one crime, according to the 1993 General Social Survey (GSS), in the previous year; this is the same proportion as was reported in 1988. However, women were more likely to be victimized than men, with rates of 151 per 100,000 compared to 136 per 100,000 for victims aged 15 and over. The GSS also indicated however a major disjunction between the reality and the perception of crime. While the crime rate has not changed in the last five years, according to the GSS, 46% of the respondents believed that it had increased, compared to 43% who thought it had remained the same, and 4% who thought it had decreased. Women, however, were more fearful of crime than men (Gartner and Doob, 1994). Crime is therefore gender specific in many different types of ways: frequency, victimization and fear among them

Furthermore the process of victimization starts early. Female children are three times more likely to be sexually abused than males (Committee on Sexual Offences, Vol. I, 1984: 198).

One topic that has been the subject of considerable attention recently has been the impact of the premenstrual syndrome (PMS) on crime. In 1980 and in 1981 two women in England who had been charged with murder had the charges reduced to manslaughter because the defense argued that PMS had reduced their responsibility for their actions. Both were found guilty and given probation. One woman, a barmaid, had fatally stabbed another barmaid in a row in a pub; the other drove her car into her lover. Both cases caused enormous controversies, and the legal, medical, and social implications are far-reaching (Sommer, 1984: 36-38). In Canada, however, PMS has not been recognized as a legal defence for women, furthermore its legitimacy as a defence is controversial within feminist discourse (Kendall, 1992).

But the broader issues of criminal law are the degree to which it remains oppressive of women or contributes to their autonomy. This question arises not only with issues which primarily affect women, such as wife battering, sexual assault, feticide, prostitution, pornography, and abortion, but also with reference to specific defences for women e.g., the battered women syndrome, premenstrual syndrome, post-partum depression, and rape trauma syndrome. These issues and defences require further consideration when devising models of equality for women's justice. Equal justice for unequals is not justice (Sheehy, 1987). And the authors of a recent book on women offenders in Canada reported: "We entered the correctional system as professional 'helpers,' but quickly realized that far from needing help, our 'clients' needed liberation — both economic and social — from a patriarchal system based on male dominance and male property rights" (Adelberg and Currie, 1987: 12).

Youth Crime

Youths (aged 12-17) are responsible for almost one quarter of all recorded crimes in Canada, including about 14% of all violent crime and 7% of the homicides (36 in 1993). A total of almost 127,000 youths were charged in 1993. Only 8% of the population are aged between 12 and 17, so they are three times *over represented* as criminals.

Most of those charged were male, as with adult crime; but female youths have higher charge rates than female adults. Also young women constituted 21% of those youth charged with Criminal Code offences, but 24% of youths charged with violent crime.

Youths therefore are apparently more criminal than adults now, (though less homicidal), the crime rates for young women are higher than those for adult females, but also violence levels seem to be rising: 17% of all youth charged in 1993 were accused of violence: almost doubled from 9% in 1986 (Statistics Canada 1994; see also Frank, 1992).

Criminality, however, for youths as for adults, is not evenly distributed through the population — not even the criminal population. Not only were most of those charged male, but also most were charged with several offences: 20% had two charges against them, 19% had three to five, 8% had six to ten, and 5% had more than ten charges laid against them. Most of the offences were property-related (B and E, theft, etc.), but 18% were violent. 64 young people were charged with murder/manslaughter (26) or attempted murder (38) (Doige, 1990). By my rough calculations, this means that a small minority of those charged (i.e. the 13% charged with six or more offences), were responsible for nearly half (44%) the total number of charges laid. That is a lot of trouble caused by under 5,000 adolescents!

Similar patterns have been noted in Philadelphia, where a small minority of offenders (18%) — and an even smaller minority of the population, therefore, — were responsible for a majority (52%) of the offenses. And in London, England, Donald West noted that only 7% of the total (male) cohort under study became offenders, but of the offenders, 23% accounted for 57% of all the convictions recorded; i.e. under 2% of the total sample (West, 1982: 16). This might be described, with all due respect to de Tocqueville, as "the tyranny of the minority."

The implications of this unequal distribution of crime have been drawn by the American criminologist James Q. Wilson, who has argued forcefully against Rousseauism that: "Wicked people exist. Nothing avails except to set them apart from innocent people" (1979: 87). To reduce, or at least contain the escalating crime rate, we must isolate the minority of incorrigible offenders who repeatedly commit serious crimes and are responsible for a disproportionate number of crimes: in Wilson's view, the "top" five or ten or fifteen per cent should be locked up.

Teenagers kill about 40 people every year: a small fraction of the total, and the rate has remained about the same for decades; but a series of homicides by teenagers in 1994 horrified Canadians and resulted in demands for tougher legislation. In Ottawa, three teenagers were charged with the drive-by murder of a British engineer; in Montreal a 16-year-old was convicted of killing a Korean store owner with a shotgun; in Edmonton three more teens were charged with stabbing a housewife to death in a robbery; in Whitehead, Nova Scotia, a 13-year-old shotgunned a neighbour to death for no apparent reason: "It just happened, I was angry." And a B.C. teenager was sentenced to life for the rape and murder of a six-year-old girl whom he was babysitting. All the murderers were male (*Maclean's* 15.8.94; *The Globe and Mail*, 3.9.94).

Amendments to the Young Offenders Act have included a doubling of the maximum sentence for first degree murder to 10 years; the transfer of 16-and 17-year-old violent offenders from youth courts to adult courts, and later to adult prisons; the release of young offenders names to relevant circles; compulsory treatment or therapy, hitherto voluntary; and, in general, a greater concern with the safety of the public than with the rehabilitation of the criminal.

The Young Offenders Act has been accused of letting kids get away with murder; and the conservative rather than the liberal paradigm is in the ascendant now. The "Troubled Teens" are being redefined as "Evil Men" or, less frequently, women. Nonetheless in his insightful book, *The Myth of Delinquency*, Elliott Leyton insists that the delinquent is often the last link in a chain of "triple delinquency": the first is the society's delinquency in creating an underclass of its weakest members; the second is the family's delinquency in its rejection of one or more, or all of its children: the family cannot cope; the third delinquency, the one targeted by the judicial system, is that of the raging, rejected, mourning, hopeless child. Leyton's case histories of eight such so-called delinquents detail the inexorable destruction of families and children and are sad to read; but in the finest traditions of anthropology he did meet and talk to these young men and women, and their families, counsellors, psychiatrists, etc., over an extended period of time. Furthermore his refusal to label these young people as "evil" or "amoral," and his contextualization of their situations, provides a model for others' research.

White Collar Crime

White collar crime is defined as "a crime committed by a person of respectability and high social status in the course of his occupation" (Sutherland, 1961: 9). These crimes include fraud, embezzlement, false advertising, tax evasion, price-fixing, bribery, padding expense accounts, bankruptcy frauds, bid rigging, copyright and patent infringement, cheque kiting, insurance frauds, kickbacks, stock manipulation. . . . Such offences are often extremely difficult to detect, and indeed often go undetected. Furthermore many have become so frequent that they are virtually accepted as normal ways of doing business: kickbacks are common, and the slogan "caveat emptor" implies that one should expect dishonesty, not honesty, in business dealings.

Edwin Sutherland, who pioneered the study of white collar crime back in 1949 with a study of 70 giant US corporations, argued that white collar crime is more dangerous to society than "ordinary" crime, not primarily because of the greater financial losses but because: "White collar crimes violate trust and therefore create distrust; this lowers social morale and produces social disorganization. Many of the white collar crimes attack the fundamental principles of the American institutions" (1961: 13). Yet they are penalized lightly, if at all, despite widespread criminality and persistent recidivism. He demonstrated that white collar crime by business executives is *organized:*, an insight that gives new meaning to the phrase "organized crime" (1961: 218-33). And he also tried to demolish the widespread theory that criminality is caused by poverty or personal pathologies (1961: 6-9) — quite convincingly, you may find.

Although Sutherland restricted himself to corporate crime, the concept of white collar crime includes not only corporation presidents and business executives but also, his secondary focus, bankers, doctors, lawyers, politicians, the police, shoe salesmen, used-car salesmen, accountants . . . and no doubt criminologists and professors.

Sutherland's early research in the US has been continued by Laureen Snider's contemporary research in Canada. She notes that "corporate crime is more harmful, in terms of lives destroyed and financial damage inflicted, than traditional crime. Despite this, the amount of legal attention and enforcement resources devoted to its control has been minimal, and efforts at intensifying control have been characterized more frequently by failure than success" (1993: 17). In other words, there is one law for the rich (the corporations) and another for the poor (the consumers and the environment). Profit maximization remains the norm of the corporate world, even if laws are occasionally (or even frequently) broken. (See also Keane, 1991). Crime pays.

Two examples are worth citing, one old, one new. In 1985 bank robberies netted a grand total of $2.8 million; in comparison white collar crime probably netted about $4 billion (*Maclean's* 30.6.86). A recent case in point is Julius Melnitzer, a London, Ontario lawyer, who committed the largest fraud in Canadian history during the eighties and early nineties, defrauding banks, colleagues, and friends out of over $100 million dollars before he was arrested, pleaded guilty to 43 counts of fraud and forgery, and was sentenced to nine years (Cannon, 1993). That's over ten million dollars per year in prison: probably 20 million if you count time off for good behaviour. Not a bad price, one might think. Hardly a deterrent either.

Tax evasion is now estimated to cost about $30 billion a year: enough to eliminate about two-thirds of the annual federal deficit — although admittedly tax evasion is not so much a white collar crime as virtually universal. In the service sector, home renovators, service stations, house cleaners, and hairdressers and their clients often evade the GST; cigarettes are smuggled; and the underground economy seems to have a higher rate of growth, in cash, than the gross domestic product (GDP). Furthermore offenders often feel no guilt about breaking the law (*Maclean's* 9.8.93).

White collar crime can reach to the very top. Think of the resignation of President Nixon in the USA in 1974. More recently Brazilian President Fernando Collor de Mello was suspended from office in 1992 for corruption. The former Prime Minister of Italy Bettino Craxi was sentenced in 1994 to eight and a half years in jail for fraud — but he lives in Tunis now and refuses to return to Italy! And Silvio Berlosconi was forced to resign in 1994 after being investigated for corruption. In France former Prime Minister Laurent Fabius was charged in 1994 for his role in the contaminated blood scandal. In Greece former Prime Minister Constantine Mitsotakis is standing trial for accepting a $20.5 million bribe. In Canada Bill Vander Zalm was charged with breach of trust in 1991 and forced to resign as Premier of B.C.

Organized Crime

Organized crime is now estimated to earn annual profits of about $1 trillion worldwide — more than the Canadian annual federal budget and almost equal to that of the United States. Organized crime has far exceeded the bounds of the Sicilian Mafia; it is now international, because many national criminal organizations cooperate, borders are permeable, and criminals are often better armed and paid than law enforcement officers. Vast treasures are at stake, illegally in drugs, and legally as the money is laundered. Pablo Escobar, shot and killed in November 1993 in Colombia, had built up a cocaine empire, organized the deaths of hundreds (including blowing up an airliner with 107 people on board), and became a multibillionaire: about number 60 on the Forbes 1991 list of the wealthiest people in the world. This empire has now been taken over by the Cali cartel led by the Rodriguez brothers (*Time* 13.12.93). The drug empires, like many of the other criminal empires, it may be as well to remember, ultimately depend for their existence and profit on the continued support of regular drug users, who are themselves criminals.

Organized crime has existed since the founding of New France and New England in such forms as piracy, robber barons, gangs, political embezzlements, etc. (Carrigan, 1991). Group crime, to be successful, must be well organized. But organized crime as we use the term today refers not simply to organization, but to a type of organization: criminal organizations are national or international, have a hierarchy, rules, and discipline, and are self-perpetuating and committed to profit by criminal activity (cf. Gomme, 1993:359).

The Mafia, originating in Sicily, came to Canada with the Italian immigration around the turn of the last century. The Black Hand, as they were known, first surfaced in Hamilton and Toronto, in protection and extortion rackets. With the passage of the Volstead Act in 1919 in the United States, and the beginnings of Prohibition, the opportunities for crime increased. Rocco Perri, the first Canadian "godfather," became a major supplier of alcohol to Al Capone and others in the US and made a fortune. When Prohibition was repealed in 1933 he simply imported the alcohol, much cheaper in the States, sold it illegally in Canada, and made another fortune . . . until he disappeared in 1944.

The family names ring like a litany: Commisso, Volpe, Petrula, Rivard, Cotroni, Violi — not all Italians, but all involved in the various families from the fifties on, whose fortunes waxed and waned as leaders were shot, imprisoned, or died natural deaths. Gambling, drugs, prostitution, extortion, loan-sharking, racketeering, arson, counterfeiting, pornography, auto-theft, political graft, police corruption, and murder — all these were and are the domain of the Mafia.

The Mafia are the most famous, or infamous, organized criminals; but there are others of course, from the Boyd gang of bank robbers in Toronto in the fifties to the Dubois and McSweeny gangs in Montreal in the seventies. Most recently we are seeing the new ethnic gangs: Chinese Triads, Jamaican posses, Asian and Colombian gangs, all primarily involved in the lucrative drug trade.

The motorcycle gangs began as recreational clubs after the end of World War Two, but quickly became criminal organizations with names like Hells Angels, Satan's Choice, The Grim Reapers and so on. The Hells Angels dominated this scene by the eighties through sheer violence. One enforcer, Yves (Apache) Trudeau admitted that he had killed 43 people; another, Donald Lavoie, who worked for the Dubois gang, killed 15 people, helped plan another 34 murders, and knew about another 76 murders (Carrigan, 1991: 195-96).

Crime pays, unless it kills you; and the obituary lists for organized crime are long indeed — most of these criminals are killed by their own or their rivals rather than by the police. Yet precisely because organized crime is so secret, so pervasive, so deep, so violent, and so profitable, it is extremely difficult to eradicate. The police have neither the resources nor the skills to cope with much more than street violence. The judiciary seems to favour the rights of the individual over the collectivity. And the Canadian consumer avidly buys the services which organized crime supplies: smuggled alcohol and cigarettes, drugs, pornography, gambling, prostitutes . . . and is therefore an accessory to crime, and helps to maintain organized crime in business.

THEORIES OF DEVIANCE AND CRIME

Everyone seems to have his or her own pet theories on the causes, and solutions, to problems of deviance and crime. You hear them all the time. "The courts are far too lenient"; "the police spend all their time chasing parking tickets"; "we should bring back the death penalty"; "I blame television"; "parents no longer control their children — they are too permissive or too busy"; "it's all in the genes." There are many theories, and types of theories.

Here we will briefly review a few of the more well-known types of theories, and focus particularly on sociological theories.

Religious

For most of western history, the most common theory of crime has been religious. The devil was believed to be the source of all evil, all sin, and all crime. The first crime in Christian mythology was committed in the Garden of Eden, and Eve's explanation was to blame the devil: "The serpent beguiled me" (Gen. 3: 13). The crime was disobedience to the law of God, and the punishment was expulsion from the Garden of Eden (with no discussion of deterrence or rehabilitation). The second crime followed soon afterwards, when Cain murdered Abel: the first of many murders in history.

This religious theory of crime and deviance is still widely believed, especially among fundamentalist Christians. A recent issue of *Watch Tower*, published by The Jehovah's Witnesses and entitled "How Crime and Violence will be Stopped" (Toronto: no date) states: "The Bible shows that the Devil is a powerful, invisible spirit who exercises influence on the minds of men. *He is the main instigator of crime.* . . . Nothing else can account for the *inhuman*, often *fiendish* and depraved nature of crime." (Emphasis added). The Witnesses admit the reality of other factors as causes, and "stopgap" measures as solutions, but they insist that "the only real solution" is that people "must learn to love God and to express genuine love for their fellowmen." People still blame the devil for their misdeeds; but Joseph Conrad remarks in *Under Western Eyes*: "The belief in a supernatural source of evil is not necessary; men alone are quite capable of every wickedness."

Religious and secular theories of crime may not necessarily be mutually incompatible, but clearly religious theories are incapable of empirical verification; thus they are not scientific in the usual sense of the term.

Biological

The first modern, scientific theory of crime was formulated by the Italian physician, Cesare Lombroso (1835-1909), founder of modern criminology. He described doing an autopsy on an infamous bandit, and finding a "distinct depression" on the occipital part of the skull, which, he realized, was exactly like the depressions found in "inferior animals."

> This was not merely an idea, but a revelation. At the sight of that skull, I seemed to see all of a sudden, lighted up as a vast plain under a flaming sky, the problem of the nature of the criminal — an atavistic being who reproduces in his person the ferocious instincts of primitive humanity and the inferior animals. Thus were explained anatomically the enormous jaws, high cheekbones, prominent superciliary arches, solitary lines in the palms, extreme size of the orbits, handle-shaped or sessile ears found in criminals, savages, and apes, insensibility to pain, extremely acute sight, tattooing, excessive idleness, love of orgies, and the irresistible craving for evil for its own sake, the desire not only to extinguish life in the victim, but to mutilate the corpse, tear its flesh, and drink its blood. (Cohen, 1966: 50)

Hence the Lombrosian idea of the born criminal, an evolutionary throwback to a lower species of humanity; hence also the idea of a "criminal type": that criminals can look like criminals, and that physical appearance symbolizes moral reality (Synnott, 1993: 96).

In the late 1940s, the American psychologist and physician W.H. Sheldon emphasized the connections between physique and personality, and crime. Working in a juvenile delinquents' home in Boston, he compared the physiques of 200 boys. He distinguished between endomorphs (people tending to be short and fat), ectomorphs (people tending to be tall and thin) and mesomorphs (athletic types: muscular and active). He found that most of the delinquents were mesomorphs (but not that mesomorphs were mostly delinquent), and suggested that physique was therefore a critical determinant of criminality. He believed that mesomorphs tended to develop predatory personalities because they were stronger, more active, faster, and less reflective and sensitive than others. His conclusion, that delinquency lay in "the germ plasm" implied, of course, that the solution lay in eugenics (Sheldon, 1949).

In the 1960s attention switched from physique to chromosomes: the XYY theory of crime. Women have two X chromosomes; most men have an XY chromosome pattern, but a small percentage of men have an XYY pattern. This was thought to be responsible for extreme male aggression. So when Richard Speck was indicted for the murder of eight nurses in Chicago, his defense argued that he had an XYY pattern, and was therefore not responsible for his actions. However, further research resulted in the almost complete discrediting of the theory (Wilson and Herrnstein, 1985: 101-02).

Nonetheless many scientists now argue that genes are somehow related to crime. It is well-known that criminality often runs in families: "like father, like son." The Mafia is a classic example. This has usually been explained as the effects of socialization; the father teaches the son, and perhaps his daughters, his trade. However, recent research on adopted children suggests that the family criminality may be genetically linked. A study in Sweden found that male adoptees whose biological parents are criminals are *four times* more likely to become criminals than are those whose parents are not criminals. There is even a link to types of crime. And a study of 3,718 male children adopted by non-relatives showed similar results. One-third of the boys had a biological parent who had been convicted at least once, and one-ninth had a parent with three or more convictions. Yet the conviction rate for the adoptees ranged from 33% among those whose parents had no convictions to 80% among those parents who had three or more convictions. As Jencks remarks: "The more often the biological parents had been convicted, the more often their sons had been convicted" (1987: 35). There is of course no gene for criminality, and the genetic etiology of crime is obscure; it is also fairly minimal. Children of multiple offenders were convicted of about 2.4 times more crimes than children of non-offenders: about the same as urban-rural differences. But when one compares crime rates from one country to another, or one city to another, crime rates which vary by factors of 10, 20 or 30, it is pretty obvious that genetic structure is far less significant than culture. This data seems to indicate that criminals are born *and* made; but the causal factors are complex, and most people do not become criminals, even when genetic *and* environmental factors seem to predispose them towards criminality (Mednick, 1985).

Even as researchers clarify the genetic and chemical roots of crime, however, new problems are raised. What does this imply about criminal responsibility? How can society convict an individual for a chemical imbalance? or genetic inheritance? No one suggests that biological factors of one form or another directly cause *all* crime; but it is suggested that they may sometimes be part of the total package of sociological and psychological variables which determine criminality (Coccaro, 1995).

Psychological Theories

Psychological theories tend to focus on the individual rather than the cultural or the biological etiology of crime. Two orientations can be discerned, conservative and radical. For some, the problem is, why is there crime? and why is there so *much* crime? For others the relevant questions are different: given the massive economic and social inequality in Canada, why is there not *more* crime? Why is the crime rate so *low*? Why indeed? One perspective requires a theory of deviance, the other a theory of conformity; and psychology and sociology overlap in these debates.

Sigmund Freud articulated perhaps the first psychological theory of crime, but indirectly. He was particularly interested in violence and aggression, an interest stimulated by the outbreak of World War I. He suggested that "The deepest essence of human nature consists of instinctual impulses which are of an elementary nature, which are similar in all men and which aim at the satisfaction of certain primal needs. These impulses in themselves are neither good nor bad" (Vol. 12; 1985: 68). But, in society, they do have to be curbed. Social life requires constraint and restraint of these impulses. Failure of restraint may result in crime and violence. Freud argued that: "A human being is seldom altogether good or altogether bad; he is usually 'good' in one relation and 'bad' in another, or 'good' in certain external circumstances and in others decidedly 'bad' (Vol. 12; 1985: 69). Nonetheless, the impulsive self is decidedly self-serving rather than socially responsible; and he did believe that "man is a wolf to man" (cf. Chapter 3).

This theory basically pits humans' biological imperatives and the demands for instant gratification against society, which requires the management of impulses and personal demands and the channelling of needs and wants into socially acceptable modalities.

Freud was not directly concerned with crime; but crime is explained in psychoanalytic theory by the dominance of the id and the failure of the ego to grow. Two scholars with this orientation concluded that: "The criminal carries out in his actions his *natural* unbridled *instinctual* drives; he acts as the *child* would act if only it could. . . . The only difference between the criminal and the normal individual is that the normal man partially controls his criminal drives and finds outlets for them in socially harmless activities" (Cohen, 1966: 2, emphasis added). This is the criminal as childlike adult.

This view of criminal activity as natural and instinctive is consistent with Hobbes' view. But where Hobbes located control with the sovereign, the psychoanalytic school locates it in the individual ego. Notice that the view of criminal activity as "childish" in the sense that such activity is irrational or non-rational is reminiscent of Lombroso's views; in psychoanalytic theory, the criminal is a throwback to the child; in Lombroso's theory the criminal is a throwback to the ape. The one is pre-adult, the other is pre-human.

While it is clear that childhood is a most important time in the learning of attitudes and values, critics of psychoanalytic theory point out that Freud's theory does not explain changes in crime rates, nor variations in rates from country to country, nor how various individuals react differently to an absence of love in their early lives. This does not in itself prove the theory wrong, but it may limit its utility.

A more recent, and controversial psychological theory of crime has been formulated by Samuel Yochelson and Stanton Samenow in a massive two-volume work, *The Criminal Personality* (1977). After a 16-year study of 255 men in a US federal mental institution, they concluded that criminals are criminals because of how they *think*. Criminality has nothing directly to do with socioeconomic status, nutrition, television, frustration, friendships, etc. They discovered that the criminals, regardless of ethnic origin or socioeconomic status, shared 52 "patterns of thinking," basically Hobbesian; and they believe that these patterns are determined or chosen by the age of three or four. The significance of this study, and the reason for the controversy it caused, is that the doctors insist that the environment is *not* a cause of crime. Individuals make their own decisions, and their own choices (Vol. 2: 151); and so develop a criminal personality. Criminals are responsible, totally, in this view, for crime; *not* society. They can be retrained in their thinking, but it takes a long time in therapy for people to change ways of thought developed over a lifetime; and not everyone wants to change.

The point was well illustrated by Claude Brown, author of the sixties classic *Manchild in The Promised Land*, returning to the streets of his youth in Harlem. He recalled talking to a "young blood" doing "a dime and a nickel" (15 years) for armed robbery, and trying to persuade him of the folly of his chosen lifestyle. The man explained how he thought about it all:

> I see where you comin' from, Mr. Brown," he replied, "but you got things kind of turned around the wrong way. You see, all the things that you say could happen to me is dead on the money, and that is why I can't lose. Look at it from my point of view for a minute. Let's say I go and get wiped [killed]. Then I ain't got no more needs, right? And my problems are solved. I don't need no more money, right? O.K., supposin' I get popped, shot in the spine and paralyzed for the rest of my life — that could happen playin' football, you know. Then I won't need a whole lot of money because I won't be able to go place and do nothin', right? So, I'll be on welfare, and the welfare check is all the money I'll need, right? Now if I get busted and end up in the joint pullin' a dime and a nickel, like I am, then I don't have to worry about no bucks, no clothes. I get free rent and three square meals a day. So you see, Mr. Brown, I really can't lose. (Brown, 1984: 44).

Well . . . it's one way of thinking — which also translates into action. As another man explained: "You take their stuff and you pop [shoot] 'em" (Brown, 1984: 44). To what extent such thinking is a "free choice," as Samenow and Yochelson suggest, thereby blaming the criminal (the conservative view), and to what extent it is a survival mechanism, an adaptation to a sick society (the liberal view) remains debatable. But evidently in citing "free choice" to explain why some members of a family choose a life of crime and others do not, Yochelson and Samenow do not explain cross-cultural variations in crime rates.

Perhaps the classic statement of a psychological perspective on delinquency, and one with which many readers will probably empathize, is this set of 10 rules from Dear Abby (Table 6-4). She is not a psychologist, but these rules could be converted into hypotheses and tested empirically. She puts the responsibility for delinquency on the *family*, rather than the individual; but her theory is highly compatible with the Yochelson-Samenow research in the sense that both theories focus on the individual: the criminal's free will, and the parent's socialization of the child — the *male* child in this case.

Sociological Theories

Machiavelli and Hobbes were both convinced of the criminal and evil nature of homo not so sapiens, as we have seen. Rousseau, on the other hand, was the spokesman for the opposite position: that people are basically good. For Machiavelli and Hobbes, crime is not a problem — virtue is, and the law-abiding citizen. For them, and for Machiavellians and Hobbesians, the problem is: why is

Table 6-4   Abby's 10 Rules for Raising a Juvenile Delinquent

1. Begin at infancy to give the child everything he wants. In this way he will grow up to believe the world owes him a living.

2. When he picks up bad words laugh at him. This will make him think he is cute.

3. Never give him any spiritual training. Wait until he is 21, then let him decide for himself.

4. Pick up everything he leaves lying around: books, shoes, clothes. Do everything for him so that he will be experienced in throwing all responsibility on others.

5. Quarrel with your spouse frequently in his presence. In this way he will not be shocked when the home is broken.

6. Give a child all the spending money he wants. Never let him earn his own. Why should he have things as tough as you had them?

7. Satisfy his every craving for food, drinks, and comfort. Denial may lead to frustrations.

8. Take his part against neighbors, teachers, and policemen. They are all prejudiced against your child.

9. When he gets into trouble, apologize for yourself by saying: "I never could do anything with him."

10. Prepare for plenty of headaches. You are sure to have them.

there not *more* crime? Why are people so *good*? Their answer is: *fear* of the consequences of crime. For Rousseau and his followers, however, the question is the
functionalist one: why crime? His answer is that society (not the devil — a major
paradigm shift) generates crime by its inequality and slavery. Crime is therefore
a legitimate response to inequality. This perspective was maintained and developed further by Marx, Engels, and the radical/socialist tradition. Capitalist society creates its own crime, and generates its own criminals; note that for
Rousseau, Marx, Engels and the radical tradition generally, the criminals were
the capitalists who expropriated the land, the labour, and often the wives and
the lives of the proletariat; the real crime is inequality. Machiavelli and Hobbes
locate the source of the problem in the individual; the radicals locate it firmly in
the society, as we shall see below.

The classical sociologists did not devote much time to thinking about crime
and deviance. In *The Communist Manifesto* (1848), however, Marx and Engels
described the law as merely one among many means to oppress the proletariat.
"Political power," they said, "is merely the organized power of one class for
oppressing another." And "jurisprudence is but the will of your [bourgeoisie]
class made into law." Having defined the law and the state as exploitative,
oppressive and, effectively criminal, they urged the proletariat to revolt; and
they concluded the Manifesto with a ringing cry: "Let the ruling classes tremble
at a Communistic revolution. The proletarians have nothing to lose but their
chains. They have a world to win. WORKING MEN OF ALL COUNTRIES,
UNITE!" (1967: 105, 100, 120-21). In their view, theft or violence against injustice and inequity was, and is, no crime (see also Chapters 2 and 3).

This incitement to violence was, of course, a criminal act; and Marx was ultimately forced to live in exile. Nonetheless, the Marxist perspective on laws, and
"bourgeois" law, has acted as an ideological indictment of the bourgeois or liberal theory of law and crime. Basically, what was criminal for the bourgeoisie or
the middle class was liberating and legitimate for the exploited working class.

Rousseau and Proudhon had earlier described private property as theft.
Theft of "private property" was therefore easily redefined in this paradigm as liberation.

Emile Durkheim did not subscribe to the Marxist theory, but offered a theory which scandalized his contemporaries. He suggested that crime is "an integral
part of all healthy society," that it is normal, necessary, and inevitable, and
"must no longer be conceived as an evil that cannot be too much suppressed."
Furthermore it is useful, and performs such essential social functions as initiating
social change and facilitating individuality (1895/1962: 65-74). Nonetheless,
crime should be punished because punishment is both an "expiation" of the
offence and "a weapon for social defense." The "true function (of punishment) is
to maintain social cohesion intact," argued Durkheim, not correction nor deterrence (1893/1964: 108-09). Durkheim was thus the first to discuss what are

now described as "the functions of deviance," and to describe crime as normal rather than pathological.

The functionalist sociologist Kingsley Davis argued long ago that prostitution is functional for society in many different ways, which explains why it still persists. However useful his analysis, and some of his discussion is a little quaint now, the feminist paradigm on prostitution is entirely different. Feminists have protested against the criminalization and exploitation of young women, the failure of society to provide other alternatives, the violence, and the commodification of women (Shaver, 1985, 1993).

The notion of crime or deviance as "functional" still annoys those who confuse the meaning of the term with "good" (as in the phrase "This car is still functional"). Functional does *not* mean good (or bad) necessarily, but merely "does something" or "acts." So the functions of the Lépine massacre, for example, include, after horrifying everyone, a heightened attention to male violence towards women, and to male attitudes to women, the formation of the National Panel on Violence Against Women, the passage of stiffer gun control legislation, tougher sentences against violent males, improved security at universities, changes in the city of Montreal's police department quick response policy, the reinforcement of feminist ideology on male violence, and so on. The massacre not only reinforced basic Canadian values it also resulted in social change: action.

A popular hypothesis about crime is the *frustration-aggression theory*. The theory, simply put, states that frustration produces aggression, and that aggression is caused by frustration. The frustration may be with oneself or with the environment (e.g., loss of a job); and the level of frustration determines the level of aggression. The story that illustrates the theory is the old chestnut: the boss reprimands the male worker, the worker swears at his wife, the wife slaps the child, and the child kicks the cat. I don't know what the cat does, goes after the mice perhaps. No crimes have been committed but it is an aggressive sequence, and we have all probably been at the receiving end of someone else's frustration, as well as at the giving end. At this level the theory seems persuasive. The theory was first articulated by John Dollard (1939) and has a certain commonsense appeal as an explanation of some types of crime, especially physical crimes, and his beliefs that crime rates rise during recessions (which are presumably frustrating experiences) and vary by class — the more frustrated working class having higher crime rates.

Yet this equation is a bit too simplistic surely. Aggression is a complex phenomenon. Murder may be committed in any number of emotional states: in anger or fear or coolly; and for many reasons: greed or passion, for money, to protect a good name, or for revenge; and under many circumstances: when robbing a bank, in a drunken brawl in a bar, or in a family argument. To describe this range of causality as "frustration" makes the word meaningless: it becomes synonymous with "cause"; it does not help us to understand homicide. Furthermore, frustration does not always, or even usually, end in aggression. Students may be frustrated by bad grades; but one person will jog around the track, another will get drunk, a third will complain to friends and a fourth may resolve to work harder; but few (hopefully none at all!) will punch their teachers' noses. Also in an earlier work, on race relations in the south, Dollard (1937) had clarified fairly precisely how Blacks generally contained or deflected their aggression against oppressive and exploitative Whites. Nonetheless Dollard's theory was useful, because it moved from thinking about "types of people" (Lombroso, Freud and psychological theories generally) to thinking about "types of situations," and it was an early contribution to the analysis of social pressures and stress.

At about the same time as Dollard was developing the frustration-aggression theory, Edwin H. Sutherland, a criminologist in Chicago, wrote *The Professional Thief* (1937) which reported the life of a man who had lived as a thief for 20 years. Apart from being a fascinating documentary on a way of life, Sutherland made two important points: that theft is, at this level, a profession, like medicine, law, or sociology. "The profession of theft is more than isolated acts of theft frequently and skillfully performed. It is a group-way of life and a social institution. It has techniques, codes, status, traditions and organization." Also, that "tutelage by professional thieves and recognition as a professional thief are essential and universal elements in the definition, genesis, and continued behavior of the professional thief . . . Tutelage by professional thieves is essential for the development of the skills, attitudes, codes and connections which are required in professional theft" (1937: ix-x). The profession of theft, in the career of this former pimp, then pickpocket, shoplifter and confidence man, is not genetically determined (as Lombroso and others insisted) nor due to psychological maladjustment (as Freud had implied) nor due to situational factors (Dollard). Criminal behaviour is learned, Sutherland argued, just like any other professional behaviour.

Durkheim's theory of anomie with respect to suicide was later developed by Robert Merton (1957) into a theory of deviance (see Table 6-5). He argued that crime and other forms of deviance are generated whenever there is a discrepancy between the culturally accepted goals of society (success, wealth, power in the case of North America) and the accepted, legal means to achieve these goals (i.e., hard work, a good job, education, etc.). When people perceive their blocked mobility and that the norms do not "work" (i.e., do not achieve the desired rewards), then we have a "breakdown of the social norms which is described as anomie" (1957: vii). Consequently, people begin to create their own norms and values, both as to goals and means.

Four types of response to this anomie are possible, according to Merton. The conformists have no problem: they accept the goals and the means, even if the latter do not work; they are the bedrock of the society, or the glue that keeps it

Table 6-5   Merton's Typology of Deviance

Modes of Adapting	Accepts Culturally Approved Goals	Accepts Culturally Approved Means
Conformist	Yes	Yes
Innovator	Yes	No
Ritualist	No	Yes
Retreatist	No	No
Rebel	No (creates new goals)	No (creates new means)

Source: Adapted from Merton, 1957:140

together. Innovators accept the success-goals but recognize that they cannot be achieved without innovation, often criminal. Merton cites Sutherland's work on white collar criminals and the robber barons as examples; also the famous self-report survey of 1,700 predominantly middle-class New Yorkers, 99% of whom admitted to committing various criminal offenses as adults (after age 16), averaging 18 for men and 11 for women. Crime is normal, not pathological, in this view. Merton insists that cultures and social structures *generate* crime; thus: "a cardinal American virtue, 'ambition,' promotes a cardinal American vice, 'deviant behavior.' " And, in more radical voice: "when poverty and associated disadvantages . . . are linked with a cultural emphasis on pecuniary success as a dominant goal, high rates of criminal behavior are the normal outcome" (1957: 146-47).

The ritualist may forget, neglect, or tone down the success goals, but follow the norms compulsively. The bureaucrat is Merton's classic example. But the best examples are the ritualists who will not give you a job unless you have "Canadian experience" — but you can't get this unique Canadian experience until you get a job. Such ritualism may generate an appropriate innovation: you lie. My favourite bureaucratic example is the hospital receptionist: after having tried to walk through a glass door, quite successfully, I sat dripping blood on the floor as she asked me my name, my address, my mother's maiden name, etc. I thought this could have been done later; but I was wrong. Mother's maiden name first, stitches later.

The retreatists are "*in* the society but not *of* it." These include: "psychotics, pariahs, outcasts, vagrants, vagabonds, tramps, chronic drunkards and drug addicts." They have rejected the goals and the means, and escaped from the rat race (1957: 153). Suicide is presumably the last action of many retreatists.

The rebels and revolutionaries include not only the obvious leaders, Louis Riel, Papineau and Poundmaker, and more recently the FLQ and the Mohawk warriors, as well as Lenin, Mao, Washington, and Castro — but also such "lesser" types of symbolic revolt, exemplified by the Hippies, Skins, Punks, and Rastafarians. They reject establishment goals and norms, but create their own.

Merton's theory is particularly useful in integrating different types of deviance, including crime, into one framework; and also for showing how society *creates* crime and deviance. However, this theory does not explain which type of deviance people choose. (Sutherland's theory of learning helps.) Furthermore, conceivably one could adopt more than one type of deviance at once: there probably is the occasional alcoholic priest or gambling revolutionary. Furthermore, goals and means can be difficult to differentiate: the B.A. may be a goal which is also a means to a job or to a higher degree which in turn is a means to other goals. It seems unlikely that retreatists have no goals — certainly the Hippies had goals; but then this blurs the distinction between retreatists and rebels. And surely people may reject some goals, and some means, but not all. Perhaps one could be a bit of all of these people in different roles.

Labelling theory

Labelling theory throws a somewhat different light on deviance from anomie theory. Howard Becker (1963), Edwin Schur (1965), and others have pointed out that the deviant *act* does not make a deviant; we have all committed deviant acts of one sort or another. What creates a deviant is *labelling* someone as a deviant; in some circumstances, one may label oneself. Take the case of criminal activity: there is first the commission of the act; then the person must be caught, charged, prosecuted, convicted, and sentenced. In the sentencing, the individual is officially and publicly labelled a deviant; if the person is not caught, not charged, not prosecuted, or not convicted, he or she is not labelled a deviant. Once the people are *labelled* criminals, however, they are criminals to society, to friends, relatives, and peers; and ultimately, probably to themselves, particularly if they are sentenced to prison with other criminals. Labelling by others is followed by labelling by the self. The self image of those labelled is changed. A new person is created. The principal difference between committing a criminal act and being a criminal, therefore, in this view, is the labelling process, and how far along the line it goes.

Some deviants may label themselves first, and then be labelled by society. Alcoholics may "come out of the closet" and declare themselves. In either case the objective and subjective labelling processes reinforce each other, and both tend to be reinforced by sub-cultural norms and a peer group of like-minded deviants.

It may seem a bit simple to state that labelling creates the deviant; after all, the person had to act first and be the sort of person that is labelled accurately. The significance of the theory, however, is the clarification of the distinction between committing a deviant act and being labelled a deviant; and, in the case of negative labelling (for example, being labelled as a criminal), the theory manifests the significance of our self image: we become who we are told we are, whether we want to be that or not.

Victim Theory

We started with the common notion of the criminal as evil, a villain, perhaps possessed by the devil (as in religious theories), or as somehow less than human: as an animal (Lombroso) or as childlike (Freud); and we have considered a series of complex biological, psychological, and sociological theories of crimes tending to blame either the criminal or the society (or both) for crime, in various ways. An exhaustive longitudinal study of 411 males from a working-class community in London seems to capsize these views. Donald West and his team tracked these men from aged eight to 25 and identified five key factors in determining the probability of juvenile delinquency: (1) poverty, (2) a large family (four or more siblings), (3) inept, incompetent, or abusive parents, (4) low intelligence and (5) a parent with a criminal record — and this last was the most important (1982: 29-30, 44).

The point is, that no one *chooses* to be born poor and stupid in a large family, with inept and perhaps criminal parents! These circumstances give five strokes against the poor kids as soon as they emerge into the world. West does not describe these delinquents and later, often, criminals as "victims" — this is my term; but they do seem to be victims of dysfunctional and criminogenic families and of poverty, particularly since these "adversities" are often linked, and come in constellations. Nonetheless, the predictive value of these factors is limited; most delinquents did not fit the profile, and most who did fit the profile did not become delinquents. Indeed the best predictor of all, it seems, was the verdict of teachers *and* class-mates at the age of eight, defining the most "troublesome" boys in the class (1982: 30-32). To describe the persistent "victimizers" as "victims" is no doubt polemical, but also surely useful in drawing attention to, for instance, what Leyton has called "the triple delinquencies" for so many young offenders (see also Farrington, 1987).

A particularly interesting feature of West's research is his effort to slaughter the dragon of paradigms with data and evidence. He notes that ideologies are hardening, "with conservatives calling for swift and more punitive reprisals against disruptive elements, and radicals demanding — in the name of civil liberty — that do-gooders should lay off the children and pay attention instead to the oppressive nature of capitalism. Meantime liberals are fighting a losing battle to preserve the notion of helping delinquents to cope better with the society in which they live" (1982: 2). I would peg West as a liberal, and he offers several interesting and constructive suggestions in his various books based on the evidence of the very many variables, personal, familial, and environmental, that influence delinquency and later criminality.

The good news in West's research was that most of the young lads were convicted only once or twice, the offences were usually trivial, more of a nuisance than anything else, and they usually settled down after 18; also, only seven of the adults were still practicing crime at 25 (1982: 15-19). The bad news is that love is not enough, that the "typical criminogenic family is beset by chronic problems," with neighbours, schools, the police, housing authorities, and social workers as well as in the immediate family, and that a very small minority of *families* commit a disproportionate number of crimes. Given early deprivation, therapeutic intervention must be multifaceted to be effective; there is no single, simple theory of crime, any more than there is of disease (1982: 119). Finally, West criticizes the (relatively conservative) judicial and penal authorities, who are so convinced that "nothing works" that they punish all and sundry, with very little success and no attempt at comparing the results of different types of sentences; he also criticizes sociology "which has done so much to expose the pressures that provoke offending, [but] has become associated with opposition to therapists who try to help individual offenders to modify their ineffectual and unprofitable ways of reacting" (1982: 141-42). This criticism applies particularly to critical criminology, below.

Critical Criminology

Mainstream criminologists tend to accept the legitimacy of the status quo and the criminal justice systems: this is the essence of the conservative or consensus paradigm. Adherents of critical, or new, criminology emphatically do not. Dismissing the "old" conservative and liberal criminologies as "voyeurism" and "correctionalism," the new radical criminologists have stated their principles clearly: "radical social science must neither simply describe nor prescribe (in the passive, liberal sense); it must engage in theory and research as praxis"; and "we have argued for a criminology which is normatively committed to the abolition of inequalities in wealth and power" (Taylor, Walton, Young, 1975: 24, 44). This involves "exposé criminology": exposing the venal criminality of the ruling class, and their double standards with respect to minorities and the poor. It also requires oppression analysis: clarifying the degree to which the legal system oppresses the majority. Using their examples, with data from the early seventies, they note that 96% of the crimes reported by police in the UK were crimes against property; in the US the figure was 88% (the US has a higher violent crime rate). The new criminologists argue that "in an inequitable society, crime is about property (and . . . even the various 'offences against the person' are often committed in the pursuit of property)." Such crime is surely "normal," and perhaps even legitimate: a form of self-help.

Once caught, the criminals may go to jail. In the UK one study showed that 15-20% of boys from working-class homes had been convicted of at least one offence by the age of 17, compared to 10% of boys from white collar families and only 5% of boys from professional and salaried families. In the US crafts-men, operatives, service workers and labourers constituted 59% of the popula-tion, but 87.4% of the prison population, and they were disproportionately Blacks and Latinos. Yet, as a former US Attorney General remarked: "reported bank embezzlements cost ten times more than bank robberies every year." The official statistics do not *demonstrate* the crime problem, in this view, they *camouflage* it! (Taylor, Walton and Young, 1975: 28-36).

Given the injustice of the "justice" system, particularly against the incarcer-ated poor and minorities, the central questions are, how do the authorities become authorities? and how do they translate legitimacy into legality? (Taylor, Walton and Young, 1975: 46). The "crime problem" is essentially redefined; the problem is not why do people — men — commit so many crimes? The problem is why do so many people *not* commit *more* crimes? The problem is a theory of *conformity*, not of crime. Why do the poor play by the rules in a society in which the *wealthy* lay down the law, literally, invent the rules, and change them as they will: not only the Criminal Code but also the taxation system, the welfare system, the penal system, the political system, and of course the legal system.

Laureen Snider has noted the prevailing consensus/conservative orientation of Canadian criminology, accepting of the status quo and, essentially, uncritical of the legal, judicial, and penal systems. Critical criminology, however, like con-flict theory in general, focusses on power, inequality, exploitation and repres-sion: the punitive trend in Canada, the emphasis on "traditional" crime (robbery, B. and E., etc.), "while the more widespread financial losses, personal injury, and deaths caused by crimes against health and safety laws in the work-place, crimes against the environment, and corporate crimes of all sorts, are minimized or ignored" (1991: 149).

The same or similar issues had been raised by Marx and Engels some 150 years ago, as we have seen, and the new criminologists have returned to these roots; but since their emergence in the seventies critical criminology has advanced further. A crime, in the radical view, cannot be defined by the State as an offense against the State, for many of these definitions are self-serving; and many of the most heinous crimes are committed *by* the State, from the Armenian genocide by the Turks, the Ukrainian genocide by Stalin, the Jewish holocaust by the Nazis, apartheid in South Africa and, more recently, ethnic cleansing by the Serbs. A crime is an offense against *human rights*, as declared by the United Nations.

Dr. Clyde Snow, a forensic anthropologist, who has investigated the skeletal remains of victims of state policy in Argentina, Bolivia, Chile, Guatemala and elsewhere, comments:

The great mass murderers of our time have accounted for no more than a few hundred victims. In contrast, states that have chosen to murder their own citizens can usually count their victims by the carload . . . (in Amnesty International, 1992: 11)

By the millions, would be more accurate. Amnesty International has systematically documented the torture, rape, abduction and murder of indigenous peoples, religious leaders, journalists, community workers, and children, not only in Argentina, Brazil, Bolivia, and Chile, but also in Colombia, Mexico, Guatemala, and Peru in the 1980s and in some cases the 1990s. Various incidents in the United States and Canada are also discussed (cf. Chapter 8) — and this report is just on the Americas. The same applies to Bosnia, Haïti, Sri Lanka, and China and elsewhere.

The Canadian state, in this theoretical framework, has been, and still is, criminal. State crimes include the expropriation of Native lands, the enslavement of Blacks and Indians, the deportation of the Acadians, the extermination of the Beothuks, the wars against the Indians and Métis on the Prairies, the denial of Jewish and Chinese immigration into Canada, and the deportation of the Japanese in the forties. Homelessness in Canada is a crime. Poverty is a crime. Racism is a crime. The situation of the First Nations is a crime. Pollution is a crime; yet no senior executive of any major corporation has ever gone to jail for the massive pollution of air, land, and sea; nor has the mayor and city council of any city which dumps raw sewage, e.g., Halifax, Montreal, and Victoria. And Clyde Wells, Premier of Newfoundland, described the overfishing by fishermen from Spain and Portugal as an environmental disaster; their defiance of international rulings, he said, is "international piracy" and "an offense against humanity" (*Globe and Mail* 21.11.91).

Is it possible, therefore, to refer to the "shared values" in Canada? And to the peace, civility, order, tolerance, caring, "freedom, dignity and respect, equality and fair treatment" in Canada?

CONCLUSION

There is an old story about two Samaritans walking down the road one day when they found someone lying by the side of the road, badly beaten, blood everywhere, perhaps dying. The conservative said to the other: "Whoever did this should be shot." The liberal replied: "Whoever did this needs our help."

Conservatives in general see themselves as crime-fighters and tough on crime, whereas liberals and radicals focus more on the "root causes" of crime: poverty, unemployment, family abuse, etc. Feminists, from conservative to radical, are more concerned with three issues: women as the victims, particularly of male violence, women as criminals, the double standards and systemic inequities

Table 6-6 Perspectives on Crime

Variable	Conservative	Radical	Feminist
The criminal	Predator, parasite, villain, evil, "devil."	Victim of, and exploited by, society, and *created* by society	Women offenders as, often, different from male offenders.
Rationale for crime	Personal choice. Crime is *individual.* Also it is "human nature."	Crime is often a consequence of an unequal/capitalist society and/or a dysfunctional family. Crime is *social.*	Crime and punishment are *gendered.* Note systemic victimization of women by judicial and penal systems, and men.
Solutions	Prison, execution, etc. Punishment as retribution and deterrence.	Reform or revolution and social equality: rehabilitation for criminal, and prevention as the goal of policy.	Gender equality; and social transformation (radical feminism).
Sociological concerns	How to explain crime, and different types of crime, and to reduce the crime rates. Crime is deviant.	How to explain the *lack of* crime, the *low* crime rate. In this view, the whole *society* is a crime. Focus on power and inequality: The oppression of the poor and minorities; attention to white collar and state crimes.	Different explanations for male and female offending; gender bias in law and punishment; women's special needs; reduction of male violence against women.

of the predominantly male legal and judicial systems, and especially the different needs and experiences of women and "the importance of a woman-centred approach to justice" (Shaw, 1993: 52; Adelberg and Currie, 1993). Some of the variations in balance and emphasis are presented schematically in Table 6-6, with the reminder that the paradigms are indicative rather than definitive. The three paradigms can be stereotyped as the "eye-for-an-eyers," the "wild-eyed radicals," and the "all men are jerks" syndromes, while the liberals may be dismissed as "bleeding hearts"; but such libelous labels are usually only invectives, and do not address the issues.

There is little consensus on the meaning and nature of crime, nor on what exactly the "crime problem" is. Some believe, in the tradition of Machiavelli and Hobbes, that people are basically evil, or that many people are; this tends to result in a conservative criminology, with demands for tough laws, capital punishment, and deterrent sentences. Retribution is the goal, not rehabilitation. The pendulum is swinging now to collective rights and victims' rights, as against the previous liberal emphasis on individual (i.e., criminal's) rights. And as the crime rate rises (or is believed to rise), so the conservative ideology toughens.

Others believe that people are fundamentally good, in the tradition of Rousseau, but corrupted by society, by child abuse, faulty socialization, the wrong friends, a drug habit, poverty, etc. The solutions are societal reform and the rehabilitation of the individual criminal. Liberals argue that a more equal society, with more opportunities for all, will alleviate the crime rate — there will be less *need* for crime.

Radicals argue that the whole *system* is corrupt, designed to protect the wealth of the top 10 or 20% of the population — who own 51 and 70% of the national wealth, respectively — from the other 80 or 90% of the population. The rest can go to prison, or starve in relative poverty. In this view crime has nothing to do with a good or bad human nature, but mostly with people trying to survive, with or without violence. The real "crime" is the unequal structure of the society in the first place, which penalizes the working poor, the unemployed, ethnic minorities, women, and then doubly penalizes them for trying to remedy their desperate situations.

In the radical view, reality is upside down: the oppressors are the real criminals, not the victims. The supposed bright side of Canada is in fact the shadow side.

It is axiomatic that criminals must be punished; but what constitutes crime, why crimes should be punished, and how — these are all more contested questions. Durkheim has suggested that the true function of punishment is "to maintain social cohesion intact" (1964: 108). In the radical paradigm this merely means to preserve the old, inequitable, status quo.

The three principal purposes or functions of punishment are retribution, deterrence, and rehabilitation. They may or may not be mutually exclusive, but theorists generally tend to argue for the priority of one, or more, over the other(s). Liberals tend to believe that the main goal is rehabilitation, while conservatives favour the "get tough on crime" policy, deterrence, and retribution, with capital punishment as a last resort. Not much chance of rehabilitation after that!

Retribution is conceptually based on the ancient mathematics of Mosaic law: "The punishment is to be a life for a life, an eye for an eye, a tooth for a tooth, a hand for a hand, and a foot for a foot" (Deuteronomy 19: 21). This law is still practised in Muslim countries.[2] The notion that the criminal should somehow pay back, expiate the offence, and redress the balance is fundamental to most theories of punishment.

Deterrence theory argues that sufficient punishment must, or does, deter the criminal from doing the illegal act again, and also other criminals. Retribution may work as a deterrent in Muslim countries, where the retributory punishment is brief but physically painful, as well as incapacitating — and the crime rate is low; but such policies would probably not be tolerated here, nor does anyone demand them. Prison does not seem to work as a deterrent, however, nor does the threat of capital punishment. Indeed the recidivism rate in Canadian prisons is high. One study of 14,500 male offenders in correctional facilities (the new term for prisons, it seems) found that 42% of the new male inmates in 1992 were repeat offenders, compared to only 22% of the female inmates. Furthermore a solid 14% of men had served time three or more times, compared to only 5% of the women (Solicitor General, 1994: 29). You might recall James Wilson's recommendations for incorrigible repeat offenders here; but the average cost of incarceration is $47,760 per person per year, and on any given day in 1992 almost 32,000 adults (not including youth) were locked up in federal or provincial facilities (Solicitor General, 1994: 49, 2). Prison is not very effective, and rather expensive. Opponents of imprisonment (except for violent offenders and incorrigibles) argue that prisons are merely schools, and very expensive ones at that, for more serious crime. In this view they are often a waste of taxpayers' money, and also effectively an investment in crime-education for criminals!

Liberals tend to argue that the prime purpose of prisons should be to rehabilitate criminals. Incarceration is pointless, in this view, unless prisoners are taught new marketable skills and given the opportunity to upgrade their educational qualifications so that, when they are released, they can earn a new living and turn their lives around. But if Canadians cannot provide this for free citizens outside prison, how can they do so for alleged villains (or victims) inside? and why should they do so? Isn't this throwing good money after bad? Of course not, liberals reply, it's an investment . . . and so on.

Canada has the second highest incarceration rate among the G7 countries, after the USA. Incarceration policies vary considerably from country to country, but rates are very high in the US, at more than 330 prisoners per 100,000 population, compared to Hungary (146), Canada (130), UK (92), France (84), Italy (56), Sweden (55), and Turkey (44) (Solicitor General, 1994: 4). US rates are therefore more than double Canada's, but Canada's are more than double Italy's and more than triple Turkey's.

What to do? Mosaic retribution is not acceptable. Deterrence does not work. Rehabilitation has not seriously been tried, and would be very expensive.

The solutions offered by the main political parties during the 1993 federal election campaign were basically very similar, and emphasized a "get tough on crime" policy. Specific recommendations included tougher legislation on gun control and crimes against women, toughening up the Young Offenders Act, stricter parole standards (Reform), and a ban on political appointments to the National Parole Board (i.e., on pork barrel patronage, to call a plum a pig). The N.D.P. was the only party to recommend prevention programs (*The Globe and Mail* 2.10.93).

Many researchers have noted that crime is not equally distributed throughout the population. Some individuals are far more careless and destructive of the rights and liberties of the rest of society than are others, and the few commit a disproportionate number of crimes, as we discussed earlier. Given this uneven and unequal distribution the solution seems obvious: to isolate the few multiple and repeat offenders and to put them away, for longer and longer periods with each successive offense. In this view, advocated particularly by James Q. Wilson (1979; Wilson and Herrnstein, 1985), the purpose of punishment is not retribution, nor deterrence, nor rehabilitation, but the safety and peace of the general public. This penal view is finding increasing favour in the United States. Congress passed the so-called "Three strikes and you're out" bill in 1994, requiring mandatory life imprisonment for three-time federal violent offenders. California has passed similar legislation. And the Reform Party adopted a similar policy in its platform at its annual convention in 1994 (*The Globe and Mail* 15.10.94).

Many commentators have suggested that the balance between individual rights and collective rights has swung so far in favour of the individual that convictions are sometimes absurdly difficult to gain. Suspects are released on technicalities; and convicted criminals launch appeal after appeal.

About 70% of Canadians favour capital punishment. About 30% do not. Opponents may be opposed to the taking of life under any circumstances whatsoever; some feel that the only difference between the innocent and the guilty is often, not always, the lack of sufficient money to hire top lawyers; some fear a miscarriage of justice as in the Marshall, Milgaard, and Morin cases; others just think it is barbaric for the state to execute anyone. The issue can provoke acrimonious debate. On the other side, advocates argue the equity of Mosaic law: a fair balance between crime and punishment; others think that multiple and repeat violent offenders could just be put to sleep, peacefully, with friends and family present to say goodbye, and the benefit of clergy if required — with none of the awful trauma of the electric chair in the States, or stonings to death elsewhere — just a humane gesture recognizing a sad reality. What do you think?

Crime, punishment and justice are evidently highly complex problems, with no easy solutions. Nor will criminals and crime go away, totally, for as we discussed in the beginning of this chapter, criminals are us.

ENDNOTES

1. The most useful official sources for further research are the Canadian Crime Statistics, Statistics Canada, Cat. 85-205; *Juristat*, published several times a month by the Canadian Centre for Justice Statistics, Statistics Canada, Cat. 85-002; and *Canadian Social Trends*, a quarterly published by Statistics Canada, Cat. 11-002. The homicide statistics are published occasionally in detail by Statistics Canada, Cat. 85-003, and 85-210. See also several books for more depth and detail: Hagan, 1991; Silverman, Teevan and Sacco, 1991; Jackson and Griffiths, 1991; Adelberg and Currie, 1993; Gomme, 1993.

2. The Christian ethic capsized this Mosaic law. Christ's teaching perhaps applied more to interpersonal relations than to state policy, however (cf. Matthew 5: 38-45); and capital punishment, a life for a life, is still practised in many nominally Christian countries.

SUICIDE

Suicide is surely a major social problem in Canada. 3,709 people committed suicide in 1992, giving a rate of 13.3 per 100,000 (Table 7-1). Many, many more attempted suicide. It is the fourth leading cause of death in Canada between the ages of 15 and 69: after cancer (36%), cardiovascular disease (30%), accidents (10%), comes suicide (5%); but it is the *second* leading cause of death for young males (15-34) and females (15-29), after accidents. Suicide accounts for about 2% of all deaths annually, up from 0.5% in 1921 (Strachan *et al*, 1990; Beneteau, 1988). We are perhaps used to thinking of homicide as a far more serious problem than suicide: but there were "only" 630 homicides in Canada in 1993, one-sixth the total number of suicides.

The suicide rate has tripled in Canada in the last 70 years, as Table 7-1 indicates; but the increase has not been steady. The rate jumped 74% from 5.7 per 100,000 in 1921 to 9.9 per 100,000 in 1930, at the peak of the Depression, then plummeted down to 6.4 per 100,000 by the end of the war in 1945. Since then it has more than doubled. *Social* factors like depression and war therefore affect suicide rates and, therefore, the personal decisions of individuals. Short of another major war, we can expect the suicide rate to keep climbing, and perhaps to accelerate if the current attempts to legitimate assisted suicide and euthanasia are successful.

Without wishing to be unduly alarmist or pessimistic therefore the future looks increasingly suicidal. What can be done? for ourselves and for other people . . . which in this global village is surely the same thing.

Canada is intermediate in its suicide rate when compared with other countries, as we can see in Table 7-2. The UN publishes this data annually, but not for all countries: data on African nations for instance are not available. The suicide rates for Hungary, Finland and Latvia are more than double those of Canada; while in other countries the suicide rates are half those of Canada: Barbados, Colombia, Greece, Kuwait, Mexico. It may be worth speculating on

Table 7-1   The Suicide Rate in Canada, 1921-1991(per 100,000)

1921	5.7
1925	6.9
1930	9.9
1935	8.4
1940	8.4
1945	6.4
1950	7.8
1955	7.0
1960	7.6
1965	8.8
1970	11.3
1975	12.3
1980	14.0
1985	12.9
1992	13.5

Source: Statistics Canada, 1972. *Suicide Mortality 1950-1968*. Cat. No. 84-528. Health and Welfare, 1987. *Suicide in Canada*. Cat. H39-107, p. 82. Statistics Canada, 1994. *Mortality 1991*. Cat. 84-209; *Causes of Death 1992*. Cat. No. 84-208.

the sorts of variables that cause the suicide rate to range so widely from 0.9 per 100,000 in Kuwait to 38.6 in Hungary: a factor of 43.

The national homicide rates are also included in the same table so that readers may evaluate for themselves the relation between the two, if any. Some have argued in the past that suicide and homicide rates are inversely related: that violence against the self and violence against the other are mutually exclusive, so to speak. Others believe that violence is violence, and that both rates tend to be high or low, and to fluctuate together, up and down. From the data presented here, however, I think we can see that the relationship is very complex. Both Kuwait and Greece, for instance, have low suicide and homicide rates. But Colombia has a very high homicide rate, presumably due to the drug wars, and a very low suicide rate; Mexico is similar. And although Hungary, Finland and Latvia have high suicide rates, the first two countries have low homicide rates, while Latvia is high. Almost everywhere the suicide rates are higher than the homicide rates, except in Colombia, Mexico and Barbados; but both rates are close in the USA. So it hard to tell whether the variables that influence suicide rates are the same as, or different from, those that affect homicide rates. We may not have all the answers, but no doubt we have some clues and theories, some of which will be debated here.

So many people killing themselves: Marilyn Monroe, Ernest Hemingway, Sylvia Plath, Kurt Cobain, Marc Lépine and further back in time Mark Anthony

Table 7-2 Suicide and Homicide Rates, Canada and Selected Countries by latest year available

		Suicide Rate (per 100,000)	Homicide Rate (per 100,000)
Australia	1988	13.3	2.4
Barbados	1988	4.7	7.1
Belgium	1987	22.7	1.6
Canada	1990	12.7	2.1
Colombia	1990	2.7	74.4
England and Wales	1991	7.6	0.5
Finland	1991	29.8	3.1
France	1990	20.1	1.1
Greece	1990	3.5	1.1
Hungary	1991	38.6	4.0
Ireland	1990	9.5	0.6
Israel	1989	7.8	2.4
Italy	1989	7.5	2.2
Japan	1991	16.0	0.6
Kuwait	1987	0.9	0.5
Latvia	1990	26.0	9.2
Mexico	1990	2.2	16.8
Netherlands	1990	9.7	0.9
Scotland	1991	10.3	1.5
Sweden	1990	17.2	1.3
Trinidad and Tobago	1989	14.3	8.1
USA	1989	12.2	9.1

Source: UN 1994 Demographic Yearbook: 688-709.

and Cleopatra, Socrates, Hitler. The deaths of some of these people have ripple effects on the lives of others. Kurt Cobain's suicide for instance was followed by several copycat suicides in the United States and Canada. A case in point is the three teens, one from Labrador, two from Quebec, who apparently made a suicide pact and then drove across Canada, driving into a storage locker near Vancouver and dying from carbon monoxide poisoning. One wrote: "When Kurt Cobain died, I died" (*Maclean's* 31.10.94).

Recent mass suicides include Jonestown in Guyana and in 1994, the mass murder-suicides of 53 members of the Order of the Solar Temple in Quebec and Switzerland. And recently we have seen the emergence of suicide bombers in Israel, Lebanon, India and elsewhere. Why? How can people take their own lives? Is there any theory or explanation? Obviously for all sorts of different reasons, as one might infer from the examples above. The most commonly-cited explanations, however, pain, depression, stress, brain-chemistry, whatever their validity, are so general, and so difficult to operationalize as concepts, that they are almost useless. Furthermore they only push the question further back: everyone feels stress and pain — so the question is, why do most people deal with it, and some people kill themselves?

Suicide is intensely personal and a very emotional topic for many people. It is also highly taboo. We do not discuss it much. Sports, cars, prices, the weather, the government — they all get discussed ad nauseam; but we hardly ever say "Do you ever feel like killing yourself?" Since it is so taboo, we will discuss it. Have you ever attempted suicide? How many people do you know who have committed suicide? How many who have attempted suicide? Why? How do you feel about it all? What did you learn from their, and your, experiences? Finally, do you believe that suicide is, in general, right or wrong? Why? Is it ever morally permissible do you think? Here we move into the domain of ethics. To investigate suicide it is necessary to break the taboo — which is surely a large part of the problem — and these are the sort of questions we should probably raise with ourselves and our friends: let some light in.

The decision to take one's own life is not only likely to be agonizing, it is also perhaps the most individual and personal decision that one can take. Nonetheless, even the most personal decisions are also *social* decisions. We are all social products, and whether we choose to kill ourselves or not, how we choose to do so, how many of us choose it, what we hope to achieve by suicide, even the time of day and the season of the year — all these seemingly personal decisions reflect our culture's norms and values.

This chapter is divided into three parts. First, suicide, in which we examine the data on suicide in Canada, evaluate its accuracy, and consider some of the social factors determining differential rates. Second we assess some of the theories of suicide and attempted suicide, beginning with Durkheim. We conclude by reviewing some of the recommendations to ameliorate this growing social problem, including the theory that suicide is a basic human right, and *not* a social problem.

SUICIDE IN CANADA[1]

Who commits suicide in Canada? Why? Where and how? A useful source for answers to some of these questions is the Report of the National Task Force on Suicide in Canada entitled *Suicide in Canada*, published in 1987. The Task Force identified seven high-risk populations:

- the mentally disordered
- alcoholics
- young people

- the elderly
- native peoples
- persons in custody
- the bereaved

We will consider these groups, and update the statistics at the same time where possible, but using somewhat different categories.

Gender

Suicide is principally a male problem — to the extent that it is a problem. Of the 3,709 people who committed suicide in 1992, 2,923 were male. Men kill themselves four times more often than women: 80% of all suicides are committed by males. Why? There are probably many reasons. Durkheim suggests that men are less well integrated into society, particularly single males. And men are more physically violent, according to the crime statistics, and they are even coached in violence in such sports as football, hockey and rugby. Suicide is such violence turned inward, so the Freudians have suggested. Also men use firearms more often than women: a more effective and direct method than drugs, which allow a longer time for a change of heart and also for discovery. Again, a higher proportion of men are alcoholics. The theories that try to account for these facts are many and various.

On the other hand, a far higher proportion of women *attempt* suicide: those who attempt suicide may outnumber those who successfully commit suicide by a factor of ten to one. Why do they attempt suicide? and why do they fail? They fail, it is argued, because the methods used by women are often less violent and less effective. Also the attempts are often a cry for help: an effective if dangerous mode of communication. As to why they attempt suicide, the reasons are probably similar to those for men and the theories are discussed below. Some have argued that women are more prone to depression than men, perhaps due to their double-load in our society, and/or to patriarchal oppression. Either way suicide seems in some ways—as studies of frequency, method, age, intent, and even cause indicate—to be a rather different phenomenon for women and men, even though there is no doubt also an overlap.

Suicide is not only a gendered issue, it is also highly political and the site of numerous battles between feminists and the new masculinists. Feminists point to the higher rates of *attempted* suicide as indicative of higher levels of women's stress and pain and victimization by an oppressive society. Masculinists point to the higher rates of *completed* suicide as indicative of higher levels of *men's* stress and pain. Warren Farrell, for instance, refers to men as "the suicide sex" (1993: 164); and David Thomas asks: "Aren't all these suicides telling us something about men's lives?" (1993: 14).

Age

Table 7-3 indicates that males are at far higher risk of suicide than females at all ages. But the 'worst' age for women, or at least the age when suicide rates peak is between 40 and 44; from then on life seems to get better (or perhaps attitudes to life change) and the suicide rate drops steadily for the rest of their lives. For men on the other hand the twin peaks are in youth and in old age: the highest rates are at 85+, but generally also from 80+, and from 20 to 24 — but they remain high until age 34, when they begin to drop. They rise again in the early fifties then fall, rise, fall, and skyrocket to twenty times the rate for women.

Age therefore does affect suicide rates, but not in the same way for each gender. The beginnings and the ends of adult life seem to be hardest for men, and the middle for women, for reasons that one may wish to ponder. But the *reasons* for these suicides are probably quite different in each cohort. The old do not necessarily kill themselves for the same reasons as the young.

Table 7-3   Number of Suicides and Suicide Rate by Age and Sex, Canada 1991

Age	Males		Females	
	Number	Rate(100,000)	Number	Rate (100,000)
5-9	1	0.1	-	-
10-14	19	2.0	9	1.0
15-19	217	23.0	36	4.0
20-24	322	31.7	40	4.1
25-29	351	29.9	85	7.3
30-34	362	30.0	92	7.5
35-39	308	27.7	81	7.1
40-44	277	27.1	87	8.4
45-49	212	26.2	63	7.8
50-54	177	27.1	40	6.1
55-59	144	24.1	44	7.2
60-64	141	25.1	38	6.3
65-69	121	25.1	41	7.2
70-74	84	23.7	31	6.7
75-79	63	25.2	19	5.2
80-84	43	30.8	8	3.4
85+	33	39.6	4	2.0
Total	2875	21.6	718	5.2

Source: Statistics Canada, 1994. *Mortality 1991.* Cat. No. 84-209.

Region

Canadians are not equally suicidal, therefore. The suicide rate varies widely by gender, by age, and also by region. The data are presented in Table 7-4. Overall the suicide rate in Canada in 1991 was 13.3 per 100,000, but rates ranged from a low of 7.1 in Newfoundland to a high of 40.3 in the Northwest Territories. It must be noted that all those who are killing themselves laughing at Newfie jokes are also killing themselves more often.

What factors explain this remarkable range of almost 600% between the highest and lowest rates in Canada? Again obviously there are many, and there have been no multivariate analyses of these rates in Canada; nor would these be the most appropriate methodologies anyway. Suicide is not a statistical problem. Two points can be noted: first, theorists point to the traditionalism and stability of Newfoundland, a Durkheimian-type integration of family, kin, church and work, and community, in contrast to the high anomie of the Territories, which are characterized by high transience and social isolation among many "whites," especially immigrant workers, and the cultural destruction and alienation of the First Nations. Second, the suicide rates correlate closely with crime rates and homicide rates in a tangle of pathology (Health and Welfare, 1987: 33, 35; Beneteau, 1988: 24).

Native Canadians

Native Canadians have the highest suicide rates of any ethnic group in Canada. The data apply only to status Indians and Inuit. The male suicide rate in 1986

Table 7-4   The Suicide Rate in Canada, by Province and Territory, 1991 (per 100,000)

Newfoundland	7.1
Prince Edward Island	16.9
Nova Scotia	12.6
New Brunswick	12.8
Quebec	16.3
Ontario	10.1
Manitoba	12.4
Saskatchewan	12.5
Alberta	18.3
British Columbia	14.4
Yukon	11.1
Northwest Territories	40.3
Canada	13.3

Source: Statistics Canada, 1994. *Mortality 1991*. Cat. No. 84-209.

(latest year available) was 56.3, which was almost 2.5 times the overall male rate in Canada, and the female rate (11.8) was almost double the overall rate for women. Young male Native Canadians are particularly at risk; those between the ages of 15 and 29 have suicide rates of more than 100 per 100,000 (Beneteau, 1988: 24; Health and Welfare, 1987: 33, 35).

The Royal Commission on Aboriginal Peoples has drawn attention to this situation: "aboriginal people have been dying by their own hands much too often and much too long." The Commissioners noted that this problem is tangled up with other problems, poverty, alcohol, drugs, family violence as well as issues of identity and power (*Globe and Mail* 2.2.95). Although the report is not available at the time of writing, it seems apparent that this aboriginal paradigm on suicide involves a radical critique of the entire status quo, and that it will have implications for the analysis of the rising suicide rates in the rest of Canada also.

High Risk Groups

Prisoners in federal and provincial institutions are also at high risk of suicide. In 1986 17 prisoners committed suicide, which represents a suicide rate of 60 per 100,000: about four times the national average (Beneteau, 1988: 24; cf. Health and Welfare, 1987: 35-6).

The Task Force identified those bereaved by the suicides of those whom they loved as particularly vulnerable to suicide themselves, and estimated that 40,000 to 50,000 Canadians are affected in this way every year. Some want to follow their loved ones, and do so; people feel responsible, guilty, angry, depressed, confused, and unbalanced. And people who come from families with prior suicides are nine times more likely to commit suicide themselves (Health and Welfare, 1987: 36-7).

Alcoholics and the mentally ill are also high-risk groups; indeed some argue that alcoholism is itself a form of suicide. But both concepts are very slippery. (For a clear summary of a difficult issue, see the Task Force Report, 1987: 27-30.)

People with AIDS and the HIV virus are also high-risk groups. This population was not studied by the Task Force; but anecdotal evidence and some research suggests that terminally ill individuals are much more likely to kill themselves than the general population, sometimes with the assistance of friends or doctors. Russell Ogden's study of assisted suicide among B.C. AIDS patients suggests that between 10% and 20% of the roughly 200 deaths a year from AIDS are assisted suicides – and many of them were very badly assisted by well-meaning friends (Ogden, 1994). This population of the terminally ill raises the question of decriminalizing assisted suicide and legislating and regulating euthanasia, perhaps along the lines of the practice in the Netherlands.

Every suicide creates ripples throughout the community, and the more famous and well-liked the person, the wider and deeper the waves, among family and friends, colleagues at work and neighbours, admirers and followers. Each suicide raises the threshold of tolerance of the act, anaesthetizes the population, and *normalizes* suicide; so each new generation is born into a more suicidal climate. Perhaps there is a crest at which suicide rates level off; but in some European countries the rate is three times that of Canada.

With this brief sketch of the dimensions and significance of suicide, we can proceed to the questions of *why* people commit suicide. But first we need to evaluate the statistics.

Accuracy of Data

How accurate are all these figures? Probably not very. The statistics underestimate the reality for two main reasons. First, some people try to camouflage their suicides, and no doubt succeed, perhaps to avoid the stigma on their honour, or the shame and guilt which they fear might fall on their family, or because their life insurance policies are in jeopardy. Some suicides may be a sort of sacrifice, for many people are worth more dead than alive — an appalling thought, but one that has inspired murder as well as suicide. So some so-called accidental deaths, by drowning, drug overdoses, single person traffic fatalities or hunting accidents may well be suicide.

Also, unless the victims' intentions are clear, the coroner is bound to give people the benefit of the doubt. Intent may be signified by a note, by the method (hanging, jumping), or by a past history of attempts, or by others' personal testimony in psychological autopsies. The balance of evidence may not be so compelling, however, that there is no room for doubt; and the religious beliefs and sympathies of those concerned may well sway a verdict one way or another. One study of 350 coroners in Ontario found that one-third were reluctant to certify a death as suicide, and 38% would certify the cause of death as "undetermined" even if it were *probably* a suicide (Health and Welfare, 1987: 38-9). This may contribute to some understating of the statistics (25%-33% according to Mann, 1971: 266-70), but such caution probably contributes to a slower rate of growth of suicide by failing to load the family with the factor of nine syndrome.

Parasuicide

The second problem with the data is that they only include the "obvious" methods of killing oneself quickly and deliberately; they do not include conventional patterns of *long-term self-destructive* behaviour. Gun shots can kill. So can smoking, alcohol abuse, reckless driving, and unsafe sex. They just take longer; and death is not the intended consequence of such actions: but it is highly probable. Without wishing to seem to blame the victim (who always, for some reason, remains blameless!) such behaviour can usefully be seen as *parasuicidal*.

We recognize the importance of lifestyle habits in our language: echoing Freud we might say "he's got a death-wish!" or "if she goes on like that, she's going to kill herself" or "slow down! You wanna kill yourself, O.K., but not me!"

What distinguishes parasuicides from suicides is that the parasuicides do not intend to die, consciously at least; what unites them is their high-risk activity, and the greater probability of an early death. The utility of this concept is that it clarifies some of the dimensions of voluntary danger in so many areas of our lives: eating, drinking, driving, sex, work, smoking . . . but also it negates the traditional dichotomy of suicide/not suicide. Suicide can be placed in a continuum ranging from the proverbial healthy lifestyle at one end, through our various parasuicidal predilections — I think most of us are parasuicidal in at least one way! — to successfully accomplished suicides at the other. Parasuicidal tendencies can perhaps be illustrated by the actions of those who get lung cancer after 30 years of smoking, or cirrhosis of the liver after 20 years of heavy drinking, or anorexia after two years of not eating properly, or AIDS after one night of unprotected sex. Of course parasuicides may not die from their self-destructive habits. The chain-smoker may get hit by a truck instead of lung cancer! The classic case, always mentioned, was Sir Winston Churchill, who was overweight, rarely exercised, drank excessively and smoked cigars, and lived to a ripe old age. The Churchill syndrome is often invoked by parasuicides as justification for their self-destructive lifestyles; but (excuse the pontificating) it is probably not wise to use the exception to prove the rule.

The notion of parasuicide is somewhat controversial, labeling as it does some of our more treasured and enjoyable habits as self destructive. Even more controversial, however, is the extension of the concept, in an attenuated state, to include such high-risk hobbies and sports as hang gliding, mountaineering, ice climbing, parachuting, car racing, perhaps scuba diving, and most recently bungee jumping. All have higher death rates than such other hobbies as, for instance, crocheting, or growing tomatoes. These are obviously not parasuicidal to the same degree that smoking is; they are therefore on the non/suicide side of the continuum, just — but the thrill is being so close to death, and (usually) cheating death. Deaths here may well be described as accidental, but they go with the territory. The point is that deliberately courting danger and therefore death may be macho, and may be thrilling, but it is parasuicidal — and many of the 14,000 or so accidental deaths in Canada every year could be avoided. Accidents, in this arithmetical view, are more of a social problem than suicides; plus many impulse suicides seem like accidents, and many accidents seem like suicide.

This theory of parasuicide may also take some of the stigma away from suicide itself as we realize that we are, many of us, *suicidal* (in these unexpected ways) even if we have not killed ourselves and do not intend to — yet we are doing so, by smoking, unsafe sex, drunk driving, food abuse and so on. In sum, our lifestyles can be, and often are, self-destructive, to a greater or lesser degree.

Some researchers, however, now believe that high-risk-taking individuals are more complex than just people with a death wish; the inclination to risk danger may be "hard-wired" into the brain, and is so powerful that it is like an addiction. As one climber phrased it: "What we do for kicks, most people wouldn't do if you held a gun to their heads." Sensation seeking has its downside, of course, not only in accidents but also the search for euphoria in gambling, speeding, sex, and drugs and alcohol (Roberts, 1994). In this view, therefore, the popularly regarded "death wish" is redefined as a wish to live life to the fullest . . . "even if it kills me!"

THEORIES OF SUICIDE

There are several different *types* of theories about suicide, physiological, psychological, and sociological; and various theories within each type. We will consider principally the sociological theories, but need to be aware that there are other options.

First, then, the *physiological* theories. They have the singular merit of being excellent shame and guilt-removers. If suicide is biologically programmed in one way or another, then no one is to blame but the machine itself. And this may well be. There is some evidence that there may be a biochemical component to suicide; suicide has been linked to abnormally low levels of a chemical neurotransmitter called serotonin, associated both with depression and impulsive violence (Coccaro, 1995). Researchers are working on a drug to increase the utilization of serotonin. One researcher commenting on the low levels of suicide in Italy and Ireland has speculated that this may be due in part to their higher consumption of carbohydrates in pasta and potatoes, which research indicates eventually raises serotonin levels (*Discover*, Jan. 1983: 74). Presumably the Catholic faith is also a factor. But if an apple a day keeps the doctor away, then perhaps a potato a day keeps a suicide away! Raw is best, so I'm told.

The mind-body connection is intimate, indeed total; but tracing the exact pathways and mechanisms seems as much a matter of trial and error as of scientific research. Two acquaintances of mine afflicted with clinical depression, and suicidal, were only cured by electric shock therapy. Manic depression can often be controlled by lithium, but that too can become problematic. Recent research has discovered that manic depression does have a genetic base, on the eleventh chromosome. In due course this can be detected early and cured by gene therapy. The flaw is thought to be a facilitator or a predisposing factor to suicide, rather than a determinant and direct cause.

The point of this aside on physiology is that there are biomedical factors in suicide, as well as social; and chemical or genetic "solutions" as well as social. Our professional concern however is with the social, and Durkheim was the pioneer in this research.

Durkheim's Theory of Integration

Durkheim wrote *Suicide* in 1897, apparently moved by the death through suicide of a friend of his in Paris.

Durkheim insisted that there are different *types* of suicide. "Of course, suicide is always the act of a man who prefers death to life. But the causes determining him are not the same in all cases: they are sometimes even mutually opposed" (1897/1966: 277). Suicides are not just individual, psychological phenomena, Durkheim argues, they are also *social* facts, influenced by social forces of which the individuals may be unaware; and what he attempted to do was to describe the "suicidogenic currents" (1966: 325) which sweep people along to their deaths. He began by comparing the suicide rates for various European countries from 1841 up to the 1890s, showing how they rose and fell over time, and varied from one to another, sometimes by a factor of 10. These rates say little about the individuals, but much about society: "These statistical data express the suicidal tendency with which each society is collectively afflicted" (1966: 51). The suicide rate therefore measures the "deep disturbance from which civilized societies are suffering" (1966: 391). Such rates measure the social pathology of a nation.

What are the root causes of this pathology? Durkheim argues that "man is double" (1966: 213). We are social beings and participate in group lives, by which indeed we have been created and formed: economic, political, religious, familial, neighbourhood, peer and so on; thus "in so far as we are solidary with the group and share its life, we are exposed to their influence; but so far as we have a distinct personality of our own we rebel against and try to escape them. . . . Two antagonistic forces confront each other. One, the collective force, tries to take possession of the individual; the other, the individual force, repulses it" (1966: 318-9).

There is therefore a war between society and the individual; yet a war in which there can be no winner, for there is no society without individuals, nor individuals without society. But there can be losers who commit two polar types of suicide: the egoistic suicide, committed out of "excessive individualism," which Durkheim believed to be the most frequent type of suicide in modern society, and the altruistic suicide, more frequent in "primitive" society. Egoistic suicide is committed by those who are under-integrated with the group; altruistic suicide is committed by those who are over-integrated with the group and who therefore display minimal individualism (1966: 210, 356). Survival lies in the balance.

Durkheim came to this notion of egoistic suicide by examining the statistics on suicide by religious affiliation, family situation, and changes over time. Protestants, he found, had higher suicide rates than Catholics and Jews; their greater individualism caused lesser integration. Men had higher suicide rates than women. And single men and women had higher suicide rates than married people, but married people in turn had higher suicide rates than married people with children. Why? Because their individualism and isolation levels are higher; they are less integrated with other people. The same theory applied to his historical data. Suicide rates declined in wartime, for both men and women. Why? Because, he suggested, "wars rouse collective sentiments, stimulate partisan spirit and patriotism, political and national faith, alike, and concentrating activity toward a single end, at least temporarily cause a stronger integration of society" (1966: 208). Ironically, perhaps, trying to kill others and to avoid being killed by others gives life new meaning, builds new bonds, and so self-killing declines.

In altruistic suicide, on the other hand, Durkheim gives numerous examples of people willingly sacrificing their lives for the greater good of the whole, as they perceived it: people on the threshold of old age; suttee, the custom whereby devout Hindu women threw themselves on their husband's funeral pyre; hari-kari among the Japanese; he suggested that even the early Christian martyrs "are really suicides" (1966: 227). This type of suicide is primarily to be found in "lower societies," Durkheim suggests, for in our own, "individual personality becomes increasingly free from the collective personality" — but it is still common in the army, which is highly structured, i.e., externally controlled (1966: 234). More recent examples of altruistic suicide include the Japanese Kamikaze pilots in World War II, the self-immolation of the Buddhist monks protesting the Vietnam War, the hunger strikes of the 10 I.R.A. men imprisoned in Northern Ireland, the suicide bombers in Lebanon and Israel, and in 1990, the 56 high caste Hindu students in India who killed themselves to protest new job quotas favouring lower castes. Protest suicides are relatively unusual in Canada.

Just as egoistic and altruistic suicides have different etiologies, so the suicides are committed in different emotional states: the one "feels himself useless and purposeless," and the act is accompanied by "a feeling of incurable weariness and sad depression"; the other "has a goal but one outside this life, which henceforth seems merely an obstacle to him," and the suicide "springs from hope," with "belief, enthusiasm and energy" (1966: 225-26).

A changed pattern of integration with society and others may also be hazardous to health. As Durkheim puts it: "Every disturbance of equilibrium, even though it achieves greater comfort and a heightening of general vitality, is an impulse to voluntary death" (1966: 246). He points out that the suicide rate rises in recessions, not due to increased poverty but to anomie; this is also true after widowhood and divorce. Anomic suicide "results from man's activity lacking regulation and his consequent sufferings" (1966: 258). People find it very difficult to cope with change — particularly if they have no support systems, no strong lines to others; i.e. if they have low levels of integration to society, then drastic change can be, as Durkheim would say, suicidogenic. Other crisis times today might be bankruptcy, being fired, imprisonment, severe illness.

These three types of suicide are presented in Table 7-5 in summary form. If I have treated Durkheim's theory in some detail it is partly because it was the first sociological theory, and it is still a model of research; also because it was highly imaginative: his conclusions are not obvious from the data; and finally because his work still has particular relevance for young males, as well as middle-aged and senior males, who all have peak suicide rates. "Excessive individualism," so well articulated in Paul Simon's song: "I am a rock, I am an island, and an island never cries . . ." has its costs. Rocks do not swim very well; and they split easily. The John Wayne macho ethic of self-sufficiency is not strong enough to keep all men alive and well. It can be lethal.

Durkheim does allow for mixed types of suicide; indeed many suicides are probably mixed, especially egoistic-anomic (e.g., the loners who lose their lovers, or some other centre of their lives, be it cats or a stamp collection — and both of these examples are on file). He also described a fourth type of suicide, fatalistic, but said it was rare (1966: 276).

Twentieth Century Theorists

And now for something completely different. Where Durkheim had emphasized that suicide *rates* expressed a collective death wish, Sigmund Freud was more interested in the *individual* death wish. He suggested that "probably no one finds the mental energy required to kill himself unless, in the first place, in doing so he is at the same time killing an object with whom he has identified himself, and, in the second place, is turning against himself a death-wish which had been

Table 7-5   Durkheim's Typology of Suicide

	Egoistic	Altruistic	Anomic
Type of integration with society	Under integration Excessive individualism	Over integration Excessive group loyalty	Changed integration
Psychological Attitude	Apathy Weariness	Energy of passion or will	Irritation Disgust
Goal	The self	The other	None or confused goals

Adapted from Durkheim, 1966, 293.

directed against someone else." He added that "the unconscious of all human beings is full enough of such death-wishes, even against those they love" (Vol. 9; 1979: 389). Death wishes may be directed inwards, against the self by displacement, or outwards, against others, in violence, murder or war — but they usually remain in the unconscious (Vol. 12; 1985: 86). For Freud life is a constant struggle between Eros and Thanatos, the Life instinct or force and the Death instinct, love and hate. "This struggle is what all life essentially consists of, and the evolution of civilization may therefore be simply described as the struggle for life of the human species" (Vol. 12; 1985: 314).

The notion of subconscious aggression is useful enough, and that it may be displaced from others to self, or vice versa, is also a valuable insight, although it is a little vague — for if we all have such aggression, hate, and death wishes, why don't we all commit suicide? Suicide is, after all, unusual. Yet Freud went further to suggest that many "accidents" and seemingly unintentional self-injuries, and illnesses also, are in fact *semi-suicides* (my term, not his). Suicidal or self-destructive people may not necessarily kill themselves: they must just injure themselves, or kill themselves "just a little bit." These "bungled actions" may also, quite "accidentally," result in the death of others, as he notes in a series of anecdotes (Vol. 5; 1990: 233-46). Freud therefore breaks down the simple dichotomy of suicide/not suicide, and suggests that there is a continuum, with self-injury and illness placed along this continuum, a notion that surely helps us to understand attempted suicide as well as our own occasional "bungled actions" better.

Freud wrote more about war and death than suicide; but one of his admirers, Karl Menninger, developed and expanded his notion of the self-destructive death instinct in the provocatively titled *Man against Himself* (1938). This war of the self against the self takes many forms, and may take many years. If Freud's particular insight was that "many suicides are disguised murders" (Menninger, 1938: 50), Menninger notes that people begin to commit suicide long before they actually attempt it; "self-defeating tendencies [arise] very early in the life of the individual" (1938: 21). He distinguishes between four types of suicide: immediate suicide; chronic suicide, including alcohol addiction, and even crime and other forms of partial, attenuated suicide — today we would add newer forms of addiction (drug, food, even sex) as well as the lifestyles discussed earlier; focal suicides, usually focused on specific body parts, including self-mutilation, malingering, compulsive surgery, and unconsciously purposive accidents (literal and metaphorical Freudian slips); and organic suicides, and here he tackles the vexed question of the psychic etiology of illness, disease and death. Freud had discussed the "flight into illness" long before (Vol. 9; 1979: 79), emphasizing the unity of body and mind; Menninger's theory of some diseases as self-punishment, or as a consequence of repressed hatred, or to attract attention, or as occurring at turning points is being developed further in medical sociology and psychology.

Medical anthropologists Nancy Scheper-Hughes and Margaret Lock have said that: "Sickness . . . is a form of communication — the language of the organs" (1987: 31). Menninger's point is that such sickness is sometimes self-generated and self-destructive (1938: 355).

Certainly some people do destroy themselves seemingly unintentionally: the deaths of Jimi Hendrix, Janice Joplin, Elvis Presley, River Phoenix, and Jim Morrison were all caused by, or associated with, drug abuse and/or alcohol abuse. As such they were parasuicides.

Psychologists and sociologists tend to ignore each other. This might be described as the first law of the social sciences, *pace* Comte. Freud and Menninger totally ignored Durkheim; and Jack Douglas virtually ignored them in turn. He also criticized Durkheim for stressing the structural etiology of suicide rather than the subjective meanings and motivations of the act. Beginning with Weber's concept of subjective meaning, he suggests that people attempt suicide for various reasons: to get help (if the attempt fails); to get revenge; to atone for evil done; out of shame or guilt or remorse; to reunite with a loved one; "to go home to rest at peace with God" and so on (1967: 235, 284-319). The implication is that there are not just three or four types of suicide, and their mixtures, as Durkheim and Menninger had suggested, but perhaps as many types as there are suicides: every one is different; and we need to understand what suicide *means* to the individuals, rather than to impose meanings on them.

Douglas' point is well taken I think; and we may choose to emphasize the similarities or the differences in suicides, but we must be aware of both. Psychology and sociology intersect in each instance.

One common theme among suicidal people is a bi-polar pattern of either-or thinking: all or nothing, black or white, life or death; options are constricted until there is only one solution to the problem of pain — death. Schneidman tells of one young college student who was pregnant. "Her pregnancy was such a mortal shame to her that she could not, in her words, 'bear to live.' "

> I took out a sheet of paper and began to list possible options for her. Our exchange went along these general lines: "Now let's see. You could have the baby and put it up for adoption." ("I couldn't do that.") "We could get in touch with the young man involved." ("I couldn't do that.") "You could bring the baby to term and keep it." (Another refusal.) "You could always have an abortion." ("I couldn't do that.") And I listed several other possibilities for her, but she insisted that she couldn't do any of them.

Eventually, however, she began to rank the options, and Schneidman remarked: "But suicide was no longer her first choice. We were, to my great relief, simply haggling about life" (1987: 57-8).

Haggling about life does require someone to haggle with. One suspects that the young student had few strong links to friends and family who could have helped her in her pain.

Theories of suicide abound: integration theory (Durkheim), displaced murder theory (Freud), self-destruction theory (Menninger), bi-polar thinking theory (Schneidman), or meaning theory (Douglas); all are useful, surely, and there are many others in both sociology and psychology (see Douglas, 1967).

Indeed everyone probably has their own theory to explain the high and rising Canadian suicide rate, as they/we do for the crime rate. Some blame the fractured family, especially for the impulse suicides of young people; some blame drugs and alcohol; some blame the media for glamourizing and romanticizing death in Bond and Rambo-type movies. The hospitals hide and sanitize death, so young people especially no longer know about death at first hand, and may not believe in its reality and finality. Even our language camouflages death; people do not die anymore, they pass on, they go to heaven, they go back to God. (If you know Monty Python's "Parrot Song" you know how many euphemisms there are for dying.) Supermarkets present us with dead animals neatly dissected, packaged, frozen, and labeled. We *live* on the deaths of animals; but we no longer kill our own food, usually, except for farmers, fishers, and hunters, and we have little concept of its bloody reality. We offer our guests a steak, but not a dead cow. This camouflaging or denial of death in our institutions, media, hospitals, supermarkets, and language defeats realism, it is often argued, and contributes to high suicide rates. So does the easy availability of lethal weaponry, especially guns, but also cars (by crashing or carbon monoxide poisoning), gas, poisons, high-rises, bridges, as well as sleeping pills and the ever-present drugs and alcohol. It is so easy to kill yourself here, it is a wonder that the suicide rate is not much higher.

Some suicides are romanticized as heroic: the Kamikaze pilots and I.R.A. prisoners and suicide bombers to their fellows, no doubt; but Kurt Cobain, Sylvia Plath and Marilyn Monroe? Even apparently egoistic suicides may be redefined as altruistic. Some blame the lack of sanctions against suicide: not only the lack of legal sanctions, but the lack of ethical values, which seem not to be taught much at home or at school; also, with the decline of religious faith in so many sectors of society, such values often seem to have no institutional foundation.

Some blame the so-called "American Dream," a.k.a. the American Nightmare, which is pervasive in Canada too: the emphasis on success, winning, happiness, possessions, power, and superiority. The argument is that we are taught totally unrealistic expectations, which we cannot possibly achieve, not all the time at least; so we do not develop the coping mechanisms necessary for dealing with failure, losing, being second, unhappiness, inferiority, and the negativities and harsh realities of life. And the more vulnerable individuals may opt out.

And yet . . . despite all the sociological and psychological theories . . . despite the seeming conspiracy of all sectors of society to impel and compel us to suicide . . . despite our problems, perhaps child abuse, dysfunctional families, stress, or battles with alcoholism or depression, or being beaten, fired or dumped (or all three in a bad week) . . . despite everything . . . none of us have committed suicide, yet. We manage.

ATTITUDES AND VALUES

Is suicide right or wrong, generally speaking? Most of my students believe it is wrong.

Traditionally the Christian church has always condemned suicide as a mortal sin punishable by hellfire. In the Christian view life is a gift from God: precious, unique, and to be held in trust until death. It is condemned by the sixth commandment, "Thou shalt not kill." Not even yourself. Those who did commit suicide were not only condemned, but their family was shamed, and the body could not, and usually still cannot, be buried in consecrated ground with the rest of the family. It was the final treachery of Judas. It is the sin against life.

Western states have also condemned suicide as a crime against the state. In the *Nicomachean Ethics* Aristotle argued that the suicide offends against the *polis*, and also that the suicide is a coward (1138, 1116; 1984: 1796, 1792). The Romans allowed suicide, unless it was committed to escape punishment for a crime, in which case the heirs were punished by confiscation of property and disinheritance. Tudor jurists noted that suicide was an act of felony, not only an act against Nature and against God, but also against the King "in that he [the King] has lost a subject, and he being the Head has lost one of his mystic members" (Kantorowicz, 1957: 269).

Yet Socrates drank the cup of hemlock, as ordered, to demonstrate both his compliance with the law, but also his contempt for this life and for his body. He was one philosopher who practiced what he preached. And the Romans seem to have expected suicide of their failures: the suicide perhaps compensated for the damage they had done. Brutus, one of the conspirators in the assassination of Julius Caesar in 44 B.C. fell on his sword after being defeated by Mark Antony and Octavian; Mark Antony in turn fell on his sword after being defeated by Octavian; and Cleopatra, having lost her lover and in imminent danger of capture, then took her own life.

The dominant philosophy of the Roman Empire was stoicism, a central tenet of which was *apatheia*, indifference to all but virtue, which was defined as living life according to reason. Life itself is a matter of indifference, as are riches or poverty, health or illness, pleasure or pain. Stoicism was extremely influential in the development of Christian thought; and one of the foremost stoic philosophers was the Emperor Marcus Aurelius (120-80), who in his *Meditations* was one of the first to condone suicide:

In all you do or say, recollect that at any time the power of withdrawal from life is in your hands . . .

It is possible to live on earth as you mean to live hereafter. But if men will not let you, then quit the house of life; though not with any feeling of ill-usage. The hut smokes? I move out. No need to make a great business of it. (1964: 48, 87-8)

Others might see this as defeatist or cowardly. "The hut smokes. Put out the fire! and hurry up about it!" Certainly mainstream Christian thought was in opposition to this view. After the Renaissance, however, free thinkers swam against the stream. In his essay "A Custom of the Island of Cea," Montaigne approved of suicide (1965: 251-62). So did David Hume and Schopenhauer. Kant and William James condemned it (Durkheim, 1966: 23). Nietzsche's essay "On Voluntary Death" advocates suicide:

Die at the right time: thus Zarathustra teaches . . .

I commend to you my sort of death, voluntary death that comes to me because *I* wish it . . .

And everyone who wants glory must take leave of honour in good time and practice the difficult art of — going at the right time. (Nietzsche, 1969: 97-8)

Nietzsche did not practice what he preached, but went mad and died, probably of tertiary syphilis. C'est la vie!

Albert Camus, on the other hand, argued that "even if one does not believe in God, suicide is not legitimate" (1942/1975: 7). Why not? Because even though, and precisely because, life is absurd (in his view), the human duty and privilege is to rebel: "It is essential to die unreconciled and not of one's own free will. Suicide is a repudiation" (1975: 55). He adds that: "The point is to live" (1975: 63).

As in philosophy, so in theology, the questioning continued, particularly in Protestantism. Dietrich Bonhoeffer, a leading German theologian hanged by the Nazis, argued in his *Ethics* (1949) that suicide is "wrongful" and is an offence against God — not the self, as Camus had suggested. Nonetheless his treatise is compassionate: "Suicide is a man's attempt to give a final human meaning to a life which has become humanly meaningless." Furthermore the context of the decision has to be considered in evaluating the morality of the act. And, in the final analysis, "The right to suicide is nullified only by the living God" (1966: 166-72). These reevaluations of traditional Christian dogma, and the blurring of the absolutist ten Commandments with ethical relativism and situation ethics, have also contributed to the legitimation of suicide.

These ideological developments have been institutionalized more recently in such organizations as Exit, founded in the United Kingdom, Hemlock in the

United States and, in Canada, the Right to Die Society, founded in Victoria in 1991, and Dying with Dignity, founded in Toronto in 1980. These organizations advocate the right to die with dignity, and insist on the right of the terminally ill and those in chronic pain to choose to die; they also provide techniques for bloodless deaths. Suicide, they insist, is not morally wrong; it is a rational choice. The "right to die" movement received widespread attention with the publication of Derek Humphry's best selling *Final Exit*.

Critics of the movement argue that this is the thin edge of the wedge, that old people will feel increasingly pressured to move on, that such policies are liable to abuse, that life is sacred, and that the techniques will be used more by the depressed than the so-called legitimate candidates.

At the popular end of the cultural spectrum rock groups have occasionally advocated suicide, or *seem* to have done so. Suicidal Tendencies, whose very name is enough to shock the complacent, Ozzie Osbourne and Death Metal Groups generally, probably reach more people than Nietzsche, Camus, Bonhoeffer, and Humphry put together. One of Suicidal Tendencies' tracks, "Suicide's an Alternative," talks about being sick of living and intending to die. Another track, "Suicidal Failure," describes someone's totally unsuccessful efforts to kill themselves and concludes that suicide would be fun. Suicide is not a sin, not a crime, not a waste, not a rational, or irrational, choice: it's *fun*.

The lyrics are harder and stronger, and more self involved than the protest songs of the sixties, the Beatles, Bob Dylan, Peter, Paul and Mary, and the blues before that — none ever discussed suicide. But rock groups like Suicidal Tendencies express the feelings of a new generation, or some of them; and the lyrics are also a powerful and poetic critique of society. Whether they actually *advocate* suicide is a more controversial matter. Ozzy Osbourne has been taken to court over the deaths of several teenagers for his song "Suicide Solution." Blaming heavy metal bands for teenage suicides is fairly easy; but there are other factors, including drugs, alcohol, violence, revolving fathers, craziness, a failure of nurture: a web of pathologies.

The right to die movement targets the old, the terminally ill, and those in chronic pain. Heavy Metal targets the young. And the suicide rate rises. Is that a problem? or a solution?

Recommendations

The National Task Force made 40 recommendations in its report. Recommendations range from the very general: "Alleviation of Social Conditions" such as grinding poverty, and alcohol and drug abuse — all subjects worthy of Task Force Reports in their own right — to the very specific: the clergy should be educated in the area of suicide.

Recommendations were divided into three categories, Prevention, Intervention (including hospital psychiatric services and crisis centres), and Postvention, following a completed suicide, including psychological autopsies. Particular recommendations are also directed towards the seven high-risk populations identified earlier, the Criminal Code, and research. The Task Force noted that "One of the greatest obstacles encountered by the Task Force in the preparation of this research was the lack of Canadian research on suicide." Very true. This is a major part of the problem. And recommendation #39 "Government funding should be increased for research on suicide" is critical (Statistics Canada, 1987: 38-60). The Conservative government, however, substantially cut all social science research. And the suicide rate continues to rise.

Recommendations include the following:

#17 Efforts to reduce the incidence of alcoholism should be strongly encouraged.

#20 The treatment of young people who are at risk to suicide should recognize and account for vulnerability factors and environmental influences.

#23 Comprehensive programs of care for the elderly should be implemented.

#24 . . . suicide prevention strategies for Canadian Native peoples should be based on a comprehensive and culturally oriented approach.

#40 Priority should be given to multi-centre and multi-disciplinary research. . .

I doubt that even if all these recommendations were implemented that they would make much of a dent in the rise in the suicide rates. Some are very vague, and others require such massive expenditures, on prison reform, alcoholism strategies, and the alleviation of poverty, particularly the poverty of Native peoples, that in the present climate of cutbacks they are unrealistic, even though very necessary.

Furthermore the suicides of middle-aged and older people are often carefully planned; they are not impulse suicides. Such suicides may be rational choices.

The Task Force did not present the absolute figures for the seven high-risk populations. The impulse and mimic suicides of young people, 15-24, especially males, account for a disproportionate number of total suicides and of the total number of years of life lost. This seems to me to be where we should focus our scarce resources.

Classes should be offered in suicide-prevention in high schools and universities, both for students and also for principals, teachers, and health care workers. Suicide prevention kits must be prepared for distribution and discussion. The National Film Board must produce documentaries for high schools as well as the adult population to air the topic. Once suicide is demythologized and even routinized, it loses much of its appeal, glamour, and mystique; and we can all be made more aware of the resources available and alternative coping strategies. All these recommendations remain little more than band-aids for some people and some populations, for whom more radical strategies are required. They are a minimum, but a necessary minimum.

But classrooms are cold places, and the first line of defense is family and friends, and our level and type of integration or relation with them. It is the links with other human beings which not only often seem to compel us to suicide, but also which sustain us. Alone we cannot cope . . . and especially not alone with a bottle (Chapter 9).

CONCLUSION

Suicide is extremely controversial, both as a social and as an ethical issue. Is it right or wrong? a problem or not? Or does it all depend? if so, on what? The debates continue, and are argued in the home, classroom, and courtroom. People do construct their realities differently, and construct different realities. Such conflict is to be expected; and it continues, in a knot of issues: ethical, medical, legal, and financial, and very personal.

Two Canadians illustrate the changing norms on suicide and assisted suicide, as well as euthanasia (literally, a good death, from the Greek). In Montreal, Nancy B., paralyzed from the neck down for two and a half years with the neurological disease Guillain-Barré Syndrome, requested the court to order her doctor and the hospital to disconnect her respirator. After a long pause, and a visit with Nancy B., the judge ordered the hospital to comply, arguing in January 1992 that this was neither a crime, nor suicide, nor euthanasia. The court merely recognized her right to die, and not to be kept alive artificially against her will. Nancy B. died soon afterwards, to her great relief.

In British Columbia, Sue Rodriguez died of amyotrophic lateral sclerosis, Lou Gehrig's disease, in February 1994. Physically unable to take her own life, she requested assistance so that she could control her own death. This is illegal under the Criminal Code, which carries a penalty of up to 14 years for counselling or assisting suicide (Section 224), although committing suicide is not itself a crime. In a videotaped presentation she told a parliamentary committee:

> Today, I can barely walk. There is much worse to come. I will be unable to breathe without a respirator. I will be unable to eat or swallow, unable to move without assistance. I want to ask you, gentlemen: If I cannot give consent to my own death, then whose body is this? Who owns my life? (*Maclean's* 28.2.94)

Rodriguez took her case to the Supreme Court of Canada which found 5 to 4 against her, arguing that the article of the Criminal Code protected "The young, the innocent, the mentally incompetent and the depressed" and did not infringe on her rights. Nonetheless, Rodriguez arranged for a physician to give her a powerful sedative, and she died peacefully in the presence of her friend, N.D.P. M.P. Svend Robinson.

The issue of assisted suicide remains controversial. What some see as "a health-care choice that is essentially therapeutic," others see as murder. Proponents of assisted suicide argue that you wouldn't see your dog suffer like that; that the patients' rights have priority, and that assisted suicide is widely practiced anyway and should be legalized. Indeed, in response to such arguments, euthanasia has been legalized in the Netherlands. Others note that many assisted suicides are botched, with appalling consequences, that life is a gift which must be lived, and that such legislation would be just the thin edge of the wedge and would certainly be abused and also would place immense pressure on the elderly to hurry up and die (the "need a hand?" syndrome); furthermore palliative care should be the direction of the future, and doctors are healers, not killers (*Maclean's*, 28.2.94; 14.3.94). The debate is just beginning.

At the annual convention of the Canadian Medical Association in 1994 the resolution that doctors "should specifically exclude participation in euthanasia and physician-assisted suicide" was passed by a vote of 93-74. This is such a close vote that the issue can be expected to return. Indeed this is the beginning of the medicalization of suicide.

In the United States, Dr. Jack Kevorkian (Dr. Death, as he is popularly known) has assisted in the suicides of at least 19 patients from 1990 to 1993. For much of this time there was no legislation against assisting suicide in Michigan but, since the law was changed, he is currently under indictment for homicide. The issue has attracted widespread public attention, particularly in the United States where it was the topic of cover stories by *Time* (19.3.90) and *Newsweek* (26.8.91; 6.12.93).

Rodriguez and Kevorkian have raised the issue of assisted suicide, and Robert Latimer has raised the seemingly related issue of euthanasia. The Saskatchewan farmer admitted to killing his 12-year-old daughter, Tracy. Tracy was born with severe cerebral palsy, was mentally retarded, could neither walk nor talk, but she could smile and laugh. She was in constant pain; she had recently dislocated her hip and was scheduled for surgery. While his wife and his other children were at church, Latimer took Tracy out to his pick-up truck, rigged up a system of pipes from the exhaust, switched on the ignition, and Tracy fell asleep, dying of carbon monoxide poisoning. Latimer confessed when charged, adding "I'm much happier for her now." He told the police: "My priority was to put her out of her pain. She was constantly in pain." Latimer was convicted of second degree murder and sentenced to life imprisonment with no possibility of parole for ten years. The sentence has been appealed (*Maclean's* 21.11.94; 28.11.94).

Suicide, like these other social problems, is a painful topic, and it is also complex. It runs all the way from parasuicide and semi-suicide and the routine forms of occasionally dangerous and self-destructive behaviour which give zest to life and which, for some, make life worth living, all the way to completed and attempted suicides, and the ethical and legal issues raised by assisted suicide, euthanasia, and mercy killing, including homicide.

Furthermore the definition of meanings of suicide are constantly changing, as Rodriguez and Latimer indicate. In the Christian era, suicide was, and is, a sin. In the middle ages suicide was a crime, punishable by death — so, one way or another the poor souls would get their way. In wartime, however, suicide was, in some circumstances, defined as a *duty*, especially for agents behind enemy lines. Combatants were expected to bite on the cyanide pill to ensure that they would not betray their allies under torture. Gary Powers, the pilot of a U2 spy plane shot down over the Soviet Union in 1956, was widely vilified by the American public for his *failure* to commit suicide and avoid capture as ordered. Once a crime and then a sin, suicide was decriminalized in 1972 in Canada. Now suicide is widely regarded as neither a sin nor a crime but sometimes as a *duty* and by many as a *right*, and perhaps by Heavy Metal types, as *fun*.

ENDNOTES

1. The statistics on suicide can be found in the following Statistics Canada publications: Catalogue Numbers 11-204, 82-003, 82-542, 84-203, 84-206 and 84-528. Consult also the index in the annual listing of publications by Statistics Canada.

CHAPTER 8

RACISM

Is Canada a racist country, or not? What do you think? Is racism a serious social problem in Canada? Is it increasing? decreasing? or staying about the same? And how do you measure it?[1]

Opinions will vary, as one might expect. Conflict theorists will be more inclined to answer that yes, Canada is racist, and conservatives to say that it is not. Both will certainly agree that there are some racists and some incidents every now and again; but they may not agree that such individuals and incidents define the society. Overall, however, according to a recent survey 86% of Canadians believe that there is at least "some racism" in Canada, 75% believe that racism is a serious social problem, and more than half think that racism has increased over the last few years (*Globe and Mail* 14.12.93; *Maclean's* 27.12.93). But Cecil Foster is dogmatic: "Canada is a racist country and always has been" (1991: 2). This decision was evoked by his reading of history and current racial incidents, but seems to have been provoked by a little girl telling his five-year-old son that he could not come to her birthday party because he was Black. And Adrienne Shadd, a fifth generation Black Canadian agrees: "Racism is, and always has been, one of the bedrock institutions of Canadian society, embedded in the very fabric of our thinking, our personality" (1991: 1). Emma Larocque, a Native educator, insists in similar terms, that "racism against Native (Indian, Inuit and Métis) peoples is embedded in Canadian institutions" (1991: 73). So the macro and the micro converge.

Racism is a difficult topic to research, for a number of reasons. One, it is very sensitive and personal. People often do not like to discuss their experiences in public. Some, of course, get off on it, and hold forth in righteous indignation at any and every opportunity. But many people stay silent, vent their feelings in private among friends, and refuse to discuss such issues in class, for instance, just as we might not talk about our experiences of rape or our thoughts of suicide. They are too personal, too private, too painful. Of course this makes it hard for others to learn about them.

184

Second, while poverty can in principal be measured and calculated using various economic methods, and while crime rates and suicide rates are collected and published annually by Statistics Canada (albeit with advice about degrees of inaccuracy), we have no central accounting system for racism. Nor do we have one for sexism. Both phenomena are elusive in this respect. Consequently, the data on rates of racism, the variations by province, age, gender, or socioeconomic status, the types of racism (attitudinal or behavioural, physical, verbal, economic, etc.), and rates of change in the data are almost impossible to calculate scientifically.

Thirdly the concepts of race and ethnicity are very slippery, as we shall see. The concept of race has no scientific or biological validity, yet it has immense political power. And ethnicity, understood in terms of culture (which is itself a broad enough term) may, or may not, overlap with political race. Furthermore, ethnicity is highly subjective: we can choose to identify with one group or another; and multiple ethnicity is not only possible, it is quite frequent (cf. Statistics Canada, 1993. Cat. No. C93).

But the greatest difficulty encountered in researching racism as a social problem in Canada is the sheer absence of data — which in turn is due to the failure of the federal government to fund research on such a political hot potato. Pious ethnic histories abound, stressing the important contributions of each and every group to the growth of the Canadian "family," but the harsher issues of ethnic and racial hatred and violence, physical, political, or economic, etc., remain largely unstudied.

Researching racism may be difficult, but it is not impossible; and given the polyethnic and polyracial reality of contemporary and future Canada, it is vital that we do this research. And the first requirement is to define our terms.

CONCEPTS

Five concepts are frequently used as tools in the literature on race and ethnic relations: race, ethnicity, stereotype, prejudice, and discrimination . . . and racism of course. Let us consider them in that order.

Race

The species *Homo sapiens* was classified into four groups by the famous Swedish taxonomist Linnaeus (1707-78) in his *Systema Naturae* (1738). These races, as they became known, were distinguished by their continental origins: the American, red; the European, white; the Asian, sallow; the African, black (Slotkin, 1965: 177). This division of humanity into four types, based on the coinciding of colour and continent, may seem at first glance clear, obvious and useful enough for practical purposes, even as we recognize that these races have moved around the world, and that many people are mixed.

Nonetheless this taxonomy is not without problems. How are these variants of *Homo sapiens* differentiated? And why four? In *The Descent of Man* (1871), Charles Darwin raised his objections:

> Man has been studied more carefully than any other organic being, and yet there is the greatest possible diversity amongst capable judges whether he should be classified as a single species or a race, or as two (Virey), as three (Jacquinot), as four (Kant), five (Blumenbach), six (Button), seven (Hunter), eight (Agassiz), eleven (Pickering), fifteen (Bory St. Vincent), sixteen (Desmoulins), twenty-two (Morton), sixty (Crawford) or as sixty-three, according to Burke (1981:226).

All was, and is, confusion. Are the Inuit a separate race? The Malays? The Lapps? The Pygmies? The Australian aborigines? The Bushmen of the Kalahari? And by what criteria do we differentiate: colour? height? hair type? These questions vexed the early anthropologists as they tried to classify and categorize the body of humanity (cf. Synnott and Howes, 1992). The races, as Darwin expressed it, "graduate into each other" (1981: 226); and there are no clear criteria to distinguish them, and certainly not colour.

Colours come and go in almost all the hues of the rainbow, from the paler shades of white, cream, pink, tan, beige to ochres, café au lait, cinnamons and yellows through to sepias, teak, mahogany and black, with occasional flashes or flushes of scarlet, crimson, and purple. Many so-called whites can be darker than so-called Asians or blacks, particularly those from the Mediterranean countries, and some of the so-called Americans can pass as Asians when visiting there. Colour, therefore, however useful it may be as a possible indicator of continental origin in Toronto or Vancouver, is not a criterion by which humanity can be scientifically divided into four, or more, or less, categories.

Anthropologists have tried for ages, since Blumenbach at the end of the eighteenth century, to pinpoint the exact number of races and the criterion by which they can be classified: cranial capacity, nose width, forehead angle, and then fingerprint types (three), blood-types (four), or genetic structure, but there is no such criterion — not least because there are no pure races, only human beings.

So, explains Joann Gutin, "white Americans, though ostensibly far removed from black Americans in phenotype, can be better tissue matches for them than are *other* black Americans" (1994: 73). It is not the phenotype, therefore, which may save our lives, but the genotype — which does not correspond at all with races or phenotypes.

Indeed the concept of race, which seemed originally so scientific, biological, and physical (colour), is now redefined as a political construct with no biological basis in science (Shreeve, 1994; Gould, 1994). Even for Linnaeus, race was a "moral" or political concept as well as a scientific taxonomy. His classification is also a moral ranking, as is evident from his descriptions of the four races, summarized here: (1) American, reddish; obstinate, merry, free; regulated by custom; (2) European, white; gentle, acute, inventive; governed by laws; (3) Asian, sallow; severe, haughty, avaricious; ruled by opinion; (4) Afer, black; women without shame; crafty, indolent, negligent; governed by caprice (Slotkin, 1965: 177-78). Obviously he liked whites most and blacks least and his supposedly scientific classification proved to be ethnocentric, prejudiced and racist.

The concept of race, it has become increasingly obvious, is useless as a scientific category and also dangerous as a moral category, underpinning racism. Biological traits which seem obvious to the general public, like skin colour, vary so much and range so easily along the continuum, from light to dark that they are useless as scientific markers. Ironically, at the very time that anthropologists and biologists are deconstructing the concept of race as scientifically invalid, politicians and minority leaders are *reconstructing* the concept as politically useful and economically necessary. It is now a tool to legitimize multiculturalism and equity policies for visible minorities. The concept which was once widely used to legitimize oppression is now capsized to legitimize liberation and equity.

Ethnicity

Ethnic *origin*, according to Statistics Canada, "refers to the ethnic or cultural group(s) to which an individual's ancestors belonged; it pertains to the ancestral roots or origins of the population and not to place of birth, citizenship or nationality" (Renaud and Badets, 1993: 18). Of course, these alternatives may often coincide: origin? Italian; place of birth? Italy; citizenship? Italian. Indeed the term "origin" implies a place, a nation.

Ethnic *identity*, however, may be different. The ethnic *groups* with which Canadians identify may and sometimes do exclude geographical roots, place of birth, and citizenship. People identify themselves by colour, by religion, and by language e.g., Black, Jewish, Hispanic; and all these options are recorded in the census. Ethnic identity is therefore a subjective choice to some degree. However, as ethnic identities may also be imputed to us by others, such choices are also political. Ethnic identity is not only a choice of personal identity from a range of possibilities, it is also a resource that has to be managed — a point that takes us from individual identity to ethnic and racial politics.

This is particularly evident in the example of dual or triple origins, depending on how far back one wishes to delve into ancestry. What are your ethnic origins? Can you juggle different ones? What circumstances might be conducive to ethnicity management? An Anglo-Irishman in Quebec, for instance, might insist on his Irish rather than his English roots to try and avoid the possibility of negative stereotyping — or to trade off a different stereotype. An invisibly pale person of Arabic origin might insist that she is a member of a visible minority; this could have a positive effect on hiring and promotion options. Another might claim aboriginal identity, quite correctly, for the same reason.

All of this means that ethnicity is quite as tricky a concept as race is; it is also an important component of our sense of self and our group identity or identities. *How* important it is, is likely to be a variable, from high to low, and this importance may sometimes be far more obvious to others than to oneself. This is a topic that is worth investigating further, particularly since it is so conflict-ridden and problematic.

Stereotype

The Daudlin Report defines stereotype as: "A fixed image attributing certain characteristics or habits to a specific racial or ethnic group" (1984: 144). We all have these generalizations in our mind, based perhaps on our experience, our education, or the media. They may be positive or negative. Often they are positive about the in-group, one's own, and more or less negative for the out-group. In any racial or ethnic stratification system, minorities may have positive stereotypes about the majority to which they aspire, but they may also internalize negative feelings of self-hatred from the dominant majority culture. Also stereotypes may be accurate or inaccurate as generalizations. Gordon Allport says in his classic study that stereotypes may have "a kernel of truth" (1958: 185).

Since any stereotype is indeed a generalization, it can always be dismissed as "just a generalization" — which does not mean that it is scientifically inaccurate. It is also a vast generalization to assert that "the sun rises in the east" (or even that nine times out of ten, the sun rises in the east!); or that women in Canada live longer than men.

Just as an exercise, consider your stereotypes of the following Canadian groups: the English, French, Jews, Blacks, Irish, Native Peoples, males, females, lawyers. . . . Certainly these are not necessarily homogeneous groups, but you probably attribute "certain characteristics or habits" to members of these groups, in general. Whether rightly or wrongly might be the task of a social scientist to ascertain. If these beliefs are entertained very widely and very strongly, however (and especially if they are very negative, and very inaccurate, based simply on prejudice), then stereotypes can have negative consequences for the employment, mobility and life chances of the target group.

Prejudice

A prejudice is, literally, a prejudgement. It is an attitude, in the definition of the Daudlin Report, "in which an individual passes judgement (generally unfavourable) on a person he or she does not know, usually attributing to that person a variety of characteristics which are attributed to a group of which the person is a member" (1984: 144). Someone may be prejudiced against an entire group, we should add, as well as against an individual. People may be anti-Semitic, anti-American, or anti-Russian without knowing any members of these ethnic groups personally. Allport offers a brief definition: "thinking ill of others without sufficient warrant" (1958: 7) — though he hastens to add that "biases may be *pro* as well as *con*" and that the sufficiency of the warrant is sometimes difficult to determine (1958: 7-9). The well-known phrase "I'm not prejudiced but. . . ." may usually but not always be followed by a prejudicial statement.

Prejudice does not necessarily translate into discrimination, as attitudes do not necessarily translate into behaviour. It depends on the circumstances. There are four possibilities, as Table 8-1 indicates. The individual, or the ethnic group, may be prejudiced and, consistent with that prejudice, practice discrimination against another individual or group. The obvious example is the Nazis, who hated Jews and also killed them. Second, an individual may not be prejudiced but may nonetheless discriminate against others because everyone does it, because it's conventional, and so on. X refuses to hire Y because he or she reckons Z will be upset; the landlady or landlord does not rent the apartment to members of some particular group because she or he knows that the spouse will object. Alternatively, in the third scenario, people may be very prejudiced against members of a particular group, without discriminating against them, perhaps because they are afraid they will be taken to court and sued for damages. The law does not determine how you *think*, only how you behave — and certain behaviours are illegal. Finally, of course, an individual may be prejudice-free and not discriminate either.

Deep and widespread prejudice in general serves to legitimize discriminatory behaviour against the "other" or the out-group, and thus to maintain the dominant status of the in-group. Surely all Canadians have heard negative statements about various charter groups, ethnic minorities, and visible minorities made by

Table 8-1   Prejudice and Discrimination

Prejudice	Discrimination
+	+
-	+
+	-
-	-

+ means presence of pattern
- means absence of pattern

their family, friends, colleagues, fellow workers or neighbours. Are they expressions of prejudice? or "true?"

But prejudice and discrimination are not necessarily independent of each other, as one might infer from this 2x4 table. Prejudice may cause discrimination, and discrimination may cause prejudice in a vicious circle of cause and effect, attitudes and behaviour.

Discrimination

We all discriminate all the time. We make choices. We select a black, white, or green T-shirt, based on our evaluations of the differences in price, quality, hue and so on. We may even be complimented on our discriminating taste. The word is derived from the Latin *discrimen*, meaning distinction, or difference.

Racial or ethnic discrimination is something else. The Daudlin Report defines discrimination as: "The conscious act of dealing with a person or persons on the basis of prejudicial attitudes and beliefs (rather than on the basis of individual merit). Thus prejudice is a state of mind, while discrimination is an action" (Committee, 1984: 143).

Such discrimination is outlawed by the Canadian Charter of Rights and Freedoms. The Charter asserts that:

> Every individual is equal before and under the law and has the right to equal protection and equal benefit of the law without discrimination based on race, national or ethnic origin, colour, religion, sex, age or mental or physical disability.

The Canadian Human Rights Act (1977) specifically outlaws discrimination based on race, national or ethnic origin, colour, religion, age, sex (including pregnancy or childbirth), marital status, family status, pardoned conviction, physical or mental disability (including dependence on alcohol or drugs) and, effectively, by a decision of the Ontario Court of Appeal, sexual orientation. Nonetheless jobs may legally be refused to those who cannot perform them safely, efficiently, and reliably, according to the Guide to the Act (1993: Cat. No. HR21-18); service may be refused when it cannot be offered without undue costs; and mandatory retirement at a certain age may be permissible.

The number of complaints lodged with the HRC on the basis of racial discrimination dropped from 297 in 1990, when they constituted 30% of the total number of complains lodged, to 172 in 1993, when they constituted only 14% of the complaints lodged (CHRC, 1994:106). On the face of it, this should be seen as evidence, both in numbers and proportions, of a decline in already low levels of Canadian racism. But the figures are so patently out of line with the everyday reality of hate messages, violence, and discrimination even as presented in the *Annual Report* that they become almost meaningless. Furthermore, although the CHRC does report on some of its initiatives and successes, it presents no date on the disposition of these complaints. We cannot tell, from the CHRC at any rate, whether racial discrimination is increasing or decreasing.

Racial discrimination may be illegal; but according to one survey 22% have witnessed racism in the workplace, and 18% have witnessed racially motivated violence (*The Globe and Mail* 14.12.93).

THE NATION

The 27 million people of Canada come from all over the world, as Table 8-2 indicates; Canada is the United Nations in microcosm. This ethnic and racial diversity in the composition of the population is not without its problems, however; the first of which is what all these numbers mean.

The 1991 Census asked respondents: "To which ethnic or cultural group(s) did this person's ancestors belong?" Respondents could check from a list provided and/or add their own. The results are consequently rather confusing as respondents applied a wide range of overlapping criteria in answering the question. Most people gave only one answer: the single-origin response, and usually they cited a particular nation. The top six are (or seem to be) as follows:

French	6,147,000
British	5,611,000
German	912,000
Italian	750,000
Chinese	587,000
Ukrainian	407,000

But this is problematic for several reasons. First, about 18% of the respondents gave multiple ethnicities, e.g., Black, British; second, another three-quarters of a million gave their ethnic origin as Canadian. So all the clean numbers listed above are underestimates. Also the British category includes English, Irish, Welsh, and Scottish; but Eire (the Republic of Ireland) gained its independence from Britain in 1921, and such Irish may hate to be considered British. Nonetheless the census concluded that 28% of the population claimed British origins, which is down from 34% in 1986, and that 23% of the population claimed French origins, down from 24% in 1986. Another 4% reported mixed French-English origin, and 31% said they were neither British nor French, up from 25% in 1986. Evidently the charter groups are steadily declining as a proportion of the total population. Aboriginal origins (single and multiple) were claimed by over one million individuals in 1991, a substantial increase over 1986; this probably reflects the changing ideology of aboriginal status rather than the natural increase of the population; i.e. people are defining themselves differently, but it also reflects the passage of C-31 in 1985.[2] Also Asian, Arab, and African (single origins) populations increased from 4% to 6% (1.6 million) (Statistics Canada, 1993. Cat. No. 93-315; also Renaud and Badets, 1993).

Table 8-2 therefore does present us with comprehensive data on the ethnic origin of Canadians; but precisely because ethnicity is complex, and because it is perceived differently, the data is problematic. For instance, while most people cited their country of origin as their ethnic group (Britain, France, etc.), others cited religion (Jews) or colour (Blacks) or region (West Indian, Québecois) or language (Hispanic), or mixed. The criteria of identification are legion, so the final numbers are indicative only, rather than definitive.

Numbers are political, however; and nowhere is this more evident than in the figures on mother tongue, sometimes a more acrimonious issue than ethnicity. For instance English was reported as the mother tongue for 63% of the population, and French for 25%, while 13% reported a non-official language as their mother tongue (Statistics Canada, 1992. Cat. No. 93-313). This suggests an ethno-linguistic reality very different from the ethnic diversity portrait in Table 8-2.

Canada, then, is a mosaic, a rainbow of ethnic groups of various colours, cultures, languages, and faiths; and this ethnic pluralism is recognized by the Canadian government.

Indeed Prime Minister Trudeau, following the recommendations of The Royal Commission on Bilingualism and Biculturalism, inaugurated the policy of multiculturalism in 1971:

> We are of the belief that cultural pluralism is the very essence of Canadian iden-
> tity. To say that we have two official languages is not to say that we have two
> official cultures; no culture is in and of itself more official than any other. (In
> Saouab, 1993: 4)

This was followed by the Canadian Human Rights Act (1977), which estab-lished the Canadian Human Rights Commission, the report entitled *Equality Now!* by the Committee on Visible Minorities (1984), the Canadian Multiculturalism Act (1988), and the establishment of a Department of Multiculturalism and Citizenship (1989). By 1991, 31% of Canadian population were of neither British nor French ancestry, as we mentioned in discussing Table 8-2.

Over four million residents of Canada are immigrants (1991 Census data) and they constitute about 16% of the total population: a proportion that has remained constant since the 1950s. As Table 8-3 indicates, the major source countries have been European (U.K., Italy, Poland) and the United States. But Table 8-3 also indicates that the source countries of the last census decade, 1981-91, are frequently Asian: four of the top six countries of birth. Thus, while

Table 8-2   The Canadian Population by Ethnic Origin 1991[1]

British	5,611,050	
English, Irish, Scottish, Welsh		
French	6,146,600	
French, Acadian, Québecois		
European	4,146,065	
Western:	Austrian, Belgian, Dutch, Flemish, German, Luxembourg, Swiss	
Northern:	Finnish, Danish, Icelandic, Norwegian, Swedish	
Eastern:	Estonian, Latvian, Lithuanian, Byelorussian, Czech, Slovak, Hungarian, Polish, Romanian, Russian, Ukrainian	
Southern:	Albanian, Bulgar, Croatian, Macedonian, Serbian, Slovenian, Yugoslav, Cypriot, Greek, Italian, Maltese, Portuguese, Spanish	
Other:	Basque, Jewish	
Asian		
Arab:	Egyptian, Iraqi, Lebanese, Moroccan, Magrebi; Palestinian, Syrian, Arab	
West Asian:	Afghan, Armenian, Iranian, Israeli, Kurdish, Turkish	
South Asian:	Bengali, Punjabi, Singhalese, Tamil, Bangladeshi, East Indian, Pakistani, Sri Lankan.	
East and South East Asia:	Chinese, Filipino, Burmese, Cambodian, Laotian, Thai, Vietnamese, Indonesian, Japanese, Korean, Malays	
African	30,060	
Ethiopian, Somali, Ghana		
Pacific Islands	7,215	
Fijian, Polynesian		
Latin, Central and South America	85,535	
Argentinean, Brazilian, Chilean, Colombian, Ecuadorian, Guatemalan, Hispanic, Mexican, Nicaraguan, Peruvian, Salvadoran, Uruguayan		
Caribbean	94,395	
Barbadian, Cuban, Guyanese, Haitian, Jamaican, Trinidadian and Tobagonian, West Indian		
Black	220,990	
Black, African Black		
Aboriginal	470,615	
Inuit (30,085) Métis (75,150)		
North American Indian (365,375)		
Other	780,035	
Canadian (765,095), American, Australian, New Zealander		
Multiple Origins	7,794,250	
Total:	*26,994,045*	

[1]Single origin, unless otherwise stated.

Source: Statistics Canada, 1993. *Ethnic Origin: The Nation*. Cat. No. 93-315.zz

**Table 8-3   Top 10 Countries of Birth for Recent Immigrants (1981-91)
and all Immigrants, Canada, 1991**

Recent Immigrants			All Immigrants		
1. Hong Kong	96,540	7.8	1. United Kingdom	717,745	16.5
2. Poland	77,455	6.3	2. Italy	351,620	8.1
3. P.R. of China	75,840	6.1	3. United States	249,080	5.7
4. India	73,105	5.9	4. Poland	184,695	4.3
5. United Kingdom	71,365	5.8	5. Germany	180,525	4.2
6. Vietnam	69,520	5.6	6. India	173,670	4.0
7. Philippines	64,290	5.2	7. Portugal	161,180	3.7
8. United States	55,415	4.5	8. P.R. of China	157,405	3.6
9. Portugal	35,440	2.9	9. Hong Kong	152,455	3.5
10. Lebanon	34,065	2.8	10. Netherlands	129,615	3.0
Total	1,238,455	100.0	Total	4,342,890	100.0

Source: Badets, 1993:11 from the 1991 Census.

the proportion of immigrants in Canada has remained constant for the last 40 years, the ethnic composition has changed. The percentage of immigrants in Canada who were born in Asia and the Middle East has increased from 14% in 1981 to 25% in 1991, while the proportion born in Europe has fallen from 67% in 1981 to 54% in 1991 (Badets, 1993).

Is this a problem? No, not necessarily. Indeed the experts argue that Canada needs these immigrants and their skills and capital. Furthermore Canadian immigration legislation was enacted precisely to facilitate and encourage selective migration to Canada. But is this immigration *perceived* as a problem? Yes, by some, for different reasons as we will discuss later.

Obviously Canada is becoming increasingly heterogeneous, and the face of Canada is changing colour.

But Canada is not only a mosaic or a rainbow, it is also, as John Porter (1965) noted in his classic work, a *vertical* mosaic. Every individual may be "equal before and under the law," as the Canadian Charter of Rights and Freedoms asserts; but not all individuals nor all ethnic groups are equal in wealth or power or prestige. And precisely because they are *not* equal, there is conflict between them for scarce resources. We are back in the Hobbesian world, and the conflict paradigm.

We will consider some of these issues very briefly in the following sections on the Native Peoples, the charter groups, and the visible minorities.

THE NATIVE PEOPLES

We are saying that we have the right to determine our own lives. This right derives from the fact that we were here first. We are saying that we are a distinct people, a nation of people, and we must have a special right within Canada.

Robert André

I can see our country being destroyed and my people pushed on reservations, and the white men taking over as they please.

Louise Frost, 21, Old Crow

It is very clear to me that it is an important and special thing to be an Indian. Being an Indian means being able to understand and live with this world in a very special way. It means living with the land, with the animals, with the birds and fish, as though they were your sisters and brothers. It means saying the land is an old friend, and an old friend your father knew, your grandfather knew, indeed your people always have known.

Richard Nerysoo, Fort McPherson

(Berger, 1977: 171, 36, 94)

The eloquence of these Native people addressing Thomas Berger, Chair of the MacKenzie Valley Pipeline Inquiry, speaks for itself. Indeed the Berger Inquiry (1977) was the first opportunity for the Native Peoples of Canada, the Inuit, the Indian nations, and the Métis, to talk directly to Canadians. There had been other reports on the Indians, notably the famous Hawthorn-Tremblay Report (1966), analyses *by* Indians, especially Harold Cardinal's *The Unjust Society* (1969) — a parody of Trudeau's slogan of "the Just Society" — and there would be federal and provincial reports, notably the Department of Indian Affairs and Northern Development (DIAND) report *Indian Conditions* (1980). Nonetheless the Berger Inquiry provided an important forum for aboriginal points of view and, together with the James Bay Treaty signed between the Cree and Quebec in 1975, marked a turning point in the relations between the Native Peoples and the other peoples of Canada.

The Native Peoples are not a homogeneous group, however. Under the Constitution Act (1982), the Native Peoples consist of three groups: the Inuit, the Indians, and the Métis. In 1991, according to the Census, the Inuit numbered 30,085, the Métis 75,150, and the Indians 365,375 (see Table 8-2); but this includes people of single origin only. If people with multiple origins are included, then the total native population numbers more than one million, or about 3.7% of the total population.

Apart from the three ethnic groups and those of single or multiple descent, there are also status and non-status Indians, treaty and non-treaty Indians, on-reserve and off-reserve Indians, often with different socioeconomic profiles, and different legal rights under the Indian Act (1951, revised from 1876). Furthermore the status Indians belong to 605 bands on 2,597 separate reserves speaking 53 dialects in 10 different language groups.

On the other hand these divisions do not totally divide. The Inuit are organized in the Inuit Tapirisat, founded in 1971; the status Indians are represented by the Association of First Nations, currently led by Ovide Mercredi; the Métis are organized in the Métis National Council, and the Congress of Aboriginal People, formerly the Native Council of Canada, represents particularly the off-reserve, urban, and non-status Indians; there are also various regional as well as national (e.g., Cree) organizations.

The Native Peoples are, by virtually every economic indicator, the most deprived peoples in Canada. The first nations are last. The life expectancy for status Indians is about eight years less than the Canadian average. Deaths by suicide are 2.5 times more frequent. Deaths by injury or poisoning are four times more frequent. And infant mortality rates are 1.7 times higher. Average incomes are the lowest in Canada by far, and unemployment rates are the highest, as we have seen in earlier chapters.

Alcohol proves to be a particularly intractable problem, with multiplier effects throughout the community. Alcohol abuse levels are estimated to be between 35% and 40% for the adult population and 10% to 15% for adolescents. These data are from a 1984 brief by the Federation of Saskatchewan Indian Nations and may not be generalizable beyond the Prairies. A Union of Ontario Indians brief of 1987 reports that between 50% and 60% of Native illnesses and deaths are alcohol-related. Abusive drinking results not only in ill health and even death, but also violence, family problems, and problems with the law. Imprisonment rates are very high: 25 times higher for Indian men than for non-Indian men, and 88 times higher for Indian women than for non-Indian women (Health and Welfare, 1989: 21-2. Cat. No. H39-158). The deplorable socioeconomic conditions of the First Nations may explain the drinking, and reciprocally the drinking exacerbates these conditions, in a vicious circle of alcohol, ill health, crime, violence, poverty, and death.

The socioeconomic indicators show a population suffering from multiple adversities: economic, social, health, and political — but adversities which are very slowly being alleviated. Several initiatives have been taken, by Native organizations as well as others, which may imply a sunnier future for the Native Peoples. These initiatives include, in chronological order: the 1982 Constitution Act, which affirmed "the existing aboriginal and treaty rights of the aboriginal peoples of Canada; Bill C-31 which amended the Indian Act in 1985 to recognize women's rights; Elijah Harper who, in 1991, drew national attention to the rights of the First Nations in rejecting the Meech Lake agreement; 1991 saw Manitoba's Aboriginal Justice Inquiry: a drastic critique of the justice system. In 1992 the Charlottetown Accord recognized for the first time the "inherent" right of self-government; but the Accord was rejected in a national referendum. In 1993 the Royal Commission on Aboriginal People presented its first report: *Partners in Confederation* (Cat. No. 21, 1991) and the Nunavut Act and the Nunavut Land Claims Act were both passed by Parliament to establish the Nunavut territory and government in 1999.

While we cannot consider all these initiatives in detail, cumulatively they indicate the immense efforts of Native Peoples "to determine our own lives," as Robert André insisted, and the commitment of both federal and provincial governments to support and recognize Native rights and self-government (Gardner-O'Toole and Allain, 1993a and 1993b). This is particularly evident in the settlement of Native Land Claims, the development of autonomous organizations and leadership, not only in politics but also in business, the arts, and education, and the widespread interest and pride of the general Canadian public in the Native Peoples. Indeed the Inuit and the Indians are prime symbols of Canada.

Canadian attitudes to the aboriginal peoples are complex. A national survey conducted in 1986 indicates that Canadians are relatively ill-informed about Native People and about Native events; these findings parallel an earlier 1976 survey. Efforts to measure the degree of support or sympathy for Native issues indicate that about one in five are inattentive to these issues, and that about half are inconsistent in their attitudes, but that the supportive (20%) outnumber the antagonistic (9%) by about 2:1, with 5% neutral. In general there was more support for land claims and self-government than for "special status" and "distinct society" claims. Considerable regional variation is evident in the responses, with the greatest sympathy found in Quebec and Ontario, least on the prairies, with the Atlantic provinces in between; these far outweighed slight variations by age, sex, educational level, income, and other variables (Ponting, 1988). How knowledge and attitudes may have changed since 1986 is anyone's guess. My own guess is that, given the much higher profile of the Native Peoples in Canada over the last 10 years, knowledge will have increased; but also that, given the violence at Oka and the Mercier Bridge in Quebec, the illegality of cigarette and alcohol smuggling in Ontario and the consequent reduction of taxes by both federal and provincial governments in 1993, and the political confrontation symbolized by Elijah Harper over Meech Lake in 1991 — given all this I would suspect that attitudes might have hardened. We must await the next survey in 1996. But a survey on Native Peoples' attitudes to Canada and Canadians would be particularly valuable. Their attitudes may have hardened too.

The situation of the Native People in Canada cannot be viewed in isolation from that of the Native People in the Americas. In 1992 Amnesty International published a report entitled *The Americas: Human Rights Violations against Indigenous Peoples* to mark, but certainly not to honour, the 500th anniversary of the arrival of Columbus in the Americas. These violations include mass murders, illegal executions, torture, unjust trials, rapes, the 'disappearances' . . . by death squads, the army, police and militia, settlers and miners . . . in Brazil, Colombia, Guatemala, Mexico, Peru and even Canada. Amnesty International cites in particular:

- The murder of Helen Betty Osborne, a 19-year-old Cree, in 1971 in The Pas; no one was convicted until 1986.
- The killing of John Harper in Winnipeg by a police officer in 1988.
- The conviction of Micmac Donald Marshall in 1971 in Nova Scotia for a murder he did not commit. He was released in 1982.
- The high incarceration rates of Native Canadians. In Manitoba the aboriginal peoples comprise only 12% of the population but constitute over 50% of the prison population. The Aboriginal Justice Inquiry stated: "The justice system has failed Manitoba's Aboriginal People on a massive scale" (Amnesty International, 1992: 48-9).

The list of violations in Canada is longer than these examples cited by Amnesty International; but even these, presented in the total American context, give cause for grave concern. The failure of the justice system? This symbolizes the failure of a society.

THE CHARTER GROUPS

The two charter groups, the French and the English, have been in conflict since they first arrived on these shores. The major historical conflicts have been described very briefly in Chapter 3, but these conflicts have been balanced by consensus and cooperation in forging Confederation and Canada as we know it today: the country with the highest quality of life in the entire world, according to the UNDP. Whether we stress the sunshine or the shadows, the consensus or the conflicts depends, as we know, on our personal political paradigms.

In the last two decades, following the Quiet Revolution, the Royal Commission on Bilingualism and Biculturalism, the rise of the FLQ and the declaration of the War Measures Act, several developments have served to transform relations between these two ethnic groups. These include the formation of the Parti Québecois and its victory at the polls in Quebec in 1976, the passage of the very controversial language law, Bill 101, in 1977, the failure of the referendum in 1980, the fall of the PQ in the provincial elections in 1985, and the death of the charismatic René Lévesque in 1985, which marked the end of an era. But it did not mark the end of Quebec nationalism nor separatism.

Jacques Parizeau took over the leadership of the PQ and won the 1994 provincial election on the issue of sovereignty. Meanwhile Lucien Bouchard left Mulroney's Conservatives, formed the Bloc Québecois and won 54 seats in the 1993 federal election, all of them in Quebec, with only 8% of the popular vote, sufficient to form Her Majesty's Loyal Opposition. Both the Reform Party and the Conservatives received a higher percentage of the popular vote (19% and 16% respectively), but they also received a smaller number *and* percentage of the seats: 52 seats or 18% of the total, and two seats or 1% of the total.

Both the BQ and the PQ are committed to achieving the sovereignty and independence of Quebec through another referendum, to be held during 1995. The details of sovereignty remain cloudy, the rhetoric on both sides is often inflammatory, and the polls indicate that the voters are fairly evenly divided between the Liberals and the PQ (small shifts can make big differences, as on a see-saw).

Inside Quebec, Mordecai Richler has slammed separatism, describing the exodus of "129,705 English-speaking Quebecers, reacting to restrictive language laws and growing tribalism" from 1976 to 1990 as caused by a "climate of subtle ethnic cleansing" (*The Globe and Mail* 26.5.94). Outside Quebec, on the day before, two Franco-Ontarians accused Ontario of "cultural genocide" before the Human Rights Committee of the United Nations. The complaint alleges that the lack of a French-only university and of Francophone school boards is contributing to the rapid "assimilation of the Franco-Ontarian community" (25.5.94). With allegations of "cultural genocide" and "ethnic cleansing" riding the winds of change, who needs which reality?

The two ethnic groups are not only polarizing politically, demographically, and ideologically, as the 1993 federal and 1994 Quebec provincial election results and these two examples indicate, they are also polarizing structurally or economically. The *Globe and Mail* recently commissioned Statistics Canada for data on family income by mother tongue. The results are presented in Table 8-4; but they are not easy to interpret. May I suggest that readers study the table and draw their own conclusions before proceeding any further. It is a 6 x 11 table, so study carefully, and, for best results (as the ads say) write your analysis down.

The data indicate that: (1) the French-English gap in median family income in Canada has *increased* over the last 15 years from 9.9% to 14.1%: a 42% increase; in dollar terms this is an increase from under $2,000 to over $6,000. Nationalists emphasized that this proved that Canada is not working for francophones; and they had the data to prove it — seemingly. (2) In every province for which statistics are available, the English earn more than the French, and in every province this income gap has *increased* — except for Quebec; the gap widened in favour of the English in Manitoba from 11% to 15%, in Ontario from 6% to 14%, in New Brunswick from 8% to 10%, and in Nova Scotia the gap even turned around from slightly favouring the French to easily favouring

Table 8-4 The French-English Gap, Median Family Income by Mother Tongue

	1977			1992		
	French	English	% difference	French	English	% difference
Newfoundland	-	14,989	-	-	36,876	-
Prince Edward Island	-	14,669	-	-	39,786	-
Nova Scotia	15,247	14,642	-4%	37,574	40,728	8.4%
New Brunswick	14,304	15,442	8%	39,954	42,704	9.6%
Quebec	17,311	18,735	8.2%	43,754	44,589	1.9%
Ontario	18,680	19,857	6.3%	47,875	54,325	13.5%
Manitoba	16,088	17,892	11.2%	38,972	44,813	15%
Saskatchewan	12,548	17,081	36.1%	-	42,625	-
Alberta	20,775	20,484	-1.4%	-	49,979	-
British Columbia	-	20,312	-	-	51,982	-
CANADA	17,310	19,024	9.9%	44,020	50,209	14.1%

-=Sample size too small

Source: Statistics Canada, unpublished data from
The Survey of Consumer Finances, *Globe and Mail* 23.3.94

the English: from -4% to 8%: a 12% shift. What could explain this shift, all across the country? (3) In Quebec this pattern was reversed with the gap *decreasing* from 8.2% to 1.9% — but still the English earned $835 more than the French, on average, and in a province where the French are the 80% majority. This caused some fury; but it still requires an explanation. This may be found in (4) the ratio of Quebec incomes to those in Ontario and Canada. Note that although French median family incomes in Quebec were *above* the Canadian average in 1977, they had fallen to *below* the average in 1992. Furthermore (5) while average French incomes in Quebec were 93% of those in Ontario in 1977, they had fallen to 91% by 1992. Ironically, but economically, it is more profitable to be French in Ontario than in Quebec. Similarly English incomes in Quebec declined from 98% of the Canadian English average in 1977 to 89% of this average. The economic growth rates in Ontario are evidently higher than those in Quebec. Thus it may be the relatively slow rate of economic growth in Quebec, where the majority of those whose mother tongue is French live that explains the increased English-French incomes gap, rather than the failure of federalism. Finally (6) while it is evident that the incomes gap between the English and the French in Quebec has closed dramatically in the 15 years between 1977 and 1992, this has been partly because of the emigration of the higher income English out of the province as well as to the francization of the Quebec economy.

In sum the economic gap between the English and the French has opened wider in Canada and many of the provinces, but closed in Quebec; but the gap between Quebec incomes and those of Ontario and Canada has opened wider. Quebec is falling behind. This raises the question: Is Quebec nationalism or Canadian federalism the problem? Does the data "prove" one paradigm or the other?

VISIBLE MINORITIES

The Daudlin Committee on Visible Minorities insists in the first page of its report:

> Visible minorities are, in fact, the invisible members of our society. Canada will be the ultimate loser if we do not take advantage of the skills and abilities which visible minorities have to offer. (1984: 1)

The term "visible minorities" emerged in the late seventies and early eighties with a descriptive and egalitarian purpose in mind: to avoid some of the pejorative associations of such earlier terms as "non-whites" and "Coloureds," and to draw attention to the common problems of racism faced by members of these groups.

The Daudlin Committee Report, *Equality Now!* was followed in the same year by the Abella Committee *Report on Equality in Employment* (1984) which recommended the introduction of employment equity legislation for four target populations: women, native people, the physically handicapped, and visible minorities. We are concerned in this chapter with the native people and visible minorities.

The Federal Government responded to the recommendations of both Committees for affirmative action and equity legislation and introduced successively the Employment Equity Act (1986), the Federal Contractors Program, the Public Service Employment Equity Program, the Multiculturalism Act (1991), and the Public Service Reform Act (1993).

In this legislation visible minorities are defined as those who are non-white in colour or non-Caucasian in race, other than aboriginal people. These minorities are divided into ten groups: Blacks, Chinese, Filipino, other Pacific Islanders, Indo-Pakistani, Japanese, Korean, Southeast Asians, West Asians and Arabs, and Latin Americans.

A profile of the visible minority population in Canada drawn from the 1991 Census indicates that they comprise about 9.1% of the total population; up from 6.3% in 1986 (CHRC 1994: 65). A detailed analysis of the socioeconomic situation of visible minorities in 1986 indicates the following:

Employment The unemployment rate (10.8%) was slightly higher than the Canadian average (10.3%).

Education Educational levels were higher than the Canadian average: 10% of Canadians have a university degree compared to 14% of the visible minorities.

Income Despite higher educational levels, average employment income was lower than the Canadian average in 1985.

Occupations Visible minority men were occupationally polarized, with higher proportions (12%) than the Canadian average (7%) in the relatively low-income service occupations, but also in the in the higher-income professional occupations (14% to 10%). Women, on the other hand, were more concentrated in lower income jobs than the Canadian average, especially as manual workers (21% to 13%) (Moreau, 1991a).

Obviously this raw data conceals a wide variation by national origin and/or colour. Some visible minorities are no doubt doing better than others. The national data are presented in Table 8-5.

Several features of this table deserve comment. First, in accord with the feminist paradigm, note the considerable difference between male and female average incomes for every ethnic group. Second, and more to our purpose in this chapter, consider the economic hierarchy of these ethnic groups stacked one on top of the other like pancakes, with the First Nations at the bottom. The data are "only" averages, so there is considerable overlap both within and between these groups; nonetheless the table does indicate clearly a "vertical mosaic." Also, despite widespread fears of the emergence of a racial stratification system, with whites over visible minorities, the economic reality seems to be more complex. The Arabs score well, so to speak, even higher than the British, French, and most other Europeans; yet they are one of the visible minorities targeted by the equity legislation. The South Asians are also doing well. Perhaps we should be less concerned with colour or visibility and more with targeting the specific populations which need equity most, especially the aboriginals, and also the Caribbeans and Blacks who outnumber the South Americans (often white) and the Pacific Islanders put together (see Table 8-2).

On the other hand the CHRC analysis of the equity legislation from 1987 to 1992 does show some gains made by visible minorities. In the private sector covered by the Employment Equity Act, visible minority representation increased from 5% in 1987 to 7.9% in 1992. Middle management representation increased from 4.4% to 6.7%, and senior management representation increased from 2.1% to 2.9%. This is slow but steady progress, but gaps still remain both between visible minorities and the majority, and between men and women. Visible minority males received about 94% of the salary of all male employees, but visible minority females made only 71% of the overall male rate — roughly the same as women as a whole.

Table 8-5   Average Income and Ethnic Origin by Sex, 1986

Ethnic Origins (single + multiple origins)	Males	Females
Northern Europeans	$24,447	$13,025
Arabs	$24,172	$12,806
British	$24,160	$12,926
Western Europeans	$23,765	$12,546
Eastern Europeans	$23,480	$13,181
South Asians	$23,113	$12,256
South Europeans	$21,861	$11,995
French	$21,440	$11,930
West Asians	$21,421	$11,793
East and Southeast Asians	$20,567	$13,387
Caribbeans	$19,373	$12,783
Blacks	$18,362	$12,899
Pacific Islanders	$18,357	$11,877
Latin, Central, South Americans	$17,953	$10,423
Aboriginals	$15,760	$ 9,828

Source: Statistics Canada, 1989. *Profile of Ethnic Groups.* Cat. No. 93-154.

In the Public Service visible minority representation is much lower, only 3.7% (compared to 7.9% in the private sector). The CHRC notes that this is hard to explain, despite federal hiring limits, "given the Government's declared commitment to its own job equity policy and legislative regime" (CHRC 1994: 68).

Blacks are the most visible of the visible minorities, and Frances Henry has documented in *The Caribbean Diaspora in Toronto: Learning to Live with Racism* not only the types and levels of white racism but also the coping strategies of Black West Indians in Toronto. She and her research team interviewed 134 people and talked to an additional 70 or so West Indians about their experiences of racism in employment, the education system, and the justice system, as well as their families, lifestyles, and culture. Most people have experienced some racism, often verbal harassment and name-calling, which was usually but not always ignored and which she describes as a hurdle and not a barrier (1994: 258). Nonetheless she found racism to be "the major barrier preventing incorporation of Caribbean people into Canadian mainstream society" (1994: 273), particularly for second generation youth, and she is concerned that if the barriers are not raised an underclass may develop with the possibility of social disruption. The strength of this research is that she lets people talk and, despite having to learn to live with racism, "most Caribbean migrants in Canada are satisfied with their lives in Canada" (1994: 271).

EQUITY

The equality of all human beings has been asserted by the UN in the Declaration of Human Rights: "All human beings are born free and equal, both in dignity and in rights." Despite the massive inequality prevailing world-wide then and now, the declaration remains a triumph of democratic and liberal ideology, countervailing the widespread tradition of inegalitarianism since Plato, and most obviously manifest in such ideologies as racism, sexism, and fascism, and in such practices as slavery, genocide, the Holocaust, and ethnic cleansing.

Much of the debate about visible minorities revolves around the notion of equity: a notion which has subtly replaced the notion of equality, while retaining much of its aura.

Equality, in my dictionary, means: "The same in number, size, value, degree, etc." Equity means "fairness," with the implication of justice. But both words have the same Latin root, *aequus*, meaning even or level.

Without wishing to delve too deeply into the philosophy and sociology of equality and equity, we can remember the distinctions between absolute equality or equality of results: the egalité so beloved of the French revolutionaries and of Rousseau and Marx — and the equality of opportunity so beloved of contemporary liberals.[3]

Equity does not mean equality, nor even equal opportunity. As it is being implemented in federal and provincial legislation it has implications of "catching-up" i.e., affirmative action and reverse discrimination (to give the positive and negative connotations of the term). Such legislation has two goals: to redress the impact of historical discrimination against the four target groups, and to create a society in which the component parts (occupational groups and income groups principally) *mirror* the total society: each part will be representative of the whole. The ultimate goal of the equity legislation is to eliminate racism, and sexism; and particularly to eliminate the blocks to the hiring and promotions of the four target populations.

Pay equity, defined as equal pay for work of equal value, is widely accepted as a fair and just policy. (The principal objections are practical e.g., that if it is implemented in such and such a place, the company/department etc. will be bankrupted.) Occupational equity, the privileging of certain sectors of the population at the expense of others, is more controversial. This has been discussed, in the context of gender, in Chapter 4.

By and large the target groups seem to think this is fair enough, about time, and praiseworthy. But many others do not, especially young white males, who see job prospects disappearing. Opponents argue that the equity legislation merely replaces one type of biological discrimination with another; furthermore *merit* is the prime requirement of any job, not membership of some category, however discriminated against it may have been in the past; and finally to replace *individual* rights by *group* rights is unworkable in practice — where would it end? Furthermore discrimination in the past is not redressed by reverse discrimination in the present.

Also even "Whites" have been discriminated against, the Jews, Ukrainians and Armenians in particular in this century. Do we develop a Discrimination Index and award points for suffering in the past? Obviously not.

And not all visible minorities have been equally discriminated against over the centuries. Many ethnic groups are relatively recent immigrants to Canada. Yet somehow, in the interests of equity, they have to be hired preferentially and automatically over other groups solely because of their visibility? Evidently the debates about equity indicate conflicts both of interests and of values.

The last word on this goes to Wilson Head, a Black American immigrant to Canada who worked hard for social justice and died in 1993: "It should be apparent that a democratic society faces a cruel dilemma when it promises equal opportunity to all, and yet a considerable portion of its population suffers from discrimination based on its racial classification" (CHRC 1994: 38).

RACISM

Racism may refer either to attitudes (prejudice) or behaviour (discrimination) and it may be individual and personal or systemic; but usually the term is used broadly to refer to the total package.

Why does racism exist and persist? Functionalist sociologists argue that racism, anti-Semitism and bigotry exist because they are *useful*, to many people and in many ways: they perform certain functions for individuals and society. If they did not, they would die out. "We do, in fact, enjoy certain benefits at the expense of others, and it should be made clear that we do. We must face up to the functions of discrimination and prejudice" (Levin and Levin, 1984: 50). Among the benefits which accrue to the majority are the following:

- "displacement of aggression" — basically scapegoating.
- "protection of self-esteem" — "We" are better than "Them."
- "reduction of uncertainty": all or most problems are mainly caused by "Them."
- "maintenance of occupational status."
- "maintenance of power."

(Levin and Levin, 1984: 202)

There are other functions. Marxists and radical sociologists insist that the prime functions of racism are to legitimize the hierarchy of oppression e.g., slavery, racial inequality etc. and to divide the population and therefore to rule. They also note that the *costs* of such racism may ultimately outweigh the alleged benefits for the dominant group: the prime costs being violence (criminal and/or racial), counter-racism, and perhaps rebellion and revolution (Cox, 1949). Injustice and inequality create countervailing efforts to change the status quo, by violence if necessary. This is axiomatic.

Two points might be made here: first, the devastating effects of racism on the target population. Second, that we should not see racism solely as the moral failing of an individual but also as an institutional impersonal, bureaucratic "air," a characteristic of the social structure which is, or may be, as totally oppressive of ethnic and visible minorities as is sexism (see Chapter 4).

To illustrate the human cost, this is Dolphus Shae, a Dene:

> Before I went to school the only English I knew was "hello," and when we got there we were told that if we spoke Indian they would whip us until our hands were blue on both sides. And also we were told that the Indian religion was superstitious and pagan. It made you feel inferior to the whites. . . . The first day we got to school all our clothes were taken away . . . and everybody was given a haircut which was a bald haircut. We all felt lost and wanted to go home, and some cried for weeks and weeks, and I remember one Eskimo boy every night crying inside his blanket because he was afraid that the sister might come and spank him. . . . Today, I think back on the hostel life and I feel ferocious. (Berger, 1977: 90)

Dolphus Shae began to "feel inferior to the Whites" and Rosemary Kirby says "We grew up to feel ashamed of being Eskimos, being ashamed of being "Indian" (Berger, 1977: 91). And this was taught in the school system. In the experience of Richard Nerysoo, 24:

> When I went to school in Fort McPherson I can remember being taught that the Indians were savages. We were violent, cruel and uncivilized. I remember reading history books that glorified the white man who slaughtered whole nations of Indian people. No one called the white man savages, they were heroes who explored new horizons or conquered new frontiers. . . . That kind of thinking is still going on today. (Berger, 1977: 91)

The role of the education system is complemented by that of the justice system. The Aboriginal Justice Inquiry in Manitoba concluded in 1991 that: "The justice system has failed Manitoba's Aboriginal People on a massive scale" — as we saw above.

As in the education system and the justice system, so in the political system in which aboriginals and visible minorities are underrepresented (see Chapter 3). Data on inequalities in the employment, health, and income systems have been discussed earlier. This is what is meant by *systemic* racism.

But just how racist are Canadians? The Committee on Visible Minorities states: "Research has shown that as many as 15 per cent of the population exhibit blatantly racist attitudes, while another 20-25 per cent have some racist tendencies (1984: 3). Unfortunately it does not say *what* research; and whether one should say "as many as" 15% or should say "as few as" is a judgement call, particularly since not all racists are white, presumably.

A recent survey by Ekos Research drew essentially similar conclusions, however. About 16% of Canadians are defined as hard-core xenophobes, with another 25% "flirting with intolerance" and another 25% increasingly uneasy about immigration levels. Indeed the survey found that 53% of Canadians believe that there are too many immigrants; this is up from 31% just five years earlier. This is widely described as a dramatic rise in intolerance, due partly to the recession and partly to a perceived threat to Canadian identity and culture. 60% of the respondents, for instance, agreed with the statement that "too many immigrants feel no obligation to adapt to Canadian values" (*The Globe and Mail*, 10.3.94).

On the other hand a recent report by the Economic Council of Canada found that "there was no systematic discrimination in earnings against visible minorities;" also that discrimination against blacks in face-to-face job offers in Toronto was not discernible — indeed the study, using Black and White actors, found that Blacks were hired *more* frequently (but telephone applications for jobs using "accented callers" did result in findings of discrimination); furthermore prejudice levels appear to be diminishing over time based both on their study of 62 surveys taken from 1975 to 1990 and also on attitudes to Black/White intermarriages from 1980 to 1990 (Economic Council of Canada, 1991: 28-31).

Racism may (or may not) be declining, but clearly immigration and multiculturalism are problematic. Immigration levels are now set at about 250,000 per annum; i.e., at about 1% of the population. And while Canada is known as "a community of communities," not all of these communities are as equal (as we have seen), nor as highly esteemed as others.

Environics has conducted a series of surveys over the years probing Canadian attitudes towards six ethnic minorities: Jews, Italians, Poles, Blacks, Chinese, and Pakistanis. Two questions related to prejudice were asked: "Would you say that members of the following ethnic groups have too much, just enough or not enough power in Canada today?" And: "If the party for which you normally vote nominated a candidate of . . . descent in your riding would you or would you not vote for this candidate?" Most of the respondents (over 80%) accepted the power distributions for all six groups, and said that they would vote for nominated candidates of all groups; but not all groups are equally liked, and some minorities are less tolerant than others. Also these questions would seem to have validity only for marginalized groups. If the British or French were included in these questions it would be difficult to interpret the results; assertions that they have too much power, might be interpreted as evidence of prejudice or simply as absolutely correct!

The results are tabulated in Table 8-6, but the author warns that the results are "partial and indicative, not complete and conclusive."

Results have been fairly consistent over the years, although space does not permit presentation of all the data; but there is a wide range of responses from the 4% who believe that Poles have too much power and the 6% who would not vote for an Italian candidate to the 16% who believe that Pakistanis have too much power and would not vote for one either. Multivariate analysis indicates that attitudes are influenced by the amount of contact respondents had with other groups, by education levels, by region and by ethnic group. Jewish and Chinese respondents were both more tolerant of other minorities than average. Black, Native, and French respondents were the least tolerant, perhaps because they feel most disenfranchised or least tolerated themselves. In between these extremes, the British, Poles, Ukrainians and Germans score as more tolerant, and Greeks, Pakistanis, Italians, and Dutch as less so (Buckner, 1993).

Evidently over 80% of Canadians are, or appear to be, relatively unprejudiced; and evidently the Pakistanis are the most disliked of these six groups, and they are a visible minority. But visibility is not everything. Canadians are not blanket-prejudiced, with prejudice levels rising in direct relation to visibility. Blacks, for instance, fare better than Jews on both the power and the vote questions, and the same as the Poles on the vote question. Indeed according to this survey Canadians are more anti-Semitic than anti-Black. On the other hand there seems to be a solid four to six per cent who loathe everybody!

A recent Decima poll on Canadian attitudes, conducted on behalf of the Canadian Council of Christians and Jews, inspired *Maclean's* to ask if we are "A nation of polite bigots?" The survey found that 72% of those surveyed believe

Table 8-6   Canadian Attitudes to Minorities, 1991

	"They" have Too Much Power (in percent)	Would not Vote for "them" (in percent)
Blacks	9.0	6.9
Chinese	11.5	8.6
Italians	8.7	6.0
Jews	14.6	8.1
Pakistanis	16.2	16.3
Poles	4.0	6.9
(n = 2,003)		

Source: Buckner 1993: 4, 5

that ethnic groups should adopt Canadian values and practices, and that 41% think that current immigration policy allows "too many people of different races and colours coming into Canada"; a majority (57%) said they sometimes held negative views of minority groups; half (50%) agreed with the statement "I am sick and tired of some groups complaining about racism being directed at them" and two-fifths (41%) agreed: "I am tired of ethnic minorities being given special treatment."

An anthropologist commented: "In the United States racism is up front: if they don't like you, they come out with their little handguns and pop bullets at you. But Canadians are in a state of denial when it comes to racism" (*The Globe and Mail* 14.12.93; *Maclean's* 27.12.93:42-3). Personally, I prefer denial to bullets; but there is little denial in this survey. On the contrary, with a majority admitting to occasional prejudice against minorities, racism (albeit partial, and attitudinal rather than behavioural) seems more like the norm than the exception .

Canadian attitudes are ambiguous therefore. While there is widespread concern about racism, yet also a majority confess to sometimes holding "negative views." Also there seems to be a conflict between the federal policy of multiculturalism and the public demand for conformity to Canadian norms and culture. Furthermore there also seems to be a conflict between the federal equity policy and a solid proportion of the public (41%) "tired of ethnic minorities being given special treatment."

To add to the complexity: how do we interpret this survey data? The Decima poll indicates that 41% think that current immigration policy allows "too many people of different races and colours coming into Canada." Is that racist? As it stands, it might seem so. But a recent Gallop poll reports that 45% of Canadians believe that current immigration levels are too high, i.e., too many people are coming into Canada, period, and that would include people of different races and colours — which is not a racist comment! (*La Presse* 10.1.94).

Canadian attitudes therefore seem to be enigmatic, ambiguous, and complex, at least in so far as they are reached by surveys; your own experience in the homes, bars, and streets of Canada may require other conclusions.

More research on attitudes is obviously necessary, particularly qualitative research; but still the consensus theorist might comment on how tolerant Canadians are, and the conflict theorist might deplore how racist Canadians are. Which view does the data support?

And are these attitudes, *in so far as* they are racist, or seem to be, warranted by any data? The answer to this is a qualified no, at least according to the latest Statistics Canada (1994) publication, *Canada's Changing Immigrant Population* (1994. Cat. No. 96-311). This monograph "explodes a number of myths," as the cliché has it, about Canadian immigrants, or stereotypes — but how widely held these myths or stereotypes may be, we simply do not know. At any rate, the census date indicate that immigrants work hard: overall labour force participation rates are about the same (65.2% for immigrants and 68.7 for Canadian-born) but for those who immigrated from 1961 to 1980 participation rates are at about 85% — much higher than the Canadian average (1994: 48).

Male immigrants are also more likely than the Canadian-born to be employed in professional and managerial occupations. And furthermore a higher proportion of immigrants have university degrees than Canadians (14% to 11%), and the proportion is even higher for recent (1981-91) immigrants (17% to 11%). In fairness we should also note that the immigrant population is polarized: a higher proportion also had less than grade nine education, mostly among the older population. But on average they have more years of schooling than the Canadian-born (1994: 55-6, 41, 43). Immigrants are also less likely to be criminals, as we will see below. In the cheque-book analysis of immigration, therefore, Canada reaps substantial economic benefits from immigration. If Canadian attitudes were more realistic and better informed, perhaps some Canadians would be less prejudiced.

Researching attitudes, i.e. prejudice, is not easy, but researching behaviour, i.e. racial or ethnic discrimination, is even more difficult. How much racial or ethnic discrimination individuals have had to endure, and of what type, how serious, and on what basis (colour, language, etc.) is virtually unknown. Gender discrimination has been far better researched than racial or ethnic discrimination. The occasional incidents are reported and discussed (e.g. the notorious ban on religious headwear by the Legion in 1994), and the Canadian Human Rights Commission does engage these issues, but we have no national data.

The League for Human Rights does record incidents of anti-Semitism, however, and reported a total of 256 incidents of anti-Semitic harassment and vandalism in 1993, which was a massive 31% increase over the 196 incidents reported in 1992. 1990 and 1991, years which coincided with the invasion of Kuwait and the Gulf War, also contained a high number of anti-Semitic incidents (210 and 251 respectively) (1994: 4). These numbers are no doubt an underestimate of the total, since not all incidents are reported to League offices. But most of the serious incidents are enumerated and discussed. The increase in anti-Semitic incidents and violence probably reflects the rise of the racist right and white power groups in Canada in recent years.

Warren Kinsella has researched the racist right and hate groups in Canada for about seven years, and recently published *Web of Hate* to discuss his findings: "As Canada's racist right has become increasingly visible, and increasingly violent, I believe that it has grown to become a significant social problem . . . Racism is growing in Canada" (1993: 4-5). There are about 40 hate groups in Canada, with a fluid and overlapping membership, mostly small in numbers (under 100), and some affiliated with parent organizations in the States, notably the Ku Klux Klan. While racism is not new in Canada, and anti-Semitic and white supremacist organizations did spring up across Canada in the twenties and thirties, this new crop is alarming not only because this is a fresh, well-educated generation — who seem to have misunderstood World War II — but also because it is more organized, more violent, largely home-grown, and expanding.

The depth of the hatreds is difficult for outsiders to understand: hatred of Jews, Blacks, First Nations, gays, and non-whites generally. The worst examples will *not* be reprinted here. The following will give some idea. A poster published by the Aryan Resistance Movement in B.C. displays an SS soldier with the slogan "FIGHT TERROR WITH TERROR"; it reads "We do not wish for law and order, for law and order means the continued existence of this rotten, rip-off, Capitalist Jew System. We wish for anarchy and chaos which will enable us to attack the system while the Big Brother Pigs are trying to keep the pieces from falling apart." The Western Guard, based in Toronto, and the first group to start a hate line in Canada, in 1973 broadcast such messages as: "Compared to race-mixing, an atomic war with near total destruction is preferable." "Communists are behind race-mixing, and the founders of communism were Jewish. Likewise, the leaders of the major black organizations, the National Association for the advancement of Colored People, have been Jewish." "The big lie is that Hitler is said to have gassed six million Jews, whereas the truth is he never gassed one." Their graffiti include "Racism is not evil," "More niggers, more crime — kill race mixers" and of course "White Power" (Kinsella, 1993: 53, 209).

Similar types of messages were and are promulgated by other neo-Nazi or white supremacist groups: the Nationalist Party of Canada, the Heritage Front, the Canadian Church of the Creator, the Aryan Nations and many more. These organizations are not entirely distinct however. The memberships often overlap, the leaders usually know and admire each other, meeting at trials, in the US at head offices or at Aryan fests across Canada. The Canadian Liberty Net, a telephone hate-line, for instance, broadcast messages from the Aryan Nations, Ernst Zundel, and the Heritage Front: various dialects of the same language.

Two of Canada's most noted extremists are Jim Keegstra, a former high school teacher in Ecksville Alberta, and Ernst Zundel, a holocaust-denier from Toronto who was deeply influenced by Adrien Arcand, the elderly fascist from the thirties in Quebec. Keegstra was charged in 1983 with promoting hatred against Jews and his conviction was upheld by the Supreme Court in 1990, but in a 4-3 split decision. The split was not about whether he preached hatred, but whether freedom of speech legislation *allowed* him to do so. An odd quandary for a court, for surely all freedoms are limited and conditional upon the rights of others. Zundel was charged in 1984 with spreading "false news" — lies, in other words. His conviction was overturned by the Court in 1992, to the joy of racists and the surprise and consternation of many others (Kinsella, 1993: 355-58; see also Barrett, 1991).

RACE AND CRIME

The relation between ethnicity or race and crime is a hot topic, not only emotionally (the Italian Mafia, Blacks as violent, Whites as racist — and the exercise of racism *is* a crime), with allegations of stereotypes, generalizations, and ethnic slurs, but also statistically, as we shall see. So we will dive into the deep end, present and analyze such statistics as are available, consider their considerable limitations, and air this difficult topic.

Tables 8-7 and 8-8 present the figures on homicides, by racial origin for Canada, 1980-89, and robberies and attempted robberies by racial origin for Toronto, 1992-93. Consider Table 8-7: the most obvious conclusion is that Whites are the majority of the suspects (72%) and the majority of the victims (77%). This is not really surprising since they constitute the majority of the population. Indeed these proportions may well be low since many of those listed under "Not Stated" would probably be Whites.

The second point is that the Native People, who constitute, as we have seen, about 3% of the total population, are 20% of the suspects and 14% of the victims. This is a homicide ratio of six to seven times the Canadian average and a victim ratio of almost five times the Canadian average: a double blow of incarceration and death to the Native People.

Blacks constituted only 2.9% of the suspects and only 2.5% of the victims, but since they were about 4% of the population in 1981 rising to 6% of the population in 1991, this means that they are *less* prone to commit homicide, or to be murdered, than the Canadian average. Far from being more violent than others, Blacks are less violent. The 1994 murders of Ms. Leimonis in Toronto, Constable Baylis in Toronto, and Chul Cho in Montreal, all of which were allegedly committed by young Black males can perhaps now be seen for what they are: quite exceptional not only in their circumstances but also in the colour of the suspects.

Table 8-8 tells a very different story. According to this data Blacks are or were suspects in over half of all the robberies and attempted robberies committed in Toronto. Whites, who far outnumber Blacks there, are suspects in only

Table 8-7   Homicides by Racial Origin, Canada, 1980-89

	Caucasian	Negroid	Mongoloid	Canadian Indian	Eskimo	Métis	Not stated	TOTAL
SUSPECTS	4,191	170	81	965	37	132	261	5,837
%	71.8	2.9	1.4	16.5	1.0	2.3	4.5	100
VICTIMS	4,947	158	108	796	35	93	269	6,406
%	77.2	2.5	1.7	12.4	0.5	1.5	4.2	100

Source: Canadian Centre for Justice Statistics in *Globe and Mail* 11.6.94.

Table 8-8   Robberies and Attempted Robberies by Racial Origin (Toronto, 1992-3)

	Suspects	
	Total	**%**
Aboriginal	46	0.4
Black	5,587	52.1
Oriental	543	5.1
North Asian	205	1.9
White	3,447	32.1
Unknown	900	8.4
Total	10,728	100

Source: Globe and Mail 11.6.94.

32% of these crimes. Certainly poverty is an intervening variable: the poor are perhaps more likely to commit robberies than the wealthy, and 26% of Blacks are below the poverty line in Toronto (1986 data in Moreau, 1991b); so the analysis might suggest that these are class crimes rather than race crimes, so to speak. But 22% of Chinese and 15% of Indo-Pakistanis also live below the poverty line, and they are relatively rarely cited as suspects. If poverty is a variable, then, it should apply to these other groups; but it does not, or not to the same degree.

The third set of data is from the prison system. In 1992-93, 80% of the 14,500 federal prison inmates were Caucasian, 11.9% were Aboriginal, and only 4.7% were Black (*The Globe and Mail* 11.6.94). Aboriginals were therefore over-represented and Blacks were underrepresented. Arrest, charge, conviction, and prison sentence are surely a far superior measure of criminality than merely "suspicion." By this data on race and prison, therefore, Whites are by far the most criminal race of all in absolute numbers, and about on a par with their proportion in the population. Following them are the Native Peoples, whose extremely hazardous state in Canada has already been discussed.

Another study using a different data base reached similar conclusions. Immigrants are far *less* likely to be criminals than Canadian-born Canadians, and so are non-whites. More specifically, foreign-born people constitute 20.2% of the population, but only 10.3% of the *prison* population (1989) — they are therefore *half* as likely as the Canadian born to land in jail. Similarly, while visible minorities constitute 8.5% of the total Canadian population, they constitute only 5.2% of the prison population (1989). The author noted: "If our future immigrants show no greater propensity toward crime than those already in the country, the ratio of taxpayers to criminals should become more favourable" (*The Globe and Mail* 14.7.94).

What then can we say about Table 8-8, which seems to give Blacks such a bad name, yet is also so discrepant both with Table 8-7 and with the prison statistics? The question is particularly urgent since so many homicides occur during robberies e.g., Ms. Leimonis and Mr. Cho. And here we must question the validity of the statistics, both the numbers and the attributions of race. Numerical accuracy is always a problem, as we discussed in Chapter 6. The data on robbery statistics include only those crimes reported and recorded — and many robberies are not reported and, if reported, are not recorded; even then only one-third of the suspects are eventually charged, and fewer still are convicted. Furthermore, many robberies are committed by more than one person, so there are more suspects than incidents; and the total number of suspects includes double counting, since one person may be a suspect in many different incidents. The interpretation of these statistics is therefore complex. As for race, the interpretations are even more complex. The homicide statistics by race collected by police forces from 1980 to 1989 were banned after 1990, partly because Statistics Canada could not guarantee their reliability, and partly because of politics. Police were required to distinguish six "different" races — a difficult task at the best of times, impossible in the case of mixed-race individuals, and always likely to be highly subjective. The same applies to the robbery statistics, except that only five "different" races are recognized here (cf. *The Globe and Mail* 11.6.94). The race data therefore are also unreliable: indicative rather than definitive.

Nonetheless the Jamaican posses remain problematic. Statistics on race and crime remain elusive, as are statistics on racism and other topics; but an absence of totally accurate statistics does not mean there are no problems and no methodologies. After the murder of a young (25-year-old) Jamaican crack dealer in Montreal, the *Montreal Gazette* decided to investigate the gangs. According to MUC police and Jamaican sources, four Jamaican gangs (with a *maximum* of 155 members, mostly affiliated rather than hard core) are trying to control their share of the crack and cocaine trade. Other gangs are also involved of course, including Colombians, the Mafia, and others. According to the MUC police, almost one in seven murders committed since 1990 involves a Jamaican-born resident either as suspected killer or as victim: this is 38 homicides involving these gangs and 97 attempted homicides. Toronto has six major gangs, and in 1991 more than half of the 32 homicides committed involved Jamaicans, either as victim or suspect (*Montreal Gazette* 23.7.94). In Ottawa where the Toronto and Montreal gangs are struggling for turf, four people have been killed in the 1993-94 drug wars (*Montreal Gazette* 26.7.94). All the sources add that the criminals are a tiny fraction of the total Jamaican community, that some are Canadian raised, some members are not Jamaican, a few are white, and all the usual and necessary riders to prevent a few bad apples from labeling the entire community. Nonetheless the danger is that the racist stereotype becomes a self-fulfilling prophecy.

While the US routinely collects and publishes data on crime and race, many Canadians are wary of the reliability of such data, the uses to which it might be put, and are concerned that the costs might be higher than the benefits. More bluntly, I think the main fear is that crime-race statistics will fuel racism, especially the violent crime statistics. What do you think? Can these difficulties of assessment be resolved or at least alleviated? or should race-crime data be ignored as undesirable and also unreliable? Is failure to publish more likely to fuel racism than publication perhaps? And *do* these statistics inspire racism?

CONCLUSION

All in all, race and ethnic relations are far more harmonious than they are in, say, Rwanda, Bosnia, or Ulster — and perhaps even than in the US, although some say that the polite racism in Canada is harder to deal with than the hard, overt racism in the States.

Nonetheless racism persists in Canada. It persists at the individual level, at the systemic or structural level, and it is organized. Furthermore there is some evidence that racism is growing as it is organized.

Racism also persists in many different sectors of the population. Neo-Nazi Skins have received the worst publicity, partly because of their occasional violence, but also because of their high visibility at Aryan fests of various sorts across Canada; but there are also Skins committed to fighting, actively and literally, racism in Canada. Racism has appeared in the Canadian Armed Forces in Somalia. Racism is alleged in police forces across Canada, from the false conviction of Donald Marshall in 1971 to the shooting death of Marcellus François in Montreal in 1992. Racism is evident in incidents of vandalism, harassment, and violence; in the justice system; in some of the middle class who finance racists and their defense; it is apparent in differential hiring and promotion policies, and salary structures; in language, stereotypes in the media, and some history books, and in the structure of politics. Racism is *not* everyone, everywhere all the time; but it persists. It restricts life chances, inhibits mobility, reinforces ethnic inequalities, creates ethnic conflicts, and ultimately damages not only the intended victim but also the society which tolerates it or, still more damaging in the long run, sanctions racism.

The ethnic prejudices which permeate multicultural and unequal Canada coincide along three major fault lines: English-French, visible minority-majority and Native-non Native, but also along clusters of ancient antagonisms affecting probably every ethnic minority in Canada (Irish-English, Vietnamese-Cambodian, Japanese-Chinese, etc.). We might emphasize the harmony — how we all get along OK, more or less, most of the time — or the discord and the conflict. We may stress the problems or the progress, depending on the paradigm.

ENDNOTES

1. There are many excellent texts on racism, and race and ethnic relations generally, including Driedger, 1989; McKague, 1991; Kallen, 1995; Henry, 1995; Elliott and Fleras, 1992. Also there are the annual reports of the Canadian Human Rights Commission and the League for Human Rights.

2. Bill C-31 amended the Indian Act which required Indian status women who married non-status Indians to lose their status, but it did not require Indian status men to lose their status. This was widely perceived as sex discrimination by feminists and Native women but not, on the whole, by Native chiefs. Mary Two-Axe Early of Kahnawake took the case to the Supreme Court and lost; then Sandra Lovelace, a Maliseet from New Brunswick took it to the United Nations and won. Hence Bill C-31. Since then more than 100,000 Indians have been added to the status rolls.

3. Equality of opportunity is impossible to achieve without a prior equality; but obviously efforts can be made to equalize opportunities, and to achieve greater equality for some groups.

CHAPTER 9

ALCOHOLISM

Alcohol can make you feel like a god, flying high; it can also make you feel like death. Alcohol is liquid god and demon booze: both.

The Good Book says that "A man hath no better thing under the sun than to eat and to drink and to be merry" (Eccles 8: 15). But the Good Book also says, "Woe unto them that rise up early in the morning, that they may follow strong drink" (Is 5: 11). This ambivalence in the Judaeo-Christian ethic has persisted for centuries; indeed alcohol is a most controversial subject.

Historically, Canadians (and Americans) have been divided into "Wets" and "Drys," Prohibitionists and Anti-Prohibitionists. Poets have described alcohol as the elixir of the gods and sung the joys of wine. The Romans even had a god of wine, Bacchus. Yet others have described alcohol abuse as the nation's number one drug problem, causing not joy, but death, destruction, illness, and unhappiness.

Alcohol is used in many Christian services all over the world; yet its use is prohibited in Islam. Sacrament to some is sin to others.

Alcohol is now so much a part of our social lives that "to have a drink" usually means to have a drink of alcohol. Yet alcohol is perhaps the most powerful depressant available on the open market without a medical prescription.

This ambivalence of attitudes stems in part from the contradictory consequences of alcohol use. In moderation alcohol is good for the heart, especially among the elderly, and prolongs life. Yet in excess it causes diseases of the heart and liver, exacerbates other diseases, and shortens life.

Ironically, this drug problem is extremely lucrative. The economy of alcohol not only involves billions of dollars in sales, thousands of workers, capital investment in land, shops, and warehouses, but also has multiplier effects in the advertising, bottling, and transport industries, agriculture, tourism, the restaurant business, construction, and even sports ((Health and Welfare, 1989: 1; Cat. No. H39-158). Yet it costs billions also in absenteeism, traffic accidents, deaths, crime, injuries, poor work, health care, insurance, and sheer misery. It is difficult to compute the social costs and social benefits.

Furthermore governments are ambivalent. They want to minimize the economic costs of alcohol abuse and to maximize the tax dollars — but the first policy means discouraging consumption, and the second means encouraging consumption. The number one drug problem lays golden eggs!

Philosophically, alcohol is most interesting, for it is usually described as good in moderation: good both medically and socially; but bad when taken in excess: bad both medically and socially. By incremental increases, therefore, alcohol consumption slowly curves over from good to bad. Perhaps good and bad are not moral opposites, but are very close to each other: they may be only a couple of drinks apart.

In this chapter we will consider this demon-god, and begin with the central role that alcohol plays in our social lives: social alcohol. We then consider the physiology of drinking: the alcohol content of various drinks, blood-alcohol concentrations, and the effects of alcohol on the central nervous system and behaviour. Thirdly we look at patterns of drinking in different cultures, the variations in consumption rates in Canada, and gender differences in alcohol consumption (feminist paradigms are useful when tackling this problem). We conclude with some of the most recent research on the process of alcohol dependency or addiction and a cost-benefit analysis of alcohol and alcohol abuse.

However, we begin by examining the everyday use of alcohol, and the roles of alcohol in contemporary life. We cannot understand alcoholism without understanding these roles.

SOCIAL ALCOHOL

Drinking, like the eating with which it is often associated, is probably the most important social lubricant we have. Almost all the events in our social lives are accompanied by eating or drinking or both. Indeed, we may drink alcohol for many reasons and on many occasions; but being thirsty is one of the *least* important reasons.

- We may join someone in a drink "just to be social."
- We drink to relax, especially at parties or after coming home from work.
- We drink if we're happy, perhaps to celebrate passing an exam: "Have one on me!"
- We drink if we're depressed, perhaps if we failed an exam; we drink to drown our sorrows: "Cheer up and have a drink" is another of our common drinking phrases.

- We celebrate births, weddings, divorces, birthdays, anniversaries, promotions, retirements, and even deaths with drinking. Drink, like food, marks our rites of passage and our changes of status through life.

- Victories and triumphs are celebrated with liquor: Grand Prix winners, World Cup Champions and National League heroes are all sprayed with champagne.

- Romancing is also associated with liquor. Ogden Nash's little verse is well known: "Candy is dandy/but liquor is quicker." Indeed, the stages of a romance can be marked by different drinks: the first drink may be coffee in the office or university cafeteria, then a drink (alcoholic) after work, a bottle of wine at the first dinner-date, the stereotypical night-cap to examine the etchings, and finally the champagne to celebrate bedding, marriage, house-purchase, childbirth and so on. Of course, this whole fantasy may stop at the coffee!

- We may have wine or brandy "for medicinal purposes": if we feel a cold coming on, or if we are chilled from the rain, or to settle the stomach. What could be better than a nip of brandy?

- Catholics and High Anglican denominations celebrate Holy Mass with wine.

- Business is often conducted in bars as well as in boardrooms. It seems to be easier to discuss difficult matters over a drink than over a pile of papers.

- Our social life is also alcohol-related: if we meet friends, we are likely to invite them to go for a drink; and if we can't go now, we often arrange to meet later in a bar or restaurant.

Alcohol obviously fulfills many functions in our society. Our social life, our religious life, our business life, and even our love life often revolve around shared drinking; our major sorrows and triumphs involve more drinking, alone or with others; and different stages in our life-cycle are highlighted by still more drinking. We may use alcohol to warm ourselves up, or to black out; as an aphrodisiac or as "hair of the dog"; to relax ourselves or to brace ourselves; in the Holy Mass or in a bar; as part of the family meal or as a consolation; to celebrate birth or to mourn death; to share happiness or sorrow, religion or business; to go to sleep, to wake up or just to have fun.

Madame Bollinger puts this very well: "Champagne. I drink it when I'm happy and when I'm sad. Sometimes I drink it when I'm alone. When I have company I consider it obligatory. I trifle with it if I'm not hungry and drink it when I am. Otherwise, I never touch it — unless I'm thirsty" (*Globe and Mail* 29.12.94).

It does not trivialize alcoholism to hear women, or men, laud drinking; on the contrary, it is precisely because alcohol is so important and so delightful that alcoholism is a problem, as these women told Brigid McConville (1983: 30-1):

I love drinking. Many of the best times of my life have been associated with drink — either in celebration of good things happening, or as the result of drink as a catalyst, making things happen.

Drinking is especially important to me as a way of *really talking* with my friends.

More than anything else women need to relax. Better to do it on four pints of Special than on a lifetime of tranquilizers.

It's a kind of reward. When I've had a really shitty day I promise myself a pint at the end of it.

Alcohol is a reward, a relaxant, a communication device, a catalyst . . . but it can get to be a habit, a necessity, an expense and a problem for women as for men.

Drinking is often shared. Indeed alcohol is usually shared, with the sharing often being more important than the drinking. Nonetheless, social life today almost invariably involves social pressures to drink alcohol. These pressures to drink create what one might call a climate of liquor or a "liquid culture."

And a liquid culture creates, in turn, a pressure to drink too much.

- Hospitality is often defined as pressing drinks on people and overwhelming objections or tentative refusals. Some hosts or hostesses will "freshen up" drinks while their guests are not looking.

- There are dozens of ways of trying to persuade people to drink more: "One for the road," we say; or "fill the other leg," "you can't fly on one wing" or "just a small one."

- Being able to hold one's liquor is an important part of the macho cult. It is socially defined, especially for young men, as "being a man." Drinking some-one under the table is the social equivalent of beating them at arm wrestling!

- The rounds system of buying drinks also maximizes alcohol consumption, since it means that people will often drink more than they want and more than they should, just to avoid offending the would-be purchaser, or to avoid missing a free drink, or not to get behind; that is: to be different from the group.

Drinking, in these circumstances, is intrinsically a *social* activity; so *not* to drink is to be subtly antisocial. And indeed to refuse to drink with someone may be downright insulting.

- Expense account eating may facilitate business but it also facilitates eating and drinking too much, not only at lunchtime but quite possibly at dinner as well.

- The custom of drinking toasts, whether to the bride and groom at weddings or to happiness in a friend's new apartment or house, has nothing to do with thirst, but much to do with the expression of shared values.

And the custom of *repeated* toasts, common among both the Poles and the Russians, has little to do with the expression of common values and much to do with getting drunk fast in good company.

- Alcohol "games" also result in alcohol abuse, especially in fraternities and engineering departments. There are chug-a-lug contests everywhere; there is the 100 club in which you drink 100 ounces of beer in an hour, using one-ounce shot glasses, and so on.

In sum, our social norms encourage us to drink, and some of our norms encourage us to drink too much. But they do illustrate the immense importance of alcohol in the social lives of many people, as well the possibility, or probability, of eventual alcohol abuse.

But first, a few words on what alcohol is.

THE PHYSIOLOGY OF DRINKING

Alcohol is a chemical compound, ethyl alcohol or ethanol, composed of three elements: carbon, hydrogen, and oxygen. It is produced by fermenting starch (e.g. grain, potatoes, rice) through bacterial action, and is a thin, colourless liquid with a faint odor.

The specific starches used determine the types of alcohol. Beer is produced by the fermentation of barley, cider from apple juice, and wine from grapes. Fermentation can produce an alcohol level of up to 15%, but usually beers have an alcohol content of 4-7% and wines are about double that, about 12% on average.

Spirits or hard liquors have a much higher alcohol content: about 40-45%. This is achieved by distilling the fermented alcohol. The fermented alcohol is boiled in large vats and the alcohol, which vaporizes before water, is collected by condensation in other containers.

Pure ethyl alcohol can be purchased in many stores, and a favourite party trick is to add it to punches or drinks to raise the alcohol content. Methyl alcohol or wood alcohol is chemically similar but, unfortunately, poisonous.

Spirits, or hard liquor, as distilled alcohol is described, include vodka, distilled from potatoes or grain; gin from grain flavoured with juniper berries, rum from molasses, whisky from barley (scotch), maize (bourbon), rye (Canadian and US) or potatoes (Irish Whiskey — note the different spelling!) Brandy is distilled from wine, the favourite brandy being cognac, distilled from white wine; kirsch is distilled from fermented cherry juice, and slivovitz from plums.

The alcohol contents of the various liquors vary slightly, depending on export-import regulations and national custom. Thus British beer is stronger than Canadian, in general, and Canadian beer is generally stronger than American; but there is a wide range in all these beers. Nonetheless, a shot of spirits (1-1$\frac{1}{2}$ ounces) has about the same alcohol content as a glass of wine (4-5 ounces) and a bottle of beer (12 ounces); i.e. about half an ounce of alcohol. For greater precision one would need to calculate the alcohol content of the beer, wine, or spirits, and the size of the drink. Our usual drinks, therefore, a shot of spirits, a glass of wine, or a beer have about the same alcohol content, although in different concentrations and at very different prices.

The immediate consequence of drinking alcohol is its absorption: 20% in the stomach and 80% in the intestines; from there it moves into the bloodstream and is carried all the way around the body, raising the blood-alcohol concentration (BAC), i.e., the level of alcohol in the blood.

The rate of absorption varies from individual to individual, however, and time to time. It depends on the concentration of alcohol (straight scotch is absorbed quicker than diluted scotch or beer), the rate of drinking, the amount of alcohol consumed (it takes longer to absorb more), the amount of food in the stomach (a full stomach acts as a buffer and slows down, but does not stop the process), body build (the bigger the person, the longer the process and the lower the BAC), and finally, quite possibly, mood.

This explains why the same couple of drinks can have different effects on different people — quite apart from possibly different tolerance levels; it also explains why the same couple of drinks may not bother a drinker one day, but may be catastrophic on another day (due to an empty stomach, or a different mood, or to the drinks being drunk faster). In more practical terms, absorption theory explains why trying to keep up with someone else's drinking is ill advised.

As the drinks keep coming and the alcohol is absorbed into the bloodstream, so the BAC rises. Even one beer causes a detectable BAC. However, the body — the liver specifically — can metabolize one drink an hour. Thus, so long as drinkers keep to one drink an hour, their BAC will remain low and constant, and their faculties will be relatively unimpaired. But with three or four drinks in an hour — not too difficult to imagine on a hot day or when you're tired or in good, or bad, company — then almost everyone would be considered legally "intoxicated" and all would be "impaired" in most of North America and Western Europe. Furthermore, rapid drinking not only raises the BAC, but tends to accelerate. The inhibitions have already been broken down in the first hour, and the restraining worries about drinking too much may vanish. Some people drink faster as they get drunker, and as they get drunker they drink faster, in a vicious circle.

Those ounces of alcohol add up, and soon affect behaviour. Only one drink is enough to raise many peoples' BAC up to 0.03%. If you consume two drinks in one hour you would not be allowed to drive in Scandinavian countries where the BAC limit is 0.05%. The limit is 0.08% in the United Kingdom and 0.10% to 0.15% in all the United States except Utah (where it is 0.08%) and Iowa, New Mexico, and Texas, where there are no limits, and the basic freedom to be paralytically drunk and drive is enshrined in the absence of law. In Canada the limit is 0.08%; but obviously 0.07% is not too impressive in court.

Physiologically, alcohol is a depressant; coffee is a stimulant. Thus alcohol acts as an anaesthetic on the central nervous system, slows it down, and impairs its functions. And the more depressant one drinks, the greater the impairment.

One cannot help thinking that there would be tremendous changes in drinking habits if we changed our invitations from "Have a drink" to "Have a depressant." "Another depressant anybody?" Better still: "God! I could do with a depressant!"

Chemically, alcohol is one of the most dangerous drugs known. It is addictive and, because the initial results of a few drinks are so euphoric, it is easily addictive. We seem to think that if a couple of drinks are good, one more is even better. Not true. One more may be the straw that breaks the camel's back; and the benefits are soon outweighed by the costs. Furthermore, as we have seen, it becomes progressively more difficult for drinkers to pace themselves as they become more relaxed and their brains become more anaesthetized.

The physiological effects of alcohol therefore range from mild euphoria through intoxification to coma and death, depending on the BAC. Every year people die directly and immediately from overdosing: often from chug-a-lugging a bottle of spirits. However, the more common problems of alcohol abuse stem usually from maladaptive patterns of drinking, both individual and social.

PATTERNS OF DRINKING

Peoples differ enormously in how much alcohol they consume. Table 9-1 presents alcohol consumption rates for 13 countries from 1970 to 1984, the latest year for which data is available. Canada is about in the middle, with consumption levels of roughly half that of top ranked France, and double that of bottom ranked Iceland. Muslim countries and Israel both have even lower consumption patterns than Iceland, but exact data are not available.

A couple of points are worth mentioning. First, there is an enormous range from top to bottom in the table: the French drink, on average, more than three times as much as their fellow Europeans in Iceland, and twice as much as their neighbours in Ireland and the United Kingdom. Evidently some cultures are far more liquid than others.

Second, note the direction of change. French and Italian consumption declined quite drastically between 1970 and 1984, perhaps because of some combination of factors such as tougher legislation on drinking and driving, the aging of the population, increased awareness and/or concern about health, or just increased taxes, etc. But this does indicate that there is nothing inevitable about cultural norms and practices or the addiction process. Trends can be turned around. On the other hand, these are the only two countries where consumption did decline: everywhere else it increased! Indeed in Canada consumption increased steadily from 1950, when it was only 4.4 litres of absolute alcohol per capita (Statistics Canada, 1983: 24. Cat. No. 82-540) to 8.0 litres in 1984; but consumption is now declining, reaching 6.7 litres in 1990-91 (see below).

Nations vary not only in how much they drink but also in what they drink. Wine is the most popular form of alcoholic drink in France, Italy, and Switzerland; beer is most popular in the United States, Canada, the United Kingdom, Australia, and West Germany; while in Finland, Iceland, Sweden, and Israel most alcohol is consumed in the form of spirits (Health, Education and Welfare, 1971: 17).

How people drink may be just as important as what they drink. In one of the pioneering works on alcoholism, E.M. Jellinek distinguished between French and "Anglo-Saxon" drinking styles, with Italian drinking styles and others in between. The former is characterized by steady wine drinking, but relatively little drunkenness, the latter by occasional heavy drinking of beer or spirits, with drunkenness not severely sanctioned. Both cultures have alcoholism, but with distinct etiologies (1960: 13-32). Since then the "ethnic culture" of drinking, usually male drinking, has been well researched and, if we can risk the raising of

Table 9-1   Alcohol Consumption (in litres of absolute alcohol per person), 1970, 1984

	1970	1984
France	19.6	14.2
Portugal	9.9	12.9
West Germany	11.2	11.9
Italy	14.4	11.5
Switzerland	10.5	11.1
Australia	8.2	9.3
USSR	5.0	8.4
Canada	6.5	8.0
United States	6.8	7.9
United Kingdom	5.2	7.3
Ireland	4.2	6.7
Japan	4.9	5.9
Iceland	2.7	4.0

Source: Health and Welfare, 1989:6. Cat. No. H39-158.

ethnic hackles, perhaps we can compare the stereotypical patterns of the Irish and the Italians.

The Irish tend to drink in bouts, often at weekends or paydays, and to drink with male friends in bars. The Italians, on the other hand, tend to drink regularly at home, and at meals, with the family. The Irish seem to identify heavy drinking with a macho self-image, and may become violent and aggressive; whereas the Italians identify drinking more as viniculture and as an aesthetic experience, and they often cultivate their own grapes. There are strong sanctions in Italian culture against drunkenness, and only weak ones in Irish culture; indeed there is often strong group support for convivial drinking, merriment, and indeed drunkenness. Also the Irish are inclined to drink their troubles away, and to try and drown their sorrows, preferably in whiskey or Guinness. They may not drink as often as the French and the Italians, but when they drink they are more likely to do so to get drunk. Rates of drunkenness among young males may therefore be rather high, but alcoholism rates, on the other hand, are much lower than those for the French and the Italians. In contrast to both the above groups, the Jews are, in general, very moderate drinkers, with relatively little drunkenness or alcoholism (Mann, 1971; Vaillant, 1983; Bales, 1962; Snyder, 1962; de Lint, 1971; Schmidt, 1971). These are, of course, vast generalizations, but they do serve to clarify the different cultures of drinking.

The culture of drinking is therefore an intrinsic and important element in the drinking process. People of different cultures may drink different amounts, and in different ways and for different purposes, and this may have quite different social, psychological, and physiological consequences. Hence the higher alcoholism rates of some groups, and the higher drunkenness rates of others. Drinking, drunkenness, and alcoholism are not simply individual phenomena, but are also collective and cultural phenomena which are either adaptive or maladaptive for physical health and social relations.

Given this range of patterns, both synchronic and diachronic, we will now turn to a detailed analysis of drinking in Canada.

ALCOHOL CONSUMPTION[1]

Canadians spend over *$10 billion* a year on alcohol (Statistics Canada, 1995: 5. Cat. No. 63-202) which amounts to roughly $462 per capita (15 years and over).

That same alcohol kills directly over 3,000 people per annum from diseases caused by alcohol consumption, and another 16,000 people indirectly from incidents and diseases associated with alcohol consumption, including traffic fatalities, fires, falls, suicide, as well as heart attacks and strokes (Addiction Research Foundation data in *Maclean's* 19.7.93).

So alcohol may be societal glue; but it is a very expensive glue, both in terms of cash and in terms of mortality — more like a time bomb than glue.

By comparison only 428 people died directly from drugs — although I doubt that this is a good reason to switch.

How do we create these problems for ourselves? Who drinks in Canada? How much? Why? and with what consequences?

In 1989 Statistics Canada conducted the National Alcohol and Other Drugs Survey (NADS) for Health and Welfare Canada (hereafter HWC), surveying about 12,000 adults by telephone across the country. The response rate was very high (79%), and although some underreporting of consumption is not unusual in surveys of this type, the data are believed to be accurate. The principal findings on consumption are presented below:

- 78% of adult Canadians drink (i.e. consumed at least one alcoholic beverage during the previous year). This is down slightly from the 82% of 1978 reported by the Canada Health Survey (CHS).

- Drinkers are drinking less, and also less often. In 1989, 26% of drinkers said they drank less than once a *month*, compared to 15% in 1978.

- And as for weekly drinking, almost half (47%) said they had "nothing" to drink in the previous week, 38% had 1-7 drinks, 8% had 8-14, and 8% had 14 or more drinks.

- Also a larger proportion of people have *stopped* drinking: 16% in 1989, up from 4% in 1978. This may reflect the aging of the population, as well as increased awareness of the social costs of alcohol use, and simply the high economic costs of alcohol.

- About half of the drinkers report having drunk heavily during the past year, i.e., consuming five or more drinks on one occasion.

- Average consumption in 1989 was 3.7 drinks per week, down from 5.1 in 1985: an almost suspiciously high decrease (27%).

In sum, fewer Canadians are drinking than 10 years ago, and they are drinking less alcohol, and less often, and more have stopped drinking altogether. It does seem as though alcohol use is declining; and this has implications for abuse.

Province To complete the consumption picture: the proportion of drinkers ranged from highs of 83% (BC) and 82% (Alberta) in the West to lows of 64% (PEI), 68% (Newfoundland), and 71% (Nova Scotia) in the East, with the center closer to the national average: Quebec (76%), Ontario and Saskatchewan (78%), and Manitoba (79%).

Age Young people drink more, and are more likely to drink. 18 is the legal drinking age in Quebec, Manitoba, and Alberta, and 19 everywhere else in Canada; but 74% of those aged 15-19 said they had consumed alcohol in the previous year; this peaks at 88% for those aged 20-24 and 87% for those aged 25-34 and then falls steadily to 54% of those aged 65+.

Gender More men drink than women: 84% overall compared to 72%; and also they drink more: 10% of the men had drunk 15 or more drinks in the week before the survey, compared to only 1% of the women; and 15% had drunk alcohol at least four times that week compared to only 6% of the women. And, putting age and gender together, young men (20-24) averaged 6.1 drinks per week. This total fell to 5.0 for those 65 and over, while young women consumed an average 2.2 alcoholic beverages. This total rose to 2.7 in the 45-54 age bracket, and fell to 1.9 in the 65+ group.

The overall consumption pattern in this mass of numbers is therefore fairly simple: men more than women, young more than old, and West more than East (Eliany, 1991; HWC, 1992. Cat. No. H39-251).

There are no studies published on consumption patterns in major corporations, the armed forces, the civil service, etc. When research is conducted, the data is confidential, for obvious reasons. A study of alcohol and drug use in the RCMP has recently been made available however. The report, based on a survey of 3,000 members of the RCMP in 1989, found as follows:

- 35% of the force had consumed three or more drinks a day during the previous month.

- 11% drank seven or more drinks a week (more than 1,800 of the total regular and civilian force of 16,761).

- 19% had experienced blackouts in the previous year.

- 25% blamed alcohol for negative consequences, ranging from absenteeism and lost promotional chances to disciplinary action and poor job performance.

These findings were recorded in a "Special Report" in *Maclean's* (28.3.94), coupled with two cases of fatalities caused by RCMP officers who were allegedly impaired. The report, entitled "Booze and the Badge," was not entirely fair. In particular, it failed to place alcohol use by the Mounties in context with use in the rest of Canada. While we cannot make exact comparisons, for the RCMP survey and the NAD survey have different population bases and consumption cut-off points, nonetheless 15% of Canadian drinkers consume eight plus drinks a week: a higher incidence, and presumably a greater problem than the 11% of the RCMP who consume seven plus a week. No doubt some officers do have problems with alcohol: given the job stress it would be surprising if they didn't; but to single them out, to ignore comparative data (which suggests that they may have *fewer* problems than the Canadian population in general), and to fail to report widespread problems with alcohol in all sectors of Canadian society (journalism, politicians, armed forces, etc.) seems not only unfair, sensationalistic, and irresponsible, but also nihilistic, and in keeping with a widespread tendency these days to discredit everyone.

DRINKING PROBLEMS

Alcohol use is not a risk-free activity; but how problematic is alcohol use? and when does use run into abuse? The NAD survey provides many of the answers which are summarized below. Note, however, that alcohol is a highly addictive drug, so use slides easily (and quickly) into abuse, and the social lubricant converts easily (and quickly) into a bomb, with devastating effects. Pleasures glide into pain, sunshine into shadows, benefits into costs, and life into death.

Just as alcohol is everywhere in this liquid culture, so are alcohol-related problems. 21% of current drinkers say that they have had a problem or problems due to alcohol at some time in their lives, and 12% have had such problems in the last year; this represents 10% of the total adult population, or about 1.8 million people. These problems relate to health, finances, work, marriage, social life. . . . As might be expected males report more problems than females (25% to 15%). Young people (aged 15-19) and students (overlapping categories) are likely to have reported alcohol-related problems in the last year (24% and 21% respectively). *But*, almost 90% of current drinkers had no problems with alcohol in the year preceding the survey, and almost 80% say they have *never* experienced any problems — this reminder is necessary to balance the conflict and consensus paradigms.

Heavy drinkers are particularly problematic, for themselves and for others:

- 33% of heavy drinkers (14+ drinks in the previous week) reported alcohol-related problems in the previous year compared to only 12% of those who had not consumed an alcoholic beverage in that week.

- 14% of heavy drinkers said that they had experienced financial problems caused by their own alcohol consumption in the previous year; only 4% of those who had not had a drink in the previous week reported this.

- 19% of heavy drinkers, compared to 7% of those who had not had a drink in the previous week, reported alcohol-related health problems (HWC, 1992: 216-21, 261. Cat. No. H39-251).

In sum, heavy drinkers were more than twice as likely to have experienced health problems, three times more likely to have experienced financial problems, and almost three times more likely to have experienced problems generally than those who had not been drinking in the previous week, i.e., light drinkers. Of course, the question arises, did they drink because they had problems, or did they have problems because they drank? Probably both. Causality is rarely simple, and often reciprocal. But, in default of multiple regression and path analyses, we would be in denial to refuse to accept the obvious problematic consequences of heavy drinking for the *drinker*, as well as for others. Note too that even apparently light drinkers reported a number of alcohol-related problems.

Heavy drinkers not only cause problems for themselves, they also cause problems to others:

- About four out of five Canadians (78%) report that they have at some time in their lives experienced a problem due to some one else's drinking; and almost half (45%) in the previous year.

- The list of problems is long: people have been insulted (52%), disturbed by parties (48%), been a passenger with a drunk driver (37%), had arguments (36%), been physically assaulted (20%), and 7% (about 1.4 million Canadians) have been in a traffic accident as a result of someone else's drinking; these, of course, are the ones who survived.

- Drinking and driving is not the norm, but it is not rare. 19% of current drinkers (about three million people) drove at least once in the year after consuming two or more alcoholic drinks in one hour. Men are three times more likely than women to do this (27% to 9%) and to do it more often (15% of men reported D and D on at least three occasions in the previous year, compared to 3% of women (HWC, 1992: 232, 225. Cat. No. H39-251).[2]

The NAD survey gives us some ideas on the social costs of alcohol; but this is only the tip of the iceberg.

Suicide: Alcoholism is both a form of, and a cause of, suicide. It is both "suicide by inches," as the Task Force reported; but also alcoholics have suicide rates, according to various studies, of between 7 and 40%— compared to the Canadian average of 13 per *100,000* (calculate the factor yourself!). And 25-30% of suicide completers are alcoholics (HWC, 1987: 28; Schmidt, 1971).

Disease: Alcohol abuse is a primary or related causal factor in many pathological conditions, and exacerbates other illnesses when they occur. It affects virtually all the organs and systems of the body: the heart, liver, pancreas, skin, muscle, vitamin absorption, as well as blood, the brain, and the central nervous system, causing everything from cancer and diarrhea, strokes and heart attacks to mental illness and ulcers (HWC, 1989: 23-6. Cat. No. H39-158. cf. HWC 1992: 221-2. Cat. No. H39-251).

Crime: More than half of the 5,500 criminals sent to jail since 1990 had consumed either alcohol or drugs on the day they committed the crime; and more than two-thirds had drug or alcohol problems requiring treatment when they entered prison (*Maclean's* 19.7.93. cf. HWC 1992: 238-9. Cat. No. H39-251).

Accidents: It is estimated that alcohol is a contributing factor in about 50% of all traffic fatalities and, based on an Alberta study, perhaps about 17% of all industrial accident fatalities (Health and Welfare, 1989: 23-6. Cat. No. H39-158. HWC 1992: 227. Cat. No. H39-251).

The brute loss of life is shocking, no doubt, but Health and Welfare Canada used the concept of Potential Years of Life Lost (PYLL) to clarify the extent of the problem. A person who dies at age 30, for instance, may be said to contribute 40 years of potential life lost. PYLL is a useful (but not perfect) method of calculating the human cost of alcohol; and the PYLL attributable to hazardous driving was 118,886: fully *40%* of all the PYLL between the ages of one and 70 for the top five causes of death listed for 1977 (Adler and Brusegard, 1980:54).

Future: Furthermore the ripple effects of adult alcohol abuse and alcoholism are felt not only at the time, but also affect the children of abusers and alcoholics for many years to come. Indeed a children of alcoholics (COA) syndrome is now recognized by some therapists (Cermak, 1985, 1989).

In Vaillant's study of Boston men, alcohol abusers (about one-quarter of the sample) were more likely than abstainers and moderate drinkers to have been truants at school (3-5 times), to have many alcoholic relatives (2-3 times), to have been unemployed for more than four years (2 and 7 times, respectively), to have suffered three or more injuries (2-3 times), to have spent two months in hospital (2 times), to be a heavy smoker (3 times) and to be divorced (3 times) (Vaillant, 1983: 118). Heavy drinking is a very expensive habit, economically and socially.

Alcohol is therefore horrendously expensive, in terms of lost production, property damage, medical expenses, insurance costs, crime, suicide, loss of jobs, work badly done, violence, divorce, accidents, deaths, and general pain and unhappiness. The effects of alcohol abuse persist over the generations, rippling out in space and time. They are a high price to pay for a liquid culture.

Indeed the Ontario Addiction Research Foundation estimates that substance abuse (mostly alcohol but also drugs) costs the Canadian economy about *$34 billion* in extra health care, policing and lost productivity (*Maclean's* 19.7.93. See also Health and Welfare 1989:27. Cat. No. H39-158).

On the plus side Alcoholics Anonymous has 5,275 groups in Canada with a total membership of about 95,000; and although 111,300 drivers were charged with impaired driving in 1991, this was a 31% decrease since 1981. And ARF has estimated that there are about 477,000 alcoholics in Canada (1989), down from 623,000 in 1979; the calculations were based on declining mortality statistics from cirrhosis of the liver (I know you wanted to know that) (cf. *Maclean's* 19.7.93). Also, as we have seen, fewer Canadians are drinking, and they are drinking less, on average. Consumption overall is declining. In 1990-91 182 million litres of absolute alcohol were sold in Canada — (6.7 litres *each*) — but this was a decrease of 3.2% over the previous year (Statistics Canada, 1992: 5. Cat. No. 63-202).

Yet most people are not hazardous drinkers; it is the ubiquitous 10%, in alcohol abuse as in crime, who constitute the hazard. That 10% includes the steady heavy drinkers, but also the occasional binge drinker. Indeed the rule of thumb is that 10% of adults consume 50% of all the alcohol drunk (Reid and Carpenter, 1990: 34).

ALCOHOL AND GENDER[3]

Women and men relate to alcohol differently: not totally differently, obviously, but nonetheless there are significant differences both in the quantity and the quality of the relation. To be specific, according to the 1989 NAD survey, a smaller proportion of women drink than men (72% to 84%). Second, women drink far less than men: 2.0 drinks per week on average compared to 5.3. Third, women drink less often: 36% of female drinkers consume alcohol at least once a week compared to 61% of male drinkers. Fourth, women drink less heavily: only 4% of female drinkers consumed 8-13 drinks, and 3% consumed 14+ drinks in the week preceding the survey, compared to 11% and 12% respectively for men. These interminable statistics are necessary to make the point that alcohol is not the same for women and men (Health and Welfare 1992: 12, 21, 23. Cat. No. H39-251). The findings here are very similar to those of the Canada Health Survey (1978-79), the General Social Survey (1985), and the Health Promotion Survey (1985) (see HWC, 1989. Cat. No. H39-158).

The 1990 Health Promotion Survey, based on telephone interviews with over 13,000 people, showed a similar pattern of gender differentiation, with men being more likely than women to drink, to drink more, and to drink heavily (see Table 9-2). With 24% of male drinkers consuming 8+ drinks per week

Table 9-2   Alcohol Consumption (by Type of Drinker, Number of Drinks, and Sex, Aged 15+), 1990

Type of Drinker	Male	Female
Lifetime Abstainer	5	10
Former Drinker	10	13
Current Drinker	85	77
Number of Drinks/Week		
0	26	38
1-7	35	32
8-14	13	4
15-21	6	1
22-27	2	_[1]
28+	3	_[1]
Mean Number of Drinks/Week	6.44	2.29

[1]Value too small to display.

Source: Health and Welfare, 1993:112. Cat. No. H39-263.

compared to only about 6% of female drinkers, it is clear that alcohol use and abuse is primarily a male problem.

Almost one-quarter of adult Canadians do not drink, however, and just as reasons for drinking vary, so do reasons for *not* drinking. These former drinkers (16%) and lifetime abstainers (7%) explained to the NAD survey that they did not drink because they did not like the taste of alcohol (36%), because they did not like the effect alcohol had on themselves or others (30%), because of health reasons (27%), or because they were taught not to drink (16%), because it is a waste of money (12%), for religious reasons (11%), or because they were alcoholics and had experienced problems with alcohol in the past (6%). Other reasons were cited by 17% of the sample.

While responses were very similar for both men and women, women were much more likely than men to say that they did not like the taste (44% to 23%) and to cite their upbringing (18% to 11%), while men were much more likely to say they had problems (12% to 2%) (HWC, 1992: 109-10. Cat. No. H39-251).

Women and men not only have different consumption patterns, they are also apparently motivated somewhat differently. Women are more likely than men to drink to be sociable or to enjoy meals, according to the NAD survey, while men are more likely than women to drink to feel good, to relax or to forget worries, and to feel less inhibited, i.e., to effect mood changes (HWC, 1992: 122. Cat. No. H39-251).

Such mild differences of degree, however, to be sociable or to feel good, are hardly sufficiently precise to explain such wide differentials as we have discussed in terms of both use and abuse. More qualitative research indicates other factors, including stigmatization, socialization, and physical risks.

The double standard which stigmatizes women alcoholics more strongly is stressed by Joan Curlee, an American authority on female alcoholism:

> Because the role of woman has been equated with the stabilising functions of wife and mother, the drunken woman is seen to be a special threat; no one likes to believe that the hand that rocks the cradle might be a shaky one. Even among alcoholic women themselves, it is not unusual to hear this statement: 'There is nothing so disgusting as a drunken woman' (McConville, 1983: 43).

One of the English women interviewed by McConville made a similar point rather more dramatically.

> The image of the pissed man is very different from that of the pissed woman. The bloke who goes out, gets legless, falls over, goes to sleep on the train, misses his stop and has to walk miles home at three o'clock in the morning is a 'good laugh,' 'one of the lads.' He's got a good story to tell in the office the next morning.
>
> Now a woman who does that is not seen in the same way *at all*. It's not a great story — it's a little bit . . . distasteful. It's not a joke. A woman who gets into a

right old state and falls over, *she's* not a folk hero. There's definitely a double standard (McConville, 1983: 34).

This double standard in stigmatization may inhibit women from developing this drug dependency, but it makes this dependency worse once it has developed. Alternatively, it may switch women from alcohol to prescription drugs.[4]

One woman refers to the different responsibilities "drilled into me by my mother". Her socialization taught her that "you just don't lose control":

> The reason why a lot of women don't drink so much as men is that they're frightened of losing control. I'm a teacher and at the end of term I feel I really want to get pissed, just to think of something other than work.

> But women have got kids to look after, meals to prepare, hundreds of little things to do. Even for someone like me who doesn't have kids there's always something to do, like the washing or the cleaning. I can't just lie in bed like a man can lie in bed. I've got to get up and do things. I can't waste the whole tomorrow.

> It was also drilled into me by my mother not to waste time. She told me that, as a woman, it was an absolute shame for me to waste a day lying in bed with a hangover.

> So you don't lose control. You go just far enough and no further (McConville, 1983: 33).

Another woman points to the different risks involved, male attack in particular:

> After socializing in the pub I usually have to go home on my own on the tube or the bus. For men it's okay. No one is going to bother them. But for a woman it's bad enough at night anyway, and if your vision is blurred and you're a bit queasy then you are much more vulnerable to being attacked (McConville, 1983: 33-4).

David McClelland, author of one of the classic studies on male drinking, argues emphatically:

> To dispose of one common answer to this question, men do not drink primarily to reduce their anxiety . . . Nor do men drink primarily to attain feelings of being cared for or orally gratified . . .

> Nor do men drink primarily to become incompetent, to enjoy a "time-out" period in which they will be free to act without being held accountable by society for their actions.

> Men drink primarily to feel stronger (McClelland, 1972: 333-34).

Yet women working with women problem drinkers speak in quite different terms:

> We found that the preoccupations of the drinkers in our group were very much of the kind that feminists identify as women's problems — difficulties with relationships, lack of assertiveness, the inability to express anger, and the loneliness and depression which stems from being stuck at home. . . .

> Anxiety was also a major factor. The women would describe themselves as feeling generally strung up. Whether this was a cause or a result of drinking I don't know. We had many unresolved arguments about it. For most of them their anxiety was a panic about the effort of living, the feeling that I don't fit into all this, that I'm not very good at anything, that I'm inferior. That I don't like recognizing my needs for other people. That I don't like being vulnerable. . . .

> Housing, family, restraints and money were problems for most of them. These social and political issues are inseparable from women's drinking (McConville, 1983: 134-35).

Women and men do have different roles in this society (and in every other society that we know). These roles affect drinking patterns in many ways. While men are allowed or even sometimes encouraged to get drunk, women are usually not. So women often *hide* their drinking, from husbands, children, colleagues, friends, and parents. Because this drinking is often hidden, and not expected, alcoholism is often misdiagnosed or denied or recognized late, by which time dependency is more serious. Furthermore, as Ridlon has noted: "The more alcoholic women hide because they fear censure, the more severe their disease becomes" (1988: 37). When the label, alcoholic, or alcohol-dependent, is finally applied, the degree of stigmatization is correspondingly higher than it is for a man. So to the dependency (or disease) is added the stigma, a double whammy. The effect on the woman drinker is therefore often more traumatic than for the male, so she may fall into depression. This may, in turn, reduce self esteem and cause further drinking: a triple hazard. In sum, while female alcoholism is more rare than male, it is often more extreme.

Furthermore many of the difficulties women face, which they try and resolve, or avoid, with alcohol stem precisely from the difficulties which some women face in fulfilling their appropriate roles, or in defining new ones. Consider what these women say:

> I was never myself before I got sober — I was my father's daughter, then my husband's wife, then my children's mother, but I was never me.

> I started drinking late in life. My children had grown up and left home; I was divorced. I felt alone, empty and useless.

Try being 27 years old with no husband, three kids, and a full-time job waiting on tables that doesn't even begin to pay the bills. Try that one, and maybe you'd drink too. (Health and Welfare, 1983. Cat. No. H39-68)

These personal stories illustrate the very different types of lives, roles, and expectations that the opposite sexes, so called, experience. All of these stories are personal, but all of them are also political, which is why Brigid McConville, who describes herself as "an enthusiastic and sometimes heavy drinker," says that the topic requires a feminist perspective. Her excellent book, *Women Under the Influence* is one of the few humanistic, in contrast to statistical, approaches to alcoholism. She is also one of the few writers on alcoholism, male or female, to suggest that woman's place *is* in the pub (1983: 1).

It must be clear by now that men and women drink different amounts of alcohol, for different reasons, and with very different social consequences. Thus the etiology, development, and treatment of alcoholism or alcohol dependency are also different. Indeed treatment is particularly problematic since it requires a critique of contemporary gender roles (which contribute to the alcoholism of both males *and* females in different social etiologies); and also because alcohol abuse needs to be examined in the broader contexts of food abuse (bulimia, anorexia, compulsive eating) and both legal and illegal drug abuse — all three of which show gender differentials also.

THE BATTLE WITH THE BOTTLE

Many people battle with the bottle at some time in their lives. The battle is indicated by some of the terms we use, euphemisms really, for someone who is drunk: bombed, hammered, smashed, sloshed, or simply wasted.

Some win. Some lose. Some recover. And some just keep fighting. Not surprisingly, the battle has attracted considerable attention. The authoritative work today is probably George Vaillant's *The Natural History of Alcoholism* (1983), superseding pioneer works by Jellinek (1960) and McClelland (1972) and neatly complementing the life stories in the AA (1955) text.

Vaillant tried to answer seven questions which he posed as follows:

(1) Is alcoholism a symptom or a disease? (2) Does alcoholism get progressively worse? (3) Are alcoholics, *before* they begin to abuse alcohol, different from non-alcoholics? (4) Is abstinence a necessary goal of treatment, or can insisting on abstinence sometimes be counterproductive? (5) Is returning to safe social drinking possible for some alcoholics? (6) Does treatment alter the natural history of alcoholism? (7) How helpful is Alcoholics Anonymous in the treatment of alcoholism? (1983: 2-3)

His unique contribution to these ancient debates was his longitudinal methodology: two samples of more than 600 men tracked over 40 years, one selected from Harvard, the other from a Boston junior high school, and a third sample of 100 alcohol dependent men and women drawn from a clinic and followed for eight years. The obvious flaw in the research is the small number of women in the sample, and they are not representative of the total population. The obvious advantage, however, is that he was able to track the drinking careers of so many men, and thereby answer so many of his questions, all of which have some applications for women.

First, however, we must define alcoholism — a difficult enough task since many experts believe that there are as many different alcoholisms as there are alcoholics. The World Health Organization (1951) is vague: "Alcoholism (or rather certain forms of it) is a disease process." But not all experts agree. Do they ever? One opined that "Alcoholism is no more a disease than thieving or lynching. Like these, it is the product of a distortion of habit, a way of life bred of ignorance and frustration." In this view it is a crime and a vice, a learned behaviour and a chosen habit (Vaillant, 1983: 3). Jellinek adopted a broad definition: "Any use of alcoholic beverages that causes any damage to the individual or society or both" (1960: 35). Today we would distinguish such problem drinking from addiction, which lies further along the continuum. The US National Council on Alcoholism suggests a more subjective definition: "The person with alcoholism cannot consistently predict on any drinking occasion the duration of the episode or the quantity that will be consumed" (Vaillant, 1983: 44). Vaillant adopts a commonsense sociological model: "It is the number and frequency of alcohol-related problems . . . that define the clinical phenomenon known as alcoholism" (1983: 35); and he developed a Problem Drinking Scale (Table 9-3) in which a score of 4 or higher indicates alcohol abusers. Only 28% of the Boston working-class sample and only 13% of the Harvard sample scored 4+. The American Psychiatric Association suggests a more rigourous medical, rather than sociological, model for alcohol dependence: (A) heavy consumption for at least a month, (B) social complications, (C) psychological dependence or pathological patterns (e.g., binges, blackouts), (D) tolerance or withdrawal symptoms. By these criteria only 18% of the Boston men and 5% of the Harvard men were clinically dependent (Vaillant, 1983: 27, 232).

So what is it? a symptom of a personality defect resulting in maladaptive habits? or a disease? This depends on whether we adopt a medical or a sociological model, and subjective or objective criteria. Alcoholics Anonymous adopt a medical model, at least for chronic alcoholics:

> We believe . . . that the action of alcohol in these chronic alcoholics is a manifestation of an *allergy*; that the phenomenon of craving is limited to this class and *never* occurs in the average temperate drinker. These allergic types can *never* safely use alcohol in any form at all. (Emphasis added. 1955: xxvi)

The solution is not medical, however, but spiritual: the adoption of the famous Twelve Point program, and the help of God "as we understood him."

Table 9-3   Vaillant's Problem Drinking Scale

PDS item
Employer complains
Multiple job losses
Family/friends complain
Marital problems
Medical problem
Multiple medical problems
Diagnosis by clinician
Alcohol-related arrest
3+ alcohol-related arrests
Single hospital, clinic, or AA visit
3+ visits to clinics
2+ blackouts
Going on the wagon
Morning tremulousness/drinking
Tardiness or sick leave
Admits problem with control

Source: Vaillant, 1983: 27

Vaillant's tentative answer is that alcoholism is both habit and disease: habit in that it is learned behaviour, and disease in the sense that the alcoholics have lost control of their drinking. It is not a simple disease like measles or chicken-pox, with an either/or single-factor etiology, but multi-factorial in origin, chameleon-like in its characteristics and, in its chronic stages, very difficult to treat. He adds that the point in the continuum which distinguishes alcohol abuse from alcoholism "will always be as uncertain as where in the spectrum yellow becomes green" (1983: 309). The middle is a sort of grey area (sorry) but the poles are quite distinct colours.

Is alcoholism progressive? Not in the sense that every social drinker becomes an alcoholic, obviously; but once one becomes a chronic alcoholic, which takes years (5-30 says Vaillant, depending on how hard you try I suppose), the dependency is so deep that it is difficult to reverse the process; and many cannot.

Alcoholism does not seem to be caused by a "weakness" of personality, or any other psychological variable that can be measured. The most powerful predictors of alcoholism are, according to Vaillant, "family history of alcoholism, ethnicity, and adolescent behaviour problems" (1983: 312A). Ethnicity is his polite code for English or, especially, Irish.

Most problem drinkers can and do heal themselves, with or without help. But the battle can take years, even a lifetime. Tactics and strategies vary from person to person: changing friends or sports, going on the wagon, taking disulfiram, individual or group therapy, joining AA . . . the possibilities are endless. The NAD survey found that the most frequent tactic employed by Canadians is the obvious one: limiting the number of drinks (66%), followed by changing the type of beverage (39% — I tried that: it didn't work; I just got to enjoy a wider variety of drinks!), going to bars and taverns less often (35%), getting involved in activities that did not involve drinking (27%), and more (HWC 1992: 340. Cat. No. H39-251). A battery of changes is more likely to be effective than just one.

The battle is fought not only with one's own bottle, however, but also with other people's bottles. And this battle involves the political economy of alcohol mentioned earlier, including tax policies and the costs of liquor, licensing laws, distribution laws, policing and penalties, education in the schools, and much more research.

CONCLUSION

Alcohol can bring sunshine and chemical joy into our lives, but it also casts long shadows; and the battle with the bottle, both individual and societal, is yet another dimension of the conflict paradigm, with a long history. Indeed alcohol is particularly interesting in that it has played such a central role in Canadian history.

Canada was founded on the beaver and the cod, argued Harold Innis, and we might agree with this rather prosaic formulation. But we might also argue that Canada was founded on violence, or on racism, or on patriarchy; or we could agree with Edmund Burke that society is founded on family love and affection. A case can be made for all these paradigms. But we can also suggest that Canada was founded on alcohol.

"So important was the toddy for the sailors, the woodcutters, and the fishermen" suggests Cheryl Warsh "that it could be said that much of Canada was built on Jamaican rum and local whisky. Liquor facilitated the raising of barns, the harvesting of crops, and certainly the election of governments" (1993: 4). And James Gray concurs; he opens his book *Booze: The Impact of Whisky on the Canadian West* definitively: "The name of the game was whisky. Whisky was the force which impelled the American fur-traders into the Canadian West; and it was the liquid lorelei that lured the Indians to the trading posts and their own destruction . . . whisky fuelled the engines of the political machines and corroded their steering mechanisms; whisky oiled the escalators to political success and greased the skids to oblivion" (1972: 1-2). A worthy companion to the beaver and the now threatened cod. It is now a mainstay of the Canadian economy, and also a drain on the same economy.

Yet alcohol is also central because it *intersects* with so many social problems: poverty, crime, violence, suicide, homicide, racism.[5] Alcohol use and abuse not only *cause* problems, but they are also *consequences* of problems. The cause-effect equation is difficult to compute. So is the cost-benefit equation. Alcohol brings benefits and costs, but it is extraordinarily difficult to calculate the net results. Is alcohol more of a blessing or a curse? Which has it been in your personal life?

There is another question: how can we compare the social costs of alcohol and alcoholism with the social costs of other social problems: poverty? suicide? crime? racism? Which is the *worst* of all these problems? How can we calculate? By what criteria? The numbers of dead is one obvious criterion, but not easy to apply for poverty, for instance. (The poor die younger than the rich; but poverty kills slowly). And, given the intersections and reciprocal causalities between these problems, how can we even separate them?

The questions have to be asked, even if they cannot be answered exactly, precisely because they clarify the complex nature of these social realities.

Alcohol is probably the nation's number one drug problem, perhaps the nation's number one health problem (although nicotine causes more deaths), and a serious social problem at the centre of a web of other problems. Yet alcohol abuse and alcoholism are still widely misunderstood. Alcoholism is often seen as a problem of alcoholics, defined as those individuals who have a number of persistent drinking problems; and alcoholics are often seen stereotypically as "skid row bums" or "derelicts." While it is true that such unfortunates are often alcoholics, yet they constitute only a very small minority of the total alcoholic population. Most of the half million or so alcoholics in Canada are fine upstanding citizens, the average Jack or Jill. By seeing the "bums" as the alcoholics we distance ourselves from the "normal" alcoholic and fail to observe the cultural construction of alcoholism by the liquid society. This is one point I have tried to emphasize: how our norms *create* the problem.

The other point which I think is important to note is that our norms do not just happen. They can and do change, as we have noted in this volume; and they too are generated. Alcohol is a ten billion dollar industry: it is big business. And addicts are created, not born (except for those few born with fetal alcohol syndrome, FAS). And they are created not only by themselves, but also by the entire industry which benefits from both the use *and* the abuse of alcohol. The alcohol industry therefore does have an important role to play in the structural generation of alcoholism, as the tobacco industry has for various cancers and other diseases, the firearms industry for crime rates, together with the circles of other industries (advertising media, etc. and also federal and provincial governments) that benefit from or promote the purchase of booze, smokes, guns, and other commodities which can and do contribute to our societal problems, and sometimes our premature deaths.

Not, obviously, that all such industries and businesses are immoral and should be closed down (although some do argue that point for polluters, sectors of the logging industry, the tobacco industry, etc.); merely that we should be aware that the benefits have costs, the profits also involve losses, albeit in a different ledger, and that abuse is the price we pay for use. More fundamentally while individuals do shape their own destinies, they are also formed by their cultures and their environments.

To point this out is not, I hope, to engage in that great sociological sport of capsizing the commonplace. It is to insist that *individualizing* the problem, whether it be alcoholism, poverty, or crime, or suicide, is to misunderstand it. We need to see also how the individuals and the problems are socially created (by values, habits, business, advertising, ourselves, etc.) — and so how these problems are perhaps more deeply social than at first we may have realized.

Perhaps the "thing" about alcoholism which makes it such a unique social problem is that it is so unlike poverty (which we are often born into, or fall into), or racism (which we learn or fight), or crime, which we may decide to commit: alcoholism is a function of what we choose to ingest and digest in our physical bodies. The transition from swallowing to a social problem costing, directly and indirectly, 19,000 lives per annum and (including drug abuse) $34 billion is so physical, so crass, that it has to surprise by its sheer danger.

We will leave the last word to an early settler in British North America, one by the name of Increase Mather, in 1673: "The wine is from God, but the drunkard is from the devil" (Lender and Martin, 1982: 1).

ENDNOTES

1. The principle source for data on alcohol and drug use in Canada is the National Alcohol and Other Drugs Survey of 1989: Health and Welfare, 1992, *Alcohol and Other Drug Use by Canadians* (H39-251); but see also other Health and Welfare publications, including *Alcohol in Canada* (H39-158/1989), *Licit and Illicit Drugs in Canada* (H39-159/1989), *The Health of Canada's Youth* (H39-239/1992) and *Canada's Health Promotion Survey 1990* (H39-263/1993) known by the acronym HPS90.

2. The "war on drunk driving" is an example of the fusion of the conflict and the feminist paradigms. The most well known organization in the war is MADD: Mothers, not Fathers, Against Drunk Driving (*Newsweek* 13.9.82, 4.6.84).

3. Female alcoholism has been seriously underresearched for decades; virtually all the researchers agree on this, Ridlon (1988); McConville (1983); Badiet (1976); Kinsey (1966). We mentioned this earlier in connection with the work of McClelland (1972) and Vaillant (1983). See also Greenblatt and Schukitt (1976).

4. Women are almost twice as likely to use tranquillizers as men, according to the NAD Survey, and also sleeping pills (HWC, 1989:4-5. Cat. No. H39-159). And men are almost twice as likely to have used and to use such illicit drugs as marijuana, cocaine, crack, or heroin (HWC 1992: 42, 47-8. Cat. No. H39-251).

5. Alcoholism and racism: This association is most easily demonstrated in the negative stereotypes of the drunken Irishman and the drunken Indian. But the relation goes far deeper than that: alcohol use was one of the variables determining ethnic relations both ideologically and politically. The *Moose Jaw Times* (1910?) for instance, offered a moral and ethnic hierarchy based on drinking habits: "Among the Canadians there are many who do not drink at all. Among the French there are very few who do not drink. Among the Germans and Half-breeds there are absolutely none at all" (Gray, 1976: 45-6). The "French" replied in kind, Hector Langevin suggesting that alcoholism in Quebec was a more pernicious evil even than anglicization, and the great temperance orator in Quebec in the 1840s, Father Chiniquy, preaching that God had sent the English, Irish, Scots, and Americans to punish the French for their intemperance. This early Quebec nationalism demanded sobriety first: it was a political and an economic issue as well as a moral one (Noel, 1993: 35, 38). Whatever habits distinguish one ethnic group from another can serve to legitimize racism. Even the derogatory term "Pepsis" for French Canadians refers to drinking.

CONCLUSION

Canada does not have as many serious social problems as many other countries one might think of from Afghanistan to Zaire . . . almost everywhere, in fact. So this should have been a very short book.

But the fact that other people may be worse off than oneself is little consolation to the poverty-stricken mother of two, the young man thinking of committing suicide, the victims of homicidal assaults in universities and their families, or the homeless.

Canada's problems are not famine or civil war or foreign invasion; but they are serious. What remedies are there? for violence? alcoholism? poverty? crime?

The recommendations have been around for decades, in reports from royal commissions, feminist organizations, lobby groups, community groups and, naturally, sociologists. As you can see, the problems have not gone away; and many have got worse. The suicide rate is rising. The homicide rate has stayed about the same for 20 years (which is surely surprising), but the violent crime rate has been rising rapidly. Income distribution remains as unequal as ever, but the distribution of wealth seems to be becoming more unequal.

Some problems have only recently been defined: child abuse since the sixties, violence against women since 1980, the homeless in the eighties, and now elder-abuse.

The *problem* seems to be not so much to solve these social problems, but to dampen them down, to reduce them. Thus sociologists (you) hop from crisis to crisis. As some intolerable incident in one sector occurs, media attention zeroes in on it: blanket coverage and reports ensue, experts give their opinions on television and their recommendations in editorials and books . . . but by then another appalling incident has occurred and the cycle starts again.

The recommendations depend on the paradigms of course. The topic of social problems, however, falls broadly within the conflict paradigm(s) precisely because there are perceived problems and issues which arouse public concern and require solutions. The utility of the conflict paradigm is that it spotlights the immense significance of the rich-poor division _ and also the immense significance of the cross-cutting male-female division — as well as other divisions according to the ideological orientation (ethnicity, region, etc.).

But which is "the best" paradigm? Surely that all depends on your ideology. For egalitarians, social democrats, many liberals and, at the extreme, the socialists, the only paradigm of value is the economic conflict model developed by Marx and Engels. Economic inequality is the central value: the inequality of distribution of wealth in Canada, where the wealthiest 10% own more than the other 90% put together, the 20% who own zero, the vast disparities in income, the 20% poverty rate, the large numbers of Canadians on welfare and unemployed and underemployed . . . These economic differentials have powerful implications for other social systems: they are at the heart of a web of other inequalities: representation in politics, the law and justice system, differential longevity and higher morbidity rates, education systems, health, social mobility and life chances: a vicious circle which is particularly damaging to the poor but also to the social fabric of life and society. And the poorest are the First Nations, who suffer from multiple adversities of racism, poverty, crime, alcoholism, high suicide rates, and marginalization and victimization and exploitation by the Canadian majority.

Yet *gender* inequality is the central problem for many of those in the women's movement: a position that overlaps to greater or lesser degree with the above mentioned economic inequality model. Patriarchy is the problem, with the marginalization, exploitation and victimization of women in poverty, crime, law, politics, families, suicide and attempted suicide, occupational segregation, violence, and more.

The two conflict paradigms are, as we have seen earlier, not necessarily mutually exclusive and certainly not monolithic: there are many "schools" within each paradigm. Nonetheless both are in diametrical opposition to the consensus/conservative paradigm with its emphasis on the "Canadian myth" of "freedom, dignity and respect, equality and fair treatment," and opportunity, peace, order and "shared values" (Chapter 2). Yet most Canadians *are* satisfied, despite the conflict paradigms; and according to the UN (1993) we have every right to be.

Whether the goals of sociology are to understand (Comte) or to act (Marx, feminists), depends on which of the paradigms are adopted. The two basic goals are complementary: understanding deepens with action, and action is more effective with understanding; but the activists involved are often mutually antagonistic.

MAX WEBER

Choosing between paradigms is not a matter of personal taste: chocolate, vanilla or strawberry. There *are* data. And there are consequences. And what *are* the lessons of history? But the comparison of competing paradigms and the ability to entertain several perspectives on reality brings us back to Max Weber and the Weberian paradigm. He was the first to develop, in embryonic form, the notion of the social construction of knowledge (which is what paradigms are), and now that the book is concluding, it is timely to consider our intellectual roots. The point is that consensus, conflict and feminist and masculinist paradigms are all political, value-laden definitions of reality, but it is the Weberians who try to assess them all, as we have done in this volume, without (necessarily) committing themselves to any one of them. (This may be described by activists as "sitting on the fence" or by Weberians as "keeping an open mind, and keeping the options open too!") The Weberian, at least in the social-psychological mode, is the one who, whether by conviction conservative, radical, or feminist or some mixture or blend in between, searches to see another person's point of view. Ideologues of all stripes and shades tend to be "true believers," convinced that they have the truth, the whole truth, and nothing but the truth. Weberians are perhaps more inclined to see truths in everyone — to be relativists — and this makes this paradigm very suitable for the conclusion of this volume.

It is not for any particular theory of social problems that we now turn to Weber, but for his theory of construction. For the Weberian, solutions are not the problem; definitions are. The question is, or should be, not: "What is the solution?" but "How do you define the problem?" It is not a matter of right or wrong, but how people perceive reality, which varies from individual to individual, and group to group.[1]

The founders of sociology whom we have recognized in these pages, Comte, Durkheim, Marx, Weber, Spencer, de Tocqueville and others — all cared passionately about the development and conditions of their societies, and the needs of the human condition. But it was Weber who oriented sociology towards individuals, admittedly in an impersonal sort of way.

The founders of sociology conceived of society in structural, holistic terms. Comte was concerned with the *evolution* of society and the sciences according to the law of the three stages. Durkheim was principally interested in the problem of social *cohesion* — how religion, the division of labour, and shared values maintained social unity, and how suicide exemplified the failure of that bond. And Marx was dedicated to the analysis of capital and the *revolution*. Weber, on the other hand, while he did outstanding work in macro-sociology, on bureaucracy, economy, religion and power, is equally well-known for developing the field of micro-sociology.

It is not necessary here to review all of Weber's work, but to understand his contribution to the study of social problems it will be useful to consider his perspectives on sociology. He defined the purpose of sociology as follows:

> Sociology . . . is a science which attempts the interpretive understanding of social action in order thereby to arrive at a causal explanation of its course and effects. In "action" is included all human behaviour when and insofar as the active individual attaches a subjective meaning to it. (1964: 88)

This dual emphasis on empathetic or "interpretive understanding" (verstehen) and "subjective meaning" distinguishes the humanist paradigm of Weber from Comtean positivism and Marxist determinism.[2] Thus, for Weber, the individual is the "basic unit" or "atom" for sociology:

> Interpretative sociology considers the individual and his action as the basic unit, as its "atom" . . . . The individual is . . . the upper limit and the sole carrier of meaningful conduct. . . . Such concepts as "state," "association," "feudalism," and the like, designate certain categories of human interaction. Hence it is the task of sociology to reduce these concepts to "understandable" action, that is without exception, to the action of participating individual men. (1948: 55)

He insisted that "Sociology, it goes without saying, is by no means confined to the study of 'social action'" (1964: 114). There are many types of sociology. Nonetheless this focus on the *individual* is quite different from the macro focus of the other founders of sociology.

From one point of view it could be argued that it does not much matter where sociologists start, with society or with the individual, since both are interlocked. In this view, sociologists who start with the society and sociologists who start with the individual should finally all meet up "in the middle." Yet Comte, Marx, and Durkheim never "met," despite an apparently common starting point. But furthermore, the *perspective* is quite different. For Weber, the individual actors are the interpreters and even the creators of their worlds, free and autonomous. The implications of Weber's conceptual framework were, however, more clearly spelled out by his followers in phenomenology after his death. Thus Raymond Aron has described Weber as an existentialist philosopher (1967: 191).

For Durkheim, on the other hand, the individual is a social *product*. Even a suicide is "only," for him, an item in the national suicide-rate and an expression of the national death wish. The "social fact" for Durkheim was the suicide *rate*, not the poor individual who died (1966: 51-2).

Both perspectives are no doubt useful, but they are quite different: human beings as creative actors or as created products, as free or determined.

It is perhaps worth adding that the Durkheimian perspective on suicide as a social problem has been so powerful and so useful that it was decades before Jack Douglas (1967) observed that suicide was not limited to three (or four) different types, but that it "meant" many different things to different people. This emphasis on subjective meaning and *verstehen* expresses precisely the Weberian perspective; and the practical implications of these different perspectives become clear.

The same applies to the different perspectives of Weber and Marx. Marx was a materialist who insisted that the problem was not to interpret the world but to change it. Weber, in his turn, insisted on the importance of *understanding* action and on the role of ideas in social change. Not that Weber was blind to social problems, for he was not, but the first problem is to understand how people see the world — and much of his own work was devoted to this issue. Sociological discourse seems to consist at times in arguing with your predecessors.

However, in sociology there are usually no clear victors, except to the followers of the various schools. Thus Raymond Aron confesses his own bias: "To me, Max Weber is the greatest of the sociologists; I would even say he is *the* sociologist" (1971: 245). Why? Because (1971: 191):

> No science can ever tell men how they should live or societies how they should be organized; and no science can ever tell humanity what its future is. The first negation distinguishes [Weber] from Durkheim, the second from Marx.

He adds, ironically, "Of course Weberians and Marxists have little in common; the former are found only in universities, the latter govern states" (1971: 246). Actually, I suspect that on further reflection this is only half-true. Marxists do govern states, although far fewer than they once did, but so do anti-Marxists. Basically activists govern, whether conservative or radical or stripes in between. And while Aron has a point, that the Weberian school, if indeed there is such a thing, is not so powerful as Marxism, nonetheless I think more people are interested in understanding the minutiae of behaviour and nuances of meaning of the social actors they know, than in politics, economics, and proselytizing. In this sense, Weberians are not only found in universities, they are everywhere.

Julien Freund was also an admirer of Weber. He suggested that (1968: 9):

> his sociology represents a veritable turning point in the history of that discipline; henceforth, sociology was to become a positive and empirical science in practice. Despite all protestations of faithfulness to the scientific spirit . . . the various sociologies of the nineteenth century were far more doctrinal than genuinely scientific. Thus Comte, Marx and Spencer, for example, all preferred romantic synthesis to modest, precise and cautious analysis.

Marxists would no doubt not agree; but much of Weber's work was a debate with the ghost of Marx. Thus he wrote *The Protestant Ethic* (1905), at least in part, to refute Marx's materialistic determinism, and his assumption that infrastructure determines superstructure, that ideas "merely" reflect material interests — as in Marx's famous dictum: "The dominant ideas are nothing more than the ideal expression of the dominant material relationships" (Marx, 1963: 93).

Here Weber showed, by meticulous scholarship, that Protestantism had influenced the development of capitalism. He concluded the book with a swipe at Marx and Marxists (1968: 183):

> The modern man is in general even with the best will, unable to give religious ideas a significance for culture and national character which they deserve. But it is, of course, not my aim to substitute for a one-sided materialistic an equally one-sided spiritualistic causal interpretation of culture and of history. Each is equally possible, but each, if it does not serve as the conclusion of an investigation, accomplishes equally little in the interest of historical truth.

Weber also attempted to refine Marx's simplistic, in his view, theory of class conflict with the more complex theory of triple stratification by class, party, and status group. The identification between each type of stratification and differentiation may be more or less complete; but his theory of multiple conflicts in pluralistic society goes a long way towards explaining the failure of Marx's predictions of class polarization and revolution (1968: 180-195).

What keeps society together, therefore, is not violence and the threat of violence, as Marxists have argued, nor consensus on values and structural interdependence in the division of labour, as Durkheim suggested, but the multiplicity of sectoral conflicts and problems which prevent the society splitting down one major line of cleavage. Enemies in one dimension are allies in another (Coser, 1964). It is the very multiplicity of cross-cutting cleavages — and alliances — problems and promises, which keep countries together . . . but not necessarily peaceful.

Furthermore, in Weber's view the most significant aspect of contemporary society was not class conflict but the development of bureaucracy, characterized by what he called rational-legal authority, i.e., the rules of rationality and legality, as opposed to the personal authority of autocratic leaders or to the authority of tradition. He did not expect a utopia with the dictatorship of the proletariat, but feared an "iron cage" of bureaucratic society: the dictatorship of the bureaucrats. For him bureaucracy, not capital, or anomie, or men, was the paramount social problem. "For the time being," he wrote, "the dictatorship of the official and not that of the worker is on the march" (1948: 50). And the future is a vision of cogs (in Coser, 1971: 231):

> Imagine the consequences of that comprehensive bureaucratization and rationalization which already today we see approaching. Already now . . . in all economic enterprises run on modern lines, rational calculation is manifest at every stage. By it the performance of each individual worker is mathematically measured, each man becomes a little cog in the machine and, aware of this, his own pre-occupation is whether he can become a bigger cog.

A fascinating contrast to Durkheim's view of organic solidarity! But Weber also describes a difficult dilemma: rationalization which is also inhumane; thus reason, which is humanity's greatest attribute in the tradition from Plato through Christian thinking, now may be destructive of humanity. Humans are alienated not by capital, not by patriarchy, but by reason, in this view.

Despite Weber's reservations about many aspects of Marx's work, he was nonetheless a great admirer of Marx and also of Nietzsche. He once remarked to a student of his at Munich:

> The honesty of a contemporary scholar, and above all of a contemporary philosopher, can be easily ascertained in terms of his position vis-à-vis Nietzsche and Marx. Those who do not admit that they could not do major parts of their own work without the contributions made by these two men, deceive themselves as well as others. The world in which we live intellectually has been shaped to a large extent by Marx and Nietzsche. (Coser, 1971: 250)

The world in which we live intellectually has also been shaped to a large extent by Weber — not only by his major works, important though they have been, but by his location of the individual at the heart of sociology, and his insistence on *verstehen* and the importance of subjective meanings. He only sketched the conceptual foundations of this methodology; nonetheless the development of phenomenology and indeed social psychology owe much to his originality and his focus on the individual, and their/our paradigms of social reality and social problems.

The conservatives may emphasize one set of social problems: violence, crime, absenteeism, political apathy, etc. The radicals may contradict and say that these are not social problems — they are logical and appropriate responses to an oppressive system (capitalist, patriarchal, racist, etc., depending on the paradigm) which should be destroyed. Opinions about what is the *prime* issue and problem vary, and always have: capital, men, the tyranny of the majority, human nature, or society, the devil or genetics, irrationalism (Comte), anomie, even rationalization. We have reviewed many of these debates earlier. But it is primarily the Weberian who will ask: *Who* defines *what* as a problem, *why*, *how* and *so what*? And this takes us back full circle to the beginning. But now the sociology of social problems is grounded a little more securely in the context of sociological theory and a sociology of knowledge, synthesizing the possibilities of understanding and social action with the principal paradigms.

THE FUTURE

What does the future of Canada look like? Obviously we do not know, we will have to wait and see. Our vision will be coloured, however, by the colour of our paradigmatic lenses: our understanding of history, our experience of the present, and our sense of the future, which all in turn colour our militancy or conservatism red or blue. In other words, our sense of the future determines our paradigms, but our paradigms also determine our sense of the future.

We cannot adopt here the scale of the global vision developed by Conor Cruise O'Brien in his recent book *On the Eve of the Millennium*: the attack on Enlightenment values by Islamic fundamentalism and the Christian fundamentalism epitomized by the Pope, whom he calls "the greatest ayatollah of the West," the population crisis, the resource crisis, the distribution of resources crisis, the rise of terrorism, the communications revolution and the challenge to democracy, the rise of nationalism and the disintegration of Eastern Europe, and his rather gloomy outlook for the new millennium.

Our agenda is more limited, restricted to the specifically Canadian problems discussed here. As always, however, how we see the future depends on how we see the present: whether we emphasize the "progress" or the "conflict." The UN (1993) has offered a balance sheet of human progress for industrial countries by several criteria: life expectancy and health, education, income and employment, women, the social fabric and the environment. These same criteria apply to Canada, and we have developed others, on poverty, politics, crime, suicide, etc., as we have discussed our social problems. Some people, depending on their paradigms, tend to emphasize the progress; conflict theorists tend to stress the deprivation, by class, gender, ethnicity or region depending on their viewpoint. Each paradigm is valid. Each is limited. A point of view may be interesting and very useful, but it is precisely that, only *one* point of view. Many are necessary.

Conservatives tend to see a future of increasing peace, prosperity, and progress. The three Ps. This is achieved by responsible government, fair laws, tolerance and a sense of equity plus "shared values." Things will go on as before, getting better and better for more and more people, and justifying the number one spot in the 1993 UNDP international ranking of the quality of life. We must conserve what we have: it doesn't get any better than this in this world. And most Canadians are indeed satisfied with Canada and its institutions.

Certainly this is a viable position, but it is not universal. Conflict theorists can point to major fault lines in Canadian society — including the social problems we have discussed here: the violence, the immense economic inequality, the negative consequences of poverty for children especially, and for the First Nations, and therefore for the future, the regional disparities with serious political possibilities for the future, the racism, the high and rising suicide rates, the problems with alcohol — the list could go on — and particularly gender inequality.

This last is the particular domain of feminists, but gender overlaps with and permeates every field of social life as we have seen, poverty, crime, suicide, alcoholism; politics and economics, public and private power, health and life and death. Feminists also identify fault-lines in Canada, although often different lines with different causes than those identified by radical/Marxist-type conflict theorists. Gender relations rather than class relations are the problematic, and the dynamics of their interaction is a constant source of debate.

How we see the future therefore will depend on the paradigms we adopt, at least in so far as the *categories* will be different, but whether it is rosy or dark will depend upon our personal or political optimism or pessimism. It also depends on facts and data. If we extrapolate from past trends we can suggest a few possibilities or probabilities for the future:

1. Inequality will increase. In Chapter 5 we saw that Canada is not an equal society, far from it, with the wealthiest 10% of the population owning most of the wealth (51%); but since wealth creates wealth then we can expect the rich to become richer, that is, to own a greater and greater share of the national wealth. Income differentials may remain similar, as they have done for the last 20 years, but of course the families *within* each quintile will change as they move up and down. No doubt there must be a limit to this trend, whereby fewer and fewer families accumulate a greater and greater share of the national wealth, until almost everything is owned by almost no one. But that limit has not been reached yet. Both the USA and the UK are believed to be economically more unequal than Canada. But the question is not whether this trend can be stopped, or even reversed, nor even how, so much as: what are the social costs of this economic trend? These we know. Long ago George Grant advised Canadians to look south to see if that is the future for which it dreams.

2. The crime rate and the violent crime rate have stabilized in the last year or two, but it is too early to tell if this is temporary or permanent.

3. The suicide rate will continue to rise, particularly as we are exposed to the advocates of suicide as a rational choice, and as their recipes for a successful death become more readily available to the young, the depressed, and the vulnerable.

4. Canada will be increasingly polarized between those who have jobs and those who have not. This will create, or continue, an economic polarization similar to that predicted by Marx and Engels between the "haves" and those on welfare or UI. This process was reinforced by this recession, resulting in more than 1.6 million Canadians unemployed. Indeed a secondary polarization may be emerging between those who are computer-literate and those who are not.

5. This economic polarization is complemented by a political polarization in which, reading from left to right as usual, the West voted primarily Reform in the 1993 election, Ontario voted primarily Liberal, Quebec voted primarily BQ, except for western Montreal (Anglophone) which voted primarily Liberal, and the Atlantic provinces voted primarily Liberal. This pattern: Reform, Liberal, Bloc, Liberal expresses both the massive *political* alienation from the old three-party system (Liberal, PC and NDP) and also a massive *geographic* alienation from the Ottawa-Ontario axis by the West and by Quebec.

6. This coincidence of political *and* geographic lines of cleavage makes the future integration of Canada more problematic — particularly since these two "fault" lines also coincide with a third line of cleavage, ethnicity/language, in the case of the province (or nation) of Quebec.

7. Ethnic conflict will continue at high and perhaps increasing levels. The rise of the BQ and the official status of the BQ as the opposition expresses and reinforces the power of the separatist PQ in Quebec. This conflict, despite violence in the past, may remain more verbal and political than physical.

   On the other hand conflicts between the AFN and both federal and provincial governments and police are potentially more explosive. The Oka and Kahnawake crises in 1990, the smuggling at Akwesasne, the demands for casinos, the occasional protest blockades, the continuing negotiations over land rights and sovereignty, the continuing enquiries into racism against Native peoples . . . all these issues demonstrate the complexity of the relations between the AFN and the rest of Canada, and the desperate need for change — as well as the potential areas of conflict.

8. The black economy will prosper. While this will financially benefit the few, it does undermine the economy of the future for the many. Nonetheless, times are hard, so more and more people are willing to buy smuggled, or stolen goods, to avoid paying taxes, to avoid declaring income, and perhaps to engage in smuggling and theft themselves. Certainly smuggling has been a financial boom to many Native people on Akwesasne and on other reserves, as well as to satellite non-Native individuals and businesses.

9. The gender gap will probably continue to close with respect to income and occupational distribution; but gender-competition may increase (unless the rate of growth of the economy increases to accommodate the expectations and demands of both sexes).

10. Canada is in some ways more *open* than it used to be. Problems are visible. Policies are discussed. Everyone is an amateur sociologist. And the contribution of sociologists and the discipline generally to the quality of life of Canada is something we can be proud of. Since the founding of the first departments of sociology at McGill and the University of Toronto, and the creation of the Canadian Sociology and Anthropology Association in 1965, sociologists and anthropologists have engaged in the study of living in Canada with great enthusiasm and skill. This is not the place for a history of sociology in Canada, although it certainly reflects the clash of paradigms, nor for a list of "great Canadian sociologists and anthropologists," but it is the place to recognize the relevance of social science research for creating knowledge, for political action, and for influencing policy formation (cf. Carroll *et al.*, 1992).

The future looks increasingly rough, therefore, at least in the short term; increasingly polarized between rich and poor, Quebec and Canada, the AFN and Canada, politically polarized between Liberal, Reform, and BQ, and regionally polarized also; gender polarization may also increase as women and men compete for scarce resources. And as polarization increases, *economic, political, ethnic, regional and gender*, so attitudes may harden and the potential for further and escalating conflict also increases.

Perhaps this will be dismissed as a worst-case scenario, rather than accepted as a realistic trends assessment. Obviously much depends on two intervening variables: the economy and the polity. A turn-around by both would be a best-case scenario. The *trends*, however, seem to indicate that we will have to pay serious attention to these challenges.

The next question is logical: which of all the theorists whom we have considered seems the most useful for understanding the present and the future? The principal theories as to what is the ultimate, *fundamental* problem can be summarized fairly briskly, along with the theorist, in a short list:

- the devil (religious paradigm)
- human nature (Machiavelli, Hobbes)
- society (Rousseau)
- the majority (Burke, de Tocqueville)
- capitalists and capitalism (Marx)
- irrationalism (Comte)
- anomie (Durkheim)
- rationality and bureaucracy (Weber)
- patriarchy and men (feminists)
- genetics, biology (hard sciences)

Other theorists could be added, but I think this list covers most of the main orientations to the issues that bother us and challenge us.

The first and last can be dismissed as not sociological: the devil is not readily available for interviews, obviously; nor surely is there any great need to blame the poor devil for entirely human activities. And while genetics and biology do have much to tell us about violence, suicide, alcoholism, and individual predispositions, they do not explain culture nor cultural variations.

Similarly, while the debates about whether human nature or society are the principal cause of our social problems are interesting, and are the building blocks of the conservative and radical paradigms respectively, they are a bit too vague and speculative to be very helpful. How do you operationalize the concepts to test their utility? I do not think you can.

Next we come to the broad divisions within society: who is to blame? the elite, the top, the capitalists, as Marx argued: "One capitalist always kills many"; or the majority, the mass, the mob, as first Burke and then de Tocqueville argued. Both hated the French revolution; but whereas Burke, writing at the beginning of it, emphasized the need for order, gradualism, hierarchy and unity in England, de Tocqueville was impressed by some aspects of equality in the United States: but not by the *majority* racism towards the Native people and the Blacks. Marx argued for equality; Burke and de Tocqueville for liberty. Are they antithetical goals?

Which is more problematic: the leaders or the public today in Canada? Is the majority tyrannical or the minority? Does the cream rise to the top (as Spencer argued) or the scum (as Marx thought)? Do the dregs fall to the bottom, as Spencer argued, or the gold, as the democrats like Rousseau insist? Conservatives generally hold to the cream theory and, like de Tocqueville, value liberty more than equality. Liberals and radicals tend, like good democrats, to believe in the gold theory and value equality, more than liberty.

Feminists generally seem to entertain the scum theory of patriarchal oppression; but while all aspire to *gender* equality, conservatives are more likely to tolerate this gender equality within an overall Canadian hierarchy, while radicals are more likely to demand an equal Canada.

Comte and Weber offer competing themes in their analysis of social trends. For Comte society was progressing to its third and final stage, the triumph of reason and particularly of the social sciences, epitomized by sociology. The future, in his view, is radiant. Weber, having lived through World War I, was more sceptical, and more critical of rationality, which he saw increasingly institutionalized in an inhuman and inhumane bureaucracy, extremely oppressive of freedom. Where Comte envisioned a future of love, and Spencer a future of war, Weber saw a future of cogs! Who was right?

Marx was probably the most optimistic of all these theorists for the future, and also the most pessimistic about his present. The arch theorist of economic and political alienation, some of his work on political economy is still relevant for Canada today, although few would follow him in his cry for revolution or in his utopian expectations.

Veins of pessimism and fear for the present and the future are apparent in many of the early sociologists and social thinkers: examples can be found in Durkheim's theory of anomie, the tyranny of the majority in de Tocqueville and Burke, the tyranny of the minority in Marx and Engels, the cog perspective of Weber, the perpetual war theory of Hobbes, Freud, Nietzsche and Spencer, and the male tyranny and war against women theory of Wollstonecraft and other feminists up to Greer, French, and CACSW.

Yet most Canadians are relatively content in the present, confident and optimistic for the future, and value Canada as one of the finest countries in the world, or *the* finest according to the UNDP (1994). We do have social problems, and the future is of course problematic. But Canadians have done well in resolving, containing, and alleviating our problems; and the wealth and range of research which you have reviewed in this volume testify to the continuing efforts to create a sunny Canada, as your reading of this volume testifies to your concerns. Hopefully readers are rather more informed now than they were at the beginning of the range and depth of some social problems, more ready to debate and initiate desired social changes, and especially more able to understand alternative paradigms and other peoples' points of view: conservative, liberal, Marxist, feminist or masculinist, which is so essential for effecting social change.

ENDNOTES

1.   Not that all perceptions are equally sensible, accurate, and valid — some are no doubt downright paranoid, or bigoted, or "ignorant and wrong"; based on a faulty analysis of inaccurate data perhaps. But the debates are not usually between "truth" and "falsity" so much as between powers and conflicting interests, and are therefore about "half-truths." W.I. Thomas wrote that "What is perceived to be real is real in its consequences." It is these perceptions and these social constructions of reality which are our first concern; our second concern may be the accuracy or otherwise of these perceptions.

2.   The Weberian perspective does not imply that the sociologist should be only the empathetic observer. Weber himself was actively involved in the German politics of his time as a diplomat and politician — far more so than Marx, Engels, or Durkheim ever had been. And in the end his fear of the "dictatorship of the bureaucracy" was overshadowed by the charismatic leadership which he had so brilliantly described and the rise of Adolf Hitler: the tyranny of the minority, not the majority, and the dictatorship not of the proletariat, nor of the bureaucrat, but of the dictator.

BIBLIOGRAPHY

Abella, Irving and Harold Troper, 1982. *None is Too Many*. Toronto: Lester and Orpen Dennys.

Adelberg, Ellen and Claudia Currie, 1987. *Too Few to Count*. Vancouver: Press Gang.

Adelberg, Ellen and Claudia Currie (eds.), 1993. *In Conflict with the Law: Women and the Canadian Justice System*. Vancouver: Press Gang.

Adler, R.J. and D.A. Brusegard, 1980. *Perspectives Canada III*. Ottawa. Cat. No. 11-511.

Alcoholics Anonymous, 1955. *Alcoholics Anonymous*. New York: AA World Services.

Allen, Robert, 1992. "Preliminary Crime Statistics, 1991." Statistics Canada, *Juristat* 12:4. June Cat. No. 85-002.

Allport, Gordon W., 1958. *The Nature of Prejudice*. New York: Doubleday Anchor.

Amiel, Barbara, 1994. "The Tyranny of Modern-day Feminism." *Maclean's* 11.7:13.

Amnesty International, 1992. *The Americas: Human Rights Violations against Indigenous Peoples*. London: Amnesty International Publications.

Aristotle, 1984. *The Complete Works*. Edited by Jonathan Barnes. Princeton University Press. Bollingen Series.

Armstrong, Pat and Hugh Armstrong, 1984. *The Double Ghetto*. Toronto: McLelland and Stewart.

Aron, Raymond, 1967. *Main Currents in Sociological Thought*. Vol. 2. New York: Basic Books.

Aurelius, Marcus, 1964. *Meditations*. Penguin Books.

Avard, Denise and Louise Harvey, 1989. *The Health of Canada's Children*. Ottawa: Canadian Institute of Child Health.

Badets, Jane, 1993. "Canada's Immigrants: Recent Trends." *Canadian Social Trends*. Statistics Canada. Cat. No. 11-008, Summer: 8-11.

Badgley, R.F., 1984. *Sexual Offences Against Children*. 2 Vols. Report of the Committee on Sexual Offences Against Children and Youth. Ottawa. Cat. No. J2-50.

Badiet, Patricia, 1976. "Women and Legal Drugs: A Review." in Anne MacLennan (ed.), *Women: Their Use of Alcohol and Other Legal Drugs*. Toronto: Addiction Research Foundation of Ontario:57-81.

Bales, Robert F., 1962. "Attitudes toward drinking in the Irish culture." In David J. Pittman and Charles R. Snyder (eds.), *Society, Culture and Drinking Patterns*. New York: John Wiley, pp. 157-87.

Barnes, Jonathan, 1987. *Early Greek Philosophy*. Penguin Books.

Barrett, Stanley R., 1991. "White Supremists and Neo-Fascists: Laboratories for the analysis of racism in wider society." In Ormond McKague (ed.), *Racism in Canada*. Saskatoon: Fifth House: 85-99.

Becker, Howard S., 1973 [1963]. *Outsiders*. Second Edition. New York: Free Press.

Beneteau, Renée, 1988. "Trends in Suicide." *Canadian Social Trends*. Winter: 22-24.

Berger, Peter L. and Thomas Luckmann, 1967. *The Social Construction of Reality*. New York: Anchor Books.

Berger, Thomas, 1977. *Northern Frontier, Northern Homeland*. The Report of the MacKenzie Valley Pipeline Inquiry. Vol. 1. Ottawa. Cat. No. CP 32-25.

Best, Joel (ed.), 1989. *Images of Issues: Typifying Contemporary Social Problems*. New York: Aldine de Gruytev.

Betcherman, Lita-Rose, 1973. *The Swastika and The Maple Leaf*. Don Mills, Ontario: Fitzhenry and Whiteside.

Bly, Robert, 1990. *Iron John*. New York: Addison-Wesley.

Bolaria, B. Singh and Peter S. Li, 1985. *Racial Oppression in Canada*. Toronto: Garamond Press.

Bonhoeffer, Dietrich, 1966 [1949]. *Ethics*. London: Collins, Fontana Library.

Brodie, J. and Jill Vickers, 1982. *Canadian Women in Politics: An Overview*. Canadian Research Institute for the Advancement of Women.

Brown, Claude, 1984. "Manchild in Harlem." *The New York Times Magazine*. Sept. 16:36-44, 54, 76-8.

Buckner, Taylor, 1993. "Minorities on Minorities: How Canada's Ethnic Minorities View Selected Canadian Minority Groups." Working Paper Series Number 3, Centre for Community and Ethnic Studies. Dept. of Sociology and Anthropology, Concordia University, Montreal.

Bullough, Vera L., 1974. *The Subordinate Sex: A History of Attitudes Towards Women*. Penguin Books.

Burke, Edmund, 1986 [1790]. *Reflections on the Revolution in France*. Penguin Classics.

Burrell, Gibson and Gareth Morgan, 1985. *Sociological Paradigms and Organizational Analysis*. London: Gower.

Burman, Patrick, 1988. *Killing Time, Losing Ground: Experiences of Unemployment*. Toronto: Thompson Educational Publishing.

Business Week 13.12.93, 31.1.94.

Camus, Albert, 1975 [1942]. *The Myth of Sisyphus*. Trans. by Justin O'Brien. Penguin Books.

Canadian Advisory Council on the Status of Women, 1988, 1989. *Annual Report*. Ottawa. Cat. No. LW1-1989.

Canadian Advisory Council on the Status of Women, 1988. *Women in Politics: Becoming full partners in the political process*. Ottawa.

Canadian Advisory Council on the Status of Women, 1991. "Male Violence Against Women: The Brutal Face of Inequality." Brief submitted to the House of Commons Subcommittee on the Status of Women: Violence Against Women.

Canadian Advisory Council on the Status of Women, 1992. "Re-evaluating Employment Equity." Publication Number:92-E-184.

Canadian Human Rights Commission, 1994. *Annual Report 1993*. Cat. No. HR1.

Canadian Institute of Child Health, 1989. *The Health of Canada's Children*. Ottawa.

Canadian Panel on Violence Against Women 1993. *Changing the Landscape: Ending Violence - Achieving Equality*. Cat. No. SW 45-1.

Cannon, Margaret, 1993. "The Big Steal." *Globe and Mail Report on Business Magazine* Feb.:16-28.

Cardinal, Harold, 1969. *The Unjust Society*. Edmonton: Hurtig.

Carrigan, D. Owen, 1991. *Crime and Punishment in Canada*. McClelland and Stewart.

Carroll, William, Linda Christiansen-Ruffman, Raymond F. Currie and Deborah Harrison (eds.), 1992. *Fragile Truths: 25 Years of Sociology and Anthropology in Canada*. Ottawa: Carleton University Press.

Cermak, Timmen L., 1985. *A Primer on Adult Children of Alcoholics*. Deerfield Beach, Florida: Health Communications.

Cermak, Timmen L., 1989. *A Time to Heal*. New York: Avon Books.

Chawla, Raj K., 1990. "The Distribution of Wealth in Canada and the United States." *Perspectives*. Statistics Canada. Cat. 75-001. Spring: 29-41.

Chunn, Dorothy E. and Shelley A.M. Gavigan, 1991. "Women and Crime in Canada" in Margaret A. Jackson and Curt T. Griffiths (eds.), *Canadian Criminology*. Toronto: Harcourt, Brace, Jovanovich.

Clarke, Annette M., 1986. *Work and Unemployment in St. John's*. Background Report. Royal Commission on Employment and Unemployment, Newfoundland and Labrador.

Coccaro, Emil F., 1995. "The Biology of Aggression." *Scientific American: Science and Medicine*. Jan/Feb: 28-47.

Cohen, Albert K., 1966. *Deviance and Control*. Englewood Cliffs, N.J.: Prentice-Hall.

Cohen, Percy S., 1968. *Modern Social Theory*. London: Heinemann.

Committee of the Senate and House of Commons, 1991. *Shared Values*. Cat. No. CP22-29.

Committee on Participation of Visible Minorities in Canadian Society, 1984. *Equality Now!* The Baudlin Committee. Ottawa. House of Commons. Issue No. 4, March 8.

Committee on Pornography and Prostitution, 1985. *Pornography and Prostitution in Canada*. The Fraser Report. Ottawa. Cat. No. J2-55.

Committee on Sexual Offenses Against Children and Youths, 1984. *Sexual Offenses Against Children*. The Badgley Report. Ottawa. Cat. No. J2-50.

Committee on the Status of Women, 1991. *The War Against Women*. Ottawa: House of Commons. Cat. XC 28-343/1-3.

Comte, Auguste, 1957. *A General View of Positivism*. New York: Robert Speller and Sons.

Comte, Auguste, 1966. *System of Positive Polity*. 4 Vols. Translated by Frederick Harrison. New York: Burt Franklin.

Comte, Auguste, 1975. *Auguste Comte and Positivism: The Essential Writings*. Edited by Gertrud Lenzer. Chicago: University of Chicago Press.

Coser, Lewis A., 1964. *The Functions of Social Conflict*. New York: The Free Press.

Coser, Lewis A., 1971. *Masters of Sociological Thought*. New York: Harcourt, Brace, Jovanovich.

Cox, Oliver, 1949. *Caste, Class and Race*. New York: Modern Reader.

Dahrendorf, Ralph, 1959. *Class and Class Conflict in Industrial Society*. Stanford, California: Stanford University Press.

Daly, Martin & Margo Wilson, 1988. *Homicide*. Hawthorne, New York: Aldine de Gruyter.

Daly, Martin & Margo Wilson, 1988. "Evolutionary Social Psychology and Family Homicide." *Science*. Vol. 242, 28 October: 519-24.

Darwin, Charles, 1968 [1859]. *The Origin of Species*. Penguin Books.

Darwin, Charles, 1981 [1871]. *The Descent of Man*. Princeton, N.J.: Princeton University Press.

Darwin, Francis, 1887. *The Life and Letters of Charles Darwin*. 2 Vols. London: John Murray.

Davies, James B., 1993. "The Distribution of Wealth and Economic Inequality." In James Curtis, Edward Grabb and Neil Guppy (eds.). *Social Inequality in Canada*. Scarborough, Ontario: Prentice-Hall, 105-20.

Davis, Kingsley and Wilbert E. Moore, 1945. "Some Principles of Stratification." *American Sociological Review*. April, Vol. 10, 242-7.

de Beauvoir, Simone, 1963 [1949]. *The Second Sex*. London: Knopf.

de Lint, Jan, 1971. "Alcohol Use in Canadian Society." In Craig L. Bogdell, Carl F. Grindstaff and Paul C. Whitehead (eds.), *Critical Issues in Canadian Society*. Toronto: Holt, Rinehart and Winston: 490-9.

de Tocqueville, Alexis, 1966 [1835-40]. *Democracy in America*. Translated by Henry Reeve. 2 Vols. New Rochelle, New York: Arlington House.

Delisle, Esther, 1993. *The Traitor and the Jew*. Montreal: Robert Davies.

Department of Indian Affairs and Northern Development, 1980. *Native Conditions: A Survey*. Ottawa. Cat. No. R32-45.

Descarries-Bélanger, Francine and Shirley Roy, 1991. *The Women's Movement and Its Currents of Thought*. Ottawa: Canadian Research Institute for the Advancement of Women. No. 26.

Discover, 1983. January.

Doige, Derrick, 1990. "Young Offenders." *Canadian Social Trends*. Autumn:11-14. Cat. 11-008.

Dollard, John, 1957 [1937]. *Caste and Class in a Southern Town*. New York: Doubleday Anchor.

Dollard, John, 1939. *Frustration and Aggression*. New Haven: Yale University Press.

Douglas, Jack D., 1967. *The Social Meanings of Suicide*. Princeton, N.J.: Princeton University Press.

Driedger, Leo, 1989. *The Ethnic Factor*. Toronto: McGraw-Hill Ryerson.

Durkheim, Emile, 1947 [1917]. *Elementary Forms of the Religious Life*. London: Free Press.

Durkheim, Emile, 1962 [1895]. *The Rules of Sociological Method*. The Free Press.

Durkheim, Emile, 1964 [1893]. *The Division of Labor in Society*. New York: The Free Press.

Durkheim, Emile, 1966 [1897]. *Suicide*. London: Routledge and Kegan Paul.

Dworkin, Andrea, 1988. *Letters from a War Zone*. London: Secker and Warburg.

Economic Council of Canada, 1991. *New Faces in the Crowd: Economic and Social Impacts of Immigration*. Cat. No. EC22-171.

Economic Council of Canada, 1992. *The New Face of Poverty*. Ottawa. Cat. No. EC22-186.

Eliany, Marc, 1991. "Alcohol and Drug Use." *Canadian Social Trends*. Statistics Canada. Spring: 19-26.

Elliott, Jean Leonard and Augue Fleras, 1992. *Unequal Relations*. Scarborough, Ontario: Prentice-Hall.

Engels, Frederick, 1969 [1845]. *The Condition of the Working Class in England*. London: Panther Books.

Evans-Pritchard, E.E., 1970. *The Sociology of Comte*. Manchester: Manchester University Press.

Farrell, Warren, 1993. *The Myth of Male Power*. New York: Simon and Schuster.

Farrington, David P., 1987. "What kind of research is needed to advance knowledge about the explanation, prevention and treatment of crime in Canada?" *Canadian Journal of Criminology* 29(2): 171-83.

Fekete, John, 1994. *Moral Panic: Biopolitics Rising*. Montreal: Robert Davies.

Ferguson, Ted, 1975. *A White Man's Country*. Toronto: Doubleday.

Fisher, Anne B., 1992. "When Will Women Get to the Top?" *Fortune* 21.9.92:44-56.

Forbes, 25.2.92; 8.7.92; 18.7.94.; 19.12.94

Forcese, Dennis and Stephan Richer, 1983. *Social Issues: Sociological Views of Canada*. Scarborough, Ont.: Prentice-Hall.

Fortune, 7.9.92; 28.6.93.

Foster, Cecil, 1991. *Distorted Mirror: Canada's Racist Face*. Toronto: Harper Collins.

Foucault, Michel, 1967 [1961]. *Madness and Civilization*. Trans. Richard Howard. London: Tavistock.

Foucault, Michel, 1979. *Discipline and Punish*. Trans. Alan Sheridan. New York: Vintage Books.

Foucault, Michel, 1980. *The History of Sexuality, Vol. 1. An Introduction*. Trans. Robert Hurley. New York: Vintage Books.

Frank, Anne, 1972 [1942-4]. *The Diary of a Young Girl*. New York: Simon and Schuster, Pocket Books.

Frank, Jeffrey, 1992. "Violent Youth Crime." *Canadian Social Trends*. 26:Autumn, 2-9.

Freidan, Betty, 1963. *The Feminine Mystique*. New York: Dell.

French, Marilyn, 1992. *The War Against Women*. New York: Summit Books.

Freud, Sigmund, 1979. *Case Histories II*. Pelican Freud Library. Vol. 9.

Freud, Sigmund, 1985. *Civilization, Society and Religion*. Pelican Freud Library. Vol. 12.

Freud, Sigmund, 1990. *The Psychopathology of Everyday Life*. Pelican Freud Library, Vol. 5.

Freund, Julien, 1968. *The Sociology of Max Weber*. New York: Pantheon Books.

Frideres, James S., 1988. *Native People in Canada*. Scarborough, Ontario: Prentice-Hall.

Frideres, James S., 1991. "From the Bottom Up: Institutional Structures and the Indian People." In B. Singh Bolaria (ed.). *Social Issues and Contradictions in Canadian Society*. Toronto: Harcourt, Brace, Jovanovich:108-32.

Gans, Herbert J., 1976. "The Uses of Poverty: The Poor Pay All." *Social Policy*, 2, July-August 1971, 20-24. Reprinted in Glen Gaviglio and David E. Raye (eds.), *Society as It Is*. New York: Macmillan.

Gardner-O'Toole, Elaine and Jane Allain, 1993a. "Aboriginal Self-Government." *Current Issue Review* 89-5. Cat. No. YM 32-1.

Gardner-O'Toole, Elaine and Jane Allain, 1993b. "Aboriginal Rights." *Current Issue Review* 89-11. Cat. No. YM 32-1.

Gartner, Rosemary and Anthony N. Doob, 1994. "Trends in Criminal Victimization: 1988-1993." *Juristat.* June. Cat. No. 85-002.

Gavigan, Shelley A.M., 1993. "Women's Crime: New Perspectives and Old Theories" in Ellen Adelberg and Claudia Currie (eds.), *In Conflict with the Law*. Vancouver: Press Gang Publishers.

The Gazette (Montreal). 2.2.88; 16.12.89; 9.2.90; 10.2.90; 8.4.90; 31.7.93; 28.5.94; 23.7.94; 26.7.94.

Gies, Gilbert and Ezra Stotland (Eds.), 1980. *White Collar Crime*. London: Sage.

Globe and Mail, 23.6.90; 21.11.91; 28.1.92; 22.4.92; 30.6.92; 11.3.93; 11.6.93; 27.7.93; 30.7.93; 31.7.93; 2.10.93; 14.12.93, 23.3.94; 25.5.94; 26.5.94; 11.6.94; 14.7.94; 2.2.95.

Gomme, Ian McDermid, 1993. *The Shadow Line: Deviance and Crime in Canada*. Toronto: Harcourt, Brace, Jovanovich.

Gould, Julius, 1969. "Auguste Comte" in Timothy Raison (ed.). *Founding Fathers of Social Science*. Penguin Books, 35-42.

Grabb, Edward G., 1990. *Theories of Social Inequality*. Toronto: Holt, Rinehart and Winston.

Grant, George, 1971. *Lament for a Nation: The Defeat of Canadian Nationalism*. Ottawa: Carleton Library.

Gray, James H., 1972. *Booze: The Impact of Whisky on the Prairie West*. Toronto: Macmillan.

Greenblatt, Milton and Marc A. Schukitt, 1976. *Alcoholism Problems in Women and Children*. New York: Grune and Stratton.

Greer, Germain, 1971. *The Female Eunuch*. London: Paladin.

Gutin, Joann C., 1994. "End of the Rainbow." *Discover*. Nov. 70-4.

Hagan, John, 1991. *The Disreputable Pleasures: Crime and Deviance in Canada*. Toronto: McGraw-Hill.

Hamilton, Peter, 1983. *Talcott Parsons*. London: Tavistock.

Hassett, James, 1981. "But That Would Be Wrong." *Psychology Today*. November:34-50.

Hatch, Alison J. and Karlene Faith, 1991. "The Female Offender in Canada: A Statistical Profile." in Robert A. Silverman, James J. Teevan, Jr., and Vincent F. Sacco (eds.), 1991. *Crime in Canadian Society*. 4th Ed. Toronto: Butterworths.

Hawthorn, H.B. and M-A Tremblay, 1966. *A Survey of Contemporary Indians of Canada.* (The Hawthorn-Tremblay Report). 2 Vols. Ottawa: Indian Affairs Branch.

Health and Welfare, 1983. *Women and Alcohol.* Cat. No. H39-68.

Health and Welfare, 1987. *Suicide in Canada.* Report of the National Task Force. Ottawa. Cat. No. H39-107.

Health and Welfare, 1989. *Alcohol in Canada.* Cat. No. H39-158.

Health and Welfare, 1989. *Licit and Illicit Drugs in Canada.* Cat. No. H39-159.

Health and Welfare, 1992. *Alcohol and Other Drug Use by Canadians.* Cat. No. H39-251.

Health and Welfare, 1992. *Canada's Health Promotion Survey 1990.* Cat. No. H39-263.

Health and Welfare, 1992. *The Health of Canada's Youth.* Cat. No. H39-239.

Health and Welfare, 1993. *Canada's Health Promotion Survey 1990.* Cat. No. H39-263.

Health, Education and Welfare, 1971. *Alcohol and Health.* National Institute on Alcohol Abuse and Alcoholism. Washington, D.C. Pub. No. 72-9099.

Henry, Frances, 1995. *The Caribbean Diaspora in Toronto: Learning to Live with Racism.* Toronto: University of Toronto Press.

Henry, Frances, Carol Tator, Winston Mattis and Tim Rees, 1995. *The Colour of Democracy: Racism in Canadian Society.* Toronto: Harcourt Brace.

Hiller, Harry H., 1976. *Canadian Society.* Scarborough, Ont.: Prentice-Hall.

Hitler, Adolf, 1942. *Mein Kampf.* London: Hurst and Blackett.

Hobbes, Thomas, 1960. *Leviathan.* Oxford: Blackwell.

Hoecker-Drysdale, Susan, 1992. *Harriet Martineau: First Woman Sociologist.* New York: Berg.

Horton, John, 1984. "The Dehumanization of Anomie and Alienation." *The British Journal of Sociology*, Vol. XV, No. 4, Dec. 283-300.

Humphry, Derek, 1992. *Final Exit.* New York: Dell.

Jackson, Margaret A. and Curt T. Griffiths (eds.), 1991. *Canadian Criminology.* Toronto: Harcourt, Brace, Jovanovich.

Jellinek, E.M., 1960. *The Disease Concept of Alcoholism.* New Haven: Hillhouse Press.

Jencks, Christopher, 1987. "Genes and Crime." *The New York Review.* Feb. 12:33-41.

Johnson, Holly and Karen Rodgers, 1993. "A Statistical Overview of Women and Crime in Canada" in Ellen Adelberg and Claudia Currie (eds.), *In Conflict with the Law.* Vancouver: Press Gang, 95-116.

Kallen, Evelyn, 1995. *Ethnicity and Human Rights in Canada.* Oxford: Oxford University Press.

Kanter, Rosabeth Moss, 1977. *Men and Women of the Corporation*. New York: Basic Books.

Kantorowicz, Ernst H., 1957. *The King's Two Bodies*. Princeton, N.J.: Princeton University Press.

Keane, Carl, 1991. "Corporate Crime." in Robert A. Silverman, James J. Teevan, Jr., and Vincent F. Sacco, eds., 1991. *Crime in Canadian Society*. 4th Ed. Toronto: Butterworths:223-32.

Keen, Sam, 1991. *Fire in the Belly: On Being a Man*. New York: Bantam Books.

Kendall, Kathy, 1992. "Sexual Difference and the Law: Premenstrual Syndrome as Legal Defense" in Dawn H. Currie and Valerie Raoul (eds.), *The Anatomy of Gender: Women's Struggle for the Body*. Ottawa: Carleton University Press.

Kinsella, Warren, 1994. *Web of Hate: Inside Canada's Far Right Network*. Toronto: Harper Collins

Kinsey, Barry A., 1966. *The Female Alcoholic*. Springfield, Illinois: Charles C. Thomas.

La Presse 10.1.94.

Larocque, Emma, 1991. "Racism Runs Through Canadian Society." In Ormond McKague, *Racism in Canada*. Saskatoon: Fifth House, 73-76.

League for Human Rights of B'Nai Brith, 1994, 1993. *Audit of Anti-Semitic Incidents*. 6900 Boul. Décarie, Suite 219, Montréal, Québec H3X 2T8.

Lee, Judy, 1993. "Women in Academia — A growing minority." *Perspectives on Labour and Income*. Ottawa: Statistics Canada Catalogue 75-002. Spring: 24-30.

Lender, Mark Edward and James Kirby Martin, 1982. *Drinking in America*. New York: The Free Press.

Lenski, Gerhard, 1966. *Power and Privilege*. New York: McGraw-Hill.

Lévesque, René, 1979. *My Quebec*. Toronto: Methuen.

Lévi-Strauss, Claude, 1964. *Tristes Tropiques*. New York: Atheneum.

Levin, Jack and William Levin, 1982. *The Functions of Discrimination and Prejudice*. 2nd Edition. New York: Harper and Row

Lévy-Bruhl, Lucien, 1966 [1911]. *How Natives Think*. New York: Washington Square Press.

Leyton, Elliott, 1993 [1979]. *The Myth of Delinquency: An Anatomy of Juvenile Nihilism*. Toronto: McClelland and Stewart.

Lowman, John, 1991. "Prostitution in Canada" in Margaret A. Jackson and Curt T. Griffiths (eds.), *Canadian Criminology*. Toronto: Harcourt, Brace, Jovanovich.

Lupri, Eugen, 1989. "Male Violence in the Home." *Canadian Social Trends*. Autumn, 19-21.

Luxton, Meg, 1986. *Through the Kitchen Window: The Politics of Home and Family*. Toronto: Garamond

Machiavelli, Niccolo, 1950. *The Prince and the Discourses*. New York: The Modern Library.

Maclean's. 30.6.86; 19.7.93; 2.8.93; 27.12.93; 3.1.94; 28.2.94; 10.3.94; 14.3.94; 28.3.94; 9.5.94; 15.8.94; 31.10.94; 21.11.94; 28.11.94; 12.12.94; 2.1.95; 13.3.95; 27.3.95.

Macleod, Linda, 1980. *Wife Battering in Canada: The Vicious Circle*. Ottawa: Canadian Advisory Council on the Status of Women.

Macleod, Linda, 1987. *Battered but not Beaten: Preventing Wife Battering in Canada*. Ottawa: Canadian Advisory Council on the Status of Women.

Maillé, Chantal, 1990. *Primed for Power: Women in Canadian Politics*. Ottawa: Canadian Advisory Council on the Status of Women.

Mann, W.E., 1971. "Suicide in Canada" in W.E. Mann (ed.), *Social Deviance in Canada*. Toronto: Copp Clark: 264-87.

Mann, W.E., 1971. "Alcoholism in Canada" in W.E. Mann (ed.), *Social Deviance in Canada*. Toronto: Copp Clark: 288-305.

Marchak, M. Patricia, 1975. *Ideological Perspectives on Canada*. Toronto: McGraw-Hill Ryerson.

Marshall, Katherine, 1989. "Women in Professional Occupations: Progress in the 1980s." *Canadian Social Trends*. Statistics Canada. Spring. 13-16.

Marx, Karl, 1963. *Selected Writings in Sociology and Philosophy*. Edited by T.B. Bottomore and Maximilien Rubel. Penguin Books.

Marx, Karl, 1969. *Capital*, Three Volumes. Moscow: Progress Publishers.

Marx, Karl, 1969. "The Civil War in France" in Karl Marx and Friedrich Engels. *Selected Works*, Vol. 2. Moscow: Progress Publishers, 178-246.

Marx, Karl and Friedrich Engels, 1967 [1848]. *The Communist Manifesto*. Edited by A.J.P. Taylor. Penguin Books.

Marx, Karl and Friedrich Engels, 1969. *Selected Works*. Three Volumes. Moscow: Progress Publishers.

McDiarmid, Garnet and David Pratt, 1971. *Teaching Prejudice*. Toronto: Ontario Institute for Studies in Education.

McKague, Ormond, 1991. *Racism in Canada*. Saskatoon: Fifth House.

McKay, Shona, 1992. "Boys Club." *Report on Business. The Globe and Mail*. September.

McLellan, David, 1971. *The Thought of Karl Marx*. London: Macmillan.

McLellan, David, 1978. *Friedrich Engels*. New York: Viking Press.

McLellan, David, 1983. *Karl Marx: The Legacy*. London: British Broadcasting Corporation.

Mead, George Herbert, 1934. *Mind, Self and Society*. Chicago: University of Chicago Press.

Mednick, Sarnoff, 1985. "Crime in the Family Tree." *Psychology Today*. March: 58-61.

Men and Other Reptiles, 1993. Chicago: Contemporary Books.

Menninger, Karl, 1938. *Man Against Himself*. New York: Harcourt Brace and World.

Merton, Robert, 1957. *Social Theory and Social Structure*. New York: Free Press.

Merton, Robert K. and Robert Nisbet, 1971 [1961]. *Contemporary Social Problems*. New York: Harcourt, Brace, Jovanovich.

Miles, Rosalind, 1991. *The Rites of Man*. London: Gralton Books.

Mill, J.S., 1911 [1869]. *The Subjection of Women*. New York: A. Stokes.

Millett, Kate, 1971. *Sexual Politics*. New York: Avon Books.

Moir, Anne and David Jessel, 1991. *Brain Sex*. London: Mandarin.

Montagu, Ashley (ed.), 1968. *Man and Aggression*. New York: Oxford University Paperback.

Montaigne, 1965. *The Complete Essays of Montaigne*. Trans. by Donald Frame. California: Stanford University Press.

Moreau, Joanne, 1991a. "Employment Equity." *Canadian Social Trends*. Autumn:26-8.

Moreau, Joanne, 1991b. "Changing Faces: Visible Minorities in Toronto." *Canadian Social Trends*. Ottawa: Statistics Canada. Winter:26-8.

Morgan, Nicole, 1988. *The Equality Game: Women in the Federal Public Service (1908-1987)*. Ottawa: Canadian Advisory Council on the Status of Women.

National Council of Welfare, 1979. *Women and Poverty*. October.

National Council of Welfare, 1990. *Women and Poverty Revisited*. Cat. No. H68-25.

National Council of Welfare, 1990. *Fighting Child Poverty*. Ottawa. H68-29-1991.

National Council of Welfare, 1992. *Poverty Profile 1980-90*. Ottawa. H67-1/4-1990.

National Council of Welfare, 1992. *Welfare Reform*. Ottawa.

National Council of Welfare, 1993. *Poverty Profile Update for 1991*. Ottawa. H67-1/4.

Newsweek. 13.9.82; 4.6.84; 26.8.91; 6.12.93.

Nietzsche, Friedrich, 1969 [1885]. *Thus Spoke Zarathustra*. Penguin Books.

Nietzsche, Friedrich, 1977. *A Nietzsche Reader*. Edited and Translated by R.J. Hollindale. Penguin Books.

Noël, Jan, 1993. "Dry Patriotism: The Chiniquy Crusade." In Cheryl Krasnik Warsh (ed.), *Drink in Canada*. Montreal and Kingston: McGill-Queen's University Press, 27-42.

O'Brien, Conor Cruise, 1994. *On the Eve of the Millennium*. Concord, Ontario: Anansi Press.

O'Brien, Mary, 1989. *Reproducing the World*. Boulder, Col: Westview Press.

O'Faolain, Julia and Lauro Martines (Eds.), 1973. *Not in God's Image*. New York: Harper Torchbooks.

Ogden, Russell, 1994. *Euthanasia: Assisted Suicide and AIDS*. Peroglyphics.

Oldridge, D.R., 1983. *Darwinian Impacts*. Atlantic Highlands: Humanities Press.

O'Neill, John, 1985. *Five Bodies: The Human Shape of Modern Society*. Ithaca: Cornell University Press.

Paglia, Camille, 1991. *Sexual Personae*. New York: Vintage Books.

Paglia, Camille, 1994. *Vamps and Tramps*. New York: Vintage Books.

Parliament, Jo-Anne B., 1990. "Labour Force Trends: Two Decades in Review." *Canadian Social Trends*. Statistics Canada. Autumn. 16-19.

Parsons, Elsie Clews, 1936. *Mitla: Town of Souls*. Chicago.

Parsons, Talcott, 1964 [1951]. *The Social System*. The Free Press of Glencoe.

Perry, Nancy J., 1992. "If you can't join 'em, beat 'em." *Fortune* 21.9.92:58-9.

Plato, 1963. *The Collected Dialogues*. Edited by Edith Hamilton and Huntington Cairns. Bollingen Series. Princeton, N.J.: Princeton University Press.

Popper, Karl, 1966. *The Open Society and Its Enemies*. Princeton, N.J.: Princeton University Press.

Porter, John, 1965. *The Vertical Mosaic*. Toronto: University of Toronto Press.

Ponting, Rick, 1988. "Public Opinion on Aboriginal Peoples' Issues in Canada." *Canadian Social Trends*. Ottawa: Statistics Canada. Winter: 9-17. Cat. No. 11-008.

Pratt, Tony, 1975. "Prospects for a radical criminology in the USA." In Ian Taylor, Paul Walton and Jock Young (eds.) 1975. *Critical Criminology*. London: Routledge and Kegan Paul.

Ramcharan, Subhas, 1989. *Social Problems and Issues: A Canadian Perspective*. Scarborough, Ontario: Nelson.

Reid, Larry D. and David J. Carpenter, 1990. "Alcohol-Abuse and Alcoholism" in Larry D. Reid (ed.), *Opioids, Bulimia, and Alcohol Abuse and Alcoholism*. New York: Springer-Verlag, 23-48.

Renaud, Viviane and Jane Badets, 1993. "Ethnic Diversity in the 1990s." *Canadian Social Trends*. Catalogue No. 11-008. Autumn: 17-22.

Ridlon, Florence V., 1988. *A Fallen Angel: The Status Insularity of the Female Alcoholic*. London: Associated University Presses.

Roberts, Paul, 1994. "Risk." *Psychology Today.* Nov/Dec, 50-53, 83-84.

Ross, David P., E. Richard Shillington and Clarence Lochhead, 1994. *The Canadian Fact Book on Poverty - 1994.* Ottawa: Canadian Council on Social Development.

Rousseau, Jean-Jacques, 1963. *The Social Contract and Discourses.* Translated by G.D.H. Cole. London: Dent, Everyman's Library.

Rousseau, Jean-Jacques, 1968. *The Social Contract.* Penguin.

Rousseau, Jean-Jacques, 1974 [1762]. *Emile.* Translated by Barbara Foxley. London: Dent, Everyman's Library.

Royal Commission on Aboriginal People, 1993. *Partners in Confederation.* Cat. No. Z1-1991.

Royal Commission on the Status of Women, 1970. *Report.* The Bird Report.

Royal Commission on Equality in Employment, 1984. *Report of the Commission on Equality in Employment.* The Abella Report. Ottawa. Cat. No. MP43-157.

Sarlo, Christopher, 1992. *Poverty in Canada.* Vancouver: The Fraser Institute.

Scheper-Hughes, Nancy and Margaret Lock, 1987. "The Mindful Body: A Prolegomenon to Work in Medical Anthropology." *Medical Anthropology Quarterly* (N.S.) 1,1:6-41.

Schmidt, Wolfgang, 1971. "The Prevalence of Alcoholism in Canada." In Craig L. Boydell, Carl F. Grindstaff and Paul C. Whitehead (eds.), *Critical Issues in Canadian Society.* Toronto: Holt, Rinehart and Winston: 499-508.

Schneidman, Edwin, 1987. "At the Point of No Return." *Psychology Today.* March, 55-8.

Schur, Edwin M., 1965. *Crimes Without Victims.* Englewood Cliffs, N.J.: Prentice Hall.

Senate Committee, 1971. *Poverty in Canada.* The Croll Report. Ottawa.

Senate Committee, 1980. *Child at Risk.* Ottawa. Cat. No. YC17-304.

Senate Committee, 1991. *Children in Poverty: Toward a Better Future.* Ottawa. Cat. No. YC17-342.

Shadd, Adrienne, 1991. "Institutionalized Racism and Canadian History: Notes of a Black Canadian." In Ormond McKague, *Racism in Canada.* Saskatoon: Fifth House, 1-5.

Shaver, Frances M., 1985. "Prostitution: A Critical Analysis of Three Policy Approaches." *Canadian Public Policy* XI:3:493-503.

Shaver, Frances M., 1993. "Prostitution: A Female Crime?" In Ellen Adelberg and Claudia Curvey (eds.), *In Conflict with the Law: Women and the Canadian Justice System.* Vancouver: Press Gang.

Shaw, Margaret, 1993. "Reforming Federal Women's Imprisonment" in Ellen Adelberg and Claudia Currie (eds.), *In Conflict with the Law.* Vancouver: Press Gang, 50-75.

Sheehy, Elizabeth A., 1987. *Personal Autonomy and the Criminal Law: Emerging Issues for Women.* CACSW.

Sheldon, W.H., 1949. *Varieties of Delinquent Youth*. New York: Harper.

Shreeve, James, 1994. "Terms of Estrangement." *Discover*. Nov. 57-63.

Silverman, Robert A., James J. Teevan, Jr., and Vincent F. Sacco (eds.), 1991. *Crime in Canadian Society*. 4th Ed. Toronto: Butterworths.

Slotkin, J.S., 1965. *Readings in Early Anthropology*. Chicago: Aldine.

Snider, Laureen, 1993. *Bad Business: Corporate Crime in Canada*. Scarborough, Ontario: Nelson.

Snyder, Charles R., 1962. "Culture and Jewish Sobriety." In David J. Pittman and Charles R. Snyder (eds.), *Society, Culture and Drinking*. New York: John Wiley, pp. 188-225.

Solicitor General, 1994. *Basic Facts about Corrections in Canada, 1993*. Cat. No. JS 82-17/

Sommer, Barbara, 1984. "Are All Women on Trial?" *Psychology Today*. August:36-8.

Spector, Aron, 1992. "Measuring Low Incomes in Canada." *Canadian Social Trends*. Ottawa. Statistics Canada. Summer. Cat. 11-008.

Spector, Malcolm and John I. Kitsuse, 1977. *Constructing Social Problems*. New York: Aldine de Gruyter.

Spencer, Herbert, 1961. *The Study of Sociology*. Ann Arbor: University of Michigan Press.

Spencer, Herbert, 1969 [1851]. *Social Statics*. New York: Augustus M. Kelley.

Spencer, Herbert, 1969. *The Man Versus the State*. Edited by Donald Macrae. Penguin Books.

Statistics Canada, 1972. *Suicide Mortality 1950-1968*. Cat. No. 84-528.

Statistics Canada, 1979. *The Distribution of Wealth in Canada*. Cat. 13-570.

Statistics Canada, 1981. *The Future of National Justice Statistics*. Cat. No. 85-206.

Statistics Canada, 1986. *The Distribution of Wealth in Canada, 1984*. Cat. 13-580.

Statistics Canada, 1987. *Changes in the Distribution of Wealth in Canada, 1970-84*. G. Oja. Cat. No. 13-588.

Statistics Canada, 1988. *Canadian Crime Statistics, 1987*. Ottawa. Cat. No. 85-205.

Statistics Canada, 1989. *Earnings of Men and Women, 1987*. Ottawa. Cat. No. 13-217.

Statistics Canada, 1989. *Profile of Ethnic Groups*. Cat. No. 93-154.

Statistics Canada, 1990. *Women in Canada*. Ottawa. Cat. 89-503.

Statistics Canada, 1992. *Mother Tongue*. Catalogue Number 93-313.

Statistics Canada, 1993. *Advance Statistics of Education 1993-94*. Cat. No. 81-220.

Statistics Canada, 1993. *Ethnic Origin*. Catalogue Number 93-315.

Statistics Canada, 1993. "The Violence Against Women Survey." *The Daily*. 18.11. Cat. No. 11-001.

Statistics Canada, 1994. *Causes of Death 1992*. Cat. No. 84-208.

Statistics Canada, 1994. *Canada's Changing Immigrant Population*. Cat. No. 96-311.

Statistics Canada, 1995. *Earnings of Men and Women*. Catalogue Number 13-217.

Statistics Canada, 1994. *Mortality 1991*. Cat. 84-209.

Statisitcs Canada, 1994. *Canadian Crime Statistics, 1993*. Cat. No. 85-205.

Statistics Canada, 1994. *The Labour Force*. Cat. No. 71-001.

Statistics Canada, 1995. *The Control and Sale of Alcoholic Beverages in Canada, 1990/91*. Cat. No. 63-202.

Statistics Canada and U.S. Bureau of the Census, 1993. *Challenges of Measuring an Ethnic World*. U.S. Govt. Printing Office, Washington, D.C. Cat. No. C93-099397.

Status of Women, Canada, 1991. *Living Without Fear . . . Everyone's Goal, Every Woman's Right*. Ottawa. Cat. No. SW21-12/1991.

Stein, Martha L., 1975. *Lovers, Friends, Slaves*. New York: Berkley Medallion.

Steinem, Gloria, 1993. *Revolution from Within: A Book of Self-Esteem*. New York: Little, Brown.

Stevenson, Leslie, 1987. *Seven Theories of Human Nature*. Oxford: Oxford University Press.

Stout, Cameron W., 1992. "A Degree of Change." *Perspectives*. Winter:14-18. Cat. No. 75-001.

Strachan, Jill *et al.*, 1990. "Canadian Suicide Mortality Rates: First-generation immigrants versus Canadian-born." *Health Reports*. Vol. 2, No. 4. Statistics Canada. Cat. 82-003.

Sumner, W.G., 1940 [1906]. *Folkways*. Boston: Ginn.

Sunday Times, 10.4.94.

Sutherland, Edwin, 1937. *The Professional Thief*. Chicago: The University of Chicago Press.

Sutherland, Edwin, 1961 [1949]. *White Collar Crime*. New York: Holt, Rinehart and Winston.

Synnott, Anthony and David Howes, 1992. "From Measurement to Meaning: Anthropologies of the Body." *Anthropos*, 87:147-66.

Synnott, Anthony, 1993. *The Body Social: Symbolism, Self and Society*. London: Routledge.

Tan, Jim and Patricia E. Roy, 1985. *The Chinese in Canada*. Ottawa: Canadian Historical Association.

Tawney, R.H., 1964 [1931]. *Equality*. London: Unwin Books.

Taylor, Ian, Paul Walton and Jock Young (eds.), 1975. *Critical Criminology*. London: Routledge and Kegan Paul.

Thomas, David, 1993. *Not Guilty: The Case in Defense of Men*. New York: William Morrow.

Time. 19.3.90; 13.12.93.

Trigg, Roger, 1988. *Ideas of Human Nature*. Oxford: Basil Blackwell.

Trudel, Marcel, 1960. *L'Esclavage au Canada français*. Québec: Les Presses de l'Université Laval.

Tumin, Melvin, 1953. "Some Principles of Stratification: A Critical Analysis." *American Sociological Review*, Vol. 18, April, 387-94.

Turner, Jonathan H. & Alexandra Maryanski, 1979. *Functionalism*. Menlo Park, California: Benjamin-Cummings.

United Nations, 1993. *The 1993 Human Development Report*. New York: Oxford University Press.

United Nations, 1994. *Demographic Yearbook*. New York.

US News and World Report. 28.3.94.

Vaillant, George E., 1983. *The Natural History of Alcoholism*. Cambridge, Mass.: Harvard University Press.

Veblen, Thorstein, 1953. *The Theory of the Leisure Class*. Introduction by C. Wright Mills. New York: Menton Books.

Vigod, Bernard L., 1984. *The Jews in Canada*. Ottawa: Canadian Historical Association.

Walker, James W. St. G., 1984. *The West Indians in Canada*. Ottawa: Canadian Historical Association.

Walby, Sylvia, 1990. *Theorizing Patriarchy*. Oxford: Basil Blackwell.

Ward, W. Peter, 1982. *The Japanese in Canada*. Ottawa: Canadian Historical Association.

Warsh, Cheryl Krasnick, 1993. "John Barleycorn Must Die: An Introduction to the Social History of Alcohol." In Cheryl Krasnick Warsh (ed.), *Drink in Canada*. Montreal and Kingston: McGill – Queen's University Press, 3-26.

Weber, Max, 1948. *From Max Weber: Essays in Sociology*. Edited by Hans Gerth and C. Wright Mills. London: Routledge and Kegan Paul.

Weber, Max, 1964. *The Theory of Social and Economic Organization*. New York: The Free Press.

Weber, Max, 1968. *The Protestant Ethic and the Spirit of Capitalism*. Trans. by Talcott Parsons. London: Unwin University Books.

Webber, Marlene, 1991. *Street Kids: The Tragedy of Canada's Runaways*. Toronto: University of Toronto Press.

West, D.J., 1982. *Delinquency*. London: Heineman.

Wilson, Edward O., 1979. *On Human Nature*. New York: Bantam Books.

Wilson, James Q., 1979. "Lock 'em up." In Phillip Whitten (ed.), *Readings in Sociology*. New York: Harper and Row:83-7.

Wilson, James Q. and Richard J. Herrnstein, 1985. *Crime and Human Nature*. New York: Simon and Schuster.

Wilson, Margo and Martin Daly, 1994. "Spousal Homicide." *Juristat* 14: 8. March.

Wolff, Lee and Dorota Geissel, 1994. "Street Prostitution in Canada." *Canadian Social Trends*. Summer. Cat. No. 11-008: 18-22.

Wollstonecraft, Mary, 1975 [1792]. *A Vindication of the Rights of Women*. New York: W.W. Norton.

Wright, Christine, 1992. "Homicide in Canada, 1991." *Juristat*. Vol. 12, No. 8. Statistics Canada: Canadian Centre for Justice Statistics. October. Cat. 85-002.

Wright, Christine, 1995. "Risk of Personal and Household Victimization, 1993." *Juristat*. January. Cat. No. 85-002.

Yochelson, Samuel and Stanton Samenow, 1977. *The Criminal Personality*. 2 Vols. New York: Jason Aronson.

Young, Michael, 1961. *The Rise of the Meritocracy*. Penguin Books.

Subject Index

Name Index